Mastering Visual J++

Mastering™ Visual J++

Steven Holzner

SYBEX®

San Francisco · Paris · Düsseldorf · Soest

Associate Publisher: Gary Masters
Acquisitions Manager: Kristine Plachy
Acquisitions & Developmental Editor: Suzanne Rotondo
Editor: Pat Coleman
Project Editor: Kimberley Askew-Qasem
Technical Editor: Kevin Russo
Book Designer: Catalin Dulfu
Desktop Publisher: Kris Warrenburg Design
Production Coordinator: Nathan Johanson
Indexer: Matthew Spence
Cover Designer: Design Site
Cover Photograph: The Image Bank

Screen reproductions produced with Collage Complete.
Collage Complete is a trademark of Inner Media Inc.

SYBEX is a registered trademark of SYBEX Inc.
Mastering is a trademark of SYBEX Inc.

TRADEMARKS: SYBEX has attempted throughout this book to
distinguish proprietary trademarks from descriptive terms by
following the capitalization style used by the manufacturer.

Microsoft® Internet Explorer on the CD accompanying this book
is Copyright Microsoft Corporation, 1996. All rights reserved.

Manufactured in the United States of America

10 9 8 7 6 5 4 3 2 1

To my Sweetie, Nancy, the computer expert

ACKNOWLEDGMENTS

Many thanks to the fine team at Sybex, starting with Suzanne Rotondo, Developmental Editor, and including all the others who were so key in putting together this book: Pat Coleman, Editor; Kimberley Askew-Qasem, Project Editor; Nathan Johanson, Production Coordinator; Kris Warrenburg, Desktop Publisher; and Kevin Russo, Technical Editor.

CONTENTS AT A GLANCE

TABLE OF CONTENTS

WELCOME TO VISUAL J++

Why Visual J++?

Even nonprogrammers know the name *Java* today. In fact, people who've never been on the Internet know the name *Java*. Java is the programming language that's brought the Web to life. World Wide Web pages used to be static text and images, with some embedded hyperlinks. But using Java, you can animate your Web pages with buttons, scroll bars, clickable images, even graphics animation. From the beginning, Java was a hit, and its popularity continues to increase.

You can create Java programs with Sun's Java Development Kit (JDK)—so why should you use Visual J++? The difference is something like comparing a horse and buggy to a powerful new car—both will get you where you're going, but if you want to save time and a great deal of effort, you're better off with the second option. To use the JDK, you have to edit the Java source code files yourself and run them through the Java compiler, as well as design all the menus and dialog boxes from scratch.

In Visual J++, everything is integrated to an extraordinary degree, and you can design your complete program without ever leaving the Visual J++ environment. Some other Java development packages are out there now, but truly nothing like Visual J++. Visual J++ has a complete set of tools, including the Dialog Editor, the Menu Editor, and the Bitmap Editor. It has true debugging and online help. It even has a set of Wizards that write a great deal of code for you. All in all, Visual J++ is by far the premiere Java development tool available today, and programmers are migrating to it at a rate so fast it surprises even Microsoft.

What's in This Book?

The emphasis in this book is to demonstrate Visual J++ at work. There's nothing like seeing working code if you want to get something from it. Many books start off with abstractions, programming constructs, and theory, but here we will consider Visual J++ a tool (and a fine tool at that) that the programmer uses to create programs that do something, and not as an end in itself.

Often, Java is taught from Java's point of view— that is, in terms of programming constructs such as loops, conditionals, class inheritance, and so on. That makes for very dry reading. In this book, you'll see things from a different point of view—the programmer's point of view. Instead of chapters named "If Statements," "Java Modifiers," or "Abstract Java Classes," these chapters are named "Checkboxes, Radio Buttons, and Layouts," "Menus, Dialog Boxes, and More Layouts," "Graphics Animation," and so on.

Together, we will put Visual J++ to work—for us. You'll see plenty of bite-sized examples in this book, because trying to learn Visual J++ without running it is like trying to learn to fly by reading an airplane parts manual. The examples will be short and to the point, without too many extraneous details, and here are just a few of the ones you'll see:

- Text fields and text areas
- Radio buttons and checkboxes
- Scroll bars and scrolling lists
- Clickable hyperlink-filled images (image maps)
- Menus and buttons
- Card layouts, GridBag layouts, and more
- Java panels and the Java `animator` class
- Java applications

- Debugging Java programs
- Graphics animation
- Coordinating multiple threads
- Integrating ActiveX with Java

We will use all the Wizards and editors in the process of creating working Java programs. Visual J++ has a great deal to offer us, and you'll see just about all of it in this book, from creating Visual J++ projects to letting Visual J++ write most of our code; from creating new dialog boxes in minutes to debugging interactively by single-stepping through our code. This package provides a great many tools, and you will use them fully as we create our programs. In addition, I'll include tips and notes throughout the book to add more power and expertise.

TIP

Tips look like this. Their purpose is to save you some time, and they may point out additional information that can be of help. In either case, they provide you with something extra, and I hope you'll find them worthwhile.

NOTE

This is a note, and I'll use notes to indicate points of special concern. For example, I'll explain why working with the mouse one way instead of another is important at a particular time, or what you can do with one Web browser in Java that you can't with another.

The code in this book also appears on the CD-ROM—each example program will get its own subdirectory, which means that you don't have to type anything in as we develop our examples. It's all there on the CD-ROM, ready to run.

What You'll Need

To use this book profitably, you'll need some programming experience—not much, but some. For example, if you've worked with C or BASIC before, that's fine. Although Java is an object-oriented language, you don't need object-oriented programming experience to read this book, because I'll show you how object-oriented programming works. If you have experience with C++, you have a leg up here, because you know about object-oriented programming already. If you've worked with Microsoft's Visual C++, you have even more of a head start, because Visual J++ uses the same programming environment—the Microsoft Developer Studio. And if you're familiar with Java itself, you're ready to jump right in.

You'll also need Microsoft Visual J++, of course (almost any version will do as long as it is at least as recent as Visual J++ 1.0 Gold). Visual J++ provides all the tools you'll need to work along in this book, including the Java source code editor that we'll use.

In addition, you'll need a Web browser; I'll use Microsoft Internet Explorer. Both Internet Exporer and ActiveX Control PAD are included on the CD-ROM. Because Visual J++ is configured to work with that browser, most readers will be using it. (You can configure Visual J++ to work with other Web browsers, and you'll see how to do that.) Still, the connection between Visual J++ and Internet Explorer is so close that using that browser might be a good idea even if you don't have it installed currently. For example, when we debug in Visual J++, we will actually be able to single-step through a Java program in Visual J++ while watching the results in Internet Explorer. If you do decide to use Internet Explorer, be sure you have a version that supports Java, which means version 3.0 or later. You can download the Internet Explorer for free from the Microsoft Web site at http://www.microsoft.com.

And, of course, to use your completed Java programs on the Web, you should have somewhere to host your Web pages, such as an

Internet service provider (ISP). Although Java can produce both stand-alone applications and applets (the packages that you embed in Web pages), the overwhelming majority of Java programmers target the Web in their Java development. You'll see how to embed Java applets in a Web page in the first chapter; your Internet service provider should be able to help you on how to upload your applets (this information can vary greatly from machine to machine) so that you can use them in your Web pages. Usually, you need to know where to install your Web pages and applets (which directory in the ISP computer), and then you can use an FTP (File Transfer Protocol) program to upload your files to that directory.

You can find more help with Java on the Internet. Some resources include the Microsoft Visual J++ sites:

```
http://www.microsoft.com/visualj
http://www.microsoft.com/visualj/docs
```

as well as Sun's Java sites:

```
http://www.javasoft.com
http://www.javasoft.com/doc
```

You can also check the Usenet group:

```
comp.lang.java.programmer
```

That's it. We're ready to begin. Let's start at once with our first Java programs—that is, both Java applets and applications—in Chapter 1, coming up next.

CHAPTER

ONE

1

Our First Java Examples

- Creating a Java program in the simplest way

- Using a workspace

- Using the Applet Wizard

- Creating Java applications

Welcome to Microsoft Visual J++, the most exciting method of working with Java since Sun Microsystems first introduced the language. The popularity of Java has skyrocketed as more and more Web programmers have started using it to make their Web pages actually *do* something. With Java, you can display animations in your Web pages, accept mouse clicks and text, display images, use controls such as scroll bars and checkboxes, and even support additional windows and menu bars. Visual J++ is the best way to create Java code these days—it is a fully featured development environment that really does leave the others far behind. This book will take advantage of what Visual J++ has to offer: everything from Wizards that write code for you, to editors that create dialog boxes and menus. You are going to take a guided tour through all the parts of Visual J++, from a first-rate debugger to an online help system.

In this book, you'll use Visual J++ to create and run Java programs. These programs come in two ways: as stand-alone applications, and as small programs you can embed in Web pages—applets. Of the two, applets targeted at the Web are the most popular, and I'll concentrate primarily on them.

As you use Visual J++, you'll see how to create Java applications and applets and how to embed applets in Web pages. Originally, a Java program was something you wrote all by yourself from start to finish and then used Sun's DOS-version Java compiler, `javac.exe`, to create Java executable files. We've come a long way since then, and Visual J++ is the most advanced Java tool yet, as you'll see. Many details that were tiresome when writing Java programs the old way are now handled literally with the click of a mouse. You can also modify your programs and restructure them almost automatically using Visual J++. As you'll find out if you ask almost any experienced Java programmer, this is a vast improvement over the old days.

Let's start our guided tour of Visual J++, and of Java itself, right away. Some books introduce chapters of abstractions before getting to work, but not here. I will concentrate on examples in this book—that is, in seeing things from the programmer's point of view, seeing Java at *work*—so let's begin at once with our first example.

Our First Example

Our first example will be a simple one, because we just want to get started in Visual J++ without too many details to weigh us down. You will create a small Java *applet*—the type of Java programs that you can embed in a Web page—that will display the words *Hello, World!* (a Hello, World! example is the traditional first example in programming books, and it's a good choice here because writing this applet in Java is relatively simple).

Each applet is given the amount of space (usually measured in pixels) in a Web page that it requests (you'll see how it "requests" space soon):

This rectangular box is the applet's own space that it will use for display. In this example, you will place the words *Hello, World!* in the applet, like this:

```
------------------------------------------
|                                        |
|                                        |
|            Hello, World!                |
|                                        |
|                                        |
|                                        |
------------------------------------------
```

After you create the applet, you can embed it in a Web page. When you use Visual J++, you can see your applet at work easily in Microsoft Internet Explorer 3.0, and I'll use that browser in this book (previous versions of Internet Explorer do not support Java). Let's create and run our applet now.

TIP   If you want to use a different Web browser, simply open the Visual J++ Build menu, select Settings, select the Debug tab in the Project Settings dialog box, select Browser in the Category box, and enter the name and location of the Web browser you want to use in the Browser box. But note that some features explored in this book—such as interactive debugging—may not work with a browser other than Internet Explorer.

Let's call this applet Hello. You will store the actual Java code for it in the file `Hello.java`, and Visual J++ will place the applet in a file named `Hello.class`. (Visual J++ lets your run the applet at the click of a menu item.) You will start by creating the Java source code file, `Hello.java`, now.

Creating Our Java Program in the Simplest Way

Start Visual J++ now, as shown in Figure 1.1. Visual J++ is actually one of several Microsoft applications that use the Microsoft Developer Studio. (If you have used other Developer Studio products, for example, Visual C++, you already have a leg up when it comes to learning about Visual J++, because many techniques and ideas are similar).

FIGURE 1.1:

The Visual Java Developer Studio

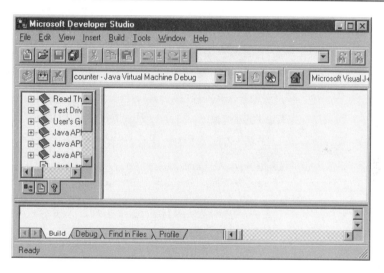

You will learn more about the Developer Studio environment throughout this book; the immediate goal is to simply create the file Hello.java. To do that, choose File ➤ New to open the New dialog box.

Visual J++ offers several types of items to create here: text files, project workspaces, resource templates, and bitmap files. You want to create a text file, so select that item and click on OK to open a new window titled Text1, as shown in Figure 1.2.

FIGURE 1.2:

Creating a new text file in
Visual J++

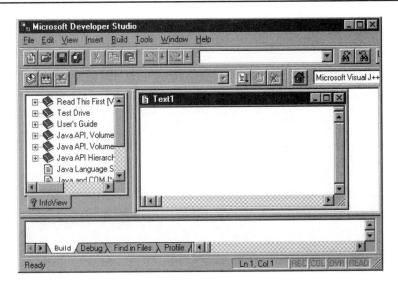

You can type your new Java program in this window. For now, type
the following text into the Text1 window (if you have programmed in
Visual C++, some of the following might seem familiar to you):

```java
import java.awt.Graphics;
class Hello extends java.applet.Applet
{
  public void paint( Graphics g )
  {
    g.drawString( "Hello, World!", 60, 30 );
  }
}
```

TIP
You'll soon see how Visual J++ can handle all these details for you,
even creating your source code files, to which you often only have
to add a few lines to customize.

This is the text of our first Java program, and soon you'll see what
each line means. After you type the text, save it to disk (choose
File ➤ Save As). Give the file the name `Hello.java`. Capitalization

counts here—be sure you type `Hello.java`, not `hello.java`. In general, the filename will match exactly (including case) the name given in the "class" statement in the file; in our case, that is `Hello`:

```
import java.awt.Graphics;

class Hello extends java.applet.Applet
{
    public void paint( Graphics g )
    {
        g.drawString( "Hello, World!", 60, 30 );
    }
}
```

Now you have created `Hello.java`, as shown in Figure 1.3. The next step is to compile this Java code into the applet `Hello.class` and see your applet at work.

FIGURE 1.3:

Your Java code is ready to go.

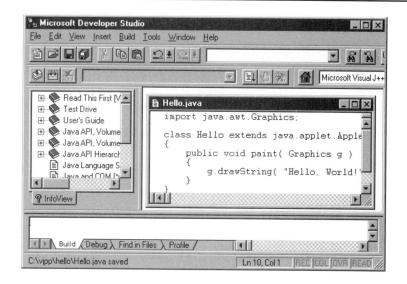

Compiling Our First Applet

Now that you have Hello.java, you can create Hello.class—the actual binary code for the applet—and see it run. To do this, choose Build ➤ Build Hello. A dialog box will appear with the message: "This build command requires an active workspace. Would you like to create a default project workspace?" Click on Yes.

NOTE Hello.java is the Java source code file, and Hello.class is the actual binary file that we call the applet. It is this binary file that you upload to your Internet service provider (ISP). Hello.class is filled with binary *bytecodes* that Java-enabled Web browsers can understand and execute.

Visual J++ displays this message in the bottom window of Visual J++, which is the output window:

```
---Configuration: Hello - Java Virtual Machine Debug---

Compiling...
Microsoft ®Visual J++ Compiler Version 1.00.6229
Copyright ©Microsoft Corp 1996. All rights reserved.

  Hello - 0 error(s), 0 warning(s)
```

The file Hello.class now exists, and you can see it at work.

Running the Applet

To see Hello.class running, choose Build ➤ Execute. If you have Microsoft Internet Explorer 3.0 installed, Visual J++ starts Explorer, and you see the results in Figure 1.4. Already, you are programming in Java.

Our first applet at work

Dissecting Our First Applet

Our first applet, Hello, runs—but what exactly did you do? Let's take a look now at the Java code that you entered for `Hello.java`, examining it line by line to get a better idea of how Java programming works (even though Visual J++ will handle many of these details for us later).

We begin with this line:

```
import java.awt.Graphics;
    .
    .
    .
```

What does this mean? This line actually points out one of the great advantages of Java programming. When you're adding menus and separate windows to your Java applets, you can imagine that it would be a great deal of work to create everything from scratch—that is, write the entire code for menu handling, separate window creation, and so forth. Instead of asking us to do so, Java comes complete with several predefined libraries. You'll see more about this later, but what you're doing is adding support from the main Java graphics library of routines to your applet. In this way, you'll be able to draw your text string Hello, World! in the applet's window.

Next, we add this line to `Hello.java`:

```
import java.awt.Graphics;

→ class Hello extends java.applet.Applet
→ {    .

        .

        .
```

Here we create a Java *class* named `Hello`. What does this mean?

Classes and Objects

If you're familiar with object-oriented programming in languages such as C++, you know about classes already. *Classes* and *objects* are two fundamental concepts in object-oriented programming. You can think of an object as a package of both code and data wrapped together in a way that makes it easy to use. For example, you might put all the screen-handling parts of a program in an object named `screen`, which holds not only all the data displayed on the screen, but also the functions needed to handle that data, for example, `drawString()` or `drawLine()`. All screen handling is hidden from the rest of the program, and, thus, the rest of the program is easier to handle. For example, a refrigerator would be far less useful if you had to regulate all the temperatures and pumps and so forth by hand at all times. When all those functions are internal and automatic to the refrigerator, the regrigerator is a much easier object to deal with and is a useful one—a "refrigerator."

A class is to an object what a cookie cutter is to a cookie—that is, a class acts something like a template or a blueprint for an object. To shape the object, you apply a class to it. In terms of programming, you might think of the relationship between a data type, such as an integer, and the actual variable itself like this, where we set up an integer named `the_data`:

```
int the_data;
```

This is the actual way you create an integer variable in Java. Here, `int` is the type of variable you are declaring, and `the_data` is the variable itself. A class has the same relationship to an object, and informally you can think of a class as an object's *type*.

<table>
<tr><td>**TIP**</td><td>As you'll see, Java supports all the standard C and C++ primitive data types: `int`, `double`, `long`, `float`, and so forth.</td></tr>
</table>

Java comes with several libraries of predefined classes, which saves you a great deal of work, and to a considerable extent, this book is an examination of these predefined and useful Java classes. These libraries are called *packages*, and one such library is called `java.awt` (where `awt` stands for Abstract Windowing Toolkit). This library holds the Graphics class, which handles the graphics work. The following line:

```
import java.awt.Graphics;
```

actually shows that you want to include the Java Graphics class and use it in your program. (In Java, displaying the text string Hello, World! is considered graphics handling.) In a minute, you'll use an object of the Graphics class for your graphics output.

Now, it's time to set up the applet itself, which is named Hello. To do this, you define a new class named `Hello`. This is the standard way to set up an applet in Java, and you might recall that the applet itself has the file extension `.class`. Each class you define in a `.java` file is exported to a `.class` file, where you can use it. You'll see more detail about this soon.

It would be quite difficult, however, to write all the code an applet class needs from scratch. For example, you would need to interact with the Web browser, reserve a section of screen, initialize the appropriate Java packages, and much more. All that functionality is built in to the Java `Applet` class, which is part of the `java.applet` package.

But how do you use the `Applet` class? You want to customize the applet to display the text string, and the `java.applet.Applet` class itself knows nothing about that. You can customize the `java.applet.Applet` class, however, by *deriving* the class `Hello` from the `Applet` class. When you do so, `java.applet.Applet` becomes the *base* class of the `Hello` class, and `Hello` becomes a class derived from `java.applet.Applet`. This gives you all the power of the `java.applet.Applet` class without the worries of writing it, and you can add what you want to this class by adding code to your derived class `Hello`.

NOTE This *inheritance* is an important part of object-oriented programming. A derived class inherits the functionality of its base class and adds more on top of it. For example, you might have a base class called, say, `chassis`. You can derive various classes from this base class called, say, `car` and `truck`. In this way, two derived classes can share the same base class, saving time and effort programmatically. Although `car` and `truck` share the same base class, `chassis`, they added different items to the base class, ending up as two quite different classes, `car` and `truck`.

In this way, you will *extend* the base class `java.applet.Applet` by creating the class `Hello` and adding on to the base class. You indicate that the `Hello` class is derived from the `java.applet.Applet` class like this—note that you use the keyword *class* to indicate that you are defining a new class:

```
  import java.awt.Graphics;

→ class Hello extends java.applet.Applet
→ {    .
       .
       .
```

Now you are starting to set up a new class, Hello, and you have given it all the power of the java.applet.Applet class (such as the ability to request space from the Web browser and to respond to many browser-created commands). But how do you add to and even alter the java.applet.Applet class to customize the Hello class? How do you display the text string? One way is by *overriding* the base class's built-in functions. When you redefine a base class's function in a derived class, the new version of the function takes over. In this way, you can customize the functions from the base class as you like them in the derived class.

For example, one function in the java.applet.Applet class is called paint(). This important function is called when the Web browser tells the applet to create its display on the screen. This happens when the applet first begins and every time it has to be redisplayed later (for example, if the Web browser was minimized and then maximized, or if some window was moved and the applet's display area was uncovered after having been covered).

The goal in the Hello class is to display the string Hello, World! on the screen, and you will override the java.applet.Applet class's paint() function to do so. You override a base class's function simply by redefining it in a new class. You'll do that now for the paint() function, noting first that the built-in functions of a class are called that class's *methods*. In this case, then, you override (that is, redefine) the paint() method like this:

```
import java.awt.Graphics;

class Hello extends java.applet.Applet
{
```

```
→   public void paint( Graphics g )
        {  .
              .
              .
```

> **NOTE** The built-in functions of a class are called *methods*. Classes can also have built-in variables—called *data members*—and even constants. Collectively, all these parts are called a class's *members*.

The keyword `public` above is called an access modifier. A class's methods can be declared `public`, `private`, or `protected`. If they are declared `public`, you can call them from anywhere in the program, not just in the class in which they are defined. If they are `private`, you can call them only from the class in which they are defined. If they are `protected`, you can call them only in the class in which they are defined and in all classes derived from that class.

Next, you indicate the *return* type of the `paint()` method. When you call a method, you can pass parameters to it, and it can return data to you. In this case, `paint()` has no return value, which you indicate as the return type *void*. Other return types are `int` for an integer return value (this variable is usually 32 bits long), `long` for a long integer (this variable is usually 64 bits long), `float` for a floating point return, or `double` for a double-precision floating point value. You can also return arrays and objects in Java.

Finally, note that you indicate that the `paint()` method is automatically passed one parameter—an object of the `Graphics` class that I will call g:

```
import java.awt.Graphics;

class Hello extends java.applet.Applet
{
→   public void paint( Graphics g )
        {  .
              .
              .
```

This `Graphics` object represents the physical display of the applet. That is, you can use the built-in methods of this object—such as `drawImage()`, `drawLine()`, `drawOval()` and others, as you will see—to draw on the screen. In this case, you want to place the string Hello, World! on the screen, and you can do that with the `drawString()` method.

How do you reach the methods of an object such as the `Graphics` object we have named g? You do so with a dot operator (.) like this: `g.drawString()`. Here you are invoking g's `drawString()` method to "draw" a string of text on the screen (text is handled like any other type of graphics in a windowing environment—that is, it is drawn on the screen rather than "printed," just as you would draw a rectangle or a circle). You supply three parameters to the `drawString()` method—the string of text you want to display, and the (x, y) location of that string's lower left corner (called the starting point of the string's *baseline*) in pixels on the screen, passed in two integer values. You can draw the string at, say, the pixel location (60, 30), where (0, 0) is the upper left corner of the applet's display:

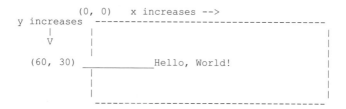

```
                 (0, 0)    x increases -->
   y increases  ---------------------------------------
        |          |                                   |
        V          |                                   |
                   |                                   |
   (60, 30)  _____    Hello, World!           |
                   |                                   |
                   |                                   |
                   ---------------------------------------
```

TIP The coordinate system in a Java program is set up with the origin (0, 0) at the upper left, with x increasing horizontally to the right, and y increasing vertically downward; this fact will be important throughout the book. If it seems backward to you, you might try thinking of it in terms of reading a page of text, like this one, where you start at the upper left and work your way to the right and down. The units of measurement in Java coordinate systems are almost always screen pixels.

Therefore, you add a call to the `drawString()` method this way:

```
import java.awt.Graphics;

class Hello extends java.applet.Applet
{
   public void paint( Graphics g )
   {
→  g.drawString( "Hello, World!", 60, 30 );
   }
}
```

Java uses the same convention as C or C++ to indicate that a code statement is finished; it ends the statement with a semicolon (;), and all code statements you see in this book will end this way.

TIP
In general, Java adheres strongly to C++ coding conventions. If you know C++, you already know a great deal of Java.

That's it, then. You have completed the code necessary for your applet, which is the code for your new class `Hello`. When the Java compiler creates `Hello.class`, the entire specification of the new class will be in that file. This is the actual binary file that you upload to your Internet service provider so that it can be included in your Web page. A Java-enabled Web browser (such as Netscape Navigator or Internet Explorer) takes this class specification, creates an object of that class, and then gives it control to display itself and, if applicable, handle user input.

But how does that work? We have not yet completed the dissection of our first example, because all we have done so far is to trace the development of `Hello.java` into `Hello.class`. How do you display the applet in Internet Explorer?

Our Applet's Web Page

You saw that Internet Explorer took the Hello applet and displayed it in a Web page like this:

How did it get there? Visual J++ created a temporary Web page and passed that on to Internet Explorer. That Web page looks like this:

```
<html>
<! NOTE - this file was generated by Microsoft Developer Studio because
    no HTML file was specified. DO NOT EDIT this file. It will be
    regenerated each time you launch your applet. To create a permanent
    HTML file,
        1. Create a new text file and save it
        2. Insert the file into your project
        3. Select "Settings..." from the "Build" menu
    a. Choose the "Debug" tab
    b. Set the "Category" to "Browser"
    c. In the "Parameters" section, select "Use parameters from HTML page"
    d. Specify the new HTML file name in the edit box for "HTML page"
>
<head>
<title>Hello</title>
</head>
<body>
<hr>
```

```
<applet
code=Hello
width=200
height=200>

</applet>
<hr>
</body>
</html>
```

You'll see later that you can design your own Web pages in which to display an applet and make Visual J++ pass them to Internet Explorer rather than to this default page. The above Web page is written in HTML (HyperText Markup Language), the language of Web pages. And although this is a book on Java programming, applets appear in Web pages, so we will take the time to briefly work through the above page to be sure you know what's going on. This will be useful when you build your own Web page .html files in which to embed applets of the kind developed in this book. If you're familiar with HTML, you can skip much of this review, but you should take a look at how to use the <applet> tag, which you use to embed applets in Web pages.

A Brief Review of HTML

Let's take apart the temporary Web page that Visual J++ created for our applet. We start with the <html> *tag*:

```
<html>
     .
     .
     .
```

Instructions in HTML pages are placed in tags like this, surrounded by angle brackets: < and >. These tags hold directions to the Web browser and are not displayed on the screen. Here, the <html> tag indicates to the Web browser that this .html file is written in HTML.

Next comes a comment added by the Visual J++ program. Comments in HTML pages are preceded by an exclamation point, like this: `<! This is a comment.>`. Here, in this comment, Visual J++ tells us that this is a temporary `.html` file and even includes instructions on how you can create your own `.html` files to display applets in Visual J++:

```
<html>
<! NOTE - this file was generated by Microsoft Developer Studio because
no HTML file was specified. DO NOT EDIT this file. It will be
regenerated each time you launch your applet. To create a permanent
HTML file,
    1. Create a new text file and save it
    2. Insert the file into your project
        3. Select "Settings..." from the "Build" menu
    a. Choose the "Debug" tab
    b. Set the "Category" to "Browser"
    c. In the "Parameters" section, select "Use parameters from HTML page"
    d. Specify the new HTML file name in the edit box for "HTML page"
>   .
    .
    .
```

Next comes the header portion of your Web page, which you declare with the `<head>` tag, ending the header section with the corresponding end header tag, `</head>` (many HTML tags are used in pairs like this, such as `<head>` and `</head>` or `<center>` and `</center>` to center text and images). In this case, the `.html` file gets the title (set up with the `<title>` tag) of "Hello" to match our applet:

```
<html>
<! NOTE - this file was generated by Microsoft Developer Studio because...>

→ <head>
→ <title>Hello</title>
→ </head>
    .
    .
    .
```

The title is the name given to a Web page, and it's usually displayed in the Web browser. For example, Internet Explorer displays a Web page's title in Explorer's title bar. Next comes the body of the Web page, where all the actual items for display will go. Visual J++ starts the page off with a ruler line (visible in Figure 1.4 , earlier in this chapter), using the `<hr>` tag:

```
<html>
<! NOTE - this file was generated by Microsoft Developer Studio because...>

<head>
<title>Hello</title>
</head>
```
➜ `<body>`
➜ `<hr>`
   .
   .
   .

Now we come to our applet. Applets are embedded with the `<applet>` tag, and here Visual J++ uses the *code* keyword to indicate that the applet is supported by the `Hello.class` file. It also indicates the size of the applet as 200 x 200 pixels this way:

```
<html>
<! NOTE - this file was generated by Microsoft Developer Studio because...>

<head>
<title>Hello</title>
</head>

<body>
<hr>
```
➜ `<applet`
➜ `code=Hello`
➜ `width=200`
➜ `height=200>`

➜ `</applet>`
   .
   .
   .

TIP

You'll see how to indicate the size of applets when we set them up in Visual J++, and in fact we can also use the `java.applet` `.Applet.resize()` method to request that the Web browser resize them.

The `<applet>` tag is important for us, so let's take a closer look at it. Here's how the `<applet>` tag works in general:

```
<APPLET
    [ALIGN = LEFT or RIGHT or TOP or TEXTTOP or MIDDLE or
    ABSMIDDLE  or BASELINE or BOTTOM or ABSBOTTOM]
    [ALT = AlternateText]
    CODE = AppletName.class
    [CODEBASE = Relative or absolute path of of .class file
]
    HEIGHT = AppletPixelsHeight
    [HSPACE = PixelSpaceToLeftOfApplet]
    [NAME = AppletInstanceName]
    [VSPACE = PixelSpaceAboveApplet]
    WIDTH = AppletPixelsWidth
 >
  [<PARAM NAME = Parameter1 VALUE = VALUE1]
  [<PARAM NAME = Parameter2 VALUE = VALUE2]
        .
        .
        .
</APPLET>
```

TIP

You can specify the path, either absolute (for example, `/usr` `/name/classes/appletname`) or relative (for example, `classes/appletname`) of the applet's `.class` file with the CODEBASE keyword. This is often useful if you want to store your applets together in a directory on your ISP's server, away from the `.html` files.

You indicate to the Web browser how much space the applet will need, using the HEIGHT and WIDTH keywords. You can also pass parameters to applets with the PARAM keyword like this: `<applet>` `PARAM today = "friday"` `</applet>`. Doing so allows you to customize an applet to fit different Web pages; you can read the parameters from inside an applet and use them. You'll see how this works in an example later in the book.

Not all Web browsers support Java. In practice, this means that those browsers simply ignore the `<applet>` tag. This, in turn, means that you can place text between the `<applet>` and `</applet>` tags that will be displayed in non-Java browsers (and not in Java-enabled browsers), like this:

```
<applet code=Hello>
Your web browser does not support Java, so you can't see my applets, sorry!
</applet>
```

Using the `<applet>` tag, you can embed applets in Web pages, as Visual J++ has done in this temporary page. You finish off the temporary page with the `</body>` and `</html>` tags this way:

```
<html>
<! NOTE - this file was generated by Microsoft Developer Studio because...>

<head>
<title>Hello</title>
</head>

<body>
<hr>
<applet
code=Hello
width=200
height=200>

</applet>
<hr>

➜ </body>
➜ </html>
```

And that completes our first example—you've gotten a glimpse into the process of creating and running an applet. This example is rudimentary, of course, and demonstrated only the easiest way to get an applet to work. Let's continue to get a better idea of how you'll be working with Visual J++ throughout the book.

Creating a Java Applet Using a Workspace

In the first example, you typed in `Hello.java` like this:

```
import java.awt.Graphics;

class Hello extends java.applet.Applet
{
   public void paint( Graphics g )
   {
     g.drawString( "Hello, World!", 60, 30 );
   }
}
```

and then you compiled and executed it, relying on Visual J++ to create both a "default project workspace" and a Web page to hold the applet. Let's take a look at how Visual J++ usually works when you create applets.

Often, you work with several files when creating an applet, including `.java` files and `.html` files. Several classes can be involved in one applet, and you can even define your own base classes, on which other classes in the applet can build. In general, then, many files may be involved in an applet. Visual J++ provides a way to coordinate all those files into what it calls *projects*.

Visual J++ Projects

To see how Visual J++ projects and project workspaces work, let's use the `Hello.java` file as the basis of a new project, `Hello.mdp` (Microsoft Developer project workspaces have the extension `.mdp`). You will end up with the same applet as before, when Visual J++ created a default project workspace for us, but this time, you will see what is happening (and since you will be creating Visual J++ projects throughout the book, this is useful).

Begin by placing `Hello.java` into a subdirectory named `c:\vjpp\hello`. Next, start Visual J++ and choose File ➤ New to open the New dialog box, which presents the same options as earlier: a new text file, project workspace, resource template, and bitmap file. Last time, you chose text file; this time, choose project workspace to open the New Project Workspace dialog box, as shown in Figure 1.5. You'll set up your new project using this dialog box. Be sure that Java Workspace is selected, as in Figure 1.5.

FIGURE 1.5:

The New Project Workspace dialog box

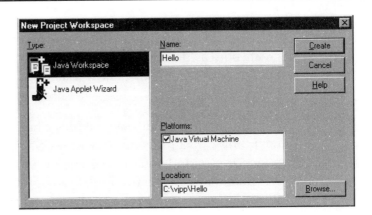

Next, type the name of the new project, **Hello**, in the Name text box, and type the location for your project files in the Location text box, as in Figure 1.5. Click on Create to create the new Visual J++

project workspace named Hello. Visual J++ organizes projects in a project workspace:

```
-------------------------------------------------
|Workspace                                       |
|                                                |
|                                                |
|                                                |
|                                                |
|                                                |
|                                                |
-------------------------------------------------
```

Usually, a project workspace contains only one project:

```
-------------------------------------------------
|Workspace                                       |
|                                                |
|                  ----------------              |
|                  |              |              |
|                  |   Project    |              |
|                  |              |              |
|                  |              |              |
|                  ----------------              |
|                                                |
|                                                |
-------------------------------------------------
```

A workspace can contain a *subproject* as well as a project:

```
-------------------------------------------------
|Workspace                                       |
|                                                |
|             ----------------                   |
|             |              |                   |
|             |   Project    |    -----------    |
|             |              |    | Subproject|  |
|             |              |    |           |  |
|             |              |    -----------    |
|             |              |                   |
|             ----------------                   |
|                                                |
-------------------------------------------------
```

A subproject can create classes needed by the main (so-called top-level project). In fact, you can have several subprojects in a workspace:

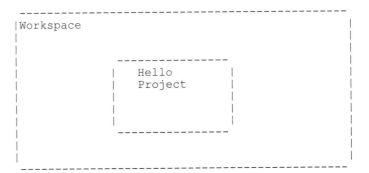

Our workspace will have only one project, named Hello:

```
-------------------------------------------------
|Workspace                                        |
|                                                 |
|               ------------------                |
|               |     Hello      |                |
|               |    Project     |                |
|               |                |                |
|               |                |                |
|               ------------------                |
|                                                 |
|                                                 |
-------------------------------------------------
```

So far, Visual J++ has created the new Hello project and the accompanying file Hello.mak, which contains all the details on how this project is to be created (that is, as an applet or as an application).

Now that you have a new project, you have to add the Hello.java file to it, since that is the source code for the applet. To do that, choose Insert ➤ Files into Project to open the Insert Files into Project dialog box, as shown in Figure 1.6.

FIGURE 1.6:

The Insert Files into
Project dialog box

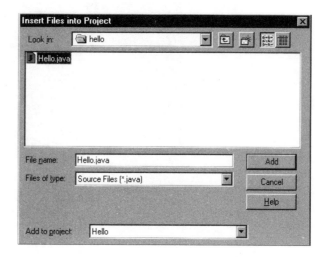

Be sure to place Hello.java in the directory of the new project (in this case, that's c:\vjpp\hello), and in the dialog box, select Hello.java and click on the Add button. This adds Hello.java to your project, and you are ready to go.

TIP

To add subprojects to a workspace, choose Insert ➤ Project. Subprojects are usually used to create classes used by the main applet or application. You can, however, also create additional classes in the main applet or application's source code file without using subprojects at all, and we'll do that often in this book.

To create Hello.class and see it at work, choose Build ➤ Build Hello, and select Execute. In the Information for Running Class dialog box, type **Hello** in the Class File Name box and then click on OK.

Figure 1.7 shows the result. The new project is a success.

FIGURE 1.7:

Our applet at work

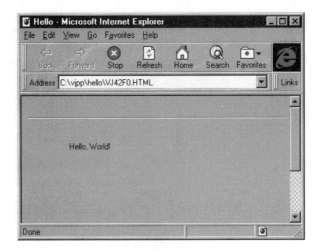

Now that you've set up your first Visual J++ project, let's look at some of the support that Visual J++ offers the project. In particular, let's look at the various ways of getting overviews and handling the files in a project.

Working with Projects: The Project Workspace Window

At this point, then, our first project is set up:

One of the advantages of Visual J++ is that it makes handling the files in a project easy—which is useful when multiple files are involved. You can get an overview by looking in the Visual J++ project workspace window, which is on the left in Figure 1.8. The `Hello files` folder contains one entry, the `Hello.java` file.

FIGURE 1.8:

The Hello project in Visual J++

This is one way to look at a project—as a collection of files. This is useful if you know which files you are dealing with, and it's most useful to organize small projects by file. When you want to open a new file, simply find that file in the list of files and then double-click on its name.

With larger projects that define many Java classes, however, it is difficult to remember what class is where—for example, was that `clock` class defined in `Clk.java` or in `Timer.java`? Sometimes it's better to organize files by content, and Visual J++ allows you to do so by looking at the project's classes in overview. To see how that works, find the three tabs—ClassView, FileView, and InfoView—at the bottom of the Project Workspace window, as shown in Figure 1.8. If you have trouble remembering which tab is which—or what the buttons in the Visual J++ toolbar do—position the mouse cursor over the tab or button (without pressing any mouse button), and a small window (called a tool tip) will appear, telling you what the button or tab does. Click on the ClassView tab now, and double-click on the `Hello Classes` folder, creating the display you see in Figure 1.9.

FIGURE 1.9:

Our Hello project's class view

Figure 1.9 shows the classes in the Hello project—that is, the single class `Hello` that you set up in `Hello.java`:

```java
import java.awt.Graphics;

class Hello extends java.applet.Applet
{
   public void paint( Graphics g )
   {
      g.drawString( "Hello, World!", 60, 30 );
   }
}
```

If you double-click on the `Hello` class in the Class View display, a window appears, opening the `Hello.java` file to the definition of the `Hello` class, as in Figure 1.9. You can do more with ClassView, however—if you click the right mouse button on a Java class in your project, a pop-up menu like the one shown in Figure 1.9 appears. Notice the choices in this menu: You can go directly to the definition of the class in code, define a new variable for the class you selected (you'll see how this works soon), define a new method for the class (as you recall, a method is a function that is part of a class), or even set up an entirely new class (one .java file can define several classes). Similarly, you can click on a file with the right mouse button while viewing the files in a project such as Hello.java (with the FileView tab), and one of the options presented is "Compile Hello.java"—and that provides an easy way to compile file by file if you want to do so in Visual J++.

NOTE It is not usually necessary to compile file by file in a Visual J++ project, because Visual J++ tracks the files that you or programs have modified since the last compilation of the project and compiles them as needed.

The other tab in the Visual J++ Project Workspace window is the InfoView tab, and clicking on it opens the InfoViewer, as shown in Figure 1.10. If you have another Developer Studio package (for example, Visual C++) installed on your computer, choose Help ➤ Open Information Title ➤ Visual J++.

The InfoViewer offers you Microsoft's online help for Visual J++, and you can either browse through the topics sequentially ("book" by "book" as shown with the book icons in Figure 1.10) or use the Search or Index items in the Visual J++ Help menu. When you request help on a particular topic, the InfoViewer opens (if that topic is listed in the help files), displaying the help text. You can also request help on any keyword in a file; simply highlight that word with the mouse and press F1.

The other major window in Visual J++ is the *output window*. It appears at the bottom of Figure 1.10 and has the Build, Debug, Find in Files, and Profile tabs.

FIGURE 1.10:

The Visual J++
Infoviewer

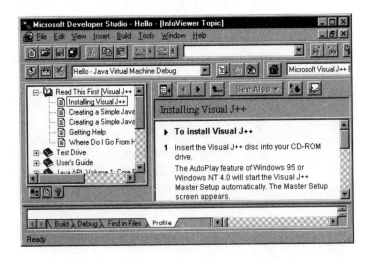

Here is where you will see the results of operations, such as compiling a class or debugging it. For example, when you compile `Hello.java` into `Hello.class`, this is where you see the message:

```
—Configuration: Hello - Java Virtual Machine Debug—-

Compiling...
Microsoft (R) Visual J++ Compiler Version 1.00.6229
Copyright (C) Microsoft Corp 1996. All rights reserved.

  Hello - 0 error(s), 0 warning(s)
```

If there are errors when you compile your project, you'll see an error message or messages in this window, along with the name of the file that contains the erroneous code and the line number of the code that caused the problem. Double-clicking on the line number in the output window opens the corresponding file so that you can edit it.

Visual J++ also has other file management tools that you'll see throughout the book. For example, you've seen how to add files to a project by choosing Insert ➤ Files into Project. You can also add `.html` files into a project, and you'll see how to do that soon. File connections can become complex in a Visual J++ project, because you can

explicitly include files in other files, and Visual J++ helps here too
(choose Build ➤ Update All Dependencies).

You now have an overview of a project. For our purposes, then, we
can think of a project as an assemblage of files:

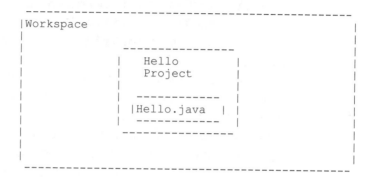

or as an assemblage of classes:

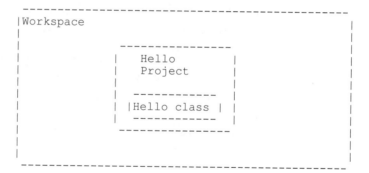

In either case, Visual J++ handles the details. Visual J++ will even
create *all* the files necessary for a project automatically with the
Applet Wizard. If you use the Visual J++ Applet Wizard, you'll
typically have to add only a few lines of code to customize an applet.
Because this is one of the most powerful features of Visual J++, let's
look at it in more detail.

Using the Applet Wizard to Create a Visual J++ Project

You may recall that when we created the Hello project's workspace, we chose File ➤ New, and Visual J++ displayed two options, Java Workspace and Java Applet Wizard, as shown in Figure 1.5. Earlier, we selected Java Workspace (that is, when creating the Hello project), let Visual J++ create the workspace, and then added the `Hello.java` file as the main file of the new project. However, Visual J++ offers a great deal of support in the Applet Wizard, which will write our project's main `.java` file for us (all except for the specific code that makes it do what we want it to do—namely, display Hello, World! in the applet's window). That is, the Applet Wizard creates a file with many comments and predefined methods that you can use—all you have to do is to add the code you want to the method in which you are interested. This is the standard way we'll set up a project in this book, so let's look at this process now.

Choose File ➤ New ➤ Project Workspace, and then click on OK. In the New Project Workspace dialog box, select Java Applet Wizard in the Type box. Next, give this new project workspace the name Hello2 in the Name box, and click on Create to open Step 1 of the Java Applet Wizard, as shown in Figure 1.11.

The Java Applet Wizard,
Step 1 of 5

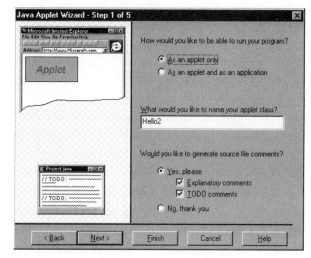

The Applet Wizard asks how you want to run your program. Be sure the As an Applet Only choice is selected, and then click on the Next button to move to Step 2, as shown in Figure 1.12.

The Java Applet Wizard,
Step 2 of 5

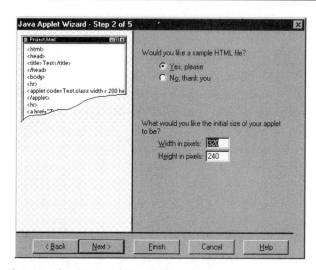

Here the Applet Wizard is asking if you want a sample `.html` file in which you can display your new applet. Leave the Yes, Please option selected. The Applet Wizard creates the following `.html` file and adds it to your project:

```
<html>
<head>
<title>Hello2</title>
</head>
<body>
<hr>
<applet
  code=Hello2.class
  id=Hello2
  width=320
  height=240 >
</applet>
<hr>
<a href="Hello2.java">The source.</a>
</body>
</html>
```

In Step 2 you can also set the size of the applet. The Java Applet Wizard asks us what size to make the applet (measured in pixels). Leave the width at 320 and the height at 240, and click on the Next button to move to Step 3, as shown in Figure 1.13.

FIGURE 1.13:

The Java Applet Wizard,
Step 3 of 5

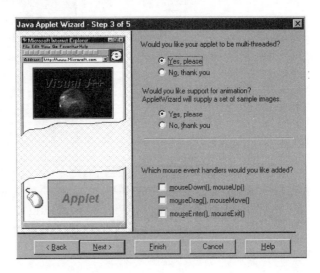

The Applet Wizard asks, "Would you like your applet to be multi-threaded?" Java supports multitasking—that is, it can divide what it does among several *threads*, or independent execution streams, that run at the same time (you'll see more about this later). Here, leave the Yes, Please option selected, as in Figure 1.13.

In addition, the Applet Wizard asks, "Would you like support for animation?" Leave the Yes, Please option selected here too. When you run your applet for the first time, you'll find that Visual J++ has added a sample animation (a circling globe). You can already see the globe in Figure 1.13.

Now, click on Next to go to Step 4. In this step, you can add *parameters* to your applet—you may recall that we can pass parameters to our applet in the ⟨applet⟩ tag:

```
<APPLET
     [ALIGN = LEFT or RIGHT or TOP or TEXTTOP or MIDDLE or ABSMIDDLE   or
➥ BASELINE or BOTTOM or ABSBOTTOM]
     [ALT = AlternateText]
     CODE = AppletName.class
     [CODEBASE = URL of .class file]
     HEIGHT = AppletPixelsHeight
     [HSPACE = PixelSpaceToLeftOfApplet]
     [NAME = AppletInstanceName]
     [VSPACE = PixelSpaceAboveApplet]
     WIDTH = AppletPixelsWidth
   >
➜ [<PARAM NAME = Parameter1 VALUE = VALUE1]
➜ [<PARAM NAME = Parameter2 VALUE = VALUE2]
          .
          .
          .

</APPLET>
```

In the applet itself, you use functions such as getParameterInfo() to work with these parameters.

TIP **You'll see later that the Applet Wizard makes it easy to get parameters that are passed to an applet from the Web page.**

We won't use any parameters here, so simply click on the Next button to go to Step 5. In this step, you can enter information about the applet that will be returned by the applet's `getAppinfo()` method (for example, when the Web browser calls this method). Here, leave the default information intact (although you can add as much as you like in the textbox displayed in this step):

```
Name: Hello2
Author: Steven Holzner
Created with Microsoft Visual J++ Version 1.0
```

Now, click on the Finish button to open the New Project Information box, which contains this information about the new project:

```
Applet class: Hello2

Applet Info:
    Name: Hello2
    Author: Steven Holzner
    Created with Microsoft Visual J++ Version 1.0

Files:
    Hello2.java: Hello2 class source code
    Hello2.html: Sample html file
    Image files for animation: img0001.gif - img0018.gif

Initial Size:
    Width in pixels: 320
    Height in pixels: 240

Features:
        + User Comments
        + TODO Comments
        + Multi Threaded
        + Simple Animation
```

Click on OK, and the Applet Wizard creates the files (note that `Hello2.mdp` is the file to open with Visual J++ when you want to open the Hello2 project):

`Hello2.java`	Java source file
`Hello2.html`	Sample `.html` file
`Hello2.ncb`	Project file
`Hello2.mak`	Build options file
`Hello2.mdp`	Developer Studio Project file

The Applet Wizard also creates a folder named `images`, in which it stores the images for the default animation it produces (a whirling globe) in the files `img001.gif` to `img018.gif`.

That's all we need for a working applet. Of course, it won't do what we want it to do until we customize the new `Hello2.java` by adding our own code, but we can already run the Hello2 applet using only the code that the Applet Wizard has created for us. In this case, you will see a whirling globe embedded in the Web page like this:

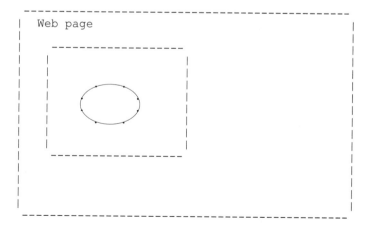

Try this new applet now. Choose Build ➤ Build Hello2 ➤ Execute. The result appears in Figure 1.14—the new applet is working, and it even displays images.

FIGURE 1.14:

Our first Applet Wizard applet

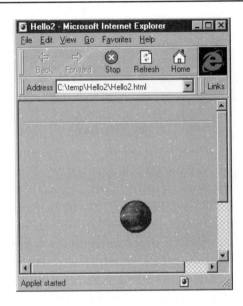

The `.java` file for this new applet appears in `Hello2.java`—as you can see, the Applet Wizard has already done a lot of work for us.

We'll dissect this new program, `Hello2.java`, in the next chapter, but for now, let's see how to modify the program to display our Hello, World! message.

Hello2.java

```
//***************************************************************************
// Hello2.java: Applet
//
//***************************************************************************
import java.applet.*;
import java.awt.*;
```

```java
//===========================================================================
// Main Class for applet Hello2
//
//===========================================================================
public class Hello2 extends Applet implements Runnable
{
  // THREAD SUPPORT:
  //   m_Hello2 is the Thread object for the applet
  //-------------------------------------------------------------------------
  Thread  m_Hello2 = null;

  // ANIMATION SUPPORT:
  //   m_Graphics used for storing the applet's Graphics context
  //   m_Images[] the array of Image objects for the animation
  //   m_nCurrImage the index of the next image to be displayed
  //   m_ImgWidth width of each image
  //   m_ImgHeight height of each image
  //   m_fAllLoaded indicates whether all images have been loaded
  //   NUM_IMAGES number of images used in the animation
  //-------------------------------------------------------------------------
  private Graphics m_Graphics;
  private Image m_Images[];
  private int   m_nCurrImage;
  private int   m_nImgWidth  = 0;
  private int   m_nImgHeight = 0;
  private boolean  m_fAllLoaded = false;
  private final int NUM_IMAGES = 18;


  // Hello2 Class Constructor
  //-------------------------------------------------------------------------
  public Hello2()
  {
    // TODO: Add constructor code here
  }


  // APPLET INFO SUPPORT:
  //   The getAppletInfo() method returns a string describing the applet's
  // author, copyright date, or miscellaneous information.
  //-------------------------------------------------------------------------
  public String getAppletInfo()
  {
```

```
      return "Name: Hello2\r\n" +
          "Author: Steven Holzner\r\n" +
          "Created with Microsoft Visual J++ Version 1.0";
}


// The init() method is called by the AWT when an applet is first loaded or
// reloaded.  Override this method to perform whatever initialization your
// applet needs, such as initializing data structures, loading images or
// fonts, creating frame windows, setting the layout manager, or adding UI
// components.
//--------------------------------------------------------------------------
public void init()
{
   // If you use a ResourceWizard-generated "control creator" class to
   // arrange controls in your applet, you may want to call its
   // CreateControls() method from within this method. Remove the following
   // call to resize() before adding the call to CreateControls();
   // CreateControls() does its own resizing.
   //-----------------------------------------------------------------------
   resize(320, 240);

   // TODO: Place additional initialization code here
}


// Place additional applet clean up code here.  destroy() is called
// when your applet is terminating and being unloaded.
//--------------------------------------------------------------------------
public void destroy()
{
   // TODO: Place applet cleanup code here
}


// ANIMATION SUPPORT:
//   Draws the next image, if all images are currently loaded
//--------------------------------------------------------------------------
private void displayImage(Graphics g)
{
   if (!m_fAllLoaded)
      return;

   // Draw Image in center of applet
```

```
    //------------------------------------------------------------------
    g.drawImage(m_Images[m_nCurrImage],
            (size().width - m_nImgWidth)   / 2,
            (size().height - m_nImgHeight) / 2, null);
    }


    // Hello2 Paint Handler
    //------------------------------------------------------------------
    {
        // ANIMATION SUPPORT:
        //   The following code displays a status message until all the
        //   images are loaded. Then it calls displayImage to display the current
        //   image.
        //------------------------------------------------------------------
        if (m_fAllLoaded)
        {
            Rectangle r = g.getClipRect();

            g.clearRect(r.x, r.y, r.width, r.height);
            displayImage(g);
        }
        else
            g.drawString("Loading images...", 10, 20);

        // TODO: Place additional applet Paint code here
    }


    //   The start() method is called when the page containing the applet
    //   first appears on the screen. The AppletWizard's initial implementation
    //   of this method starts execution of the applet's thread.
    //------------------------------------------------------------------
    public void start()
    {
        if (m_Hello2 == null)
        {
            m_Hello2 = new Thread(this);
            m_Hello2.start();
        }
        // TODO: Place additional applet start code here
    }


    //   The stop() method is called when the page containing the applet is
```

```
// no longer on the screen. The AppletWizard's initial implementation of
// this method stops execution of the applet's thread.
//--------------------------------------------------------------------------
public void stop()
{
  if (m_Hello2 != null)
  {
    m_Hello2.stop();
    m_Hello2 = null;
  }

  // TODO: Place additional applet stop code here
}


// THREAD SUPPORT
//   The run() method is called when the applet's thread is started. If
// your applet performs any ongoing activities without waiting for user
// input, the code for implementing that behavior typically goes here. For
// example, for an applet that performs animation, the run() method controls
// the display of images.
//--------------------------------------------------------------------------
public void run()
{
  m_nCurrImage = 0;

  // If re-entering the page, then the images have already been loaded.
  // m_fAllLoaded == TRUE.
  //--------------------------------------------------------------------------
  if (!m_fAllLoaded)
  {
    repaint();
    m_Graphics = getGraphics();
    m_Images   = new Image[NUM_IMAGES];

    // Load in all the images
    //--------------------------------------------------------------------------
    MediaTracker tracker = new MediaTracker(this);
    String strImage;

    // For each image in the animation, this method first constructs a
    // string containing the path to the image file; then it begins
    // loading the image into the m_Images array.  Note that the call to
```

```java
   // getImage will return before the image is completely loaded.
   //------------------------------------------------------------------
   for (int i = 1; i <= NUM_IMAGES; i++)
   {
      // Build path to next image
      //---------------------------------------------------------------
      strImage = "images/img00" + ((i < 10) ? "0" : "") + i + ".gif";
      m_Images[i-1] = getImage(getDocumentBase(), strImage);

      tracker.addImage(m_Images[i-1], 0);
   }


   // Wait until all images are fully loaded
   //------------------------------------------------------------------
   try
   {
      tracker.waitForAll();
      m_fAllLoaded = !tracker.isErrorAny();
   }
   catch (InterruptedException e)
   {
      // TODO: Place exception-handling code here in case an
      //    InterruptedException is thrown by Thread.sleep(),
      //    meaning that another thread has interrupted this one
   }

   if (!m_fAllLoaded)
   {
      stop();
      m_Graphics.drawString("Error loading images!", 10, 40);
      return;
   }


   // Assuming all images are same width and height.
   //------------------------------------------------------------------
   m_nImgWidth  = m_Images[0].getWidth(this);
   m_nImgHeight = m_Images[0].getHeight(this);
}
repaint();
```

```
while (true)
{
  try
  {
    // Draw next image in animation
    //----------------------------------------------------------------
    displayImage(m_Graphics);
    m_nCurrImage++;
    if (m_nCurrImage == NUM_IMAGES)
      m_nCurrImage = 0;

    // TODO:  Add additional thread-specific code here
    Thread.sleep(50);
  }
  catch (InterruptedException e)
  {
    // TODO: Place exception-handling code here in case an
    //    InterruptedException is thrown by Thread.sleep(),
    //    meaning that another thread has interrupted this one
    stop();
  }
}


  // TODO: Place additional applet code here

}
```

To customize this applet, you can add a string of text to it like this:

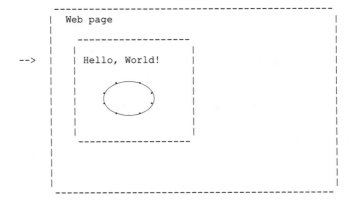

Modifying an Applet Wizard–Produced Java File

You can display the Hello, World! message in the Hello2 class's paint() method, as we did with the Hello class earlier. To do that, you need to find the paint() method in the file Hello2.java, and because there can be dozens of methods in a file, Visual J++ makes that easy. In the Project Workspace window, select the ClassView tab and click on the Hello2 icon, as shown in Figure 1.15. There you can see all the methods in this class, including the paint() method. To open Hello2.java directly to the paint() method, double–click on its entry in the Project Workspace window. The paint() method appears in the Developer Studio's main window, as shown in Figure 1.15.

FIGURE 1.15:

Finding the Hello2 class's paint() method

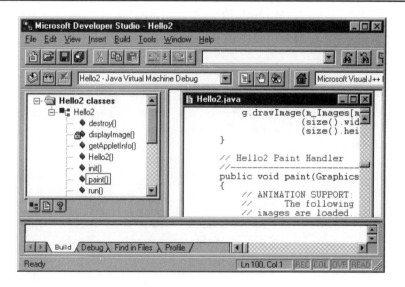

Here's how the paint() method looks now (that is, after the Applet Wizard created it):

```
public void paint(Graphics g)
{
    // ANIMATION SUPPORT:
```

```
//   The following code displays a status message until all the
// images are loaded. Then it calls displayImage to display the current
// image.
//--------------------------------------------------------------------
if (m_fAllLoaded)
{
   Rectangle r = g.getClipRect();

   g.clearRect(r.x, r.y, r.width, r.height);
   displayImage(g);
}
else
   g.drawString("Loading images...", 10, 20);

// TODO: Place additional applet Paint code here

}
```

You might notice a few things here. First, Java uses the same one-line comments that you see in C++:

```
public void paint(Graphics g)
{
→// ANIMATION SUPPORT:
→//The following code displays a status message until all the
→// images are loaded. Then it calls displayImage to display the current
→// image.
         .
         .
         .
```

When you use a double slash (//), Visual J++ ignores everything on the rest of the line (that is, everything to the right of the double slash). In addition, much Java syntax is the same as C++ syntax. For example, you see here an if...else combination that displays the message "Loading images..." before the images that make up the whirling globe have been loaded into the applet and then displays the whirling globe (elsewhere in the program, the variable m_fAllLoaded is set to TRUE when the images are loaded and the globe is ready to be displayed):

```
public void paint(Graphics g)
{
    // ANIMATION SUPPORT:
    //   The following code displays a status message until all the
    // images are loaded. Then it calls displayImage to display the current
    // image.
    //-------------------------------------------------------------------
➜   if (m_fAllLoaded)
    {
       Rectangle r = g.getClipRect();

       g.clearRect(r.x, r.y, r.width, r.height);
       displayImage(g);
    }
➜   else
       g.drawString("Loading images...", 10, 20);
            .

            .

            .
```

Finally, you might notice an additional line (starting TODO) at the end of the paint() method as the Applet Wizard set it up:

```
public void paint(Graphics g)
{
    // ANIMATION SUPPORT:
    //   The following code displays a status message until all the
    // images are loaded. Then it calls displayImage to display the current
    // image.
    //-------------------------------------------------------------------
    if (m_fAllLoaded)
    {
       Rectangle r = g.getClipRect();

       g.clearRect(r.x, r.y, r.width, r.height);
       displayImage(g);
    }
    else
       g.drawString("Loading images...", 10, 20);

➜   // TODO: Place additional applet Paint code here

}
```

This is how the Applet Wizard indicates that you can modify the methods it has already written, and you'll find the Applet Wizard TODO's throughout Hello2.java. In this case, you want to display the Hello, World! message as before. You do so with our previous line of code:

```
public void paint(Graphics g)
{
    // ANIMATION SUPPORT:
    //   The following code displays a status message until all the
    // images are loaded. Then it calls displayImage to display the current
    // image.
    //-------------------------------------------------------------------
    if (m_fAllLoaded)
    {
        Rectangle r = g.getClipRect();

        g.clearRect(r.x, r.y, r.width, r.height);
        displayImage(g);
    }
    else
        g.drawString("Loading images...", 10, 20);

    // TODO: Place additional applet Paint code here

➜   g.drawString( "Hello, World!", 60, 30 );
}
```

The new version of this applet appears in Figure 1.16. As you can see, it displays not only the whirling globe, but also the Hello, World! message.

FIGURE 1.16:

The new Hello2 applet

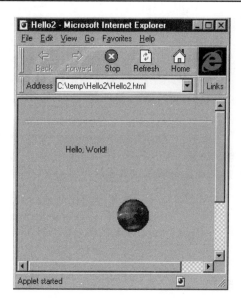

Besides applets that go into Web pages, it's also possible to create Java *applications*. Unlike applets, these programs don't need to work with a Web browser. It's as easy to create an application as an applet, so let's take a quick look at that now.

Java Applications

Java applications don't differ much from applets. You can use the Applet Wizard to create this example application, which we will call helloapp.

Choose File ➤ New ➤ Project Workspace. In the New Project Workspace box, be sure that Java Applet Wizard is selected in the Type box, and type **helloapp** in the Name box. Click on the Create button to start the Applet Wizard.

When the Applet Wizard asks, "How would you like to be able to run your program?" click on the "As an applet and as an application" button. That's all you need—click on the Finish button to create a new application. The Applet Wizard creates two new .java files—helloapp.java, our source code file for the application, and helloappFrame.java, which handles the "frame" window (it's called a frame window because it has a frame that can be resized) in which you can display your new application.

> **TIP**
>
> Although there are far more Java applets in use than Java applications, a big advantage of a Java application is that it runs on so many computer platforms. If you are thinking of targeting different operating systems and hardware with an application you'd like to write, Java is a good programming language choice.

The *main()* Method

All that is really different here from the hello applet is that the Applet Wizard has given our application a method called main(). This is necessary in Java applications because it provides the starting point of the program. If, however, you run this application as an applet in a Web page (which you can), the main() method is ignored. In the main() method, the program creates a new frame window from the new helloappFrame class and starts the application in it:

```
public static void main(String args[])
{
    // Create Toplevel Window to contain applet helloapp
    //------------------------------------------------------------------
    helloappFrame frame = new helloappFrame("helloapp");

    // Must show Frame before we size it so insets() returns valid values
    //------------------------------------------------------------------
    frame.show();
    frame.hide();
    frame.resize(frame.insets().left + frame.insets().right  + 320,
 frame.insets().top  + frame.insets().bottom + 240);
```

```
      // The following code starts the applet running within the frame window.
      // It also calls GetParameters() to retrieve parameter values from the
      // command line, and sets m_fStandAlone to true to prevent init() from
      // trying to get them from the HTML page.
      //------------------------------------------------------------------------
→         helloapp applet_helloapp = new helloapp();

→         frame.add("Center", applet_helloapp);
→         applet_helloapp.m_fStandAlone = true;
→         applet_helloapp.init();
→         applet_helloapp.start();
→         frame.show();
    }
```

The major difference between an applet and an application is the use of the `main()` method. You can modify the `paint()` method of our application as you did before to display the message Hello, World! this way:

```
   // helloapp Paint Handler
   //-----------------------------------------------------------------------
public void paint(Graphics g)
{
    // ANIMATION SUPPORT:
    //   The following code displays a status message until all the
    // images are loaded. Then it calls displayImage to display the current
    // image.
    //-----------------------------------------------------------------------
    if (m_fAllLoaded)
    {
       Rectangle r = g.getClipRect();

       g.clearRect(r.x, r.y, r.width, r.height);
       displayImage(g);
    }
    else
       g.drawString("Loading images...", 10, 20);

→      g.drawString("Hello, World!", 10, 10);
       // TODO: Place additional applet Paint code here
    }
```

Now build the application by choosing Build ➤ Build helloapp.

To run this application without the Web browser, choose Build ➤ Settings and select the Debug tab in the Project Settings dialog box. In the Debug/Execute Project Under dialog box, click on the Stand-Alone Interpreter button and then click on OK. Now, choose Build ➤ Execute helloapp to run the application.

If you prefer, you can also run the new application using the jview application viewer that comes with Visual J++. This program, `jview.exe`, is a command-line program (that is, you run it in a DOS window), which Visual J++ places in `c:\windows`. To view the application at work, then, change to the directory that contains the application's `.class` files and type:

```
C:\vjpp\helloapp>c:\windows\jview helloapp
```

This produces the result shown in Figure 1.17—now we've gotten a program to run without a Web browser. The code for this application appears in `helloapp.java`.

FIGURE 1.17:

Our first Java application

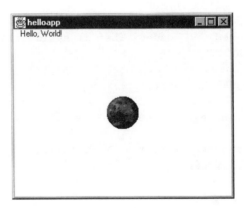

helloapp.java

```java
//*****************************************************************************
// helloapp.java: Applet
//
//*****************************************************************************
import java.applet.*;
import java.awt.*;
import helloappFrame;


//=============================================================================
// Main Class for applet helloapp
//
//=============================================================================
public class helloapp extends Applet implements Runnable
{
    // THREAD SUPPORT:
    //    m_helloapp is the Thread object for the applet
    //-------------------------------------------------------------------------
    Thread  m_helloapp = null;

    // ANIMATION SUPPORT:
    //    m_Graphics     used for storing the applet's Graphics context
    //    m_Images[]     the array of Image objects for the animation
    //    m_nCurrImage   the index of the next image to be displayed
    //    m_ImgWidth     width of each image
    //    m_ImgHeight    height of each image
    //    m_fAllLoaded   indicates whether all images have been loaded
    //    NUM_IMAGES     number of images used in the animation
    //-------------------------------------------------------------------------
    private Graphics m_Graphics;
    private Image m_Images[];
    private int   m_nCurrImage;
    private int   m_nImgWidth  = 0;
    private int   m_nImgHeight = 0;
    private boolean  m_fAllLoaded = false;
    private final int NUM_IMAGES = 18;

    // STANDALONE APPLICATION SUPPORT:
    //    m_fStandAlone will be set to true if applet is run standalone
    //-------------------------------------------------------------------------
    boolean m_fStandAlone = false;
```

```
// STANDALONE APPLICATION SUPPORT
// The main() method acts as the applet's entry point when it is run
// as a standalone application. It is ignored if the applet is run from
// within an HTML page.
//---------------------------------------------------------------------
public static void main(String args[])
{
   // Create Toplevel Window to contain applet helloapp
   //------------------------------------------------------------------
   helloappFrame frame = new helloappFrame("helloapp");

   // Must show Frame before we size it so insets() will return valid values
   //------------------------------------------------------------------
   frame.show();
   frame.hide();
   frame.resize(frame.insets().left + frame.insets().right  + 320,
           frame.insets().top  + frame.insets().bottom + 240);

   // The following code starts the applet running within the frame window.
   // It also calls GetParameters() to retrieve parameter values from the
   // command line, and sets m_fStandAlone to true to prevent init() from
   // trying to get them from the HTML page.
   //------------------------------------------------------------------
   helloapp applet_helloapp = new helloapp();

   frame.add("Center", applet_helloapp);
   applet_helloapp.m_fStandAlone = true;
   applet_helloapp.init();
   applet_helloapp.start();
   frame.show();
}


// helloapp Class Constructor
//---------------------------------------------------------------------
public helloapp()
{
   // TODO: Add constructor code here
}
```

```
// APPLET INFO SUPPORT:
  //   The getAppletInfo() method returns a string describing the applet's
  // author, copyright date, or miscellaneous information.
  //------------------------------------------------------------------------
  public String getAppletInfo()
  {
    return "Name: helloapp\r\n" +
         "Author: Steven Holzner\r\n" +
         "Created with Microsoft Visual J++ Version 1.0";
  }



  // The init() method is called by the AWT when an applet is first loaded or
  // reloaded.  Override this method to perform whatever initialization your
  // applet needs, such as initializing data structures, loading images or
  // fonts, creating frame windows, setting the layout manager, or adding UI
  // components.
  //------------------------------------------------------------------------
  public void init()
  {
    // If you use a ResourceWizard-generated "control creator" class to
    // arrange controls in your applet, you may want to call its
    // CreateControls() method from within this method. Remove the following
    // call to resize() before adding the call to CreateControls();
    // CreateControls() does its own resizing.
    //----------------------------------------------------------------------
    resize(320, 240);

    // TODO: Place additional initialization code here
  }

  // Place additional applet clean up code here.  destroy() is called
  // when your applet is terminating and being unloaded.
  //------------------------------------------------------------------------
  public void destroy()
  {
    // TODO: Place applet cleanup code here
  }

  // ANIMATION SUPPORT:
  //   Draws the next image, if all images are currently loaded
  //------------------------------------------------------------------------
```

```java
private void displayImage(Graphics g)
{
  if (!m_fAllLoaded)
    return;

  // Draw Image in center of applet
  //-------------------------------------------------------------------
  g.drawImage(m_Images[m_nCurrImage],
          (size().width  - m_nImgWidth)  / 2,
          (size().height - m_nImgHeight) / 2, null);
}

// helloapp Paint Handler
//-------------------------------------------------------------------
public void paint(Graphics g)
{
  // ANIMATION SUPPORT:
  //   The following code displays a status message until all the
  //   images are loaded. Then it calls displayImage to display the current
  //   image.
  //-------------------------------------------------------------------
  if (m_fAllLoaded)
  {
    Rectangle r = g.getClipRect();

    g.clearRect(r.x, r.y, r.width, r.height);
    displayImage(g);
  }
  else
    g.drawString("Loading images...", 10, 20);

  g.drawString("Hello, World!", 10, 10);
  // TODO: Place additional applet Paint code here
}

//   The start() method is called when the page containing the applet
// first appears on the screen. The AppletWizard's initial implementation
// of this method starts execution of the applet's thread.
//-------------------------------------------------------------------
public void start()
{
```

```
   if (m_helloapp == null)
   {
     m_helloapp = new Thread(this);
     m_helloapp.start();
   }
   // TODO: Place additional applet start code here
}


//   The stop() method is called when the page containing the applet is
// no longer on the screen. The AppletWizard's initial implementation of
// this method stops execution of the applet's thread.
//-------------------------------------------------------------------------
public void stop()
{
   if (m_helloapp != null)
   {
     m_helloapp.stop();
     m_helloapp = null;
   }

   // TODO: Place additional applet stop code here
}


// THREAD SUPPORT
//   The run() method is called when the applet's thread is started. If
// your applet performs any ongoing activities without waiting for user
// input, the code for implementing that behavior typically goes here. For
// example, for an applet that performs animation, the run() method controls
// the display of images.
//-------------------------------------------------------------------------
public void run()
{
   m_nCurrImage = 0;

   // If re-entering the page, then the images have already been loaded.
   // m_fAllLoaded == TRUE.
   //----------------------------------------------------------------------
   if (!m_fAllLoaded)
   {
     repaint();
     m_Graphics = getGraphics();
     m_Images   = new Image[NUM_IMAGES];
```

```
// Load in all the images
//------------------------------------------------------------------
MediaTracker tracker = new MediaTracker(this);
String strImage;

// For each image in the animation, this method first constructs a
// string containing the path to the image file; then it begins
// loading the image into the m_Images array.  Note that the call to
// getImage will return before the image is completely loaded.
//------------------------------------------------------------------
for (int i = 1; i <= NUM_IMAGES; i++)
{
  // Build path to next image
  //------------------------------------------------------------------
  strImage = "images/img00" + ((i < 10) ? "0" : "") + i + ".gif";
  if (m_fStandAlone)
    m_Images[i-1] = Toolkit.getDefaultToolkit().getImage(strImage);
  else
    m_Images[i-1] = getImage(getDocumentBase(), strImage);

  tracker.addImage(m_Images[i-1], 0);
}

// Wait until all images are fully loaded
//------------------------------------------------------------------
try
{
  tracker.waitForAll();
  m_fAllLoaded = !tracker.isErrorAny();
}
catch (InterruptedException e)
{
  // TODO: Place exception-handling code here in case an
  //    InterruptedException is thrown by Thread.sleep(),
  //    meaning that another thread has interrupted this one
}

if (!m_fAllLoaded)
{
  stop();
```

```
            m_Graphics.drawString("Error loading images!", 10, 40);
            return;
        }


        // Assuming all images are same width and height.
        //------------------------------------------------------------------
        m_nImgWidth  = m_Images[0].getWidth(this);
        m_nImgHeight = m_Images[0].getHeight(this);
    }
    repaint();

    while (true)
    {
      try
      {
        // Draw next image in animation
        //--------------------------------------------------------------
        displayImage(m_Graphics);
        m_nCurrImage++;
        if (m_nCurrImage == NUM_IMAGES)
          m_nCurrImage = 0;

        // TODO:  Add additional thread-specific code here
        Thread.sleep(50);
      }
      catch (InterruptedException e)
      {
        // TODO: Place exception-handling code here in case an
        //   InterruptedException is thrown by Thread.sleep(),
        //   meaning that another thread has interrupted this one
        stop();
      }
    }
  }


  // TODO: Place additional applet code here

}
```

What's Next?

Note that we still haven't examined all that the Applet Wizard has built into the `Hello2.java` file; and a great deal of power is buried in all the unexamined portions. We'll take a look at what the Applet Wizard created for us as we dissect `Hello2.java` in the next chapter.

CHAPTER

TWO

2

Visual J++ Text Fields

- The `getAppletInfo()` method

- The `init()` method

- The `displayImage()` method

- The `paint()` method

- The `start()`, `stop()`, and `run()` methods

In this chapter, we're going to start adding *controls* to our applets. Controls are the interactive items you find in applets—for example, text boxes, buttons, scroll bars, and scrolling list boxes—and they're a powerful part of Java programs. In this chapter, we're going to start with one of the most important and fundamental controls, text boxes, which are called *text fields* in Java. A text field is simply a box on the screen that can hold and display text. The user can place text in it, and so can we. For example, in the next chapter, when I discuss how to use Java buttons in programs, you'll see how to create an applet that has a text field and a Click Me button like this:

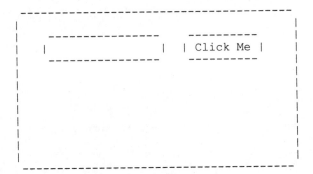

When the user clicks on the Click Me button, the applet places the Hello, World! message in the text field like this:

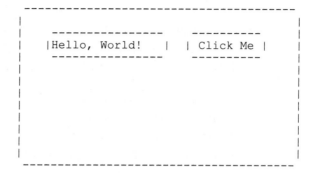

In this way, you use text fields to hold and display text in Java programs, which is an important task. Any text-based output can go into text fields. For example, you might want to report on the results of a search, or you might want to indicate to the user which options are currently set, or you can even accept messages that the user types and that your applet records. Any Windows user can attest to the hundreds of uses for text fields. Using controls such as text fields is a strong technique in Java—in fact, using the included controls is often the whole point of an applet.

Before working with text fields, however, we'll dig deeper into the Java source code file that the Applet Wizard created for us in the last chapter, `Hello2.java`. Getting an overview of what the Applet Wizard can do will be important as we continue our guided tour of Java. We will create almost all the programs in this book by using the Visual J++ Applet Wizard, so seeing exactly what that tool creates for us will be crucial.

What Makes *Hello2.java* Tick?

We used the Applet Wizard in the last chapter to create the Hello2 applet, which displayed both a whirling globe and the Hello, World! message. The Applet Wizard placed a great deal of Java support for us in `Hello2.java`, and it will be helpful to get an overview of that. Most of the actual Java code in this file will not make a great deal of sense right now, but that's fine, because we just want an overview of the type of AppletWizard-created files we'll be working with.

Don't worry about the details (a large part of this book is about the details, as well as sections coming up in this chapter). The listing appears in `Hello2.java`, and it's typical of the program *skeleton* that the Applet Wizard creates for us. That is, we can use the Applet Wizard to create the rough framework of the applet's code, but it's up to us to work on that framework, adding the code we need to make what we want actually work. This will be our typical programming practice: We will use the Applet Wizard to create a program skeleton, and then we'll add code to it. Let's look through `Hello2.java` now so that we can become familiar with the various parts of what the Applet Wizard has created; knowing the structure of that skeleton will make it possible to modify it when you write your own applets.

Declaring Our New Class

In the first section of this file, you declare the new `Hello2` class, deriving it from the Java `Applet` class (which, as you saw in the last chapter, deals with the Web browser and sets up the applet's space in the Web page):

```
//******************************************************************************
// Hello2.java: Applet
//
//******************************************************************************
import java.applet.*;
import java.awt.*;


//==============================================================================
// Main Class for applet Hello2
//
//==============================================================================
```

```
→ public class Hello2 extends Applet implements Runnable
  {
    // THREAD SUPPORT:
    //   m_Hello2 is the Thread object for the applet
    //-----------------------------------------------------------------------
    Thread  m_Hello2 = null;

    // ANIMATION SUPPORT:
    //   m_Graphics       used for storing the applet's Graphics context
    //   m_Images[]       the array of Image objects for the animation
    //   m_nCurrImage     the index of the next image to be displayed
    //   m_ImgWidth       width of each image
    //   m_ImgHeight      height of each image
    //   m_fAllLoaded     indicates whether all images have been loaded
    //   NUM_IMAGES       number of images used in the animation
    //-----------------------------------------------------------------------
    private Graphics m_Graphics;
    private Image m_Images[];
    private int   m_nCurrImage;
    private int   m_nImgWidth  = 0;
    private int   m_nImgHeight = 0;
    private boolean m_fAllLoaded = false;
    private final int NUM_IMAGES = 18;
          .
          .
          .
```

Notice the words implements Runnable—those keywords here add multithreaded support to the applet, as you'll see when we cover multitasking in the *Image Handling* chapter.

> **NOTE** A *thread* is an execution stream in Java. That is, a multitasking program that can do several things at once has two or more of these threads working at the same time. You'll see a great deal more about this in the *Image Handling* chapter.

The Java Numeric Data Types

Notice also all the variables defined for use in the program:

```
private Graphics m_Graphics;
private Image  m_Images[];
private int   m_nCurrImage;
private int   m_nImgWidth  = 0;
private int   m_nImgHeight = 0;
private boolean  m_fAllLoaded = false;
private final int NUM_IMAGES = 18;
     .
     .
     .
```

Here you see variables of type Graphics (you have already seen the Java Graphics class), Image (another built-in Java class), integers, a boolean variable (boolean variables can take two values: TRUE or FALSE), and another integer. You will find that the numeric data types in Java are the same as most standard C or C++ implementations. The built-in Java numeric data types such as int and float appear in Table 2.1.

TABLE 2.1: The Java Numeric Data Types

Type	Bits	Means
byte	8	Holds a byte of data
short	16	Short integer
int	32	Integer value
long	64	Long integer
float	32	Floating-point value
double	64	Double-precision floating-point value
char	16	Unicode character
boolean	—	Takes TRUE or FALSE values

Another thing to notice is that these variables appear right after the declaration of the new `Hello2` class and outside any class method. That means they are accessible from any method in the class; in other words, these variables are considered *global* to the class.

TIP

It is usually good to keep the number of global class variables to a minimum. Because these variables can be reached anywhere, there is always the possibility of conflict with another variable of the same name in one of your methods. Using too many global variables goes directly against the spirit of object-oriented programming, which was originally developed to handle larger programs by getting variables and methods out of the global space and placing them in objects to clear the global space of clutter. At certain times you will need global variables in your classes, but those variables that can be made part of individual methods should be placed in those methods.

Note that you can declare a class's data as `private, protected,` or `public,` just as you can for a class's methods. Here, all the above variables are declared as `private`, which means they are accessible only to the methods in objects of this class.

Java Class Constructors

Next in `Hello2.java` is the class's *constructor*:

```
// Hello2 Class Constructor
//-------------------------------------------------------------
public Hello2()
{
  // TODO: Add constructor code here
} .
  .
  .
```

Constructors are popular methods in object-oriented programming. A constructor for a particular class is simply a method that runs automatically when you create an object of that class, and its purpose is to initialize that object as you want it. Simply put, constructors are used to initialize objects. A class's constructor is called when a new object is being created of that class, and you can set the object up as you like. In this case, you won't place any code in the `Hello2` class's constructor. (You will see much more about constructors in the next chapter.)

> **TIP**
>
> The Applet Wizard has also added a method called `destroy()` to our applet, and this method is sort of the opposite of a constructor, because it is called when the applet is about to end. Although languages such as C++ have *destructors,* which are the exact opposite of constructors, Java does not directly support true destructors.

The *getAppletInfo()* Method

Next, the Applet Wizard has included the method `getAppletInfo()`:

```
// APPLET INFO SUPPORT:
// The getAppletInfo() method returns a string describing the applet's
// author, copyright date, or miscellaneous information.
//--------------------------------------------------------------------

public String getAppletInfo()
{
   return "Name: Hello2\r\n" +
       "Author: Steven Holzner\r\n" +
       "Created with Microsoft Visual J++ Version 1.0";
}     .
      .
      .
```

This method is designed to return data about the applet to the Web browser or to other applets. This function returns an object of the Java class `String`. This is a text string holding information about the applet. Java uses the same format control codes as C or C++; here, \r\n represents a carriage-return newline (linefeed) pair. As almost anyone who has programmed in C can attest, it's a good idea to have a native (that is, built-in) string class to handle text strings (strings in C are handled as unwieldy arrays of characters). The Java String class not only provides a convenient way of storing strings, but also provides many methods to manipulate strings, and you'll find that useful. The methods of the Java String class appear in Table 2.2.

TABLE 2.2: The Java String Class Methods

Method	Does This
String()	Constructs a new String
String(String)	Constructs a new String, copying String
String(char[])	Constructs a new String from an array of chars
String(char[], int, int)	Constructs a new String made of the specified subarray of chars
String(byte[], int, int, int)	Constructs a new String made of the specified subarray of bytes
String(byte[], int)	Constructs a new String from the specified array of bytes
String(StringBuffer)	Construct a new String from the string buffer
charAt(int)	Returns the character at specified position
compareTo(String)	Compares this String to another
concat(String)	Concatenates string to end of specified String
copyValueOf(char[], int, int)	Returns String equal to the specified character array
copyValueOf(char[])	Returns String equal to specified char array

TABLE 2.2: The Java `String` Class Methods (continued)

Method	Does This
`endsWith(String)`	Determines if `String` ends with a suffix
`equals(Object)`	Compares `String` to specified object
`equalsIgnoreCase(String)`	Compares `String` to another, ignoring case
`getBytes(int, int, byte[], int)`	Gets chars from `String` to specified byte array
`getChars(int, int, char[], int)`	Gets chars from `String` to specified char array
`hashCode()`	Returns hashcode for this `String`
`indexOf(int)`	Returns index in this `String` of first occurrence of specified character
`indexOf(int, int)`	Returns index in this `String` of first occurrence the specified character, starting at given position
`indexOf(String)`	Returns index in `String` of first occurrence of specified substring
`indexOf(String, int)`	Returns index in this `String` of first occurrence of specified substring
`intern()`	Returns `String` equal to this `String` but guaranteed to be from the unique `String` pool
`lastIndexOf(int)`	Returns index in `String` of last occurrence of specified character
`lastIndexOf(String)`	Returns index in this `String` of last occurrence of specified substring
`lastIndexOf(String, int)`	Returns index in `String` of last occurrence of specified substring
`length()`	Returns length of the `String`
`regionMatches` `(int, String, int, int)`	Indicates if a region of `String` matches specified part of the specified `String`
`replace(char, char)`	Replaces all occurences of old char with new char

TABLE 2.2: The Java `String` Class Methods (continued)

Method	Does This
`startsWith(String)`	Indicates if `String` starts with some prefix
`substring(int)`	Returns substring of this `String`
`substring(int, int)`	Returns substring of `String` of given length
`toCharArray()`	Converts `String` to a character array
`toLowerCase()`	Converts characters in `String` to lowercase
`toString()`	Converts data to a `String`
`toUpperCase()`	Converts characters in `String` to uppercase
`trim()`	Trims leading and trailing white space
`valueOf(Object)`	Returns a `String` representing the `String`'s value
`valueOf(char[])`	Returns a `String` equal to specified char array
`valueOf(boolean)`	Returns a `String` object representing the state of the specified boolean value
`valueOf(char)`	Returns a `String` that contains a single char
`valueOf(int)`	Returns a `String` object representing value of specified integer
`valueOf(long)`	Returns a `String` object representing value of the specified long
`valueOf(float)`	Returns a `String` object representing value of the specified float
`valueOf(double)`	Returns a `String` object representing value of the specified double

<blockquote>
TIP

Some of the more useful Java `String` class methods in Table 2.2 are `substring()`, `toLowerCase()`, and `replace()`. The Java `String` class is one of the most useful of all, even including the `valueOf()` methods, which allow you to convert numeric values to strings in one simple expression.
</blockquote>

The *init()* Method

Next in `Hello2.java` comes the `init()` method. You will find this method useful—as you'll see shortly—to set up the controls you want to use in your applet. This method is called when the applet is loaded the first time or when it is loaded back in:

```
// The init() method is called by the AWT when an applet is first loaded or
// reloaded.  Override this method to perform whatever initialization your
// applet needs, such as initializing data structures, loading images or
// fonts, creating frame windows, setting the layout manager, or adding UI
// components.
//--------------------------------------------------------------------------
public void init()
{
   // If you use a ResourceWizard-generated "control creator" class to
   // arrange controls in your applet, you may want to call its
   // CreateControls() method from within this method. Remove the following
   // call to resize() before adding the call to CreateControls();
   // CreateControls() does its own resizing.
//--------------------------------------------------------------------------
   resize(320, 240);

   // TODO: Place additional initialization code here
}
         .
         .
         .
```

The counterpart of the `init()` method is the `destroy()` method. This method is called when the applet is being unloaded, and you can place clean-up code there:

```
// Place additional applet clean up code here.  destroy() is called
// when your applet is terminating and being unloaded.
//-------------------------------------------------------------------
public void destroy()
{
   // TODO: Place applet cleanup code here
}
         .
         .
         .
```

The *displayImage()* Method

You may recall that the Applet Wizard automatically built in to our program a whirling globe animation. This method, displayImage(), is part of that support, and you'll see more about this when I cover graphics animation:

```
// ANIMATION SUPPORT:
//   Draws the next image, if all images are currently loaded
//-----------------------------------------------------------
private void displayImage(Graphics g)
{
   if (!m_fAllLoaded)
      return;

   // Draw Image in center of applet
   //-----------------------------------------------------------
   g.drawImage(m_Images[m_nCurrImage],
         (size().width - m_nImgWidth)  / 2,
         (size().height - m_nImgHeight) / 2, null);
}
         .
         .
         .
```

When we work with graphics animation, you'll see that this method will be useful and, in fact, handles graphics animation better than the usual Java techniques.

The *paint()* Method

Next comes the `paint()` method, which you've already seen. This method handles the actual display of the applet in the Web browser, and we've placed our code here to display the Hello, World! message:

```
// Hello2 Paint Handler
//--------------------------------------------------------------------
public void paint(Graphics g)
{
   // ANIMATION SUPPORT:
   //   The following code displays a status message until all the
   // images are loaded. Then it calls displayImage to display the current
   // image.
   //------------------------------------------------------------------
   if (m_fAllLoaded)
   {
      Rectangle r = g.getClipRect();

      g.clearRect(r.x, r.y, r.width, r.height);
      displayImage(g);
   }
   else
      g.drawString("Loading images...", 10, 20);

   // TODO: Place additional applet Paint code here

      g.drawString( "Hello, World!", 60, 30 );
}
      .
      .
      .
```

The `paint()` method will be important throughout this book, because that's where you display what you want on the screen. This method is called when the applet is first displayed or when it (or a part of it) needs to be redrawn, as is the case when the Web browser is minimized and then restored and then has to redisplay the contents of the Web page. You will be seeing a lot of this method.

The *start()*, *stop()*, and *run()* Methods

The next three methods, start(), stop(), and run(), are used for multithreading (multitasking) support, and you'll see more about that when I cover multitasking. In the start() method, you start threads; in the stop() method, you stop them; and the run() method holds the code that the start() and stop() methods are to execute:

```
//The start() method is called when the page containing the applet
// first appears on the screen. The AppletWizard's initial implementation
// of this method starts execution of the applet's thread.
//-------------------------------------------------------------------------
public void start()
{
   if (m_Hello2 == null)
   {
     m_Hello2 = new Thread(this);
     m_Hello2.start();
   }
   // TODO: Place additional applet start code here
}

//The stop() method is called when the page containing the applet is
// no longer on the screen. The AppletWizard's initial implementation of
// this method stops execution of the applet's thread.
//-------------------------------------------------------------------------
public void stop()
{
   if (m_Hello2 != null)
   {
     m_Hello2.stop();
     m_Hello2 = null;
   }

   // TODO: Place additional applet stop code here
}

// THREAD SUPPORT
//The run() method is called when the applet's thread is started. If
```

```
// your applet performs any ongoing activities without waiting for user
// input, the code for implementing that behavior typically goes here. For
// example, for an applet that performs animation, the run() method controls
// the display of images.
//--------------------------------------------------------------------------
public void run()
{
   m_nCurrImage = 0;

   // If re-entering the page, then the images have already been loaded.
   // m_fAllLoaded == TRUE.
   //-----------------------------------------------------------------------
   if (!m_fAllLoaded)
   {
      repaint();
         .
         .
         .
   [animation handling removed for brevity]
         .
         .
         .
      stop();
   }
}
```

And that completes our survey of the type of file that the Applet Wizard creates for us, except for the last line, which points the way for us:

```
   // TODO: Place additional applet code here
      .
      .
      .
}
```

That will be our task in this book—adding code to the skeleton version of our programs that the Applet Wizard has created. Here, then, is an overview of the methods created for us by the Applet Wizard in our applet—typical of what you'll see from the Applet Wizard before you start customizing the applet:

```
---------------------------------------------------------------------
|                  Typical Java Applet Wizard Program               |
|-------------------------------------------------------------------|
| public class the_class extends Applet                             |
| {                                                                 |
|     constructor           <--Class Constructor                    |
|     getAppletInfo()       <--Returns info about the applet        |
|     init()                <--initialization code goes here        |
|     destroy()             <--exit code goes here                  |
|     paint()               <--handes the paint event for screen refreshes |
|     start()               <--launch threads here                  |
|     stop()                <--halt threads here                    |
|     run()                 <--thread code goes here                |
| }                                                                 |
---------------------------------------------------------------------
```

Now that you have a feeling for the code environment we'll be working in throughout the book, let's start working with the control that we want to put to work in this chapter—text fields. This control makes up a great deal of the programming we'll be doing in this book, so we'll begin with text fields now.

Text Fields

The first control we add to our applets is the text field. A text field is simply a box that can hold text, familiar to all Windows users (text fields are also called text boxes and edit controls). Our goal might be to place a text field in our applet like this:

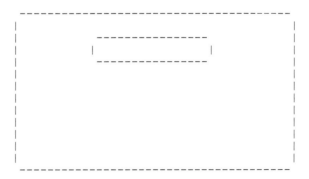

In fact, we can start the text field out with our Hello, World! message like this:

```
 ---------------------------------------------
|                                             |
|               -----------------             |
|              |Hello, World!    |            |
|               -----------------             |
|                                             |
|                                             |
|                                             |
|                                             |
|                                             |
|                                             |
|                                             |
 ---------------------------------------------
```

After this text field appears, the user can edit the text, using the mouse and keyboard. Let's create this new applet now.

> **TIP**
>
> Sometimes you may not want the user to edit the text you display in a Java program. In that case, you can use the `TextField` `setEditable()` method, which allows you to make text fields read-only. In addition, you can use *label* controls, instead of text fields. Label controls display text that cannot be altered by the user, and you'll see these controls soon.

Start Visual J++, and choose File ➤ New to start the Applet Wizard as we did in the last chapter. Give this new applet the name text. This time, we won't need animation or multithreaded support because we're not creating a graphics animation or a multitasking applet. Therefore, in Step 3 of the Applet Wizard, answer the question "Would you like your applet to be multi-threaded?" by clicking on the No, Thank You option, as shown in Figure 2.1. This removes both multithreading and animation support from the program. Then, click on the Finish button to create the new applet's code.

FIGURE 2.1:

Removing animation and multithreading support in the Applet Wizard

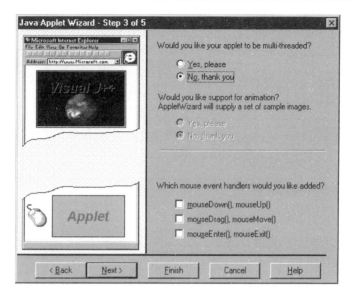

After the Applet Wizard creates our new text project, select the ClassView tab in the Project Workspace window, and double-click on the entry for the new `text` class. This opens the file `text.java` to the definition of our new class:

```
public class text extends Applet
{       .
        .
        .
```

This is where the class is defined, and you can place class global variables available to all methods right here. In particular, we want to set up a text field, and we do that by declaring an object of the Java class `TextField`. Let's name our object of that class `text1`:

```
public class text extends Applet
{
➜   TextField text1;
        .
        .
        .
```

NOTE Note the distinction between the terms `TextField` and `text1`. `TextField` is the Java class, and `text1` is the object of that class that we will actually work with. In this way, declaring objects is much like declaring any other kind of variable.

The methods of the Java class `TextField`, which is the class we will use for text fields, appear in Table 2.3.

TABLE 2.3: Java `TextField` Class Methods

Method	Does This
`TextField()`	Constructs the `TextField`
`TextField(int)`	Constructs the `TextField` with specified number of columns
`TextField(String)`	Constructs the `TextField` with specified initial text
`TextField(String, int)`	Constructs a `TextField` with specified text and number of columns
`addNotify`	Creates `TextField`'s peer—the peer lets you change the appearance of the `TextField` without changing its function
`echoCharIsSet()`	Returns true if `TextField` has a character set supporting echoing
`getColumns()`	Returns the number of columns in the `TextField`
`getEchoChar()`	Returns the character used for echoing
`getSelectionStart()`	Returns an integer holding the start location of the selection
`getSelectionEnd()`	Returns an integer holding the end location of the selection
`getText()`	Gets the `TextField`'s actual text
`minimumSize(int)`	Returns minimum size needed for `TextField` with specified number of columns
`minimumSize()`	Returns minimum size needed for `TextField`
`paramString()`	Returns parameter string for `TextField`

TABLE 2.3:   Java `TextField` Class Methods (continued)

Method	Does This
`preferredSize(int)`	Returns preferred size for `TextField` with given number of columns
`preferredSize()`	Returns preferred size needed for `TextField`
`select(int, int)`	Sets the selection and selection length
`setEchoCharacter(char)`	Sets echo character for the `TextField`
`setEditable(boolean)`	Sets the `TextField` to read-only
`setText(String)`	Sets the `TextField`'s actual text

TIP   The `getText()` and `setText()` methods in the `TextField` class are the usual ways to get text from a text field or set the text in that text field.

Now we've declared an object of type `TextField` and called that object `text1`. However, all we've actually done is to set aside the space for our new `TextField` object named `text1`. Creating Java controls is a two-step process: You first declare the new object as we have done above, and then you have to actually create the new object, using the Java `new` operator.

The Java *new* Operator

The Java `new` operator is just like the `new` operator in C++, and it is used to allocate memory (for objects, variables, arrays—anything you like). If you know C, the `new` operator largely replaces `malloc()`, `calloc()`, and all the memory allocation functions, and it is much easier to work with.

NOTE
Although the standard memory-allocating functions such as `malloc()` and `calloc()` in C really are functions, the new operator is indeed an operator (like +, -, and so on), not a function. This operator is a built-in part of Java and does not come from any class library or package.

Let's put the `new` operator to work. We'll create our new object named `text1` in our applet's `init()` method, which currently only holds the line `resize(320, 240)`, like this:

```
public void init()
{
    // If you use a ResourceWizard-generated "control creator" class to
    // arrange controls in your applet, you may want to call its
    // CreateControls() method from within this method. Remove the following
    // call to resize() before adding the call to CreateControls();
    // CreateControls() does its own resizing.
    //---------------------------------------------------------------------
    resize(320, 240);

    // TODO: Place additional initialization code here
}
```

TIP
To reach the `init()` method, open the entry for the `text` class in ClassView, find the `init()` entry, and double-click on it. This will open `text.java` to the definition of the `init()` method.

We now need to create our new `TextField` object here, and you do that like this:

```
      public void init()
      {
        resize(320, 240);
→         text1 = new TextField;
          .
          .
          .
```

This creates a new `TextField` object and places it in our `text1` variable. This is a two-step process that you'll see many times in this book: You first declare a control's object, and then you use the `new` operator to create it in the `init()` method.

The above new line of code creates a new text field, but it's only one character wide. To make the text field, say, 20 characters wide, you can pass a value of 20 to the `TextField` class's constructor (as you saw earlier, a constructor is called when an object is created to perform initialization, and you can customize the object by passing data to the constructor, provided that a constructor exists to take data in the format you want to pass it, such as an integer value here). You do that like this:

```
public void init()
{
    resize(320, 240);
→   text1 = new TextField(20);
        .
        .
        .
}
```

This makes our new text field 20 characters wide. If you wanted to set up an initial string in the text field instead of using a set number of characters, you could just pass that string to `TextField`'s constructor, which takes a string, like this :

```
text1 = new TextField("Hello, World!");
```

Overloaded Functions and Methods

If you are not familiar with C++, this might seem odd: How can you call a function with a numeric value such as 20 *or* a string such as Hello, World!? In Java, as in C++, you can *overload* functions. You can set up a function to be called with different types and numbers of parameters. The Java compiler determines which version of the function to call depending on the parameters—and how many of them—you pass. Thus, both these lines are valid Java code:

```
text1 = new TextField(20);
text2 = new TextField("Hello, World!");
```

NOTE   Don't confuse overloading funtions with overriding them. When you overload a function, the function can be called with different parameter lists. When you override a function, the version of the function that appears in the class's base class is redefined.

Now that we've created our new text field, the next step is to *add* it to the applet's display. Starting in the next chapter, you'll see that Java handles the display of controls automatically—that is, Java handles what's called the *layout* of controls automatically, although we will take more control of this process as time goes on. To add our text field to that display, you use the add() method like this, where you add the new control text1 to the applet's layout:

```
public void init()
{
   resize(320, 240);
   text1 = new TextField(20);
→    add(text1);
      .
      .
      .
}
```

At this point, then, our new text field appears in the applet:

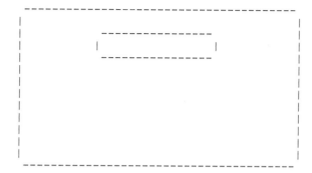

We might add text to the text field like this, using the `TextField` class's `setText()` method (see Table 2.3):

We place that text into the text field like this:

```
public void init()
{
    resize(320, 240);
    text1 = new TextField(20);
    add(text1);
        text1.setText("Hello, World!");
}
```

We could also have placed this text into the text box by passing it to the text field's constructor this way:

```
text1 = new TextField("Hello, World!");
```

> **NOTE**
>
> The syntax here—`text1.setText("Hello, World!");`—is the standard way of executing an object's internal method (here, that's the `setText()` method of the `text1` object) with the dot operator (.). Again, this is standard C++ terminology, but if you're not used to it, it might take a while before it becomes second nature. In general, if you want to execute, say, a method named `the_method()`, which is a member function of an object named `the_object`, the correct syntax is: `the_object.the_method();`.

We've now created a new text field and added it to the applet's display. To build the new applet, choose Build ➤ Build Text. To run it, choose Build ➤ Execute. The result appears in Figure 2.2.

FIGURE 2.2:

Our first text field applet

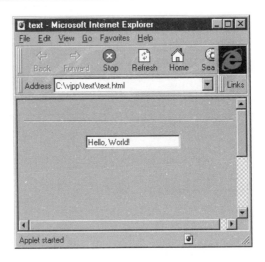

Our first text field applet is a success—you can see our string, which the user can edit, in Figure 2.2. The listing for this applet appears in `text.java`.

TIP

The Applet Wizard often "customizes" applets with messages such as "Created with Microsoft Visual J++ Version 1.0," which appears drawn across the applet's display. To remove those messages, comment them out (with a double slash, **//**) like this in the `paint()` method: `g.drawString("Created with Microsoft Visual J++ Version 1.0", 10, 20);`. This will prevent that line from appearing.

text.java

```
//****************************************************************************
// text.java: Applet
//
//****************************************************************************
import java.applet.*;
import java.awt.*;


//============================================================================
// Main Class for applet text
//
//============================================================================
public class text extends Applet implements Runnable
{
    TextField text1;

    // THREAD SUPPORT:
    //    m_text is the Thread object for the applet
    //--------------------------------------------------------------------------
    Thread  m_text = null;


    // text Class Constructor
    //--------------------------------------------------------------------------
    public text()
    {
        // TODO: Add constructor code here
    }

    // APPLET INFO SUPPORT:
    //    The getAppletInfo() method returns a string describing the applet's
```

```
// author, copyright date, or miscellaneous information.
//--------------------------------------------------------------------------
public String getAppletInfo()
{
    return "Name: text\r\n" +
         "Author: Steven Holzner\r\n" +
         "Created with Microsoft Visual J++ Version 1.0";
}



// The init() method is called by the AWT when an applet is first loaded or
// reloaded.  Override this method to perform whatever initialization your
// applet needs, such as initializing data structures, loading images or
// fonts, creating frame windows, setting the layout manager, or adding UI
// components.
//--------------------------------------------------------------------------
public void init()
{
    // If you use a ResourceWizard-generated "control creator" class to
    // arrange controls in your applet, you may want to call its
    // CreateControls() method from within this method. Remove the following
    // call to resize() before adding the call to CreateControls();
    // CreateControls() does its own resizing.
//--------------------------------------------------------------------------
    resize(320, 240);
    text1 = new TextField(20);
    add(text1);
    text1.setText("Hello, World!");

    // TODO: Place additional initialization code here
}

// Place additional applet clean up code here.  destroy() is called
// when your applet is terminating and being unloaded.
//--------------------------------------------------------------------------
public void destroy()
{
    // TODO: Place applet cleanup code here
}

// text Paint Handler
//--------------------------------------------------------------------------
```

```
public void paint(Graphics g)
{
   // TODO: Place applet paint code here
   //g.drawString("Running: " + Math.random(), 10, 20);
}


//   The start() method is called when the page containing the applet
// first appears on the screen. The AppletWizard's initial implementation
// of this method starts execution of the applet's thread.
//-------------------------------------------------------------------------
public void start()
{
   if (m_text == null)
   {
     m_text = new Thread(this);
     m_text.start();
   }
   // TODO: Place additional applet start code here
}


//   The stop() method is called when the page containing the applet is
// no longer on the screen. The AppletWizard's initial implementation of
// this method stops execution of the applet's thread.
//-------------------------------------------------------------------------
public void stop()
{
   if (m_text != null)
   {
     m_text.stop();
     m_text = null;
   }

   // TODO: Place additional applet stop code here
}


// THREAD SUPPORT
//   The run() method is called when the applet's thread is started. If
// your applet performs any ongoing activities without waiting for user
// input, the code for implementing that behavior typically goes here. For
// example, for an applet that performs animation, the run() method controls
// the display of images.
//-------------------------------------------------------------------------
```

```
public void run()
{
   while (true)
   {
      try
      {
         repaint();
         // TODO:  Add additional thread-specific code here
         Thread.sleep(50);
      }
      catch (InterruptedException e)
      {
         // TODO: Place exception-handling code here in case an
         //    InterruptedException is thrown by Thread.sleep(),
         //    meaning that another thread has interrupted this one
         stop();
      }
   }
}



   // TODO: Place additional applet code here

}
```

> **TIP** Java text fields support the standard Windows editing shortcuts such as ^V to paste from the clipboard, ^X to cut selected text, ^C to copy selected text, and so on.

We've come far in this chapter: We've been able to dissect our first Applet Wizard-created applet, and we've been able to write a new applet that displays a working text field. The text field is our first Java control. When you place a text field in an applet, the user can type text in it, delete the text in it, and so on. Our example text field is fully functional.

What's Next?

Creating and using text fields is a good start. However, that's only part of the story. The next step is all about using buttons that we can click on to make things happen. Understanding how to use Java buttons is a crucial part of Java programming, because they are such common user interface controls. Just about everyone knows and uses buttons—when you click on a button, something is supposed to happen. Let's look into that in the next chapter.

CHAPTER
THREE

3

Visual J++ Buttons

- Adding a button to an applet

- Using Java events

- Setting up multiple buttons

- Adding buttons and text areas

You have already seen a little about handling text fields in the last chapter. In this chapter, you'll see how you can control what happens even more, by using buttons. Windows users are familiar with buttons: When you click on a button on the screen, you are directing the program to take some action. For example, you might click on a button to copy marked text, or to paste text, or to cut it. Buttons are important user interface tools in Java, and you'll see how to use them in this chapter.

Using buttons and text fields together is a natural. For example, you might set up a new applet with a text field and a Click Me button:

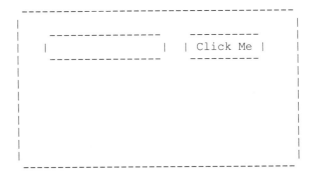

When the user clicks on the button, the program might display a message such as "No problem" in the text field:

```
 ------------------------------------------
|                                          |
|   ----------------     ----------        |
|  |No problem      |   | Click Me |       |
|   ----------------     ----------        |
|                                          |
|                                          |
|                                          |
|                                          |
|                                          |
|                                          |
|                                          |
 ------------------------------------------
```

Let's create this example now. Use the Applet Wizard to create a new (non-multithreaded) project named button. This creates and opens button.java, the support file for our new class.

NOTE Don't forget to comment out this line in our new applet's paint() method: g.drawString("Created with Microsoft Visual J++ Version 1.0", 10, 20);. Use the double slash to prevent this line from appearing in the middle of the applet.

You start by adding the text field for the new applet, which, like before, you can name text1. You declare that new control at the beginning of the class's declaration (this is where you will place all the control's declarations, making them global class variables because, as you'll see, you need to reach them from more than one method):

```
public class button extends Applet
{

    TextField text1;
        .
        .
        .
```

Next, you create the new text field with the `new` operator and add it to the applet's display with the `add()` method:

```
public void init()
{
   resize(320, 240);
➜  text1 = new TextField(20);
➜  add(text1);

   // TODO: Place additional initialization code here
}
```

This adds support for the text field. Next, we add the button.

Adding a Button to an Applet

Here, you want to add a new button that will have the caption Click Me:

```
 ---------------------------------------
|                                       |
|  -----------------    ----------      |
|  |               |    | Click Me |    |
|  -----------------    ----------      |
|                                       |
|                                       |
|                                       |
|                                       |
|                                       |
|                                       |
|                                       |
 ---------------------------------------
```

You do so with the Java `Button` class, naming the new button object `button1` and declaring it at the beginning of the class, as you do with all controls:

```
public class button extends Applet
{

    TextField text1;
→   Button button1;
        .
        .
        .
```

You can add a new variable such as *button1* to a class by clicking the right mouse button when the mouse pointer is over the class's entry in ClassView. This opens the pop-up menu you saw in the *Our First Java Examples* chapter, and you can select the Add Variable item in that menu, opening the Add Variable dialog box. You fill out the Variable type, Variable name, and, optionally, the Initial value boxes, and click on OK. However, it's usually easier just to add the new variable yourself in code—letting Visual J++ add a new button, for example, would not add the following code in `init()`, which you would have to do yourself.

The methods of the Java `Button` class appear in Table 3.1.

TABLE 3.1:   Java `Button` Class Methods

Method	Does This
`Button()`	Constructs a `Button`
`Button(String)`	Constructs `Button` with a label
`addNotify()`	Creates peer of the `Button`; the peer allows us to change the appearance of the `Button`
`getLabel()`	Returns the `Button`'s caption
`paramString()`	Returns the parameter string of `Button`
`setLabel(String)`	Sets the `Button`'s caption

TIP

You can set a button's caption on-the-fly with `setLabel()`, **allowing you to change the options you offer to the user as required.**

Next, you create that button and add it to the applet. You can give the button a Click Me caption by passing that text to the `Button` class's constructor this way:

```
public void init()
{
   resize(320, 240);
   text1 = new TextField(20);
   add(text1);
➜    button1 = new Button("Click Me");
➜    add(button1);

   // TODO: Place additional initialization code here
}
```

Now you have two controls: the text field and the button. The next step is to actually connect the button to the text field in code.

Using Java Events

When the user clicks on a button, types text, uses the mouse, or performs any other interface-related action in an applet, an interface *event* occurs. If you have programmed in Windows, you probably know about such interface events already. When an event occurs in an applet, such as when the user clicks the mouse, the applet is notified and can take the appropriate action. That's the way programming goes in *GUI* (Graphics User Interface) programs such as those written for Windows. The program responds to user events when they happen, because the user directs the program flow by manipulating the controls in the applet. In this case, you can find out which events—such as mouse movements or button clicks—occur as the applet runs by using an *action()* method. This method is called when an interface event occurs. You can add an `action()` method to an applet simply by editing `button.java` and adding this code by hand for the new method (although we will put this new method right under the `init()` method in the `button.java` file, you can place it anywhere in a class's definition):

```
public boolean action (Event e, Object o){
    .
    .
    .
}
```

This is the empty shell of a method named `action()` that returns a boolean value (`TRUE` or `FALSE`) and that takes two parameters: an object of the `Event` class, which we name e, and an object of the Java `Object` class, which we name o. The `Event` object tells you what kind of event occurred, as shown in Table 3.2, and the object o will tell you more about the event. You can add a new method such as `action()` to a class by clicking the right mouse button when the mouse pointer is over the class's entry in ClassView. This opens its pop-up menu; select Add Method to open the Add Method dialog box. Fill in the required fields, and click on OK to create the shell of the new method. However, it's usually easier just to add the new method yourself in code.

The *target* member of the Event object tells you what kind of control created the event, and you start the code by checking to find out if this control was a button. You can do that with an `if` statement and the `instanceof` keyword like this, where we check the class of the control that created the Java event:

```
public boolean action (Event e, Object o){

    if(e.target instanceof Button){
        .
        .
        .
    }
}
```

TABLE 3.2:   ID values for Events

ID Value	Means
ACTION_EVENT	Action event occurred
GOT_FOCUS	Got the focus
KEY_ACTION	Keyboard event
KEY_ACTION_RELEASE	Keyboard release event
KEY_PRESS	Key press event
KEY_RELEASE	Key release event
LOST_FOCUS	Lost the focus
MOUSE_DOWN	Mouse down
MOUSE_DRAG	Mouse drag
MOUSE_ENTER	Mouse enter
MOUSE_EXIT	Mouse exit
MOUSE_MOVE	Mouse move
MOUSE_UP	Mouse up
SAVE_FILE	File save event
SCROLL_ABSOLUTE	Absolute scroll
SCROLL_LINE_DOWN	Line down scroll
SCROLL_LINE_UP	Line up scroll
SCROLL_PAGE_DOWN	Page down scroll
SCROLL_PAGE_UP	Page up scroll
WINDOW_DEICONIFY	Deiconify window
WINDOW_DESTROY	Destroy window
WINDOW_EXPOSE	Expose window
WINDOW_ICONIFY	Iconify window
WINDOW_MOVED	Window moved

If the control that created the Java event is of the Java `Button` class, the code you place in the code block—the code surrounded by the { and } braces following the `if` statement—is executed.

if Statements in Java

In Java, `if` statements work as they do in just about any other programming language: If the expression in the parentheses of the `if` statement is true, the code in the code block is executed:

```
if(conditional){

[code block]

}
```

You don't yet know, however, that it was your button that was clicked. To check that, you can get the caption of the control that created the event. Do so by creating an object of the Java `String` class named, for example, `caption`, and initialize it to the caption of the control that caused the Java event. That looks like this:

```
    public boolean action (Event e, Object o){
➡       String caption = (String)o;
            .

            .

            .

        if(e.target instanceof Button){

        }
    }
```

NOTE

Note the expression (String) in the line String caption = (String)o;. This is called a *cast*, and it functions by temporarily converting the type of a variable to a new type. That is, we are treating the object named o as a string here so that we can create a new string from it. (If it is not possible to cast a variable into the new type you want, Visual J++ will inform you.)

Now, you can check if the caption of the button that caused the Java event was "Click Me" using the Java equality operator, which returns a value of TRUE if the two items you are comparing are equal (the equality operator in Java is the same as in C or C++: ==, as, for that matter, is the inequality operator, !=, which returns TRUE if the two items being compared are not equal):

```
public boolean action (Event e, Object o){
    String caption = (String)o;
    if(e.target instanceof Button){
➡️      if(caption == "Click Me"){
            .
            .
            .
        }
    }
    return true;
}
```

If the caption of the button that was clicked was "Click Me," you know that the user clicked your Click Me button. In that case, you want to place the message "No problem" in the text field text1. You can do so with the setText() method. First, set up a new string with the text "No problem" in it, and then place it in the text field as required. That looks like this:

```
public boolean action (Event e, Object o){
    String caption = (String)o;
➡️  String message = "No problem";
    if(e.target instanceof Button){
        if(caption == "Click Me"){
```

```
➡        text1.setText(message);
       }
     }
   }
```

Finally, you return a value of TRUE from the `action()` method. This indicates that you have handled the event successfully:

```
public boolean action (Event e, Object o){
   String caption = (String)o;
   String message = "No problem";
   if(e.target instanceof Button){
     if(caption == "Click Me"){
       text1.setText(message);
     }
   }
➡  return true;
 }
```

Our new applet is complete. Build it now and run it, as shown in Figure 3.1. You can see the new button there—click it now to see the "No problem" message appear in the text field. Our applet is a success.

FIGURE 3.1:

Our button applet supports buttons and text fields.

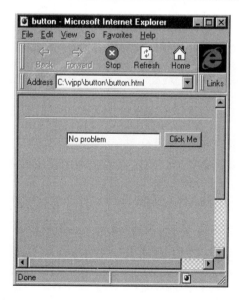

The code for this applet appears in `button.java`.

button.java

```
//****************************************************************************
// button.java: Applet
//
//****************************************************************************
import java.applet.*;
import java.awt.*;


//============================================================================
// Main Class for applet button
//
//============================================================================
public class button extends Applet
{

   TextField text1;
   Button button1;

   // button Class Constructor
   //--------------------------------------------------------------------------
   public button()
   {
      // TODO: Add constructor code here
   }


   // APPLET INFO SUPPORT:
   //   The getAppletInfo() method returns a string describing the applet's
   // author, copyright date, or miscellaneous information.
   //--------------------------------------------------------------------------
   public String getAppletInfo()
   {
      return "Name: button\r\n" +
           "Author: Steven Holzner\r\n" +
           "Created with Microsoft Visual J++ Version 1.0";
   }


   // The init() method is called by the AWT when an applet is first loaded or
   // reloaded.  Override this method to perform whatever initialization your
   // applet needs, such as initializing data structures, loading images or
   // fonts, creating frame windows, setting the layout manager, or adding UI
```

```
// components.
//----------------------------------------------------------------
public void init()
{
   // If you use a ResourceWizard-generated "control creator" class to
   // arrange controls in your applet, you may want to call its
   // CreateControls() method from within this method. Remove the following
   // call to resize() before adding the call to CreateControls();
   // CreateControls() does its own resizing.
//----------------------------------------------------------------
   resize(320, 240);
        text1 = new TextField(20);
        add(text1);
        button1 = new Button("Click Me");
        add(button1);

   // TODO: Place additional initialization code here
}


public boolean action (Event e, Object o){
        String caption = (String)o;
        String message = "No problem";
        if(e.target instanceof Button){
             if(caption == "Click Me"){
text1.setText(message);
             }
        }
        return true;
}



// Place additional applet clean up code here.  destroy() is called
// when your applet is terminating and being unloaded.
//----------------------------------------------------------------
public void destroy()
{
   // TODO: Place applet cleanup code here
}

// button Paint Handler
//----------------------------------------------------------------
public void paint(Graphics g)
```

```
{
   //g.drawString("Created with Microsoft Visual J++ Version 1.0", 10, 20);
}

//   The start() method is called when the page containing the applet
// first appears on the screen. The AppletWizard's initial implementation
// of this method starts execution of the applet's thread.
//-----------------------------------------------------------------------
public void start()
{
   // TODO: Place additional applet start code here
}

//   The stop() method is called when the page containing the applet is
// no longer on the screen. The AppletWizard's initial implementation of
// this method stops execution of the applet's thread.
//-----------------------------------------------------------------------
public void stop()
{
}



   // TODO: Place additional applet code here

}
```

So far, you've seen how to add both a text field and a button to an applet. Now let's turn to the next case—multiple buttons.

Setting Up Multiple Buttons

So far, we've had only one button in our applet, but, of course, real applets may have many buttons. For example, later in this book, we'll develop a drawing applet that lets the user draw rectangles, circles, ovals, and more using the mouse. In that applet, the user selects the type of figure to draw by clicking on various buttons labeled "Rectangle," "Oval," and so on. In our code, we'll have to be able to keep straight which button the user clicks on.

Let's set up a new applet that has a No button, a Problem button, and a text box like this:

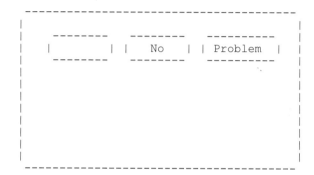

When the user clicks on the No button, we can display "No" in the text box:

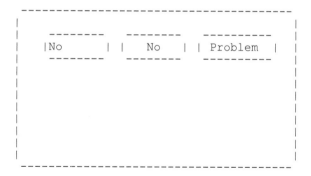

When the user clicks on the Problem button, we can display that string in the text box:

```
---------------------------------------------------
|                                                 |
|     ---------    ---------    -----------       |
|    |problem |  |   No    |  |  Problem  |       |
|     ---------    ---------    -----------       |
|                                                 |
|                                                 |
|                                                 |
|                                                 |
|                                                 |
|                                                 |
|                                                 |
 ---------------------------------------------------
```

This will give us the chance to see how to keep buttons separate, and you'll see a new and faster method of determining which button was clicked. Let's put this together now. Let's create a new project called `buttons` with the Applet Wizard, disabling animation and multithreading support.

You'll need two buttons, `button1` and `button2`, and a text field, `text1`. We'll add those to the beginning of our class definition like this:

```
public class buttons extends Applet
{
➜    TextField text1;
➜    Button button1, button2;
        .
        .
        .
```

Next, let's create and add those controls to the applet in the `init()` method as we did in the last two examples:

```
public void init()
{
    // If you use a ResourceWizard-generated "control creator"
➥ class to
    // arrange controls in your applet, you may want to call its
```

```
   // CreateControls() method from within this method. Remove
➥ the following
   // call to resize() before adding the call to CreateControls();
   // CreateControls() does its own resizing.
   //-------------------------------------------------------------
   resize(320, 240);
➜     text1 = new TextField(20);
➜     add(text1);
➜     button1 = new Button("No");
➜     add(button1);
➜   button2 = new Button("Problem");
➜   add(button2);
 }
```

At this point, you've added all the controls you need to the applet:

```
----------------------------------------
|                                        |
|     --------   --------   ----------   |
|    |        | |   No   | | Problem  |  |
|     --------   --------   ----------   |
|                                        |
|                                        |
|                                        |
|                                        |
|                                        |
|                                        |
----------------------------------------
```

Now it's time to get the new controls working. As before, we'll do that with the action() method, so type that into our class now:

```
public boolean action (Event e, Object o){
        .
        .
        .
 }
```

In the previous example, we checked to see if the control clicked was in fact a button, and then we checked to see if the button's caption matched that of the Click Me button. You can do this more directly by using the Java equals keyword. To check if the clicked button was button1, for example, you check the e.target member against our actual button object, button1:

```
public boolean action (Event e, Object o){
→    if(e.target.equals(button1)){
        .
        .
        .
    }

}
```

In case button1 was clicked, you want to place the text "No" in the text field text1, and you do so like this:

```
public boolean action (Event e, Object o){
   if(e.target.equals(button1)){
→     text1.setText("No");
   }
}
```

You can do the same for button2, which places the text "problem" in text1 this way:

```
public boolean action (Event e, Object o){
   if(e.target.equals(button1)){
      text1.setText("No");
   }
→  if(e.target.equals(button2)){
→     text1.setText("problem");
   }   .
       .
       .
}
```

Finally, you return a value of TRUE, indicating that you handled the Java events:

```
public boolean action (Event e, Object o){
   if(e.target.equals(button1)){
```

```
        text1.setText("No");
      }
      if(e.target.equals(button2)){
        text1.setText("problem");
      }
➜      return true;
  }
```

Our applet is complete. You can build and execute it now, as in Figure 3.2. As we designed it, when the user clicks on the No button, "No" appears in the text field; when the user clicks on the Problem button, "problem" appears in the text field. Our applet is working. The listing for this applet appears in buttons.java.

FIGURE 3.2:

Our multibutton applet is functional.

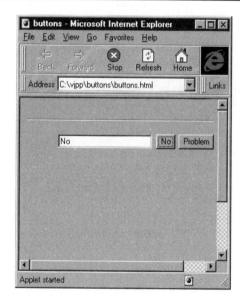

buttons.java

```
//************************************************************************
// buttons.java:  Applet
//
//************************************************************************
import java.applet.*;
```

```java
import java.awt.*;

//=============================================================================
// Main Class for applet buttons
//
//=============================================================================
public class buttons extends Applet
{
  TextField text1;
  Button button1, button2;

  // buttons Class Constructor
  //---------------------------------------------------------------------------
  public buttons()
  {
    // TODO: Add constructor code here
  }

  // APPLET INFO SUPPORT:
  //   The getAppletInfo() method returns a string describing the applet's
  // author, copyright date, or miscellaneous information.
  //---------------------------------------------------------------------------
  public String getAppletInfo()
  {
    return "Name: buttons\r\n" +
        "Author: Steven Holzner\r\n" +
        "Created with Microsoft Visual J++ Version 1.0";
  }


  // The init() method is called by the AWT when an applet is first loaded or
  // reloaded.  Override this method to perform whatever initialization your
  // applet needs, such as initializing data structures, loading images or
  // fonts, creating frame windows, setting the layout manager, or adding UI
  // components.
  //---------------------------------------------------------------------------

  public void init()
  {
    // If you use a ResourceWizard-generated "control creator" class to
    // arrange controls in your applet, you may want to call its
    // CreateControls() method from within this method. Remove the following
    // call to resize() before adding the call to CreateControls();
```

```
   // CreateControls() does its own resizing.
   //-----------------------------------------------------------------
   resize(320, 240);
   text1 = new TextField(20);
   add(text1);
   button1 = new Button("No");
   add(button1);
   button2 = new Button("Problem");
   add(button2);

   // TODO: Place additional initialization code here
}

public boolean action (Event e, Object o){
   if(e.target.equals(button1)){
       text1.setText("No");
   }
   if(e.target.equals(button2)){
       text1.setText("problem");
   }
   return true;
}


// Place additional applet clean up code here.  destroy() is called
// when your applet is terminating and being unloaded.
//-----------------------------------------------------------------
public void destroy()
{
   // TODO: Place applet cleanup code here
}


// buttons Paint Handler
//-----------------------------------------------------------------
public void paint(Graphics g)
{
   //g.drawString("Created with Microsoft Visual J++ Version 1.0", 10, 20);
}


//   The start() method is called when the page containing the applet
// first appears on the screen. The AppletWizard's initial implementation
// of this method starts execution of the applet's thread.
//-----------------------------------------------------------------
```

```
public void start()
{
   // TODO: Place additional applet start code here
}

//   The stop() method is called when the page containing the applet is
// no longer on the screen. The AppletWizard's initial implementation of
// this method stops execution of the applet's thread.
//-----------------------------------------------------------------------
public void stop()
{
}




   // TODO: Place additional applet code here

}
```

While we're working on text fields and buttons, we can take a look at the multiline text field called a text area. This is how Java supports text that takes up more than one line.

Adding Buttons and Text Areas

A text area really works the same as a text field does, but it can have several lines:

You use this control to display multiple lines of text, such as a set of instructions or a large amount of text that the user will edit. Text fields can do the same job, but for large amounts of text—especially text that has carriage returns or paragraphs—text areas are the way to go. Let's put together an example applet using a text area. When the user clicks on a Click Me button, a "No problem" message appears in the text area, like this:

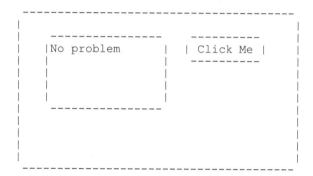

You handle this much as you would handle a text field. As with the previous examples in this chapter, you simply add a button, button1, to the applet. Next, you add a text area object of the Java class TextArea, calling that object, for example, textarea1:

```
public class textarea extends Applet
{
    TextArea textarea1;
    Button button1;
        .
        .
        .
```

The Java TextArea class methods appear in Table 3.3.

TABLE 3.3: TextArea Class Methods

Method	Does This
TextArea()	Constructs the TextArea
TextArea(int, int)	Constructs TextArea with indicated rows and columns
TextArea(String)	Constructs TextArea with indicated text
TextArea(String, int, int)	Constructs TextArea with indicated text and rows and columns
addNotify()	Creates TextArea's peer
appendText(String)	Appends string to end of TextArea
getColumns()	Gets number of columns in TextArea
getRows()	Gets number of rows in TextArea
insertText(String, int)	Inserts text at indicated location
minimumSize()	Gets minimum size of TextArea
paramString()	Gets string of parameters for TextArea
preferredSize()	Gets preferred rows and columns of TextArea
replaceText(String, int, int)	Replaces text from start to end
setText(String)	Sets the Text Area's actual text

As we did in our previous button and text field examples, we will create and add the new text area to our applet's layout. This time we will pass a width of 20 characters to the text area's constructor, and we will pass a height of 8 text rows this way:

```
public void init()
{
    resize(320, 240);
➜   textarea1 = new TextArea(8, 20);
➜   add(textarea1);
➜   button1 = new Button("Click Me");
➜   add(button1);
}
```

Next, we can place our "No problem" text into the text area when the user clicks on the button. We could use `setText()` to set the text of our text area as we did for text fields, but this time, let's use the `insertText()` method.

> **TIP**
>
> The `insertText()` method, which let's you insert text at a specific location, is unique to text areas—text fields do not have this method. With `insertText()`, you treat all the text in the text area as one long string, each character counting as one place, and you indicate the position where you want to insert your new text by passing that location as an integer to `insertText()`.

We can insert text at a specified position in the text area. In this case, we'll place the "No problem" message at the beginning of the text area, so we pass a location of 0:

```
public boolean action (Event e, Object o){
    String message = "No problem";
    if(e.target.equals(button1)){
        textarea1.insertText(message, 0);
    }
    return true;
}
```

Now, run the new applet, as shown in Figure 3.3. As you can see, our new text area is working. Now we can support not only buttons and text fields, but text areas as well. If you edit the text in the text area, you'll find out that it supports multiple lines and that you can use the Enter key as you type. The listing for this applet appears in `textarea.java`.

FIGURE 3.3:

Our text area example supports a multiple-row text box.

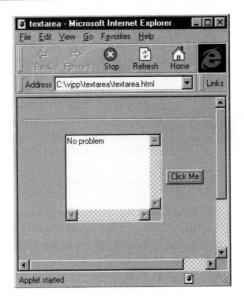

textarea.java

```
//*****************************************************************************
// textarea.java: Applet
//
//*****************************************************************************
import java.applet.*;
import java.awt.*;

//=============================================================================
// Main Class for applet textarea
//
//=============================================================================
public class textarea extends Applet
{
   TextArea textarea1;
   Button button1;

   // textarea Class Constructor
   //---------------------------------------------------------------------------
   public textarea()
   {
```

```
   // TODO: Add constructor code here
}


// APPLET INFO SUPPORT:
//   The getAppletInfo() method returns a string describing the applet's
// author, copyright date, or miscellaneous information.
//--------------------------------------------------------------------
public String getAppletInfo()
{
   return "Name: textarea\r\n" +
        "Author: Steven Holzner\r\n" +
        "Created with Microsoft Visual J++ Version 1.0";
}



// The init() method is called by the AWT when an applet is first loaded or
// reloaded.  Override this method to perform whatever initialization your
// applet needs, such as initializing data structures, loading images or
// fonts, creating frame windows, setting the layout manager, or adding UI
// components.
//--------------------------------------------------------------------
public void init()
{
   // If you use a ResourceWizard-generated "control creator" class to
   // arrange controls in your applet, you may want to call its
   // CreateControls() method from within this method. Remove the following
   // call to resize() before adding the call to CreateControls();
   // CreateControls() does its own resizing.
//--------------------------------------------------------------------
   resize(320, 240);

   // TODO: Place additional initialization code here

   textarea1 = new TextArea(8, 20);
   add(textarea1);
   button1 = new Button("Click Me");
   add(button1);
}

public boolean action (Event e, Object o){
   String message = "No problem";
   if(e.target.equals(button1)){
```

```
        textarea1.insertText(message, 0);
    }
    return true;
}

// Place additional applet clean up code here.  destroy() is called
// when your applet is terminating and being unloaded.
//-------------------------------------------------------------------------
public void destroy()
{
    // TODO: Place applet cleanup code here
}

// textarea Paint Handler
//-------------------------------------------------------------------------
public void paint(Graphics g)
{
    //g.drawString("Created with Microsoft Visual J++ Version 1.0", 10, 20);
}

//   The start() method is called when the page containing the applet
// first appears on the screen. The AppletWizard's initial implementation
// of this method starts execution of the applet's thread.
//-------------------------------------------------------------------------
public void start()
{
    // TODO: Place additional applet start code here
}

//   The stop() method is called when the page containing the applet is
// no longer on the screen. The AppletWizard's initial implementation of
// this method stops execution of the applet's thread.
//-------------------------------------------------------------------------
public void stop()
{
}


    // TODO: Place additional applet code here

}
```

What's Next?

For the moment, that's it for the guided tour of how to use buttons. We've come far in this chapter, using buttons with text fields, as well as buttons with text areas. We also handled multiple buttons and placed text in text fields under program control. We're off to a good start. Let's turn now to the next chapter, in which we start working with ways to arrange our text fields and buttons and other controls— in Java programs—when we work with Java layouts.

CHAPTER
FOUR

4

Java Layouts

- Using the Java `Label` control

- Reading numeric values from text fields

- Placing numeric values in text fields

- Installing and using the GridLayout manager

Checkboxes and radio buttons are meant to be handled in *groups*. You often use checkboxes to choose one or more selections from a group of selections, and radio buttons are even more group-oriented—they are often used to allow the user to select one option among many. And they are exclusive options too—when you click on one radio button in the group, all the other radio buttons are often supposed to be cleared.

When we start handling controls in groups, their arrangement in our programs becomes important, and we'll start working on that in this chapter. You handle this with a technique known as *laying out* controls in Java, and to investigate this, we'll start with a small calculator example.

You may have been surprised (and even pleased) to see in the last chapter that we did not need to do anything special to place text fields and buttons in our applets—Java handled the placement of controls for us. That is both good and bad—it's good if things work out the way you want them, but bad if what you have in mind is not the same as what Java has in mind. You'll see an example of this soon.

In fact, we have been using Java's default *layout manager*, the FlowLayout manager. Layout managers direct the placement of controls in an applet. You can select a layout manager to use, which gives much needed flexibility. Often, the default layout manager does not arrange controls the way you want them.

Let's take a look at an example. In the following case, we will build a small multiplying calculator applet. All we'll do is take two integers from the user, multiply them together, and display the result, but this will demonstrate how to handle both text and numeric input, as well as how to use layout managers. Let's get started.

Our Multiplying Calculator Example

Our goal is simply to create a Java applet that acts as a multiplying calculator. We can make this calculator out of text fields and buttons: one text field for the first number to multiply, one for the second, and one for the answer. The user can enter values into the text fields and click on a button marked with an equals sign to see the result. For example, to multiply 3 x 3, the user can enter that data in the first two text fields:

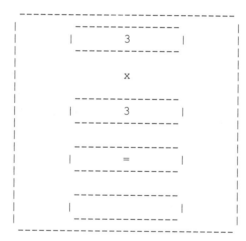

Then, when the user clicks on the Equals button, the result is displayed in the bottom text field:

```
-------------------------------
|    -------------------        |
|    |        3        |        |
|    -------------------        |
|                               |
|             x                 |
|                               |
|    ------------------         |
|    |        3        |        |
|    ------------------         |
|                               |
|    ------------------         |
|    |        =        |        |
|    ------------------         |
|                               |
|    ------------------         |
|    |        9        |        |
|    ------------------         |
-------------------------------
```

You may wonder at first how to place a multiplication symbol between the top two text boxes (to indicate we'll multiply the two values in the text boxes). You might assume that we'll use `drawString()` as we did in our first Java example, but in fact we'll place the multiplication symbol in a new type of control—a `Label` control. `Label` controls are like any other controls—they simply display text and nothing more. The methods of the `Label` control appear in Table 4.1. Specifically, we can give the controls in our multiplying calculator these names:

```
---------------------------------
|    -----------------      |
|    |      3        |      |    <--   text1
|    -----------------      |
|                           |
|    -----------------      |
|    |      x        |      |    <--   timeslabel
|    -----------------      |
|                           |
|    -----------------      |
|    |      3        |      |    <--   text2
|    -----------------      |
|                           |
|    -----------------      |
|    |      =        |      |    <--   button1
|    -----------------      |
|                           |
|    -----------------      |
|    |      9        |      |    <--   answertext
|    -----------------      |
---------------------------------
```

TABLE 4.1: The Label Class Methods

Method	Does This
Label()	Constructs an empty Label
Label(String)	Constructs a Label with indicated text
Label(String, int)	Constructs a Label with indicated text and alignment (RIGHT, CENTER, or LEFT)
addNotify()	Creates a peer for the Label
getAlignment()	Gets alignment of Label
getText()	Gets the text of the Label
paramString()	Returns parameter string of Label
setAlignment(int)	Sets alignment for Label
setText(String)	Sets text in Label

TIP

You can set the text of a Label control with the setText() method just as you can in a text field. You can also align the text in the label to the right, left, or center by passing one of the Label class's predefined constants to the setAlignment() method: Label.RIGHT, Label.LEFT, or Label.CENTER.

Let's start this project now. Create a new project named calculat now, using the Applet Wizard, and leave out support for animation and multithreading. Next, open the new class named calculat in Visual J++:

```
public class calculat extends Applet
{    .
     .
     .
```

First, you add all the controls—three text fields, a `Label` control, and a button—like this:

```
public class calculat extends Applet
{
```
→   `TextField text1, text2, answertext;`
→   `Label timeslabel;`
→   `Button button1;`
```
        .
        .
        .
```

The Java *Label* Control

Java `Label` controls are very useful, as their name indicates, when you want to label anything, including other controls. They provide an easy way to display text without having to worry about redrawing that text when the applet is uncovered or redisplayed. In this case, our `Label` control will hold the multiplication symbol.

Next, we have to initialize these controls in the `init()` method, so open that method as the Applet Wizard has created it for us now:

```
public void init()
{
   resize(320, 240);
        .
        .
        .
```

Our first job is to add the top text field, `text1`. You do that like this in the `init()` method:

```
public void init()

{
   resize(320, 240);
```
→   `text1 = new TextField(10);`

→   `add(text1);`

.
.
.

When you use the `add()` method, you are adding controls to the applet using the default layout manager, which is called the FlowLayout manager.

Next, we can add the multiplication symbol that is supposed to appear between the top two text fields.

We've already declared the `Label` control that will display the multiplication symbol as an object of the Java class `Label`, and we called it `timeslabel`:

```
public class calculat extends Applet
{
    TextField text1, text2, answertext;
→   Label timeslabel;
    Button button1;
        .
        .
        .
```

Now, in the `init()` method, you can create this label object and add it to the applet's layout. That looks like this:

```
public void init()
{
    resize(320, 240);

    text1 = new TextField(10);
    add(text1);

→   timeslabel = new Label("x");
→   add(timeslabel);
        .
        .
        .
```

Now we add the other controls:

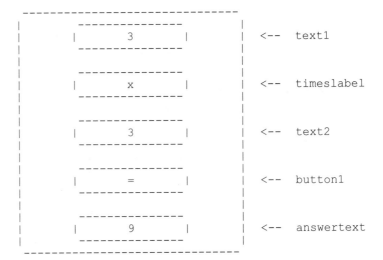

In `init()`, that looks like this:

```
public void init()
{
   resize(320, 240);

   text1 = new TextField(10);
   add(text1);

   timeslabel = new Label("x");
   add(timeslabel);

      text2 = new TextField(10);
      add(text2);

      button1 = new Button("=");
      add(button1);

      answertext = new TextField(10);
      add(answertext);
   }
```

At this point, then, we've added all the controls we'll need. The next step is to connect the controls to the code and make our multiplying calculator work.

Making Our Calculator Work

We make our calculator work by responding when the user clicks on the Equals button. To do that, we add an `action()` method to the applet (we will place this method right after the `init()` method):

```
public boolean action (Event e, Object o){

}
```

When the user clicks on the Equals button, we want to read the two integers in the top two text fields, multiply them, and display the result in the bottom text field (the `answer` text field):

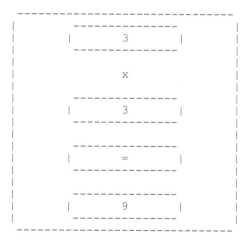

First, we need to verify that the Equals button (button1) was the button that the user clicked:

```
public boolean action (Event e, Object o){
    if(e.target.equals(button1)){
        .
        .
        .
    }
}
```

If the Equals button was clicked, we should go on to read the integers the user placed in the top two text fields, text1 and text2. But how do you do that?

Reading Numeric Values from Text Fields

You saw in the last chapter that you can place text in a text field with the setText() method. To read text, you can use the text field getText() method like this: text1.getText(). This returns the string of text in the text field text1. For example, if the user has placed 4 in text1, you get 4 back—but how do you convert that text to the actual number 4? You do so with the Java Integer class.

The Java Integer class has a method called parseInt() that takes text and returns an integer value. For example, you can get the text in the text field text1 this way:

```
text1.getText()
```

And you can convert that text to an integer value this way:

```
Integer.parseInt(text1.getText())
```

Besides the parseInt() method, Java also has a parseLong() method and a parseNumbers() method for floating point values. You can do other things with classes too. For example, if you want to check the maximum or minimum possible values an integer can hold, simply look at that class's constants named MAX_VALUE or MIN_VALUE like this: `int big_number = Integer.MAX_VALUE;`.

In our applet, we can now take the integer in `text1`, multiply it by the integer in `text2`, and store the result in a new integer called `product` like this:

```
public boolean action (Event e, Object o){
    if(e.target.equals(button1)){
→       int product = Integer.parseInt(text1.getText()) *
        Integer.parseInt(text2.getText());
            .
            .
            .
    }
}
```

TIP

You might be surprised (unless you program in C++) that you can declare new variables, such as `product`, right in the middle of code and not necessarily at the beginning of the function. This is a useful aspect of Java. If you declare variables in a specific block of code (blocks of code are set apart with { and }), the variables you declare inside that block of code are created when you enter that block and are destroyed when you leave. In practical terms, that means you can declare variables as you like throughout a Java program.

Now that we have the answer we want to display in the integer named `product`, we want to convert that value to a string so that we can display it in the `answer` text field.

Placing Numeric Values in Text Fields

At this point, the problem is converting an integer value (in the variable named `product`) into a string that you can display in the text field `answertext`. The Java `String` class will help here, because it has a method called `valueOf()` that is designed for just this case. When you pass a number to the `valueOf()` method, you get back a string of text representing that number. That looks like this (note that you return `TRUE` from the `action()` method at the end of the code as well, indicating that you've handled the event):

```
public boolean action (Event e, Object o){
   if(e.target.equals(button1)){
       int product = Integer.parseInt(text1.getText()) *
           Integer.parseInt(text2.getText());
     answertext.setText(String.valueOf(product));
   }
   return true;
}
```

TIP

The `String` class method `valueOf()` is overloaded to handle not only `integers`, but also `longs`, `doubles`, and `floats`.

The listing for this applet appears in `calculat.java`. Build the applet and run it, creating the display shown in Figure 4.1.

FIGURE 4.1:

Our multiplying calculator in default layout

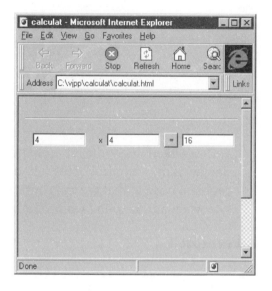

As you can see, the calculator functions, but it looks all wrong—the controls are all on one line. That's because we are using the default FlowLayout layout manager. This layout manager simply adds controls to an applet like you might add text to a document in a word processor—row by row, like words on a page:

When the FlowLayout layout manager comes to the end of a row, it simply wraps the next controls around to the next line:

That's been fine for us up until now, but our multiplying calculator demands more control of the layout. Let's see about fixing the problem now so that we can control the positions of our controls the way we want them in Java programs.

calculat.java, Version 1

```
//********************************************************************
// calculat.java: Applet
//
//********************************************************************
import java.applet.*;
import java.awt.*;


//====================================================================
// Main Class for applet calculat
//
//====================================================================
public class calculat extends Applet
{
  TextField text1, text2, answertext;
  Label timeslabel;
  Button button1;


  // calculat Class Constructor
  //-----------------------------------------------------------------
```

```
public calculat()
{
  // TODO: Add constructor code here
}

// APPLET INFO SUPPORT:
//   The getAppletInfo() method returns a string describing the applet's
// author, copyright date, or miscellaneous information.
//--------------------------------------------------------------------------
public String getAppletInfo()
{
  return "Name: calculat\r\n" +
       "Author: Steven Holzner\r\n" +
       "Created with Microsoft Visual J++ Version 1.0";
}


// The init() method is called by the AWT when an applet is first loaded or
// reloaded.  Override this method to perform whatever initialization your
// applet needs, such as initializing data structures, loading images or
// fonts, creating frame windows, setting the layout manager, or adding UI
// components.
//--------------------------------------------------------------------------
public void init()
{
  // If you use a ResourceWizard-generated "control creator" class to
  // arrange controls in your applet, you may want to call its
  // CreateControls() method from within this method. Remove the following
  // call to resize() before adding the call to CreateControls();
  // CreateControls() does its own resizing.
  //------------------------------------------------------------------------
  resize(320, 240);

  text1 = new TextField(10);
  add(text1);

  timeslabel = new Label("x");
  add(timeslabel);

  text2 = new TextField(10);
  add(text2);

  button1 = new Button("=");
```

```
    add(button1);

    answertext = new TextField(10);
    add(answertext);

}

public boolean action (Event e, Object o){
    if(e.target.equals(button1)){
        int product = Integer.parseInt(text1.getText()) *
➡ Integer.parseInt(text2.getText());
        answertext.setText(String.valueOf(product));
    }
    return true;
}

// Place additional applet clean up code here.  destroy() is called
// when your applet is terminating and being unloaded.
//--------------------------------------------------------------------------
public void destroy()
{
    // TODO: Place applet cleanup code here
}

// calculat Paint Handler
//--------------------------------------------------------------------------
public void paint(Graphics g)
{
    //g.drawString("Created with Microsoft Visual J++ Version 1.0", 10, 20);
}

//   The start() method is called when the page containing the applet
// first appears on the screen. The AppletWizard's initial implementation
// of this method starts execution of the applet's thread.
//--------------------------------------------------------------------------
public void start()
{
    // TODO: Place additional applet start code here
}

//   The stop() method is called when the page containing the applet is
// no longer on the screen. The AppletWizard's initial implementation of
```

```
// this method stops execution of the applet's thread.
//------------------------------------------------------------------------
public void stop()
{
}




    // TODO: Place additional applet code here

}
```

Now let's take a look at a new layout manager—the GridLayout manager. You can use this layout manager to place the controls where you want them.

Our Multiplying Calculator with GridLayout

This is the way we want our calculator to look, with the controls placed vertically, not horizontally:

```
-----------------------------------
|          ---------------          |
|         |      3        |         |
|          ---------------          |
|                                   |
|                x                  |
|                                   |
|          ---------------          |
|         |      3        |         |
|          ---------------          |
|                                   |
|          ---------------          |
|         |      =        |         |
|          ---------------          |
|                                   |
|          ---------------          |
|         |      9        |         |
|          ---------------          |
-----------------------------------
```

We can do that by replacing the default FlowLayout manager in our applet with another layout manager—the GridLayout manager.

The GridLayout Manager

The FlowLayout manager simply places controls in an applet one by one, "wrapping" them at the end of a row. The GridLayout manager, on the other hand, is often more useful, because it places controls in a grid like this:

```
 ---------------------------
|         |         |         |
|-------|-------|-------|
|         |         |         |
|-------|-------|-------|
|         |         |         |
|-------|-------|-------|
|         |         |         |
 ---------------------------
```

We can add the multiplying calcuator's controls to our applet in a grid of dimensions 9×3 (rows $\times$ columns) like this to arrange them vertically:

The way you do this is to install the GridLayout manager in our applet and then add the controls to it. As you add controls to the layout manager, it places them in the grid, one after the other, row by row; that is, it creates a grid with the dimensions you give it, and it's up to you to place something in every location in the grid. You have to fill all the entries in the grid, not just the entries that hold the controls you want to display (in other words, you can't leave any of the grid entries empty). One way of solving this problem is to use a set of empty labels that act as spacers. We can add those labels now, giving them these names:

```
-----------------------------------------------------
|              |  ------------  |                    |
|    fill1     | |      3     | |      fill2         |
|              |  ------------  |                    |
|--------------|----------------|--------------------|
|              |  ------------  |                    |
|    fill3     | |      x     | |      fill4         |
|              |  ------------  |                    |
|--------------|----------------|--------------------|
|              |  ------------  |                    |
|    fill5     | |      3     | |      fill6         |
|              |  ------------  |                    |
|--------------|----------------|--------------------|
|              |                |                    |
|   spacer1    |    spacer2     |     spacer3        |
|              |                |                    |
|--------------|----------------|--------------------|
|              |  ------------  |                    |
|    fill7     | |      =     | |      fill8         |
|              |  ------------  |                    |
|--------------|----------------|--------------------|
|              |                |                    |
|   spacer4    |    spacer5     |     spacer6        |
|              |                |                    |
|--------------|----------------|--------------------|
|              |  ------------  |                    |
|    fill9     | |      9     | |      fill10        |
|              |  ------------  |                    |
-----------------------------------------------------
```

We add these labels to the `calculat` class like this:

```
public class calculat extends Applet
{
    TextField text1, text2, answertext;
    Label timeslabel, fill1, fill2, fill3, fill4, fill5, fill6,
       fill7, fill8, fill9, fill10;
    Label spacer1, spacer2, spacer3, spacer4, spacer5, spacer6;
    Button button1;
    .
    .
    .
```

Now we can install the GridLayout manager as our new layout manager.

Installing the GridLayout Manager

You install the GridLayout manager (replacing the default FlowLayout manager) in the init() method before you add any controls to the layout. In this case, we want a grid of 9 rows and 3 columns, and we set that up with the setLayout() method this way:

```
public void init()
{
  resize(320, 240);

→   setLayout(new GridLayout(9, 3));
    .

    .

    .
```

That's all there is to it—now our applet uses a grid layout. You add the other controls, including the spacer labels, this way:

```
public void init()
{
  resize(320, 240);

  setLayout(new GridLayout(9, 3));

→     fill1 = new Label();
→     add(fill1);
→     text1 = new TextField(10);
→     add(text1);
→     fill2 = new Label();
→     add(fill2);

→     fill3 = new Label();
→     add(fill3);
→     timeslabel = new Label("x", Label.CENTER);
→     add(timeslabel);
→     fill4 = new Label();
```

```
➜        add(fill4);

➜        fill5 = new Label();
➜        add(fill5);
➜        text2 = new TextField(10);
➜        add(text2);
➜        fill6 = new Label();
➜        add(fill6);

➜        spacer1 = new Label();
➜        add(spacer1);
➜        spacer2 = new Label();
➜        add(spacer2);
➜        spacer3 = new Label();
➜        add(spacer3);

➜        fill7 = new Label();
➜        add(fill7);
➜        button1 = new Button("=");
➜        add(button1);
➜        fill8 = new Label();
➜        add(fill8);

➜        spacer4 = new Label();
➜        add(spacer4);
➜        spacer5 = new Label();
➜        add(spacer5);
➜        spacer6 = new Label();
➜        add(spacer6);

➜        fill9 = new Label();
➜        add(fill9);
➜        answertext = new TextField(10);
➜        add(answertext);
➜        fill110 = new Label();
➜        add(fill110);

    }
```

Now our controls will be aligned vertically. Build the new version of the calculat applet now and run it, as shown in Figure 4.2. As you can see, our controls are placed as we want them—our grid layout example is a success. The code for this applet appears in the `calculat.java` version 2 listing.

FIGURE 4.2:

Our multiplying calculator with a grid layout

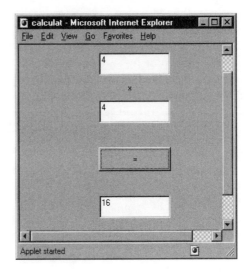

calculat.java, Version 2 (with layout)

```
//*************************************************************************
// calculat.java: Applet
//
//*************************************************************************
import java.applet.*;
import java.awt.*;


//=========================================================================
// Main Class for applet calculat
//
//=========================================================================
public class calculat extends Applet
{
    TextField text1, text2, answertext;
```

```
Label timeslabel, fill1, fill2, fill3, fill4, fill5, fill6, fill7, fill8,
fill9, fill10;
Label spacer1, spacer2, spacer3, spacer4, spacer5, spacer6;
Button button1;


// calculat Class Constructor
//--------------------------------------------------------------------------
public calculat()
{
   // TODO: Add constructor code here
}


// APPLET INFO SUPPORT:
//   The getAppletInfo() method returns a string describing the applet's
// author, copyright date, or miscellaneous information.
//--------------------------------------------------------------------------
public String getAppletInfo()
{
   return "Name: calculat\r\n" +
        "Author: Steven Holzner\r\n" +
        "Created with Microsoft Visual J++ Version 1.0";
}



// The init() method is called by the AWT when an applet is first loaded or
// reloaded.  Override this method to perform whatever initialization your
// applet needs, such as initializing data structures, loading images or
// fonts, creating frame windows, setting the layout manager, or adding UI
// components.
//--------------------------------------------------------------------------
public void init()
{
  // If you use a ResourceWizard-generated "control creator" class to
  // arrange controls in your applet, you may want to call its
  // CreateControls() method from within this method. Remove the following
  // call to resize() before adding the call to CreateControls();
  // CreateControls() does its own resizing.
  //------------------------------------------------------------------------
```

```
resize(320, 240);

setLayout(new GridLayout(9, 3));

fill1 = new Label();
add(fill1);
text1 = new TextField(10);
add(text1);
fill2 = new Label();
add(fill2);

fill3 = new Label();
add(fill3);
timeslabel = new Label("x", Label.CENTER);
add(timeslabel);
fill4 = new Label();
add(fill4);

fill5 = new Label();
add(fill5);
text2 = new TextField(10);
add(text2);
fill6 = new Label();
add(fill6);

spacer1 = new Label();
add(spacer1);
spacer2 = new Label();
add(spacer2);
spacer3 = new Label();
add(spacer3);

fill7 = new Label();
add(fill7);
button1 = new Button("=");
add(button1);
fill8 = new Label();
add(fill8);

spacer4 = new Label();
add(spacer4);
spacer5 = new Label();
```

```
        add(spacer5);
        spacer6 = new Label();
        add(spacer6);

        fill9 = new Label();
        add(fill9);
        answertext = new TextField(10);
        add(answertext);
        fill10 = new Label();
        add(fill10);

        // TODO: Place additional initialization code here
    }

    public boolean action (Event e, Object o){
        if(e.target.equals(button1)){
            int product = Integer.parseInt(text1.getText()) *
Integer.parseInt(text2.getText());
            answertext.setText(String.valueOf(product));
        }
        return true;
    }
}

    // Place additional applet clean up code here.  destroy() is called
    // when your applet is terminating and being unloaded.
    //-----------------------------------------------------------------------------
    public void destroy()
    {
        // TODO: Place applet cleanup code here
    }

    // calculat Paint Handler
    //-----------------------------------------------------------------------------
    public void paint(Graphics g)
    {
        //g.drawString("Created with Microsoft Visual J++ Version 1.0", 10, 20);
    }

    //   The start() method is called when the page containing the applet
    // first appears on the screen. The AppletWizard's initial implementation
    // of this method starts execution of the applet's thread.
    //-----------------------------------------------------------------------------
```

```
public void start()
{
   // TODO: Place additional applet start code here
}

//   The stop() method is called when the page containing the applet is
// no longer on the screen. The AppletWizard's initial implementation of
// this method stops execution of the applet's thread.
//------------------------------------------------------------------------
public void stop()
{
}



   // TODO: Place additional applet code here

}
```

What's Next?

Now that you have some familiarity with layouts, we will press on to work with checkboxes and radio buttons, two controls that are often used in special layouts to form them into groups, as you'll see soon. Because of the layout expertise you've acquired in this chapter, you'll be able to group controls as you want them in the next chapter.

CHAPTER
FIVE

5

Checkboxes, Radio Buttons, and Panels

- ■ Using checkboxes

- ■ Inserting radio buttons

- ■ Using panels

- ■ Creating a new panel

In this chapter, we're going to take a look at how to use some popular Java controls: checkboxes and radio buttons. As mentioned in the last chapter, checkboxes and radio buttons are often used together in groups, and you'll see how to use Java layouts to group them as you want them in this chapter. In addition, you'll see that an important method of grouping controls is through the use of *panels*, which may be thought of as controls that contain other controls.

We'll begin this chapter by taking a look at checkboxes and radio buttons, followed by some work with panels, and end with an example that brings together layouts, panels, checkboxes, and radio buttons.

Using Checkboxes

Checkboxes are those small boxes with which Windows users are familiar. When a user clicks on a checkbox, it stays clicked, and you can set various options in your programs by using checkboxes. For example, if you're selling pizza, your applet can include checkboxes for all the items you might put on pizzas—pepperoni, sausage, onions, black olives, and so on. Users can indicate which items they want by checking the appropriate checkboxes.

We will begin our exploration of checkboxes with a simple check-box example. In this case, we'll place a number of checkboxes in our applet:

```
-------------------------------------------------------------
|                                                           |
|  |_|  check 1    |_|  check 2     |_|  check 3    |_|  check 4  |
|                                                           |
|          -------------------------------------           |
|          |                                     |         |
|          -------------------------------------           |
|                                                           |
|                                                           |
-------------------------------------------------------------
```

When the user clicks on one of these checkboxes—for example, checkbox 2—you can indicate that in a text field like this:

```
-------------------------------------------------------------
|                                                           |
|  |_|  check 1    |v|  check 2     |_|  check 3    |_|  check 4  |
|                                                           |
|          -------------------------------------           |
|          |You clicked check box 2              |         |
|          -------------------------------------           |
|                                                           |
|                                                           |
-------------------------------------------------------------
```

This will get us started with checkboxes, and we'll be able to go on to more complex examples later.

Create a new project now, named `check`, with the Applet Wizard—disabling animation support and multitasking support—and open the new class named `check`:

```
public class check extends Applet
{    .
     .
     .
```

Now we can declare the four checkboxes we'll need—naming them `checkbox1` through `checkbox4`—and the text field, called `text1`, that we'll use to report what happens when the user clicks on a checkbox. You create checkboxes with the Java Checkbox class, so we declare our four checkboxes like this:

```
public class check extends Applet
{
➜       Checkbox checkbox1, checkbox2, checkbox3, checkbox4;
➜       TextField text1;
        .
        .
        .
```

The Java Checkbox class methods appear in Table 5.1.

TABLE 5.1:   The Checkbox Class Methods

Method	Does This
Checkbox()	Constructs Checkbox without a label
Checkbox(String)	Constructs Checkbox with indicated text
Checkbox(String, CheckboxGroup, boolean)	Constructs Checkbox with indicated text, indicated Checkbox group, and indicated state (set or not)
addNotify()	Creates the peer of a Checkbox
getCheckboxGroup()	Returns a Checkbox group
getLabel()	Gets the label of this Checkbox
getState()	Returns set or not set state of Checkbox
paramString()	Returns parameter string of Checkbox
setCheckboxGroup (CheckboxGroup)	Sets Checkbox's CheckboxGroup to the indicated group
setLabel(String)	Sets Checkbox label's text
setState(boolean)	Sets Checkbox to indicated set state

As with other controls, we actually create and add the new check-boxes to our applet in the `init()` method, so we open that method now:

```
public void init()
{
  // If you use a ResourceWizard-generated "control creator" class to
  // arrange controls in your applet, you may want to call its
  // CreateControls() method from within this method. Remove the following
  // call to resize() before adding the call to CreateControls();
  // CreateControls() does its own resizing.
  //---------------------------------------------------------------------
  resize(320, 240);
    .
    .
    .
```

All we have to do here is to add the checkboxes and the text field. You add the checkbox `checkbox1` like this:

```
    public void init()
    {
      resize(320, 240);
➜    checkbox1 = new Checkbox("check 1");
➜    add(checkbox1);
        .
        .
        .
```

You can label the checkbox (here that label is `check 1`) by passing a string to the `Checkbox` class's constructor, as we have done above. All that remains now is to add the other checkboxes and the text field:

```
    public void init()
    {
      resize(320, 240);
      checkbox1 = new Checkbox("check 1");
      add(checkbox1);
➜    checkbox2 = new Checkbox("check 2");
➜    add(checkbox2);
➜    checkbox3 = new Checkbox("check 3");
```

```
→     add(checkbox3);
→     checkbox4 = new Checkbox("check 4");
→     add(checkbox4);
→     text1 = new TextField(40);
→     add(text1);

    }
```

Now our new checkboxes are installed:

The next step is to connect them to the code, and we do that as before when we worked with buttons; we'll do so with the `action()` method. We'll add that method now to our applet:

```
public boolean action (Event e, Object o){

    }
```

This method will be called if the user clicks on a checkbox. We can examine which checkbox was clicked in the same way we dealt with standard buttons (radio buttons are later—standard buttons were Chapter 1), with the `equals()` method. That looks like this for `checkbox1`:

```
    public boolean action (Event e, Object o){
→         if(e.target.equals(checkbox1)){
              .
              .
              .
        }
    }
```

If checkbox1 was clicked, we can place a "You clicked check box 1" message in the text field this way, using the TextField setText() method:

```
public boolean action (Event e, Object o){
    if(e.target.equals(checkbox1)){
➔       text1.setText("You clicked check box 1");
    } .
            .
            .
}
```

In the same way, we can respond to clicks on the other checkboxes like this (note that you can also write this with a series of if-else clauses):

```
public boolean action (Event e, Object o){
    if(e.target.equals(checkbox1)){
        text1.setText("You clicked check box 1");
    }
➔   if(e.target.equals(checkbox2)){
➔       text1.setText("You clicked check box 2");
➔   }
➔   if(e.target.equals(checkbox3)){
➔       text1.setText("You clicked check box 3");
➔   }
➔   if(e.target.equals(checkbox4)){
➔       text1.setText("You clicked check box 4");
➔   }
    return true;
}
```

Build the new applet now and run it, as shown in Figure 5.1. As you can see, when the user clicks on a checkbox, our applet responds and indicates what happened. Our checkbox example works exactly as we planned. The code for this applet appears in check.java below.

FIGURE 5.1:

Our checkbox example
applet

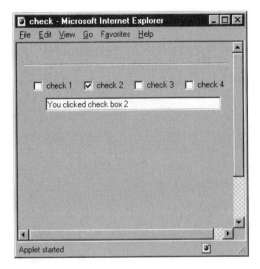

TIP

To see if a checkbox is clicked at any time, you can use the `getState()` method like this: `checkbox1.getState()`, which returns `TRUE` if the checkbox is checked, and `FALSE` otherwise. This is how you can examine which checkboxes the user has clicked. This means, for example, that you can modify our present applet to indicate when the user has unchecked (not just checked) a checkbox simply by using `getState()` in the `action()` method.

check.java

```
//*****************************************************************************
// check.java:  Applet
//
//*****************************************************************************
import java.applet.*;
import java.awt.*;

//=============================================================================
// Main Class for applet check
//
//=============================================================================
public class check extends Applet
{
    Checkbox checkbox1, checkbox2, checkbox3, checkbox4;
    TextField text1;

    // check Class Constructor
    //-------------------------------------------------------------------------
    public check()
    {
        // TODO: Add constructor code here
    }

    // APPLET INFO SUPPORT:
    //    The getAppletInfo() method returns a string describing the applet's
    // author, copyright date, or miscellaneous information.
    //-------------------------------------------------------------------------
    public String getAppletInfo()
    {
        return "Name: check\r\n" +
            "Author: Steven Holzner\r\n" +
            "Created with Microsoft Visual J++ Version 1.0";
    }


    // The init() method is called by the AWT when an applet is first loaded or
    // reloaded.  Override this method to perform whatever initialization your
    // applet needs, such as initializing data structures, loading images or
    // fonts, creating frame windows, setting the layout manager, or adding UI
    // components.
```

```
//-----------------------------------------------------------------
public void init()
{
  // If you use a ResourceWizard-generated "control creator" class to
  // arrange controls in your applet, you may want to call its
  // CreateControls() method from within this method. Remove the following
  // call to resize() before adding the call to CreateControls();
  // CreateControls() does its own resizing.
  //-----------------------------------------------------------------
  resize(320, 240);
  checkbox1 = new Checkbox("check 1");
  add(checkbox1);
  checkbox2 = new Checkbox("check 2");
  add(checkbox2);
  checkbox3 = new Checkbox("check 3");
  add(checkbox3);
  checkbox4 = new Checkbox("check 4");
  add(checkbox4);
  text1 = new TextField(40);
  add(text1);

  // TODO: Place additional initialization code here
}


public boolean action (Event e, Object o){
   if(e.target.equals(checkbox1)){
       text1.setText("You clicked check box 1");
   }
   if(e.target.equals(checkbox2)){
       text1.setText("You clicked check box 2");
   }
   if(e.target.equals(checkbox3)){
       text1.setText("You clicked check box 3");
   }
   if(e.target.equals(checkbox4)){
       text1.setText("You clicked check box 4");
   }
   return true;
}


  // Place additional applet clean up code here.  destroy() is called
```

```
// when your applet is terminating and being unloaded.
//--------------------------------------------------------------------
public void destroy()
{
   // TODO: Place applet cleanup code here
}

// check Paint Handler
//--------------------------------------------------------------------
public void paint(Graphics g)
{
   //g.drawString("Created with Microsoft Visual J++ Version 1.0", 10, 20);
}

//   The start() method is called when the page containing the applet
// first appears on the screen. The AppletWizard's initial implementation
// of this method starts execution of the applet's thread.
//--------------------------------------------------------------------
public void start()
{
   // TODO: Place additional applet start code here
}

//   The stop() method is called when the page containing the applet is
// no longer on the screen. The AppletWizard's initial implementation of
// this method stops execution of the applet's thread.
//--------------------------------------------------------------------
public void stop()
{
}


   // TODO: Place additional applet code here

}
```

You now have a good introduction to checkboxes, and our applet works as we planned—we've supported a number of checkbox controls in this applet and acted appropriately when the user checked them, indicating that we can handle these new controls. Now let's turn to the other controls that act much like checkboxes: radio buttons.

Inserting Radio Buttons

Radio buttons (also called option buttons) are much like checkboxes, but there is an important difference. You can check a number of checkboxes at the same time:

```
------------------------------------------------------------
|                                                          |
|  |‾| check 1    |v̅| check 2     |v̅| check 3    |v̅| check 4 |
|         ------------------------------------------        |
|        |                                          |       |
|         ------------------------------------------        |
|                                                          |
|                                                          |
------------------------------------------------------------
```

Radio buttons, however, operate in a group, and you can click on only one of them at a time:

```
------------------------------------------------------------
|                                                          |
|  ( ) option 1   (*) option 2    ( ) option 3   ( ) option 4 |
|         ------------------------------------------        |
|        |                                          |       |
|         ------------------------------------------        |
|                                                          |
|                                                          |
------------------------------------------------------------
```

Radio buttons are useful when you want the user to select only *one* of a number of options. For example, if you are selling five package tours to tropical islands, you can let the user select from among these tours using radio buttons. When the user clicks on the Package 1 radio button, you can display information about that tour. When the user clicks on the Package 2 radio button, you can switch to that tour's information, hiding the information about Package 1. To do this, you group radio buttons and allow the user to select only one at a time.

To associate radio buttons, you use a CheckboxGroup object. When you add radio buttons to a group, the CheckboxGroup class's internal methods ensure that only one of the radio buttons is checked at any time—you don't have to worry about "unchecking" radio buttons when one of a group is checked.

To see this at work, we can write a new applet much like our checkbox applet to display radio buttons instead of checkboxes. When the user clicks on one of the radio buttons, we can report that event like this:

```
 ------------------------------------------------------------
|                                                            |
|  ( ) option 1   (*) option 2    ( ) option 3   ( ) option 4 |
|                                                            |
|          ---------------------------------------          |
|          |You clicked radio button 2           |          |
|          ---------------------------------------          |
|                                                            |
|                                                            |
 ------------------------------------------------------------
```

To do this, create a new project now named radio, and open the new class named radio like this:

```
public class radio extends Applet
{    .
     .
     .
```

You might be expecting a new Java class called, say, RadioButton. In Java, however, radio buttons are actually checkboxes that have been added to a checkbox group. When you add checkboxes to a checkbox group, they change their appearance and become radio buttons. This means that we should create four new `Checkbox` objects for our radio controls:

```
public class radio extends Applet
{
➜   Checkbox checkbox1, checkbox2, checkbox3, checkbox4;
➜   TextField text1;
        .
        .
        .
```

Next, we will need an object of class `CheckboxGroup` to add our checkboxes to (so that they can act in a coordinated fashion). The `CheckboxGroup` class methods appear in Table 5.2. In our applet, we declare a new object of class `CheckboxGroup` that we can name `checkboxgroup1`:

```
public class radio extends Applet
{
➜   CheckboxGroup checkboxgroup1;
    Checkbox checkbox1, checkbox2, checkbox3, checkbox4;
    TextField text1;
        .
        .
        .
```

TABLE 5.2:   The `CheckboxGroup` Class Methods

Method	Does This
CheckboxGroup()	Creates a CheckboxGroup
getCurrent()	Gets current selection
setCurrent(Checkbox)	Sets current selection to indicated Checkbox
toString()	Returns string of CheckboxGroup's options

Next, we will set up our controls in the init() method, which looks like this right now (as the Applet Wizard set it up for us):

```
public void init()
{
    resize(320, 240);
        .
        .
        .

}
```

First, we create our new CheckboxGroup object, checkbox1:

```
public void init()
{
    resize(320, 240);
➜        checkboxgroup1 = new CheckboxGroup();
        .
        .
        .
```

Now we are ready to add radio buttons to this new checkbox group. We do that when we create each checkbox, passing the CheckboxGroup object to the constructor of the checkbox class. This attaches the new checkbox to the checkbox group and turns that checkbox into a radio button. For example, we add the first radio button like this (the last parameter indicates if the radio button should appear initially checked, and we pass a value of FALSE to indicate that it should appear unchecked initially):

```
public void init()
{
    resize(320, 240);
    checkboxgroup1 = new CheckboxGroup();
➜   checkbox1 = new Checkbox("option 1", checkboxgroup1, false);
➜   add(checkbox1);
        .
        .
        .
```

Now we can add the rest of the radio buttons and the text field that we'll use to report on user activities:

```
public void init()
{
   resize(320, 240);
   checkboxgroup1 = new CheckboxGroup();
   checkbox1 = new Checkbox("option 1", checkboxgroup1, false);
   add(checkbox1);
→  checkbox2 = new Checkbox("option 2", checkboxgroup1, false);
→  add(checkbox2);
→  checkbox3 = new Checkbox("option 3", checkboxgroup1, false);
→  add(checkbox3);
→  checkbox3 = new Checkbox("option 4", checkboxgroup1, false);
→  add(checkbox3);
→  text1 = new TextField(40);
→  add(text1);

}
```

At this point, we've installed our radio buttons. The next step is to respond when they are clicked, and we do that just as we did in our previous example on checkboxes, in an action() method. Here, we simply report back to the user in our text field, indicating which radio button was clicked:

```
public boolean action (Event e, Object o){
→     if(e.target.equals(checkbox1)){
→        text1.setText("You clicked radio button 1");
→     }
→     if(e.target.equals(checkbox2)){
→        text1.setText("You clicked radio button 2");
→     }
→     if(e.target.equals(checkbox3)){
→        text1.setText("You clicked radio button 3");
→     }
→     if(e.target.equals(checkbox4)){
→        text1.setText("You clicked radio button 4");
→     }
→     return true;
   }
```

Build this new radio button applet and run it, as shown in Figure 5.2. Only one radio button can be selected at a time. When the user clicks on a new radio button, the one that had been selected before is cleared, and the just-clicked radio button is selected instead. Our radio button example is a success. The code for this applet appears in `radio.java`.

FIGURE 5.2:

Our radio button example applet

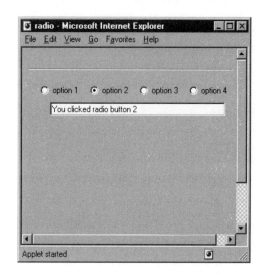

radio.java

```
//************************************************************************
// radio.java:  Applet
//
//************************************************************************
import java.applet.*;
import java.awt.*;


//========================================================================
// Main Class for applet radio
//
//========================================================================
public class radio extends Applet
{
```

```
CheckboxGroup checkboxgroup1;
Checkbox checkbox1, checkbox2, checkbox3, checkbox4;
TextField text1;

// radio Class Constructor
//--------------------------------------------------------------------------
public radio()
{
  // TODO: Add constructor code here
}

// APPLET INFO SUPPORT:
//   The getAppletInfo() method returns a string describing the applet's
// author, copyright date, or miscellaneous information.
//--------------------------------------------------------------------------
public String getAppletInfo()
{
  return "Name: radio\r\n" +
      "Author: Steven Holzner\r\n" +
      "Created with Microsoft Visual J++ Version 1.0";
}


// The init() method is called by the AWT when an applet is first loaded or
// reloaded.  Override this method to perform whatever initialization your
// applet needs, such as initializing data structures, loading images or
// fonts, creating frame windows, setting the layout manager, or adding UI
// components.
//--------------------------------------------------------------------------
public void init()
{
  // If you use a ResourceWizard-generated "control creator" class to
  // arrange controls in your applet, you may want to call its
  // CreateControls() method from within this method. Remove the following
  // call to resize() before adding the call to CreateControls();
  // CreateControls() does its own resizing.
  //------------------------------------------------------------------------
  resize(320, 240);
  checkboxgroup1 = new CheckboxGroup();
  checkbox1 = new Checkbox("option 1", checkboxgroup1, false);
  add(checkbox1);
  checkbox2 = new Checkbox("option 2", checkboxgroup1, false);
```

```
add(checkbox2);
checkbox3 = new Checkbox("option 3", checkboxgroup1, false);
add(checkbox3);
checkbox3 = new Checkbox("option 4", checkboxgroup1, false);
add(checkbox3);
text1 = new TextField(40);
add(text1);

// TODO: Place additional initialization code here
}

public boolean action (Event e, Object o){
   if(e.target.equals(checkbox1)){
       text1.setText("You clicked radio button 1");
   }
   if(e.target.equals(checkbox2)){
       text1.setText("You clicked radio button 2");
   }
   if(e.target.equals(checkbox3)){
       text1.setText("You clicked radio button 3");
   }
   if(e.target.equals(checkbox4)){
       text1.setText("You clicked radio button 4");
   }
   return true;
}


// Place additional applet clean up code here.  destroy() is called
// when your applet is terminating and being unloaded.
//-------------------------------------------------------------------------
public void destroy()
{
   // TODO: Place applet cleanup code here
}


// radio Paint Handler
//-------------------------------------------------------------------------
public void paint(Graphics g)
{
   //g.drawString("Created with Microsoft Visual J++ Version 1.0", 10, 20);
}


//   The start() method is called when the page containing the applet
```

```
// first appears on the screen. The AppletWizard's initial implementation
// of this method starts execution of the applet's thread.
//-------------------------------------------------------------------------
public void start()
{
   // TODO: Place additional applet start code here
}

//   The stop() method is called when the page containing the applet is
// no longer on the screen. The AppletWizard's initial implementation of
// this method stops execution of the applet's thread.
//-------------------------------------------------------------------------
public void stop()
{
}




   // TODO: Place additional applet code here

}
```

Now you have some experience in handling both checkboxes and radio buttons. The next step is to see them at work in an applet, arranged into groups as they are normally. To do that, we'll first look at how to arrange controls in *panels*, and then we'll arrange the panels of controls as we want them in an applet.

Using Panels

Layout managers are only part of the story when it comes to organizing controls in an applet. Another part of the story concerns the Panel class. A *panel* is simply a rectangular region that contains controls, and it's useful when you want to group controls and place the new group of controls apart from other controls in your applet (for

example, you might have a control "panel" of special controls to
adjust colors and fonts in your applet).

**Despite their name, panels do not have any predefined outlines
that appear around them in an applet. They are really only constructs to arrange controls, not GUI objects.**

Here, we will design a panel with four buttons and then display
that panel in an applet like this:

```
 -------------------------------------------------------------
|                                                             |
|    ---------------------                                    |
|   |   -----------------   |                                 |
|   |  | This is button 1 |  |                                |
|   |   -----------------   |                                 |
|   |   -----------------   |                                 |
|   |  | This is button 2 |  |                                |
|   |   -----------------   |                                 |
|   |   -----------------   |                                 |
|   |  | This is button 3 |  |                                |
|   |   -----------------   |                                 |
|   |   -----------------   |                                 |
|   |  | This is button 4 |  |                                |
|   |   -----------------   |                                 |
|    ---------------------                                    |
|                                                             |
 -------------------------------------------------------------
```

In many ways, you can think of a panel as a new control that contains other controls. We can add another panel to our applet just
as easily as we added the first one:

```
 -------------------------------------------------------------
|                                                             |
|    ---------------------        ---------------------       |
|   |   -----------------   |    |   -----------------   |    |
|   |  | This is button 1 |  |   |  | This is button 1 |  |   |
|   |   -----------------   |    |   -----------------   |    |
|   |   -----------------   |    |   -----------------   |    |
|   |  | This is button 2 |  |   |  | This is button 2 |  |   |
|   |   -----------------   |    |   -----------------   |    |
|   |   -----------------   |    |   -----------------   |    |
|   |  | This is button 3 |  |   |  | This is button 3 |  |   |
|   |   -----------------   |    |   -----------------   |    |
|   |   -----------------   |    |   -----------------   |    |
|   |  | This is button 4 |  |   |  | This is button 4 |  |   |
|   |   -----------------   |    |   -----------------   |    |
|    ---------------------        ---------------------       |
|                                                             |
 -------------------------------------------------------------
```

This is perfect for groups of controls such as radio buttons or checkboxes, because it keeps the group of controls together. Let's see this at work now as we create a new example that uses panels.

Creating a New Panel

Create a new applet named panels now. We will construct the example I outlined above, so our first job is to create a new type of panel with the four buttons we want in it. You can do that by deriving a class named `buttonpanel` from the Java `Panel` class—add this code to the end of the `panels.java` file now in Visual J++:

```
class buttonpanel extends Panel {
    .
    .
    .
}
```

> **TIP**
>
> You can add a new class to a project in Visual J++ by clicking on the class's entry in ClassView with the right mouse button and then selecting Create New Class. Doing so creates the skeleton of the new class for you in its own file and adds that file to the project. You can also do this by choosing Insert ➤ New Java Class. However, for relatively small classes, such as our `buttonpanel` class, it's easier to keep everything in one file, adding the new class definition yourself.

This is the first time that we have created a new class in our programs, but as you can see, it's easy to do so. Our new class will be used by the main applet class, and because we are defining this new class in the same file as the applet's code, we won't have to use the Java `import` statement to import this new class.

We add the four buttons as we have added controls in the past—by first declaring them at the beginning of our new class's definition:

```
class buttonpanel extends Panel {
→       Button button1, button2, button3, button4;
        .
        .
        .

}
```

And now we will create and add the new buttons to this panel. It turns out that we do not do that in the panel's init() method, but in its constructor (because the Panel class does not support an init() method). A Java (or C++) constructor is run when an object of the class is created, and we define it as just a method with the exact same name of the class itself. In this case, that's buttonpanel, so we set up the constructor for this class and name that constructor buttonpanel():

```
class buttonpanel extends Panel {
    Button button1, button2, button3, button4;

→       buttonpanel(){
        .
        .
        .

    }
}
```

That's our new class's constructor, and in that constructor we create and add the new buttons, like this:

```
class buttonpanel extends Panel {
    Button button1, button2, button3, button4;

    buttonpanel(){
→       button1 = new Button("This is button 1");
→       add(button1);
→       button2 = new Button("This is button 2");
→       add(button2);
→       button3 = new Button("This is button 3");
→       add(button3);
```

```
➜        button4 = new Button("This is button 4");
➜        add(button4);
     }
  }
```

Now we've created the new panel class `buttonpanel`. A panel of this class will look like this:

```
    ---------------------
   |  -----------------  |
   | | This is button 1 | |
   |  -----------------  |
   |  -----------------  |
   | | This is button 2 | |
   |  -----------------  |
   |  -----------------  |
   | | This is button 3 | |
   |  -----------------  |
   |  -----------------  |
   | | This is button 4 | |
   |  -----------------  |
    ---------------------
```

We can treat these new panels much as we treat controls in our applet. For example, to add two of these panels to the applet as `buttonpanel1` and `buttonpanel2`, you start by declaring them like this in the applet's main class, `panels`:

```
public class panels extends Applet
{
➜        buttonpanel buttonpanel1, buttonpanel2;
         .
         .
         .
```

Next, you have to initialize these button panels in the `init()` method. We will use the GridLayout manager to make these panels appear side by side, so we first install that manager:

```
public void init()
{
    // If you use a ResourceWizard-generated "control creator" class to
    // arrange controls in your applet, you may want to call its
    // CreateControls() method from within this method. Remove the following
```

```
   // call to resize() before adding the call to CreateControls();
   // CreateControls() does its own resizing.
   //------------------------------------------------------------------
   resize(320, 240);
➜  setLayout(new GridLayout(1, 2));
                  .

                  .

                  .
```

Now you create and add two button panels, buttonpanel1 and buttonpanel2, of the new class, buttonpanel, to our applet:

```
 public void init()
 {
    // If you use a ResourceWizard-generated "control creator" class to
    // arrange controls in your applet, you may want to call its
    // CreateControls() method from within this method. Remove the following
    // call to resize() before adding the call to CreateControls();
    // CreateControls() does its own resizing.
    //------------------------------------------------------------------
    resize(320, 240);
    setLayout(new GridLayout(1, 2));
➜   buttonpanel1 = new buttonpanel();
➜   buttonpanel2 = new buttonpanel();
➜   add(buttonpanel1);
➜   add(buttonpanel2);

 }
```

And that's all there is to it—you've now created a new panel type, added controls to the panel, and added panels of that type to the applet. The result of all this appears in Figure 5.3, and as you can see, we have successfully installed two panels in our applet. Our panels applet is a success. The code for this applet appears in panels.java.

FIGURE 5.3:

Our panel example
supports Java panels.

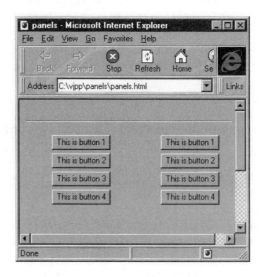

panels.java

```
//*****************************************************************************
// panels.java: Applet
//
//*****************************************************************************
import java.applet.*;
import java.awt.*;


//=============================================================================
// Main Class for applet panels
//
//=============================================================================
public class panels extends Applet
{
    buttonpanel buttonpanel1, buttonpanel2, buttonpanel3;

  // panels Class Constructor
  //---------------------------------------------------------------------------
  public panels()
  {
```

```
   // TODO: Add constructor code here
}


// APPLET INFO SUPPORT:
//   The getAppletInfo() method returns a string describing the applet's
// author, copyright date, or miscellaneous information.
//-------------------------------------------------------------------------
public String getAppletInfo()
{
   return "Name: panels\r\n" +
        "Author: Steven Holzner\r\n" +
        "Created with Microsoft Visual J++ Version 1.0";
}



// The init() method is called by the AWT when an applet is first loaded or
// reloaded.  Override this method to perform whatever initialization your
// applet needs, such as initializing data structures, loading images or
// fonts, creating frame windows, setting the layout manager, or adding UI
// components.
//-------------------------------------------------------------------------
public void init()
{
   // If you use a ResourceWizard-generated "control creator" class to
   // arrange controls in your applet, you may want to call its
   // CreateControls() method from within this method. Remove the following
   // call to resize() before adding the call to CreateControls();
   // CreateControls() does its own resizing.
   //---------------------------------------------------------------------
   resize(320, 240);
   setLayout(new GridLayout(1, 2));
   buttonpanel1 = new buttonpanel();
   buttonpanel2 = new buttonpanel();
   add(buttonpanel1);
   add(buttonpanel2);

   // TODO: Place additional initialization code here
}


// Place additional applet clean up code here.  destroy() is called
// when your applet is terminating and being unloaded.
//-------------------------------------------------------------------------
```

```
public void destroy()
{
   // TODO: Place applet cleanup code here
}

// panels Paint Handler
//--------------------------------------------------------------------------
public void paint(Graphics g)
{
   g.drawString("Created with Microsoft Visual J++ Version 1.0", 10, 20);
}

//   The start() method is called when the page containing the applet
// first appears on the screen. The AppletWizard's initial implementation
// of this method starts execution of the applet's thread.
//--------------------------------------------------------------------------
public void start()
{
   // TODO: Place additional applet start code here
}

//   The stop() method is called when the page containing the applet is
// no longer on the screen. The AppletWizard's initial implementation of
// this method stops execution of the applet's thread.
//--------------------------------------------------------------------------
public void stop()
{
}




   // TODO: Place additional applet code here

}

class buttonpanel extends Panel {
    Button button1, button2, button3, button4;

    buttonpanel(){
        button1 = new Button("This is button 1");
        add(button1);
```

```
button2 = new Button("This is button 2");
add(button2);
button3 = new Button("This is button 3");
add(button3);
button4 = new Button("This is button 4");
add(button4);
        }
}
```

As you can see, panels are a powerful technique for grouping controls. We'll use this technique in our next example, in which we bring the whole chapter together by using radio buttons, checkboxes, panels, and layouts to create an applet that uses all these components.

The "PCs for All" Example

Now we're going to tie everything in this chapter together with the discussion on layouts from the last chapter. Let's say that you've been hired by a computer superstore, PCs for All, to do a little Java programming. In particular, this company wants to embed an applet in its Web page giving users the prices of various computer systems. That applet might look something like this, in which the user selects from various system packages, indicating the components in each system, and the program indicates the price of the selection:

```
 -----------------------------------------------------------
|                                                           |
|    ( ) System Package 1        [ ] CPU1 system            |
|                                                           |
|    ( ) System Package 2        [ ] SVGA screen            |
|                                                           |
|    ( ) System Package 3        [ ] CDROM  (6x)            |
|                                                           |
|    ------------------                                     |
|    |                |                                     |
|    ------------------                                     |
 -----------------------------------------------------------
```

For example, if the user clicks on the System Package 1 radio button, we set the corresponding checkboxes to indicate what's in this system and indicate the total price in a text field:

```
-----------------------------------------------------------
|                                                         |
|   (*) System Package 1          [v] CPU1 system         |
|                                                         |
|   ( ) System Package 2          [v] SVGA screen         |
|                                                         |
|   ( ) System Package 3          [ ] CDROM  (6x)         |
|                                                         |
|   ------------------                                    |
|   |Price: $3000     |                                   |
|   ------------------                                    |
-----------------------------------------------------------
```

If the user then clicks on another radio button, the other radio buttons are cleared, a new set of system components is indicated, and a new price appears:

```
-----------------------------------------------------------
|                                                         |
|   ( ) System Package 1          [v] CPU1 system         |
|                                                         |
|   ( ) System Package 2          [v] SVGA screen         |
|                                                         |
|   (*) System Package 3          [v] CDROM  (6x)         |
|                                                         |
|   ------------------                                    |
|   |Price: $4000     |                                   |
|   ------------------                                    |
-----------------------------------------------------------
```

We can place the controls in this applet in two panels like this:

```
--------Panel1--------------------Panel2----------
|   --------------------          ----------------    |
|   | ( ) System Package 1 |      | [ ] CPU1 system  |    |
|   |                      |      |                  |    |
|   | ( ) System Package 2 |      | [ ] SVGA screen  |    |
|   |                      |      |                  |    |
|   | ( ) System Package 3 |      | [ ] CDROM  (6x)  |    |
|   |                      |      |                  |    |
|   |   ----------------   |      |                  |    |
|   | |                | | |      |                  |    |
|   |   ----------------   |      |                  |    |
|   --------------------          ----------------    |
--------------------------------------------------
```

To see this in action, create a new applet now with Applet Wizard, naming the applet PCs4All. We will begin by designing the new panels, starting with the panel that has the radio buttons and the text field:

```
--------------------
| ( )  System Package 1 |
|                       |
| ( )  System Package 2 |
|                       |
| ( )  System Package 3 |
|                       |
|   ------------------   |
| |                | |  |
|   ------------------   |
--------------------
```

As we did in our previous panels applet, we derive a new class named, in this case, systempanel, from the Java Panel class (add this new class at the end of the PCs4All.java file):

```
class systempanel extends Panel
{

}
```

Now we add the controls we'll need (since this panel holds radio buttons, we'll need a `CheckboxGroup` object):

```
class systempanel extends Panel
{
→    CheckboxGroup CGroup;
→    Checkbox system1, system2, system3;
→    TextField pricetextfield;
         .
         .
         .
}
```

And we add our controls to the new `Panel` class in that class's constructor:

```
class systempanel extends Panel
{
   CheckboxGroup CGroup;
   Checkbox system1, system2, system3;
   TextField pricetextfield;

   systempanel(){
→      CGroup = new CheckboxGroup();
→      add(system1 = new Checkbox("System Package 1", CGroup, false));
→      add(system2 = new Checkbox("System Package 2", CGroup, false));
→      add(system3 = new Checkbox("System Package 3", CGroup, false));
→      pricetextfield = new TextField(15);
→      add(pricetextfield);
   }
}
```

That's it—we've set up our first panel:

```
 ---------------------
| ( ) System Package 1 |
|                      |
| ( ) System Package 2 |
|                      |
| ( ) System Package 3 |
|                      |
|  ------------------  |
| |                  | |
|  ------------------  |
 ---------------------
```

The other panel we need looks like this, with three labeled checkboxes:

```
        ------------------
        | [ ] CPU1 system  |
        |                  |
        | [ ] SVGA screen  |
        |                  |
        | [ ] CDROM  (6x)  |
        |                  |
        |                  |
        |                  |
        ------------------
```

We can call this new `panel` class `componentpanel` and add the definition of this new class to the end of the `PCs4All.java` file. All we'll need in this new class are three labeled checkboxes, so that class looks like this:

```
class componentpanel extends Panel
{
    Checkbox component1, component2, component3;

    componentpanel(){
        add(component1 = new Checkbox("CPU1 system"));
        add(component2 = new Checkbox("SVGA screen"));
        add(component3 = new Checkbox("CDROM  (6x)"));
    }
}
```

At this point, our new panels are ready to add to the `PCs4All` class. Open that class now in Visual J++ and declare a panel of each of our new panel classes:

```
public class PCs4All extends Applet
{
➜   systempanel Panel1;
➜   componentpanel Panel2;
        .
        .
        .
```

Now you can create and add those panels to the applet. To make sure they appear side by side, we'll use the GridLayout manager. We install that manager now in the applet's init() method:

```
public void init()
{
    // If you use a ResourceWizard-generated "control creator" class to
    // arrange controls in your applet, you may want to call its
    // CreateControls() method from within this method. Remove the following
    // call to resize() before adding the call to CreateControls();
    // CreateControls() does its own resizing.
    //-------------------------------------------------------------------
    resize(320, 240);
→   setLayout(new GridLayout(1, 2));
        .
        .
        .
```

Then we simply add our two new panels like this:

```
public void init()
{
    resize(320, 240);
    setLayout(new GridLayout(1, 2));
→     Panel1 = new systempanel();
→     Panel2 = new componentpanel();
→     add(Panel1);
→     add(Panel2);

}
```

At this point, our applet will appear like this:

```
 --------------------------------------------------------------
|                                                              |
|   ( ) System Package 1           [ ] CPU1 system             |
|                                                              |
|   ( ) System Package 2           [ ] SVGA screen             |
|                                                              |
|   ( ) System Package 3           [ ] CDROM  (6x)             |
|                                                              |
|     ------------------                                       |
|   |                    |                                     |
|   | ------------------ |                                     |
|                                                              |
 --------------------------------------------------------------
```

However, we haven't done anything yet to make this applet functional—we still need to connect the buttons. Start that process by adding the `action()` method to our applet:

```
public boolean action (Event e, Object o){
        .
        .
        .
}
```

Now let's handle what happens when the user clicks on the System Package 1 radio button. That button's name is `system1`, but it turns out that we can't just check to see if `system1` was clicked like this:

```
    public boolean action (Event e, Object o){
➡       if(e.target.equals(system1)){ //wrong!!!
        .
        .
        .
        }
    }
```

The `system1` radio button is *not* an object defined in our applet's class. It is an object internal to the `panel1` object. For that reason, we have to address `system1` as `panel1.system1` in our applet, not just as `system1`. The correct usage is this:

```
    public boolean action (Event e, Object o){
➡       if(e.target.equals(Panel1.system1)){
        .
        .
        .
        }
    }
```

This is an important point, because it illustrates how to address the internal members of other objects—as `object.member` (if `member` is public and we can get access to it), again using the dot operator.

NOTE   If you're ever puzzled when Visual J++ says it can't find a certain object that you know is in your applet, it may be that you haven't addressed the object properly. For example, you may have referred to it as `button1`, **not as** `panel1.button1`.

If, in fact, the `system1` button was clicked, we want to set the checkboxes to indicate what is in this PC system:

```
-----------------------------------------------------------
|                                                         |
|   (*) System Package 1         [v] CPU1 system          |
|                                                         |
|   ( ) System Package 2         [v] SVGA screen          |
|                                                         |
|   ( ) System Package 3         [ ] CDROM  (6x)          |
|                                                         |
|   ------------------                                    |
|   |Price: $3000      |                                  |
|   ------------------                                    |
-----------------------------------------------------------
```

The checkboxes are actually objects internal to the `Panel2` object that we have named `component1` to `component3`, so you address them as `Panel2.component1` to `Panel2.component5`. You can use the checkbox method `setState()` to set the checkboxes as you want them—passing a value of TRUE makes them appear checked, and a value of FALSE makes them appear unchecked:

```
public boolean action (Event e, Object o){
    if(e.target.equals(Panel1.system1)){
→       Panel2.component1.setState(true);
→       Panel2.component2.setState(true);
→       Panel2.component5.setState(false);
        .
        .
        .
    }
}
```

We also set the price of the user's selection in the text field in Panel1:

```
public boolean action (Event e, Object o){
   if(e.target.equals(Panel1.system1)){
      Panel2.component1.setState(true);
      Panel2.component2.setState(true);
      Panel2.component5.setState(false);
➡️       Panel1.pricetextfield.setText("Price: $3000.");
   }    .
              .
              .
              .
   }
```

In this way, we've handled the System Package 1 radio button. The other system package buttons are the same with different options, so activating them looks like this:

```
public boolean action (Event e, Object o){
   if(e.target.equals(Panel1.system1)){
      Panel2.component1.setState(true);
      Panel2.component2.setState(true);
      Panel2.component5.setState(false);
      Panel1.pricetextfield.setText("Price: $3000.");
   }
➡️   if(e.target.equals(Panel1.system2)){
➡️      Panel2.component1.setState(true);
➡️      Panel2.component2.setState(false);
➡️      Panel2.component5.setState(true);
➡️      Panel1.pricetextfield.setText("Price: $3500.");
➡️   }
➡️   if(e.target.equals(Panel1.system3)){
➡️      Panel2.component1.setState(true);
➡️      Panel2.component2.setState(true);
➡️      Panel2.component5.setState(true);
➡️      Panel1.pricetextfield.setText("Price: $4000.");
➡️   }
   return true;
   }
```

We've completed our PCs4All example applet, which uses panels, checkboxes, radio buttons, and a grid layout. Run the completed applet now, as shown in Figure 5.4. When the user clicks on various system options, the corresponding price and component list are indicated. Our applet is a success. The code for this applet appears in PCs4All.java.

FIGURE 5.4:

Our PCs4All example

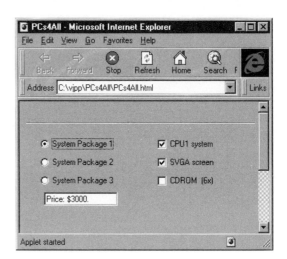

PCs4All.java

```
//**********************************************************************************
// PCs4All.java:  Applet
//
//**********************************************************************************
import java.applet.*;
import java.awt.*;


//==================================================================================
// Main Class for applet PCs4All
//
//==================================================================================
public class PCs4All extends Applet
{
    systempanel Panel1;
```

```
  componentpanel Panel2;

// PCs4All Class Constructor
//-----------------------------------------------------------------------------
public PCs4All()
{
   // TODO: Add constructor code here
}


// APPLET INFO SUPPORT:
//   The getAppletInfo() method returns a string describing the applet's
// author, copyright date, or miscellaneous information.
//-----------------------------------------------------------------------------
public String getAppletInfo()
{
   return "Name: PCs4All\r\n" +
        "Author: Steven Holzner\r\n" +
        "Created with Microsoft Visual J++ Version 1.0";
}



// The init() method is called by the AWT when an applet is first loaded or
// reloaded.  Override this method to perform whatever initialization your
// applet needs, such as initializing data structures, loading images or
// fonts, creating frame windows, setting the layout manager, or adding UI
// components.
//-----------------------------------------------------------------------------
public void init()
{
   // If you use a ResourceWizard-generated "control creator" class to
   // arrange controls in your applet, you may want to call its
   // CreateControls() method from within this method. Remove the following
   // call to resize() before adding the call to CreateControls();
   // CreateControls() does its own resizing.
   //-----------------------------------------------------------------------------
   resize(320, 240);
   setLayout(new GridLayout(1, 2));
   Panel1 = new systempanel();
   Panel2 = new componentpanel();
```

```java
      add(Panel1);
      add(Panel2);

}

public boolean action (Event e, Object o){
   if(e.target.equals(Panel1.system1)){
       Panel2.component1.setState(true);
       Panel2.component2.setState(true);
       Panel2.component5.setState(false);
       Panel1.pricetextfield.setText("Price: $3000.");
   }
   if(e.target.equals(Panel1.system2)){
       Panel2.component1.setState(true);
       Panel2.component2.setState(false);
       Panel2.component5.setState(true);
       Panel1.pricetextfield.setText("Price: $3500.");
   }
   if(e.target.equals(Panel1.system3)){
       Panel2.component1.setState(true);
       Panel2.component2.setState(true);
       Panel2.component5.setState(true);
       Panel1.pricetextfield.setText("Price: $4000.");
   }
   return true;
}



// Place additional applet clean up code here.  destroy() is called
// when your applet is terminating and being unloaded.
//-------------------------------------------------------------------------
public void destroy()
{
   // TODO: Place applet cleanup code here
}

// PCs4All Paint Handler
//-------------------------------------------------------------------------
public void paint(Graphics g)
{
```

```
    //g.drawString("Created with Microsoft Visual J++ Version 1.0", 10, 20);
  }

  //   The start() method is called when the page containing the applet
  // first appears on the screen. The AppletWizard's initial implementation
  // of this method starts execution of the applet's thread.
  //------------------------------------------------------------------------
  public void start()
  {
     // TODO: Place additional applet start code here
  }

  //   The stop() method is called when the page containing the applet is
  // no longer on the screen. The AppletWizard's initial implementation of
  // this method stops execution of the applet's thread.
  //------------------------------------------------------------------------
  public void stop()
  {
  }




     // TODO: Place additional applet code here

}

class componentpanel extends Panel
{
  Checkbox component1, component2, component3;

  componentpanel(){
      add(component1 = new Checkbox("CPU1 system"));
      add(component2 = new Checkbox("SVGA screen"));
      add(component3 = new Checkbox("CDROM  (6x)"));
  }
}

class systempanel extends Panel
{
    CheckboxGroup CGroup;
    Checkbox system1, system2, system3;
```

```
TextField pricetextfield;

systempanel(){
   CGroup = new CheckboxGroup();
   add(system1 = new Checkbox("System Package 1", CGroup, false));
   add(system2 = new Checkbox("System Package 2", CGroup, false));
   add(system3 = new Checkbox("System Package 3", CGroup, false));
   pricetextfield = new TextField(15);
   add(pricetextfield);
}
}
```

What's Next?

Having mastered radio buttons and checkboxes, we'll turn now to other powerful Java controls—scroll bars, scrolling lists, and more in the next chapter. As any Windows user knows, scroll bars and scrolling lists (list boxes you can scroll) form an integral part of windowed programming, and we'll put these new controls to work for us now.

CHAPTER
SIX

6

Scroll Bars, Scrolling Lists, and Choice Controls

- The Scroll Bar layout

- The `choice` control

- Scrolling lists

- The GridBag layout

- GridBag constraints

- Customizing the Visual J++ Web page

In this chapter, we're going to continue our guided tour of Visual J++ by examining several controls: scroll bars, scrolling lists, and choice controls. I'll also discuss some additional Java layout techniques. Layouts are an important part of Java programming, and you'll become more familiar with what Visual J++ has to offer here. Finally, you'll see how to use the built-in Visual J++ support for applet *parameters*—values that you can pass an applet from data placed in the `<applet>` tag in an HTML page. Visual J++ adds a great deal of support for parameters, and using parameters, you can customize an applet to work in many different Web pages without having to recompile it. Let's get to work at once, starting with scroll bars.

Scroll Bars

The two types of scroll bar controls are horizontal and vertical, and you'll see both here. For example, we could create a new applet scrolls that contained both types of scroll bars:

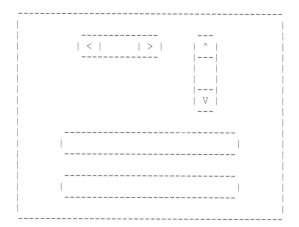

When the user moves a scroll bar, you can report on the new horizontal and vertical positions of the bars in two text fields:

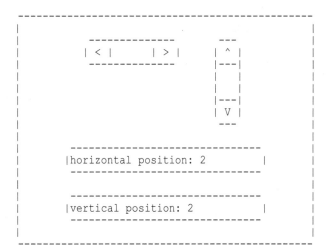

This will be an easy example, so let's put it together now. Create a new applet with the Applet Wizard named scrolls now. Begin by adding the two text fields we'll need, text1 and text2, and the two scroll bars, scroll1 and scroll2, which are objects of the Java Scrollbar class:

```
public class scrolls extends Applet
{
 TextField text1, text2;
 Scrollbar scroll1, scroll2;
     .
     .
     .
```

The Java Scrollbar class's methods appear in Table 6.1.

TABLE 6.1: The Scrollbar Class's Methods

Method	Does This
Scrollbar()	Constructs a Scrollbar (vertical)
Scrollbar(int)	Constructs a Scrollbar with specified orientation: Scrollbar.HORIZONTAL or Scrollbar.VERTICAL
Scrollbar (int, int, int, int, int)	Constructs a Scrollbar with given orientation, initial value, scroll thumb size, and minumum and maximum values
addNotify()	Adds the Scrollbar's peer
getLineIncrement()	Gets line-by-line increment for Scrollbar
getMaximum()	Gets maximum setting of Scrollbar
getMinimum()	Gets minimum setting of Scrollbar
getOrientation()	Gets orientation of Scrollbar
getPageIncrement()	Gets page-by-page increment for Scrollbar
getValue()	Gets current value of Scrollbar
getVisible()	Gets the visible portion of Scrollbar
paramString()	Gets string parameters for Scrollbar; this method's access is protected
setLineIncrement(int)	Sets line-by-line increment for Scrollbar
setPageIncrement(int)	Sets page-by-page increment for Scrollbar
setValue(int)	Sets value of Scrollbar to given value
setValues (int, int, int, int)	Sets values for Scrollbar

In the init() method, we will add our scroll bars and text fields to the applet. We start by constructing the horizontal scroll bar, scroll1, by passing these parameters to its constructor (see Table 6.1). The parameters are its orientation (you use the predefined Scrollbar class constants `Scrollbar.HORIZONTAL` or `Scrollbar.VERTICAL`; these constants are built into the `Scrollbar` class), the scroll bar's initial value (that is, the location of the little scroll box—called the *thumb* in the scroll bar), the size of the scroll thumb in pixels, and the scroll bar's minimum possible value (we'll use 1) and its maximum possible value (we'll use 100):

```
public void init()
{
    // If you use a ResourceWizard-generated "control creator" class to
    // arrange controls in your applet, you may want to call its
    // CreateControls() method from within this method. Remove the following
    // call to resize() before adding the call to CreateControls();
    // CreateControls() does its own resizing.
    //-------------------------------------------------------------------------
    resize(320, 240);
➜   scroll1 = new Scrollbar(Scrollbar.HORIZONTAL, 1, 10, 1, 100);
➜   add(scroll1);
        .
        .
        .
```

> **TIP**
>
> You can change a scroll bar's maximum and minimum possible values while your applet is running by using the `setValues()` method. You can also scroll the scroll bar from code with the `setValue()` method. (It's a common error to confuse `setValue()` with `setValues()`, but note that these are two different methods.)

In this way, we've created a new horizontal scroll bar whose values can range from 1 to 100, and whose initial value is 1.

In the same way, we create a similar scroll bar, `scroll2`, that has the same value range but is vertical:

```
public void init()
{
    resize(320, 240);
    scroll1 = new Scrollbar(Scrollbar.HORIZONTAL, 1, 10, 1, 100);
```

```
      add(scroll1);
  →   scroll2 = new Scrollbar(Scrollbar.VERTICAL, 1, 10, 1, 100);
  →   add(scroll2);
              .
              .
              .
```

Finally, we add the two text fields we'll need to report the scroll bars' positions:

```
public void init()
{
    resize(320, 240);
    scroll1 = new Scrollbar(Scrollbar.HORIZONTAL, 1, 10, 1, 100);
    add(scroll1);
    scroll2 = new Scrollbar(Scrollbar.VERTICAL, 1, 10, 1, 100);
    add(scroll2);
  → text1 = new TextField(40);
  → add(text1);
  → text2 = new TextField(40);
  → add(text2);

}
```

The scroll bars now appear in our applet. The next step is to connect them to code, and you might think we do that with an action() method. If you've done Windows programming, however, you know that scroll bars are always just a little bit different. In this case, you use the Java method handleEvent(). This event handler takes one parameter—an object of the Java Event class (add this code to scrolls.java now):

```
    public boolean handleEvent(Event e){

    }
```

You can determine which scroll bar caused the event just as you would with a button or a checkbox. To see if scroll1 was scrolled, you can do this:

```
    public boolean handleEvent(Event e){
```

```
➜          if(e.target.equals(scroll1)){
               .
               .
               .
           }
       }
```

Our first step is to set the scroll bar's thumb position to the place where the user scrolled it. That might seem funny, but it turns out that unless you update the scroll bar's thumb yourself, it will spring back to its original position when the user releases it. You have to move it yourself because the user may have moved the thumb to a location that is considered "forbidden," and Java allows you the option of not accepting the user's scroll actions in that case. To set the thumb's new location, you use the `Scrollbar` class's `setValue()` method, and to get its current value, you use the `getValue()` method. To place the thumb at the location where the user moved it, execute this code:

```
public boolean handleEvent(Event e){
   if(e.target.equals(scroll1)){
➜          scroll1.setValue(scroll1.getValue());
           .
           .
           .
       }
   }
```

> **NOTE** Don't forget to set the scroll bar thumb to its new value when it has been scrolled. If you don't, it will appear to "jump" back on its own when you release it, and that's frustrating.

Since `scroll1`, the horizontal scroll bar, was scrolled, you can display the new setting of that scroll bar in the text field `text1`. To do so, you convert the value of `scroll1` to an integer and display it in `text1` this way:

```
public boolean handleEvent(Event e){
    if(e.target.equals(scroll1)){
      scroll1.setValue(scroll1.getValue());
➜       text1.setText("horizontal position:" +
➥ String.valueOf(scroll1.getValue()));
    }
            .
            .
            .
```

> **TIP** You can concatenate—that is, join—strings in Java with the + operator as in the line: `text1.setText("horizontal position:" + String.valueOf(scroll1.getValue ()));`.

And you do the same for `scroll2` in this way:

```
public boolean handleEvent(Event e){
    if(e.target.equals(scroll1)){
      scroll1.setValue(scroll1.getValue());
      text1.setText("horizontal position:" +
➥ String.valueOf(scroll1.getValue()));
    }
➜     if(e.target.equals(scroll2)){
➜        scroll2.setValue(scroll2.getValue());
➜        text2.setText("vertical position:" +
➥ String.valueOf(scroll2.getValue()));
➜     }  .
            .
            .

}
```

At the end of the `handleEvent()` method, you normally return a value you get from the `Scrollbar` class's original `handleEvent()` method. To return this value, you simply pass the `Event` object `e` to the method `super.handleEvent()`, which passes the `Event` object back to the Scrollbar class's—that is, the base class's—handleEvent() method:

```
public boolean handleEvent(Event e){
   if(e.target.equals(scroll1)){
      scroll1.setValue(scroll1.getValue());
      text1.setText("horizontal position:" + String.valueOf(scroll1.getValue()));
   }
   if(e.target.equals(scroll2)){
      scroll2.setValue(scroll2.getValue());
      text2.setText("vertical position:" + String.valueOf(scroll2.getValue()));
   }
   return super.handleEvent(e);
}
```

> **TIP**
>
> The super keyword refers to the base class from which the current class is derived, and it's useful when you want to pass data back to the base class so that it can take the appropriate action.

> **TIP**
>
> You can actually get access to the object that caused an event from the Event object passed to handleEvent() and action() methods. For example, to get the new value of scroll1 if that scroll bar was scrolled, you can either use this scroll1.getValue() or ((Scrollbar)e.target).getValue(). You use a Java *cast* operator (just as you do in C or C++) here—that is, "(Scrollbar)"—to make sure the compiler knows that the class of the e.target object is the Java Scrollbar class.

Our scroll bar applet is ready to go. Run it now, as shown in Figure 6.1. As you can see, the user can move the scroll bar thumbs, and the new position is reported in the text fields. Our scrolling applet is a success—now we're using scroll bars. The code for this applet appears in scrolls.java.

FIGURE 6.1:

Our scroll bar example
applet

scrolls.java

```
//*****************************************************************************
// scrolls.java:  Applet
//
//*****************************************************************************
import java.applet.*;
import java.awt.*;


//=============================================================================
// Main Class for applet scrolls
//
//=============================================================================
public class scrolls extends Applet
{
 TextField text1, text2;
 Scrollbar scroll1, scroll2;

  // scrolls Class Constructor
  //---------------------------------------------------------------------------
  public scrolls()
  {
    // TODO: Add constructor code here
  }
```

```
// APPLET INFO SUPPORT:
//   The getAppletInfo() method returns a string describing the applet's
// author, copyright date, or miscellaneous information.
//--------------------------------------------------------------------------
public String getAppletInfo()
{
   return "Name: scrolls\r\n" +
         "Author: Steven Holzner\r\n" +
         "Created with Microsoft Visual J++ Version 1.0";
}


// The init() method is called by the AWT when an applet is first loaded or
// reloaded.  Override this method to perform whatever initialization your
// applet needs, such as initializing data structures, loading images or
// fonts, creating frame windows, setting the layout manager, or adding UI
// components.
//--------------------------------------------------------------------------
public void init()
{
   // If you use a ResourceWizard-generated "control creator" class to
   // arrange controls in your applet, you may want to call its
   // CreateControls() method from within this method. Remove the following
   // call to resize() before adding the call to CreateControls();
   // CreateControls() does its own resizing.
   //--------------------------------------------------------------------------
   resize(320, 240);
   scroll1 = new Scrollbar(Scrollbar.HORIZONTAL, 1, 10, 1, 100);
   add(scroll1);
   scroll2 = new Scrollbar(Scrollbar.VERTICAL, 1, 10, 1, 100);
   add(scroll2);
   text1 = new TextField(40);
   add(text1);
   text2 = new TextField(40);
   add(text2);

   // TODO: Place additional initialization code here
}

public boolean handleEvent(Event e){
   if(e.target.equals(scroll1)){
```

```
      scroll1.setValue(scroll1.getValue());
      text1.setText("horizontal position:" +
➡ String.valueOf(scroll1.getValue()));
    }
    if(e.target.equals(scroll2)){
      scroll2.setValue(scroll2.getValue());
      text2.setText("vertical position:" + String.valueOf(scroll2.getValue()));
    }
    return super.handleEvent(e);
  }


  // Place additional applet clean up code here.  destroy() is called
  // when your applet is terminating and being unloaded.
  //-------------------------------------------------------------------------
  public void destroy()
  {
    // TODO: Place applet cleanup code here
  }


  // scrolls Paint Handler
  //-------------------------------------------------------------------------
  public void paint(Graphics g)
  {
    //g.drawString("Created with Microsoft Visual J++ Version 1.0", 10, 20);
  }


  //   The start() method is called when the page containing the applet
  // first appears on the screen. The AppletWizard's initial implementation
  // of this method starts execution of the applet's thread.
  //-------------------------------------------------------------------------
  public void start()
  {
    // TODO: Place additional applet start code here
  }


  //   The stop() method is called when the page containing the applet is
  // no longer on the screen. The AppletWizard's initial implementation of
  // this method stops execution of the applet's thread.
  //-------------------------------------------------------------------------
```

```
public void stop()
{
}



// TODO: Place additional applet code here

}
```

A special Java layout manager—the BorderLayout manager—is perfect for use with scroll bars (although not even many Java experts are aware of it!). Let's see how this layout handles scroll bars for us in a way that adds a great deal of power to our applets.

A Scroll Bar Layout Example

The BorderLayout manager allows you to surround an applet with scroll bars like this:

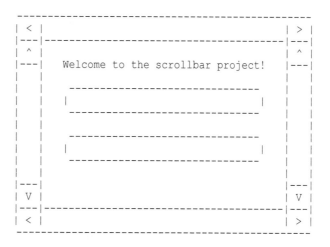

When the user scrolls the horizontal or vertical scroll bars, you can report the new settings of the scroll bars in two text fields like this:

Let's see this in action. Create a new applet now with the Visual J++ Applet Wizard named sbars. You declare the controls you need— two horizontal scroll bars hScroll1 and hScroll2, and two vertical scroll bars, vScroll1 and vScroll2—this way:

```
public class sbars extends Applet
{
    Scrollbar hScroll1, hScroll2, vScroll1, vScroll2;
        .
        .
        .
```

In addition, you need to display two text fields in the center of the applet—but the BorderLayout manager can place only one control in the center of the layout. To accomodate this, we will place our two text fields in a panel of a new class named textfieldpanel and named panel1:

```
public class sbars extends Applet
{
    Scrollbar hScroll1, hScroll2, vScroll1, vScroll2;
```

➜   `textfieldpanel panel1;`

        .

        .

        .

Let's create our `textfieldpanel` class now. Add this code to the end of the `sbars.java` file:

```
class textfieldpanel extends Panel {

}
```

You saw how to work with panels in the previous chapter. All we need here are two text fields, which we can call `text1` and `text2`. We can also add a label that reads"Welcome to the scrollbar project!" this way:

```
class textfieldpanel extends Panel {
        Label label1;
        TextField text1, text2;

        textfieldpanel(){
          label1 = new Label("Welcome to the scrollbar project!");
          add(label1);
          text1 = new TextField(40);
          add(text1);
          text2 = new TextField(40);
          add(text2);
        }
}
```

Now that the new panel class is ready, we can set up the new layout. This layout will consist of four scroll bars surrounding a central panel, and as you'll see, that's easy to set up with the BorderLayout manager. First, we install that as our new layout manager in the applet's `init()` method:

```
public void init()
{
   // If you use a ResourceWizard-generated "control creator" class to
   // arrange controls in your applet, you may want to call its
   // CreateControls() method from within this method. Remove the following
```

```
// call to resize() before adding the call to CreateControls();
// CreateControls() does its own resizing.
//--------------------------------------------------------------
resize(320, 240);
```

➜
```
setLayout(new BorderLayout());
   .
   .
   .
```

You can now add controls to this new layout. When you add controls to the BorderLayout manager, you specify where the new control goes—around the edges of the applet, which are designated north, east, south, and west, or in the center, like this:

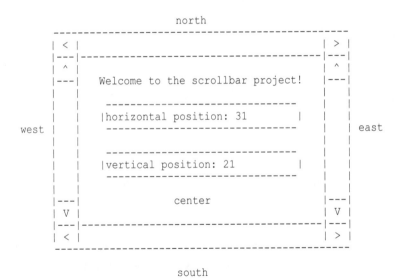

For example, you create and add a scroll bar on the top of the applet—the north position—like this:

```
public void init()
{
    resize(320, 240);
```

```
    setLayout(new BorderLayout());

➜   hScroll1 = new Scrollbar(Scrollbar.HORIZONTAL, 1, 1, 1, 200);
➜   add("North", hScroll1);
        .
        .
        .
```

You continue, adding the other scroll bars and the `panel1` object in the center of our applet:

```
public void init()
{
    resize(320, 240);
    setLayout(new BorderLayout());
    hScroll1 = new Scrollbar(Scrollbar.HORIZONTAL, 1, 1, 1, 200);
    add("North", hScroll1);
➜   vScroll1 = new Scrollbar(Scrollbar.VERTICAL, 1, 1, 1, 200);
➜   add("West", vScroll1);
➜   hScroll2 = new Scrollbar(Scrollbar.HORIZONTAL, 1, 1, 1, 200);
➜   add("South", hScroll2);
➜   vScroll2 = new Scrollbar(Scrollbar.VERTICAL, 1, 1, 1, 200);
➜   add("East", vScroll2);
➜   panel1 = new textfieldpanel();
➜   add("Center", panel1);

}
```

Now our scroll bars are laid out correctly. All that remains is to connect them to our code in the `handleEvent()` method; so add this code to `sbars.java`:

```
public boolean handleEvent(Event e){

}
```

Let's handle the top scroll bar—hScroll1—now. If that scroll bar was scrolled, we update the scroll bar's thumb like this:

```
   public boolean handleEvent(Event e){
→  if(e.target.equals(hScroll1)){
→     hScroll1.setValue(hScroll1.getValue());
→  }
         .
         .
         .
   }
```

Note that you should coordinate the two horizontal scroll bars (that is, if the user scrolls one, you should update the other as well). That looks like this in code:

```
   public boolean handleEvent(Event e){
      if(e.target.equals(hScroll1)){
         hScroll1.setValue(hScroll1.getValue());
→        hScroll2.setValue(hScroll1.getValue());
      }
         .
         .
         .
   }
```

Finally, you can report the new horizontal scroll bar position in the appropriate text field like this:

```
   public boolean handleEvent(Event e){
      if(e.target.equals(hScroll1)){
         hScroll1.setValue(hScroll1.getValue());
         hScroll2.setValue(hScroll1.getValue());
→        panel1.text1.setText("horizontal position:" + ↵
   String.valueOf(hScroll1.getValue()));
      }
   }
```

Our top scroll bar is ready to go. You can add the other scroll bars in a similar way, like this:

```
public boolean handleEvent(Event e){
  if(e.target.equals(hScroll1)){
     hScroll1.setValue(hScroll1.getValue());
```

```
        hScroll2.setValue(hScroll1.getValue());
        panel1.text1.setText("horizontal position:" +
➥ String.valueOf(hScroll1.getValue()));
    }
➜   if(e.target.equals(vScroll1)){
➜       vScroll1.setValue(vScroll1.getValue());
➜       vScroll2.setValue(vScroll1.getValue());
➜       panel1.text2.setText("vertical position:" +
➥ String.valueOf(vScroll1.getValue()));
➜   }
➜   if(e.target.equals(hScroll2)){
➜       hScroll2.setValue(hScroll2.getValue());
➜       hScroll1.setValue(hScroll2.getValue());
➜       panel1.text1.setText("horizontal position:" +
➥ String.valueOf(hScroll2.getValue()));
➜   }
➜   if(e.target.equals(vScroll2)){
➜       vScroll2.setValue(vScroll2.getValue());
➜       vScroll1.setValue(vScroll2.getValue());
➜       panel1.text2.setText("vertical position:" +
➥ String.valueOf(vScroll2.getValue()));
➜   }
    return super.handleEvent(e);
}
```

Our `sbars` applet is finished. Run the `sbars` applet now, as shown in Figure 6.2. As you can see, scroll bars surround the central panel. When the user scrolls the scroll bars, the new horizontal and vertical positions appear in the text fields, as shown in Figure 6.2. Our sbars applet is a success. The code for this applet appears in `sbars.java`.

FIGURE 6.2:

Our sbars applet supports four scroll bars.

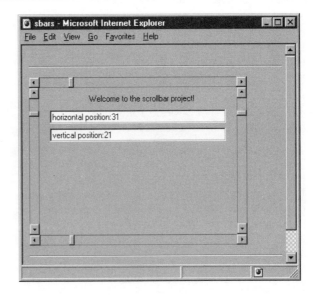

| TIP | If you want to move controls around in the central panel in response to the action of the surrounding scroll bars, use the control's `move()` method (which most Java controls have). This can give the user the impression of scrolling the controls around inside the applet. |

sbars.java

```
//********************************************************************************
// sbars.java:  Applet
//
//********************************************************************************
import java.applet.*;
import java.awt.*;


//================================================================================
// Main Class for applet sbars
//
//================================================================================
```

```
public class sbars extends Applet
{
    Scrollbar hScroll1, hScroll2, vScroll1, vScroll2;
    textfieldpanel panel1;

    // sbars Class Constructor
    //--------------------------------------------------------------------------
    public sbars()
    {
        // TODO: Add constructor code here
    }


    // APPLET INFO SUPPORT:
    //    The getAppletInfo() method returns a string describing the applet's
    // author, copyright date, or miscellaneous information.
    //--------------------------------------------------------------------------
    public String getAppletInfo()
    {
        return "Name: sbars\r\n" +
               "Author: Steven Holzner\r\n" +
               "Created with Microsoft Visual J++ Version 1.0";
    }


    // The init() method is called by the AWT when an applet is first loaded or
    // reloaded.  Override this method to perform whatever initialization your
    // applet needs, such as initializing data structures, loading images or
    // fonts, creating frame windows, setting the layout manager, or adding UI
    // components.
    //--------------------------------------------------------------------------
    public void init()
    {
        // If you use a ResourceWizard-generated "control creator" class to
        // arrange controls in your applet, you may want to call its
        // CreateControls() method from within this method. Remove the following
        // call to resize() before adding the call to CreateControls();
        // CreateControls() does its own resizing.
        //--------------------------------------------------------------------------
        resize(320, 240);

        setLayout(new BorderLayout());
```

```
    hScroll1 = new Scrollbar(Scrollbar.HORIZONTAL, 1, 1, 1, 200);
    add("North", hScroll1);

    vScroll1 = new Scrollbar(Scrollbar.VERTICAL, 1, 1, 1, 200);
    add("West", vScroll1);

    hScroll2 = new Scrollbar(Scrollbar.HORIZONTAL, 1, 1, 1, 200);
    add("South", hScroll2);

    vScroll2 = new Scrollbar(Scrollbar.VERTICAL, 1, 1, 1, 200);
    add("East", vScroll2);

    panel1 = new textfieldpanel();
    add("Center", panel1);

}


public boolean handleEvent(Event e){
  if(e.target.equals(hScroll1)){
      hScroll1.setValue(hScroll1.getValue());
      hScroll2.setValue(hScroll1.getValue());
      panel1.text1.setText("horizontal position:" +
         String.valueOf(hScroll1.getValue()));
  }
  if(e.target.equals(vScroll1)){
      vScroll1.setValue(vScroll1.getValue());
      vScroll2.setValue(vScroll1.getValue());
      panel1.text2.setText("vertical position:" +
         String.valueOf(vScroll1.getValue()));
  }
  if(e.target.equals(hScroll2)){
      hScroll2.setValue(hScroll2.getValue());
      hScroll1.setValue(hScroll2.getValue());
      panel1.text1.setText("horizontal position:" +
         String.valueOf(hScroll2.getValue()));
  }
  if(e.target.equals(vScroll2)){
      vScroll2.setValue(vScroll2.getValue());
      vScroll1.setValue(vScroll2.getValue());
      panel1.text2.setText("vertical position:" +
         String.valueOf(vScroll2.getValue()));
  }
```

```
      return super.handleEvent(e);
   }


   // Place additional applet clean up code here.  destroy() is called
   // when your applet is terminating and being unloaded.
   //-------------------------------------------------------------------------
   public void destroy()
   {
      // TODO: Place applet cleanup code here
   }


   // sbars Paint Handler
   //-------------------------------------------------------------------------
   public void paint(Graphics g)
   {
      //g.drawString("Created with Microsoft Visual J++ Version 1.0", 10, 20);
   }


   //   The start() method is called when the page containing the applet
   // first appears on the screen. The AppletWizard's initial implementation
   // of this method starts execution of the applet's thread.
   //-------------------------------------------------------------------------
   public void start()
   {
      // TODO: Place additional applet start code here
   }


   //   The stop() method is called when the page containing the applet is
   // no longer on the screen. The AppletWizard's initial implementation of
   // this method stops execution of the applet's thread.
   //-------------------------------------------------------------------------
   public void stop()
   {
   }




   // TODO: Place additional applet code here

}
```

```
class textfieldpanel extends Panel {
    Label label1;
    TextField text1, text2;

    textfieldpanel(){
        label1 = new Label("Welcome to the scrollbar project!");
        add(label1);
        text1 = new TextField(40);
        add(text1);
        text2 = new TextField(40);
        add(text2);
    }
}
```

The *choice* Control

The choice control is really just the drop-down list box with which Windows users are familiar. For example, if you have a choice control, the user sees the first choice in the choice control and an arrow button next to it:

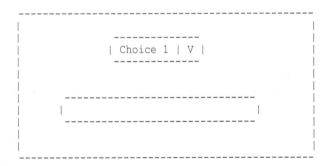

When the user clicks on the arrow button, the list of choices opens:

```
-------------------------------------------------
|                                               |
|               ---------------                 |
|             | Choice 1  | V |                 |
|             |Choice 2|----                     |
|             |Choice 3|                          |
|             |Choice 4|                          |
|               --------                         |
|         -----------------------------          |
|       |                           |            |
|         -----------------------------          |
|                                               |
|                                               |
-------------------------------------------------
```

When the user selects a choice (by double-clicking on it), you can display the result in a text field:

```
-------------------------------------------------
|                                               |
|               ---------------                 |
|             | Choice 2  | V |                 |
|               ---------------                 |
|                                               |
|                                               |
|         -----------------------------          |
|       |You chose: Choice 2          |          |
|         -----------------------------          |
|                                               |
-------------------------------------------------
```

We will put this to work in a minute. As it turns out, choice controls give us the opportunity to explore another facet of Visual J++—handling parameters. Parameters are values that you can pass to an applet and use to customize the applet's behavior. For example, you might pass the items that the choice control is to display. In this way, you can use the same applet with the same choice control in many different Web pages.

Let's see how this all works. Create a new applet named choices. Here, we'll pass the choices that the choice control is to display as parameters embedded in the applet's Web page; so do not skip over the fourth step in the Applet Wizard this time—this is how you add parameters to Applet Wizard applets.

The fourth step in the Visual J++ Applet Wizard appears in Figure 6.3. We will add four parameters to our applet example: `choice1`, `choice2`, `choice3`, and `choice4`. Each of these parameters corresponds to a string expression: Choice 1, Choice 2, Choice 3, and Choice 4, respectively. To add these parameters to our applet, type the names of the parameters, `choice1` to `choice4` in the Applet Wizard's Name column, as shown in Figure 6.3. Next, type the string that each parameter represents, Choice 1 to Choice 4, in the column labeled Def-Value, as shown in Figure 6.3. The Applet Wizard adds the other information you see in Figure 6.3. If you want to give a description to any parameter that you can retrieve in the applet's code, place that in the Description column. That's it—now click on the Finish button to create our applet.

FIGURE 6.3:

The Applet Wizard Step 4 of 5 window

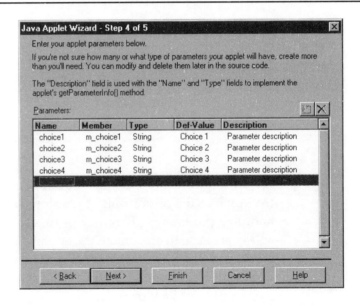

The values we have selected for our parameters are placed in the sample `.html` file that the Applet Wizard makes for us, like this:

```
<html>
<head>
```

```
<title>choices</title>
</head>
<body>
<hr>
<applet
  code=choices.class
  id=choices
  width=320
  height=240 >
  <param name=choice1 value="Choice 1">
  <param name=choice2 value="Choice 2">
  <param name=choice3 value="Choice 3">
  <param name=choice4 value="Choice 4">
</applet>
<hr>
<a href="choices.java">The source.</a>
</body>
</html>
```

If you want to, you can have many different sets of parameters in many different Web pages, and still use the same applet. In this way, you can easily customize the applet's behavior.

Now let's add our `choice` control and see how to retrieve the parameters we set up with the Visual J++ Applet Wizard. We begin by adding the controls—a `choice` control and a text field—this way:

```
public class choices extends Applet
{
  Choice choice1;
  TextField text1;
      .
      .
      .
```

The methods of the Java `Choice` class appear in Table 6.2.

TABLE 6.2: The Choice Class's Methods

Method	Does This
Choice()	Constructs an empty Choice control
addItem(String)	Adds an item to the control
addNotify()	Creates the Choice's peer
countItems()	Gets number of items in the control
getItem(int)	Gets string at indicated position in Choice control
getSelectedIndex()	Gets index of the selected item
getSelectedItem()	Gets string representation of Choice control
paramString()	Gets parameter string of the control
select(int)	Selects item at given postion
select(String)	Selects item with given text

The Visual J++ Applet Wizard has already added considerable support for parameters to the applet. For example, it has set aside four strings, PARAM_choice1 to PARAM_choice4, to hold the names of the four parameters we've set up, choice1 to choice4:

```
// Parameter names.  To change a name of a parameter, you need only make
// a single change.  Simply modify the value of the parameter string below.
//-----------------------------------------------------------------------------
private final String PARAM_choice1 = "choice1";
private final String PARAM_choice2 = "choice2";
private final String PARAM_choice3 = "choice3";
private final String PARAM_choice4 = "choice4";
        .
        .
        .
```

TIP In Java, the final keyword you see in the above code makes a variable into a constant, which cannot change its value.

In the `init()` method, the Applet Wizard has already added the code necessary to read in our four parameters and place their contents in the strings `m_choice1` to `m_choice4` like this:

```
public void init()
{
  // PARAMETER SUPPORT
  //The following code retrieves the value of each parameter
  // specified with the <PARAM> tag and stores it in a member
  // variable.
  //-------------------------------------------------------------
  String param;

  // choice1: Parameter description
  //-------------------------------------------------------------
  param = getParameter(PARAM_choice1);
  if (param != null)
    m_choice1 = param;

  // choice2: Parameter description
  //-------------------------------------------------------------
  param = getParameter(PARAM_choice2);
  if (param != null)
    m_choice2 = param;

  // choice3: Parameter description
  //-------------------------------------------------------------
  param = getParameter(PARAM_choice3);
  if (param != null)
    m_choice3 = param;

  // choice4: Parameter description
  //-------------------------------------------------------------
  param = getParameter(PARAM_choice4);
  if (param != null)
    m_choice4 = param;
          .
          .
          .
```

This makes it very simple—now all we have to do to get the first parameter is to look in the variable m_choice1, to get the second parameter look in m_choice2, and so on. We can add our own code now to declare our choice control, which we might name choice1:

```
public void init()
{
    // PARAMETER SUPPORT
    //   The following code retrieves the value of each parameter
    // specified with the <PARAM> tag and stores it in a member
    // variable.
    //---------------------------------------------------------------
    String param;
            .
            .
            .

    // If you use a ResourceWizard-generated "control creator" class to
    // arrange controls in your applet, you may want to call its
    // CreateControls() method from within this method. Remove the following
    // call to resize() before adding the call to CreateControls();
    // CreateControls() does its own resizing.
    //---------------------------------------------------------------
    resize(320, 240);
➜   choice1 = new Choice();
            .
            .
            .
```

To add the choices our choice control is to display (that is, those strings now held in m_choice1 to m_choice4), we use the Choice class's addItem() method this way:

```
    public void init()
    {   .
            .
            .
        resize(320, 240);
        choice1 = new Choice();
➜       choice1.addItem(m_choice1);
➜       choice1.addItem(m_choice2);
➜       choice1.addItem(m_choice3);
```

```
→       choice1.addItem(m_choice4);
            .
            .
            .
    }
```

Now we add the `choice` control to our applet's layout, as well as the text field we'll need to report which choice the user made:

```
    public void init()
    {   .
            .
            .
      resize(320, 240);
      choice1 = new Choice();
      choice1.addItem(m_choice1);
      choice1.addItem(m_choice2);
      choice1.addItem(m_choice3);
      choice1.addItem(m_choice4);
→     add(choice1);
→     text1 = new TextField(40);
→     add(text1);

    }
```

At this point, our `choice` control and text field appear. The next step is to display the user's choice, and you do that by adding an `action()` method:

```
    public boolean action (Event e, Object o){
            .
            .
            .
    }
```

Here, we just make sure that our `choice1` control caused the Java event:

```
    public boolean action (Event e, Object o){
→     if(e.target.equals(choice1)){
            .
            .
            .
      }
    }
```

And if so, we want to display the user's selection. We find that selection and place it in the string that we name *caption* in this way:

```
public boolean action (Event e, Object o){
    String caption = (String)o;
    if(e.target.equals(choice1)){
        .
        .
        .
    }
}
```

All that is left is to display the new choice the user has just made in the text field, which you do like this:

```
public boolean action (Event e, Object o){
    String caption = (String)o;
    if(e.target.equals(choice1)){
        text1.setText("You chose: " + caption);
    }
    return true;
}
```

Our choices applet is ready to go. Run it now, as shown in Figure 6.4. As you can see, our `choice` control is active—we've read in the parameters from the Web page and presented them to the user. When the user makes a selection from the `choice` control, we display that selection in the text field. Our choices applet is a success. The code for this applet appears in `choices.java`.

FIGURE 6.4:

Our choices applet
supports a choice
control.

choices.java

```
//*********************************************************************************
// choices.java:  Applet
//
//*********************************************************************************
import java.applet.*;
import java.awt.*;


//=================================================================================
// Main Class for applet choices
//
//=================================================================================
public class choices extends Applet
{
   Choice choice1;
   TextField text1;

   // PARAMETER SUPPORT:
   //   Parameters allow an HTML author to pass information to the applet;
   // the HTML author specifies them using the <PARAM> tag within the <APPLET>
   // tag.  The following variables are used to store the values of the
```

```
// parameters.
//--------------------------------------------------------------------------

// Members for applet parameters
// <type>   <MemberVar>  = <Default Value>
//--------------------------------------------------------------------------
private String m_choice1 = "Choice 1";
private String m_choice2 = "Choice 2";
private String m_choice3 = "Choice 3";
private String m_choice4 = "Choice 4";

// Parameter names.  To change a name of a parameter, you need only make
// a single change.  Simply modify the value of the parameter string below.
//--------------------------------------------------------------------------
private final String PARAM_choice1 = "choice1";
private final String PARAM_choice2 = "choice2";
private final String PARAM_choice3 = "choice3";
private final String PARAM_choice4 = "choice4";

// choices Class Constructor
//--------------------------------------------------------------------------
public choices()
{
   // TODO: Add constructor code here
}

// APPLET INFO SUPPORT:
//   The getAppletInfo() method returns a string describing the applet's
// author, copyright date, or miscellaneous information.
//--------------------------------------------------------------------------
public String getAppletInfo()
{
   return "Name: choices\r\n" +
       "Author: Steven Holzner\r\n" +
       "Created with Microsoft Visual J++ Version 1.0";
}

// PARAMETER SUPPORT
//   The getParameterInfo() method returns an array of strings describing
// the parameters understood by this applet.
//
// choices Parameter Information:
```

```
//   { "Name", "Type", "Description" },
//-----------------------------------------------------------------------
public String[[ getParameterInfo()
{
   String[[ info =
   {
      { PARAM_choice1, "String", "Parameter description" },
      { PARAM_choice2, "String", "Parameter description" },
      { PARAM_choice3, "String", "Parameter description" },
      { PARAM_choice4, "String", "Parameter description" },
   };
   return info;
}


// The init() method is called by the AWT when an applet is first loaded or
// reloaded.  Override this method to perform whatever initialization your
// applet needs, such as initializing data structures, loading images or
// fonts, creating frame windows, setting the layout manager, or adding UI
// components.
//-----------------------------------------------------------------------
public void init()
{
   // PARAMETER SUPPORT
   //   The following code retrieves the value of each parameter
   // specified with the <PARAM> tag and stores it in a member
   // variable.
   //-----------------------------------------------------------------------
   String param;

   // choice1: Parameter description
   //-----------------------------------------------------------------------
   param = getParameter(PARAM_choice1);
   if (param != null)
      m_choice1 = param;

   // choice2: Parameter description
   //-----------------------------------------------------------------------
   param = getParameter(PARAM_choice2);
   if (param != null)
      m_choice2 = param;

   // choice3: Parameter description
```

```
//----------------------------------------------------------------------
param = getParameter(PARAM_choice3);
if (param != null)
  m_choice3 = param;

// choice4: Parameter description
//----------------------------------------------------------------------
param = getParameter(PARAM_choice4);
if (param != null)
  m_choice4 = param;

// If you use a ResourceWizard-generated "control creator" class to
// arrange controls in your applet, you may want to call its
// CreateControls() method from within this method. Remove the following
// call to resize() before adding the call to CreateControls();
// CreateControls() does its own resizing.
//----------------------------------------------------------------------
resize(320, 240);
choice1 = new Choice();
choice1.addItem(m_choice1);
choice1.addItem(m_choice2);
choice1.addItem(m_choice3);
choice1.addItem(m_choice4);
add(choice1);
text1 = new TextField(40);
add(text1);

}


public boolean action (Event e, Object o){
  String caption = (String)o;
  if(e.target.equals(choice1)){
    text1.setText("You chose: " + caption);
  }
  return true;
}

// Place additional applet clean up code here.  destroy() is called
// when your applet is terminating and being unloaded.
//----------------------------------------------------------------------
```

```
public void destroy()
{
   // TODO: Place applet cleanup code here
}


// choices Paint Handler
//-------------------------------------------------------------------------
public void paint(Graphics g)
{
   //g.drawString("Created with Microsoft Visual J++ Version 1.0", 10, 20);
}


//   The start() method is called when the page containing the applet
// first appears on the screen. The AppletWizard's initial implementation
// of this method starts execution of the applet's thread.
//-------------------------------------------------------------------------
public void start()
{
   // TODO: Place additional applet start code here
}


//   The stop() method is called when the page containing the applet is
// no longer on the screen. The AppletWizard's initial implementation of
// this method stops execution of the applet's thread.
//-------------------------------------------------------------------------
public void stop()
{
}




   // TODO: Place additional applet code here

}
```

Scrolling Lists

A scrolling list presents just that to the user—a scrolling list of choices that the user can select from or scroll, using the up and down arrows that appear at right in the list control:

```
 --------------------------------------------------
|        ----------------                          |
|       |            | ^ |                         |
|       | Choice 1   |---|                         |
|       |            | V |                         |
|        ----------------                          |
|                                                  |
|        ------------------------------            |
|       |                              |           |
|        ------------------------------            |
|                                                  |
|                                                  |
 --------------------------------------------------
```

For example, the user can scroll down to the second choice, like this:

```
 --------------------------------------------------
|        ----------------                          |
|       |            | ^ |                         |
|       | Choice 2   |---|                         |
|       |            | V |                         |
|        ----------------                          |
|                                                  |
|        ------------------------------            |
|       |                              |           |
|        ------------------------------            |
|                                                  |
|                                                  |
 --------------------------------------------------
```

If the user selects this choice (that is, double-clicks on it), we can report that selection in a text field like this:

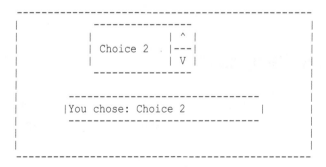

```
 --------------------------------------------------
|        ----------------                          |
|       |            | ^ |                         |
|       | Choice 2  . |---|                        |
|       |            | V |                         |
|        ----------------                          |
|                                                  |
|        ------------------------------            |
|       |You chose: Choice 2           |           |
|        ------------------------------            |
|                                                  |
|                                                  |
 --------------------------------------------------
```

It is easy to implement a choice control applet, so let's do that now. Create a new applet named slists for our scrolling list applet, and open the applet's main class. Here, we can add the two controls we'll use, the scrolling list itself—an object of class List named list1, and a text field named text1—like this:

```
public class slists extends Applet
{
→    List list1;
→    TextField text1;
         .
         .
         .
```

The Java List class's methods appear in Table 6.3.

TABLE 6.3:   The List Class's Methods

Method	Does This
List()	Creates a List with no items
List(int, boolean)	Creates a List with given number of lines; boolean is true if multiple selections are allowed
addItem(String)	Adds item to end of List
addItem(String, int)	Adds item to given position in List
addNotify()	Creates the peer for the control
allowsMultipleSelections()	Is true if control allows multiple selections
clear()	Clears the entries in the control
countItems()	Gets number of items
delItem(int)	Deletes item
delItems(int, int)	Deletes a number of items
deselect(int)	Deselects item at indicated position
getItem(int)	Gets item at indicated position
getRows()	Gets number of visible lines

TABLE 6.3: The List Class's Methods (continued)

Method	Does This
getSelectedIndex()	Gets selected item (-1 if no item is selected)
getSelectedIndexes()	Gets selected indexes in the control
getSelectedItem()	Gets selected item
getSelectedItems()	Gets selected items
getVisibleIndex()	Gets index of item that is visible
isSelected(int)	True if item at given index is selected
makeVisible(int)	Makes item at given location visible
minimumSize(int)	Gets minimum dimensions for given number of rows
minimumSize()	Gets minimum dimensions for List
paramString()	Gets parameter string of List
preferredSize()	Gets preferred dimensions for control
removeNotify()	Removes peer from control
replaceItem(String, int)	Replaces item at given index
select(int)	Selects item at given index
setMultipleSelections(boolean)	Sets if control should allow multiple selections

In the init() method, we simply add our new list control this way, indicating (see how to use the List class's constructors in Table 6.3) that we want two lines in our list control and that we will allow multiple selections by passing a second parameter and setting it to TRUE:

```
public void init()
{
   // If you use a ResourceWizard-generated "control creator" class to
   // arrange controls in your applet, you may want to call its
   // CreateControls() method from within this method. Remove the following
   // call to resize() before adding the call to CreateControls();
   // CreateControls() does its own resizing.
```

```
//-------------------------------------------------------------------
    resize(320, 240);

→   list1 = new List(2, true);
        .
        .
        .
```

Now we add the selections in the list in the same way as with the choice control—using the addItem() method:

```
    public void init()
    {
       resize(320, 240);

       list1 = new List(2, true);
→      list1.addItem("Choice 1");
→      list1.addItem("Choice 2");
→      list1.addItem("Choice 3");
→      list1.addItem("Choice 4");
            .
            .
            .
```

Next, we add the list and the text field like this:

```
    public void init()
    {
       resize(320, 240);

       list1 = new List(2, true);
       list1.addItem("Choice 1");
       list1.addItem("Choice 2");
       list1.addItem("Choice 3");
       list1.addItem("Choice 4");
→      add(list1);
→      text1 = new TextField(40);
→      add(text1);
    }
```

Now the applet displays the scrolling `list` control and the text field. Our next step is to make the scrolling list active with an `action()` method:

```
public boolean action (Event e, Object o){

}
```

We begin by checking to make sure that our scrolling list, `list1`, really caused the event:

```
public boolean action (Event e, Object o){
    if(e.target.equals(list1)){
        .
        .
        .
    }
}
```

If so, we can get the currently selected item in the scrolling list just as we did for the `choice` control:

```
public boolean action (Event e, Object o){
    String caption = (String)o;
    if(e.target.equals(list1)){
        .
        .
        .
    }
}
```

All that remains is to display that choice in the text field, and that looks like this in code:

```
public boolean action (Event e, Object o){
    String caption = (String)o;
    if(e.target.equals(list1)){
        text1.setText("You chose: " + caption);
    }
    return true;
}
```

Our scrolling list applet is ready to run. Run it now as shown in Figure 6.5. The user can scroll up and down the list, and when the user makes a selection, we report what that selection is, as shown in Figure 6.5. Our slists applet is a success. The code for this applet appears in `slists.java`.

FIGURE 6.5:

Our scrolling list applet

slists.java

```
//**************************************************************************
// slists.java: Applet
//
//**************************************************************************
import java.applet.*;
import java.awt.*;


//==========================================================================
// Main Class for applet slists
//
//==========================================================================
public class slists extends Applet
{
```

```java
List list1;
TextField text1;

// slists Class Constructor
//--------------------------------------------------------------------------
public slists()
{
   // TODO: Add constructor code here
}


// APPLET INFO SUPPORT:
//    The getAppletInfo() method returns a string describing the applet's
// author, copyright date, or miscellaneous information.
//--------------------------------------------------------------------------
public String getAppletInfo()
{
   return "Name: slists\r\n" +
        "Author: Steven Holzner\r\n" +
        "Created with Microsoft Visual J++ Version 1.0";
}



// The init() method is called by the AWT when an applet is first loaded or
// reloaded.  Override this method to perform whatever initialization your
// applet needs, such as initializing data structures, loading images or
// fonts, creating frame windows, setting the layout manager, or adding UI
// components.
//--------------------------------------------------------------------------
public void init()
{
   // If you use a ResourceWizard-generated "control creator" class to
   // arrange controls in your applet, you may want to call its
   // CreateControls() method from within this method. Remove the following
   // call to resize() before adding the call to CreateControls();
   // CreateControls() does its own resizing.
   //--------------------------------------------------------------------------
   resize(320, 240);

   list1 = new List(2, true);
   list1.addItem("Choice 1");
   list1.addItem("Choice 2");
   list1.addItem("Choice 3");
```

```
    list1.addItem("Choice 4");
    add(list1);
     text1 = new TextField(40);
    add(text1);
}

public boolean action (Event e, Object o){
    String caption = (String)o;
    if(e.target.equals(list1)){
        text1.setText("You chose: " + caption);
    }
    return true;
}


// Place additional applet clean up code here.  destroy() is called
// when your applet is terminating and being unloaded.
//-----------------------------------------------------------------------------
public void destroy()
{
    // TODO: Place applet cleanup code here
}


// slists Paint Handler
//-----------------------------------------------------------------------------
public void paint(Graphics g)
{
    //g.drawString("Created with Microsoft Visual J++ Version 1.0", 10, 20);
}


//   The start() method is called when the page containing the applet
// first appears on the screen. The AppletWizard's initial implementation
// of this method starts execution of the applet's thread.
//-----------------------------------------------------------------------------
public void start()
{
    // TODO: Place additional applet start code here
}


//   The stop() method is called when the page containing the applet is
// no longer on the screen. The AppletWizard's initial implementation of
// this method stops execution of the applet's thread.
//-----------------------------------------------------------------------------
```

```
public void stop()
{
}
```

```
// TODO: Place additional applet code here
```

```
}
```

A GridBag Layout Example–the Phone Applet

In this last example of the chapter, we'll explore what is probably the most powerful native Java layout of all—the GridBag layout. This layout manager lets you specify the position of controls more exactly than any other layout manager we've seen.

For example, using the GridBagLayout manager, we can create an applet that provides the user with a phone directory. We can place the names of people in buttons at the top of the applet like this:

When the user clicks on a button, we can display the corresponding phone number in a text area this way:

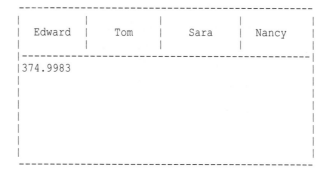

We'll give this new layout a try. With the Applet Wizard, create a new applet now named phone. We add the controls we'll need—buttons button1 to button4, and a text area named text1:

```
public class phone extends Applet
{
```

➡   `Button button1, button2, button3, button4;`
➡   `TextArea text1;`
```
        .
        .
        .
```

Now let's set up our new GridBagLayout manager to see how it works. We do that by creating a new object of the GridBagLayout class named gridbag, like this in the init() method:

```
public void init()
{
    // If you use a ResourceWizard-generated "control creator" class to
    // arrange controls in your applet, you may want to call its
    // CreateControls() method from within this method. Remove the following
    // call to resize() before adding the call to CreateControls();
    // CreateControls() does its own resizing.
    //------------------------------------------------------------------------
    resize(320, 240);
```
➡   `GridBagLayout gridbag = new GridBagLayout();`
```
        .
        .
        .
```

The way we specify how we want our controls to be arranged under the GridBagLayout manager is with an object of the Java class `GridBagConstraints`, as you'll see. We use this object to arange the controls in a GridBag layout. Let's create an object of that class now and name it `constraints`:

```
public void init()
{
    resize(320, 240);
    GridBagLayout gridbag = new GridBagLayout();
➜   GridBagConstraints constraints = new GridBagConstraints();
        .
        .
        .
```

Now we can install our new GridBag layout in our applet:

```
public void init()
{
    // If you use a ResourceWizard-generated "control creator" class to
    // arrange controls in your applet, you may want to call its
    // CreateControls() method from within this method. Remove the following
    // call to resize() before adding the call to CreateControls().
    // CreateControls() does its own resizing.
    //-----------------------------------------------------------------------
    resize(320, 240);
    GridBagLayout gridbag = new GridBagLayout();
    GridBagConstraints constraints = new GridBagConstraints();
➜   setLayout(gridbag);
        .
        .
        .
```

The next step is to start specifying how we want controls to be "constrained" in our new layout.

GridBag Constraints

GridBag layouts work with the relative "weights" of controls in the x and y directions—for example, since all these buttons have the same width, they each have the same x weight, like this:

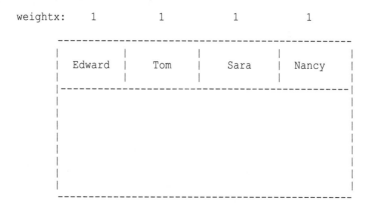

However, if one control is twice as wide as the others, it will have double the x weight:

You specify x and y weights with the `weightx` and `weighty` members of the `GridBagConstraints` object that we have named `constraints`. Because all buttons have the same height, they have the same value for `weighty`, which we can just set to one:

```
public void init()
{
    resize(320, 240);
    GridBagLayout gridbag = new GridBagLayout();
    GridBagConstraints constraints = new GridBagConstraints();
    setLayout(gridbag);
→   constraints.weighty = 1;
        .
        .
        .
```

We can specify that the controls in our applet be stretched to fill their allotted space in the layout, and we do that by setting the fill member of our `constraints` object. We could set this data member to the constant `GridBagConstraints.HORIZONTAL` to stretch controls horizontally, we could use the constant `GridBagConstraints.VERTICAL` to stretch them vertically, or we could use `GridBagConstraints.BOTH` to stretch them in both dimensions to fill the allotted space. In this case, we'll stretch controls in both dimensions:

```
public void init()
{
    resize(320, 240);
    GridBagLayout gridbag = new GridBagLayout();
    GridBagConstraints constraints = new GridBagConstraints();
    setLayout(gridbag);
    constraints.weighty = 1;
→   constraints.fill = GridBagConstraints.BOTH;
        .
        .
        .
```

TIP In the Java naming convention, the built-in data members of a class are referred to with small letters, and constants use capital letters. Therefore, we know the fill member of a `GridBagConstraints` object is a variable and that `GridBagConstraints.VERTICAL` is a built-in constant of the class.

At this point, we're ready to add our first button to the GridBag. We do so by giving this first button an x weight of 1, creating the new button, button1, and giving it the caption of the first name in our phone directory, Edward:

```
public void init()
{
   resize(320, 240);
   GridBagLayout gridbag = new GridBagLayout();
   GridBagConstraints constraints = new GridBagConstraints();
   setLayout(gridbag);
   constraints.weighty = 1;
   constraints.fill = GridBagConstraints.BOTH;

➜     constraints.weightx = 1;
➜     button1 = new Button("Edward");
       .
       .
       .
```

Adding this button to the GridBag layout is a two-step process. First, we set up the GridBag's constraints, using our constraints object, and then we add the control itself. That looks like this:

```
public void init()
{
   resize(320, 240);
   GridBagLayout gridbag = new GridBagLayout();
   GridBagConstraints constraints = new GridBagConstraints();
   setLayout(gridbag);
   constraints.weighty = 1;
   constraints.fill = GridBagConstraints.BOTH;

➜  constraints.weightx = 1;
➜  button1 = new Button("Edward");
➜  gridbag.setConstraints(button1, constraints);
➜  add(button1);
     .
     .
     .
```

We add the remaining buttons like this:

```
public void init()
{
   resize(320, 240);
   GridBagLayout gridbag = new GridBagLayout();
   GridBagConstraints constraints = new GridBagConstraints();
   setLayout(gridbag);
   constraints.weighty = 1;
   constraints.fill = GridBagConstraints.BOTH;

   constraints.weightx = 1;
   button1 = new Button("Edward");
   gridbag.setConstraints(button1, constraints);
   add(button1);

   constraints.weightx = 1;
   button2 = new Button("Tom");
   gridbag.setConstraints(button2, constraints);
   add(button2);

   constraints.weightx = 1;
   button3 = new Button("Sara");
   gridbag.setConstraints(button3, constraints);
   add(button3);

   constraints.weightx = 1;
   button4 = new Button("Nancy");
   constraints.gridwidth = GridBagConstraints.REMAINDER;
   gridbag.setConstraints(button4, constraints);
   add(button4);
               .
               .
               .
```

Note in particular this line that we use when adding the final button to the row of buttons:

```
constraints.gridwidth = GridBagConstraints.REMAINDER;
```

This tells the GridBag layout that we are done with the current row of controls and that it should take the remainder of the space left for the current (and last) button in this row.

Now that the top row (all buttons) is complete, we add the next row, which is made up of the `text area` control. Again, we set `constraints.gridwidth` to `GridBagConstraints.REMAINDER`, this time to indicate that there is only one item in this row, the text area:

```
public void init()
{
    resize(320, 240);
    GridBagLayout gridbag = new GridBagLayout();
    GridBagConstraints constraints = new GridBagConstraints();
    setLayout(gridbag);
    constraints.weighty = 1;
    constraints.fill = GridBagConstraints.BOTH;
        .
        .
        .
    text1 = new TextArea();
    constraints.gridwidth = GridBagConstraints.REMAINDER;
    gridbag.setConstraints(text1, constraints);
    add(text1);

}
```

Now our GridBag layout is set up. All that remains is to display the correct phone number when the user clicks on a button in our applet. As you might expect, that looks like this in an `action()` method (add this code to `phone.java` now):

```
public boolean action(Event e, Object o){
    if(e.target.equals(button1)){
        text1.setText("376.9983");
    }
    if(e.target.equals(button2)){
        text1.setText("376.8889");
    }
    if(e.target.equals(button3)){
        text1.setText("376.7582");
```

```
    }
    if(e.target.equals(button4)){
       text1.setText("376.6563");
    }
    return true;
  }
```

Our applet is complete. Run it now, as shown in Figure 6.6. As you can see, our controls appear as we want them and where we want them. We've set up a GridBag layout successfully. When you click on a button, the corresponding phone number appears. Our phone directory is a success. The code for this applet appears in phone.java.

FIGURE 6.6:

Our GridBag phone directory applet

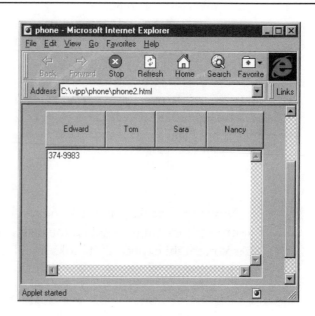

phone.java

```
//***********************************************************************
// phone.java:  Applet
//
//***********************************************************************
import java.applet.*;
import java.awt.*;

//=======================================================================
// Main Class for applet phone
//
//=======================================================================
public class phone extends Applet
{

   Button button1, button2, button3, button4;
   TextArea text1;

   // phone Class Constructor
   //--------------------------------------------------------------------
   public phone()
   {
      // TODO: Add constructor code here
   }


   // APPLET INFO SUPPORT:
   //   The getAppletInfo() method returns a string describing the applet's
   // author, copyright date, or miscellaneous information.
   //--------------------------------------------------------------------
   public String getAppletInfo()
   {
      return "Name: phone\r\n" +
            "Author: Steven Holzner\r\n" +
            "Created with Microsoft Visual J++ Version 1.0";
   }


   // The init() method is called by the AWT when an applet is first loaded or
   // reloaded.  Override this method to perform whatever initialization your
   // applet needs, such as initializing data structures, loading images or
   // fonts, creating frame windows, setting the layout manager, or adding UI
```

```java
// components.
//--------------------------------------------------------------------------
public void init()
{
  // If you use a ResourceWizard-generated "control creator" class to
  // arrange controls in your applet, you may want to call its
  // CreateControls() method from within this method. Remove the following
  // call to resize() before adding the call to CreateControls();
  // CreateControls() does its own resizing.
  //--------------------------------------------------------------------------
  resize(320, 240);
  GridBagLayout gridbag = new GridBagLayout();
  GridBagConstraints constraints = new GridBagConstraints();
  setLayout(gridbag);
  constraints.weighty = 1;
  constraints.fill = GridBagConstraints.BOTH;

  constraints.weightx = 1;
  button1 = new Button("Edward");
  gridbag.setConstraints(button1, constraints);
  add(button1);

  constraints.weightx = 1;
  button2 = new Button("Tom");
  gridbag.setConstraints(button2, constraints);
  add(button2);

  constraints.weightx = 1;
  button3 = new Button("Sara");
  gridbag.setConstraints(button3, constraints);
  add(button3);

  constraints.weightx = 1;
  button4 = new Button("Nancy");
  constraints.gridwidth = GridBagConstraints.REMAINDER;
  gridbag.setConstraints(button4, constraints);
  add(button4);

  text1 = new TextArea();
  constraints.gridwidth = GridBagConstraints.REMAINDER;
  gridbag.setConstraints(text1, constraints);
```

```
    add(text1);

}

public boolean action(Event e, Object o){
   if(e.target.equals(button1)){
       text1.setText("376.9983");
   }
   if(e.target.equals(button2)){
       text1.setText("376.8889");
   }
   if(e.target.equals(button3)){
       text1.setText("376.7582");
   }
   if(e.target.equals(button4)){
       text1.setText("376.6563");
   }
   return true;
}

// Place additional applet clean up code here.  destroy() is called
// when your applet is terminating and being unloaded.
//--------------------------------------------------------------------
public void destroy()
{
   // TODO: Place applet cleanup code here
}

// phone Paint Handler
//--------------------------------------------------------------------
public void paint(Graphics g)
{
   //g.drawString("Created with Microsoft Visual J++ Version 1.0", 10, 20);
}

//   The start() method is called when the page containing the applet
// first appears on the screen. The AppletWizard's initial implementation
// of this method starts execution of the applet's thread.
//--------------------------------------------------------------------
public void start()
{
```

```
   // TODO: Place additional applet start code here
}

//   The stop() method is called when the page containing the applet is
// no longer on the screen. The AppletWizard's initial implementation of
// this method stops execution of the applet's thread.
//--------------------------------------------------------------------------
public void stop()
{
}




   // TODO: Place additional applet code here

}
```

Since the phone directory applet is a rather nice applet, let's take one more step and see how we can create and use a custom `.html` file with that applet.

TIP Using several Web pages to display the applet you are creating is a useful Visual J++ technique. By seeing the applet in a variety of surroundings, you can design it to fit those surroundings better.

Customizing the Visual J++ Web Page

Visual J++ has already created this sample `.html` file for use with our phone applet, and that `.html` file is called `phone.html`. It looks like this:

```
<html>
<head>
```

```
<title>phone</title>
</head>
<body>
<hr>
<br>
<br>
<applet
  code=phone.class
  id=phone
  width=320
  height=240 >
</applet>
<hr>
</body>
</html>
```

However, you might want to modify that a little to see how the applet's appearance should be customized with other Web pages. You can do so by indicating to Visual J++ that it should use another .html page as the default for this project. For example, let's add a displayed header that reads "Phone Directory" and center both that and our applet like this, modifying the original phone.html into phone2.html:

```
<html>
<head>
<title>phone</title>
</head>
<body>
<hr>
→ <center>
→ <h1>Phone Directory</h1>
  <br>
  <br>
  <applet
    code=phone.class
    id=phone
    width=320
    height=240 >
  </applet>
→ </center>
  <hr>
```

```
</body>
</html>
```

How do you tell Visual J++ to use `phone2.html`? You choose Build ➤ Settings to open the Settings dialog box, select the Debug tab, and click on Browser in the Category drop-down list box. Then, just fill in the HTML page text box, as shown in Figure 6.7.

FIGURE 6.7:

Setting the default .html file for an applet

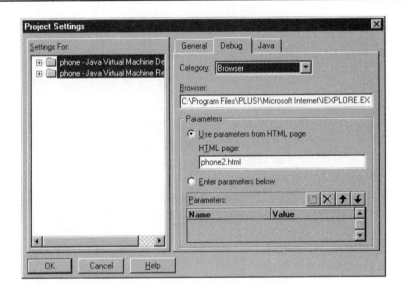

Now when we run the applet, Visual J++ will use our new Web page, as shown in Figure 6.8. We've been able to install a new Web page as our project's default.

FIGURE 6.8:

Loading and using a
customized Web page
with Visual J++

What's Next?

That about wraps it up for this chapter. You've learned about some
key VJ++ topics: how to use scroll bars, scrolling lists, choice controls, the border layout, the GridBag layout, applet parameters, and
more. Let's turn now to the next chapter in which we start to explore
some powerful Java techniques—pop-up windows, menus, and dialog boxes.

CHAPTER
SEVEN

Windows and Menus

■ Creating pop-up windows

■ Using the Menu Editor

■ Creating a resource template

■ Using the Resource Wizard to create a menu

In this chapter, we'll explore the process of creating pop-up windows and menus in Visual J++. These are powerful techniques. Using the procedures in this chapter, you can add new windows entirely separate from the applet that you can pop up as required, as well as add menus to such windows. You can display information—both images and text—in pop-up windows, and you can even display and use controls. Menus are familiar to any Windows user: Using menus, you can allow the user to select from among many items, and when not called for, those items can be hidden. We will get started at once by seeing how to support pop-up windows in Java.

Creating Pop-Up Windows

We might start by seeing how to pop a new window onto the screen. For example, we can create an applet like this, with a Make Window Visible button and a Make Window Invisible button:

```
 ------------------------------------------------------------
|                                                            |
|                                                            |
|    --------------------      --------------------          |
|   |Make window visible|     |Make window invisible|        |
|    --------------------      --------------------          |
|                                                            |
|                                                            |
|                                                            |
|                                                            |
|                                                            |
|                                                            |
 ------------------------------------------------------------
```

When the user clicks on the Make Window Visible button, we can display a new (free-floating) window with a No Problem message in it like this:

```
 -------------------------------------------------------
|                                                       |
|                                                       |
|     ------------------       --------------------     |
|    |Make window visible|    |Make window invisible|   |
|     ------------------       --------------------     |
|                                             --------------
|                                            |--------------|
|                                            |  No problem  |
|                                            |              |
|                                            |              |
|                                            |              |
|                                             --------------
 -------------------------------------------------------
```

When the user clicks on the Make Window Invisible button, we can hide the window again. Let's put this together now. Create a new applet with the Applet Wizard named wnds. Open the applet's main class now:

```
public class wnds extends Applet
{     .
      .
      .
```

Start by declaring the two buttons that you will use, `button1` and `button2`:

```
    public class wnds extends Applet
    {
➜      Button button1, button2;
         .
         .
         .
```

The next step is to declare a window object so that you can work with it, showing it to the user and hiding it when required. We might call this new window object `window1`. This object will be based on the Java `Frame` class, which creates a frame window on the screen.

> **NOTE** Frame windows are called frame windows because they support a frame surrounding the window that often may be resized.

This means we should derive our own class—named `demoframe`—from the `Frame` class. In this case, the declaration of our window object looks like this:

```
public class wnds extends Applet
{
    Button button1, button2;
➔   demoframe window1;
        .
        .
        .
```

Now it's up to us to create the new `demoframe` class, because our `window1` object is an object of this class. We add this code to the end of the `wnds.java` file now, where we declare a new class named `demoframe`, derived from the `Frame` class:

```
class demoframe extends Frame {
        .
        .
        .

}
```

The Java `Frame` class's methods appear in Table 7.1.

TABLE 7.1: The Java `Frame` Class's Methods

Method	Does This
`Frame()`	Constructs a `Frame` (starts as invisible)
`Frame(String)`	Constructs `Frame` with given title
`addNotify()`	Creates `Frame`'s peer
`dispose()`	Disposes of the object
`getCursorType()`	Gets cursor type
`getIconImage()`	Gets icon for `Frame`
`getMenuBar()`	Gets menu bar for `Frame`
`getTitle()`	Gets title of `Frame`
`isResizable()`	Gets true if user can resize `Frame`
`paramString()`	Gets parameter string of object
`remove(MenuComponent)`	Removes given menu bar from object
`setCursor(int)`	Sets cursor to a given cursor
`setIconImage(Image)`	Sets image to show when `Frame` is iconized
`setMenuBar(MenuBar)`	Sets menu bar for object
`setResizable(boolean)`	Sets object's resizable flag
`setTitle(String)`	Sets title for `Frame` to given title

We'll need a constructor for this new class. The base class, `Frame`, has a constructor that takes the title we want in the window's title bar as an argument. We can take that argument in our `demoframe` constructor (recall that a constructor is just a method with the same name as the class) and pass it back to the `Frame` class's constructor by calling the `super()` method:

```
class demoframe extends Frame {
```

```
→   demoframe(String title){
→     super(title);
              .
              .
              .

      }
    }
```

Next, we can add the text that we want in this window: No problem. We can do that with a label like this:

```
class demoframe extends Frame {

→   Label label1;

    demoframe(String title){
      super(title);
→     label1 = new Label("No problem");
→     add(label1);
      }
    }
```

Unlike applets, windows and dialog boxes in Java have no default layout manager. Thus, we should add our own, and we might use the GridLayout manager this way:

```
class demoframe extends Frame {

    Label label1;

    demoframe(String title){
      super(title);
→       setLayout(new GridLayout(1, 1));
      label1 = new Label("No problem");
      add(label1);
      }
    }
```

And that's it—our new demoframe window class is ready to go.

Now we're ready to work with `window1`, our new pop-up window, in our applet. First, we add the two new buttons (Make Window Visible and Make Window Invisible) to the applet in its `init()` method:

```
public void init()
{
    // If you use a ResourceWizard-generated "control creator" class to
    // arrange controls in your applet, you may want to call its
    // CreateControls() method from within this method. Remove the following
    // call to resize() before adding the call to CreateControls();
    // CreateControls() does its own resizing.
    //------------------------------------------------------------------------
    resize(320, 240);
→   button1 = new Button("Make window visible");
→   add(button1);
→   button2 = new Button("Make window invisible");
→   add(button2);
        .
        .
        .
```

At this point, then, you create `window1`, having declared it earlier. You do so like this, passing a title to the `demoframe` class's constructor:

```
    public void init()
    {
        resize(320, 240);
        button1 = new Button("Make window visible");
        add(button1);
        button2 = new Button("Make window invisible");
        add(button2);
```

```
➜        window1 = new demoframe("Hello World!");
                   .
                   .
                   .
         }
```

We've set up our constructor so that this title is just passed back to the Java `Frame` class's constructor. We also give the new window an initial size (in pixels) using its `resize()` method this way:

```
public void init()
{
   resize(320, 240);
   button1 = new Button("Make window visible");
   add(button1);
   button2 = new Button("Make window invisible");
   add(button2);

   window1 = new demoframe("Hello World!");
➜  window1.resize(100, 100);
   }
```

All that remains is to connect our buttons to make the window appear or disappear on command.

To show a window, you use its `show()` method, and to hide it, you use its `hide()` method. Thus, you can make buttons functional by adding an `action()` method this way, where we show or hide the window, `window1`, like this:

```
public boolean action (Event e, Object o){
   if(e.target.equals(button1)){
➜     window1.show();
   }
   if(e.target.equals(button2)){
➜     window1.hide();
   }
   return true;
}
```

And that's it—our wnds applet is ready to run. Build this applet now and run it, as shown in Figure 7.1. When the user clicks on the Make Window Visible button, the pop-up window appears, as also shown in Figure 7.1. Now you've seen how to support free-floating, pop-up windows. The code for this applet appears in wnds.java.

FIGURE 7.1:

Our wnds applet supports a pop-up window.

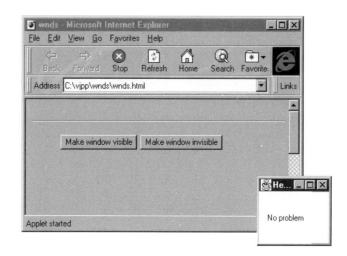

wnds.java

```
//*****************************************************************************
// wnds.java: Applet
//
//*****************************************************************************
import java.applet.*;
import java.awt.*;

//=============================================================================
// Main Class for applet wnds
//
//=============================================================================
public class wnds extends Applet
{
   Button button1, button2;
```

```
demoframe window1;

// wnds Class Constructor
//--------------------------------------------------------------------------
public wnds()
{
  // TODO: Add constructor code here
}

// APPLET INFO SUPPORT:
//   The getAppletInfo() method returns a string describing the applet's
// author, copyright date, or miscellaneous information.
//--------------------------------------------------------------------------
public String getAppletInfo()
{
   return "Name: wnds\r\n" +
        "Author: Steven Holzner\r\n" +
        "Created with Microsoft Visual J++ Version 1.0";
}


// The init() method is called by the AWT when an applet is first loaded or
// reloaded.  Override this method to perform whatever initialization your
// applet needs, such as initializing data structures, loading images or
// fonts, creating frame windows, setting the layout manager, or adding UI
// components.
//--------------------------------------------------------------------------
public void init()
{
  // If you use a ResourceWizard-generated "control creator" class to
  // arrange controls in your applet, you may want to call its
  // CreateControls() method from within this method. Remove the following
  // call to resize() before adding the call to CreateControls();
  // CreateControls() does its own resizing.
  //--------------------------------------------------------------------------
  resize(320, 240);
  button1 = new Button("Make window visible");
  add(button1);
  button2 = new Button("Make window invisible");
  add(button2);

  window1 = new demoframe("Hello World!");
```

```
   window1.resize(100, 100);
}

// Place additional applet clean up code here.  destroy() is called
// when your applet is terminating and being unloaded.
//-------------------------------------------------------------------------

public boolean action (Event e, Object o){
   if(e.target.equals(button1)){
      window1.show();
   }
   if(e.target.equals(button2)){
      window1.hide();
   }
   return true;
}

public void destroy()
{
   // TODO: Place applet cleanup code here
}

// wnds Paint Handler
//-------------------------------------------------------------------------
public void paint(Graphics g)
{
   //g.drawString("Created with Microsoft Visual J++ Version 1.0", 10, 20);
}

//   The start() method is called when the page containing the applet
// first appears on the screen. The AppletWizard's initial implementation
// of this method starts execution of the applet's thread.
//-------------------------------------------------------------------------
public void start()
{
   // TODO: Place additional applet start code here
}

//   The stop() method is called when the page containing the applet is
// no longer on the screen. The AppletWizard's initial implementation of
// this method stops execution of the applet's thread.
//-------------------------------------------------------------------------
```

```
public void stop()
{
}




// TODO: Place additional applet code here

}

class demoframe extends Frame {
  Label label1;
  demoframe(String title){
    super(title);
    setLayout(new GridLayout(1, 1));
    label1 = new Label("No problem");
    add(label1);
  }
}
```

Seeing how to support pop-up windows is a good start. We will now see how another powerful aspect of Java works: menus.

Adding Menus

In Java, menus and dialog boxes need to be attached to a frame window like the one we've just developed. That means we should start our menu example with a frame window, which we can display or hide. We can use the same two buttons in our new menu applet to show or hide the needed frame window:

```
---------------------------------------------------------
|                                                       |
|                                                       |
|    --------------------      ----------------------   |
|    |Make window visible|     |Make window invisible|  |
|    --------------------      ----------------------   |
|                                                       |
|                                                       |
|                                                       |
|                                                       |
|                                                       |
|                                                       |
|                                                       |
---------------------------------------------------------
```

When the user clicks on the Make Window Visible button, we can display the new frame window that will support our menu. If we give the menu system a menu named File, the user can open that menu to display two items that we will add: No and Problem:

```
---------------------------------------------------------
|                                               |
|                                               |
|    --------------------      --------------------   |
|    |Make window visible|     |Make window invisible|  |
|    --------------------      --------------------   |
|                                               |
|                                               |
|                                  --------------- |
|                                  |File Edit    | |
|                                  |-  ----------| |
|                                  || No       | | |
|                                  || Problem  | | |
|                                  |  -------- | |
|                                  |           | |
|                                  ------------- |
---------------------------------------------------------
```

When the user selects one of these two choices, we can display the selection in the frame window like this:

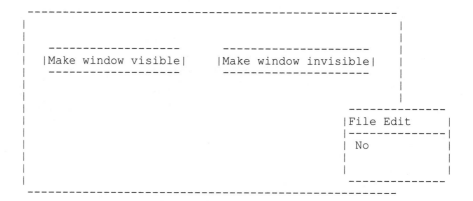

Let's put this to work now. Create a new applet called menus with the Applet Wizard. In Step 3, when the Applet Wizard asks, "Would you like your applet to be multi-threaded?" click on Yes, Please because the Visual J++ support for menus requires this. Do not, however, request support for animation (that is, click on the No, Thank You option button when asked about animation).

Now that our project is created, instead of the usual first step—opening the applet's main class and working on it—we'll create the menu we need. This menu will be a separate Java class, and we can create it with the Visual J++ Menu Editor.

Using the Menu Editor

Let's create the menu now. You might create two menus, File and Edit, like this:

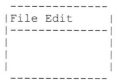

```
 --------------
|File Edit     |
|--------------|
|             |
|             |
|             |
 --------------
```

We can give the File menu two items, No and Problem:

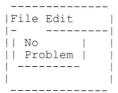

```
 --------------
|File Edit     |
|-  ---------- |
|| No       |  |
|| Problem  |  |
|  ---------   |
|             |
 --------------
```

And we can give the Edit menu two items: No and Worries:

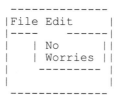

```
 --------------
|File Edit     |
|----  ------- |
|   | No     | |
|   | Worries| |
|    --------- |
|             |
 --------------
```

Creating a Resource Template

Let's see how this works now. To begin, choose File ➤ New to open the New dialog box, and then select Resource Template. This creates a *resource template* for our project (you'll see what that means in a minute). Now choose Insert ➤ Resource Item to open the Insert Resource dialog box. Click on the Menu icon in the Resource Type box, and then click on OK.

This opens two new windows: a resource template window displaying the new file Templ1.rct, and the Visual J++ Menu Editor, as shown in Figure 7.2. The .rct extension stands for resource template. When we create dialog boxes or menus in Visual J++, we first create a resource template. The Visual J++ Resource Wizard will convert the resource template into the correct Java support file(s) for us. That is, menus are usually created in Java code, and the Resource Wizard will create the .java files we need to add to our project.

FIGURE 7.2:

The Visual J++
Menu Editor

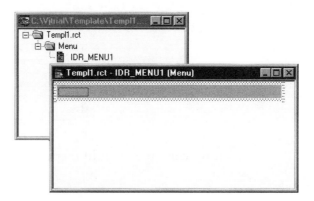

We start work in the Menu Editor by pressing Alt+Enter, which displays the Menu Properties window, as shown in Figure 7.3. Give this new menu the ID menuclass as shown in Figure 7.3, and then close the Properties window.

FIGURE 7.3:

Our new menu's
Properties window

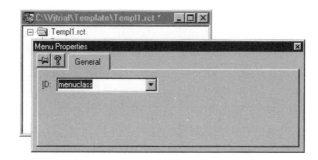

We want a new File menu with two items, No and Problem, and we want a new Edit menu with two items, No and Worries. To create a new File menu, highlight the dotted box at left in the new menu bar in the Menu Editor (see Figure 7.2) and type **File**. Doing this opens the MenuItem Properties window, as shown in Figure 7.4.

FIGURE 7.4:

The MenuItem Properties
window

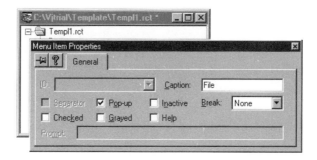

As you can see, the caption of our new menu, File, appears in the Caption box of the Properties window. Close the Properties window now, and you'll see our new File menu in the menu bar we are designing, as shown in Figure 7.5.

FIGURE 7.5:

Our new File menu before being filled

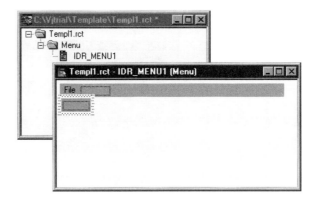

A new dotted box represents the first item in the File menu now. Select that box, as shown in Figure 7.5, and type **No**, and close the Properties window that opens. Move down to the next menu item and type **Problem**. Close the Properties window again, and you'll see the File menu in Figure 7.6.

FIGURE 7.6:

Our new File menu

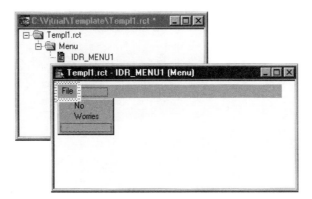

Now repeat the process for the Edit menu, adding two new items to it: No and Worries. Close the Menu Editor, leaving the `Templl .rct` window open. Save this file now by choosing File ➤ Save As in the Visual J++ menu.

TIP   By default, when you save a new `.rct` file, with File ➤ Save, Visual J++ puts the file in one of its internal directories. Use Save As instead, and be sure the `.rct` file is stored with the rest of your project's files.

Using the Visual J++ Resource Wizard to Create a Menu

Now we're ready to convert our new resource template, `Templ1 .rct`, into a Java class that we can use in our menus applet. Choose Tools ➤ Java Resource Wizard to open the Java Resource Wizard, as shown in Figure 7.7.

FIGURE 7.7:

The Visual J++ Resource Wizard

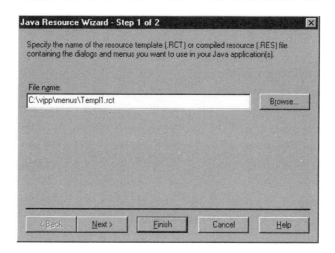

Be sure you select the `Templ1.rct` file, as shown in Figure 7.7, and click on the Finish button. The Resource Wizard creates the file `menuclass.java` (`menuclass` was the ID we gave our menu), and this file provides the Java support for the new menu. The code appears in `menuclass.java`.

menuclass.java

```
//--------------------------------------------------------------
// menuclass.java:
//   Implementation for menu creation class menuclass
//
//--------------------------------------------------------------
import java.awt.*;

public class menuclass
{
  Frame    m_Frame            = null;
  boolean m_fInitialized = false;

  // MenuBar definitions
  //------------------------------------------------------------
  MenuBar mb;

  // Menu and Menu item definitions
  //------------------------------------------------------------
  Menu m1; // File
  MenuItem ID_FILE_NO;// No
  MenuItem ID_FILE_PROBLEM;  // Problem
  Menu m4; // Edit
  MenuItem ID_EDIT_NO;// No
  MenuItem ID_EDIT_WORRIES;  // Worries

  // Constructor
  //------------------------------------------------------------
  public menuclass (Frame frame)
  {
     m_Frame = frame;
  }

  // Initialization.
  //------------------------------------------------------------
  public boolean CreateMenu()
  {
     // Can only init controls once
     //------------------------------------------------------------
     if (m_fInitialized || m_Frame == null)
```

```
      return false;

   // Create menubar and attach to the frame
   //----------------------------------------------------------
   mb = new MenuBar();
   m_Frame.setMenuBar(mb);

   // Create menu and menu items and assign to menubar
   //----------------------------------------------------------
   m1 = new Menu("File");
   mb.add(m1);
      ID_FILE_NO = new MenuItem("No");
      m1.add(ID_FILE_NO);
      ID_FILE_PROBLEM = new MenuItem("Problem");
      m1.add(ID_FILE_PROBLEM);
   m4 = new Menu("Edit");
   mb.add(m4);
      ID_EDIT_NO = new MenuItem("No");
      m4.add(ID_EDIT_NO);
      ID_EDIT_WORRIES = new MenuItem("Worries");
      m4.add(ID_EDIT_WORRIES);

   m_fInitialized = true;
   return true;
   }
}
```

Now we're ready to use the new `menuclass.java` file. We first insert that new file into the menus project. To do that, choose Insert ➤ Files into Project to open the Insert Files into Project dialog box, select the `menuclass.java` file, and click on Add. This adds the new Visual J++ menu support—that is, the new Java class `menuclass`—to our project.

You indicate to Visual J++ that the applet will require this class by importing it, adding this code to the top of the `menus.java` file:

```
//*************************************************************
// menus.java:  Applet
//
//*************************************************************
import java.applet.*;
```

```
  import java.awt.*;
→ import menuclass;
        .
        .
        .
```

Now we're ready to use our new `menuclass`. To create the new menus applet, we will need two buttons, a frame window to attach the menu to, and an object of the new menuclass:

```
---------------------------------------------------------
|                                                       |
|                                                       |
|   --------------------    ----------------------      |
|   |Make window visible|   |Make window invisible|     |
|   --------------------    ----------------------      |
|                                              |        |
|                                              |        |
|                                      -----------------|
|                                      |File Edit       |
|                                      |-    ---------   |
|                                      || No         |  |
|                                      || Problem    |  |
|                                      |  ---------      |
|                                      |              |  |
|                                      ----------------  |
|                                                       |
---------------------------------------------------------
```

We'll call the buttons `button1` and `button2`, we'll call our new menu object `menu`, and we'll call the new frame window `frame`, of class `menuframe`. We declare those objects in our applet now:

```
public class menus extends Applet implements Runnable
{
    // THREAD SUPPORT:
    //m_menus  is the Thread object for the applet
    //-----------------------------------------------------------
    Thread  m_menus = null;
→   Button button1, button2;
→   menuclass menu;
→   menuframe frame;
        .
        .
        .
```

We can create our new frame window class, `menuframe`, now. We simply derive this new class from the Java `Frame` class like this (add this new class at the end of the menus.java file):

```
class menuframe extends Frame
{
  menuframe(String title)
  {
    super(title);
    resize(200, 200);
  }
}
```

Now you're ready to create the new objects in the init() function. You create the new frame window, named frame, like this:

```
public void init()
{
    // If you use a ResourceWizard-generated "control creator" class to
    // arrange controls in your applet, you may want to call its
    // CreateControls() method from within this method. Remove the following
    // call to resize() before adding the call to CreateControls();
    // CreateControls() does its own resizing.
    //--------------------------------------------------------------------
    resize(320, 240);
→   frame = new menuframe("menu test");
→   frame.resize(100, 100);
        .
        .
        .
```

Next, attach the menu to it by passing the new frame window to the menuclass class's constructor. Do so like this:

```
public void init()
{
  resize(320, 240);
  frame = new menuframe("menu test");
  frame.resize(100, 100);

→    menu = new menuclass(frame);
        .
        .
        .
```

There's one more step—we have to create the menu itself by calling the menu object's `CreateMenu()` method. We do that like this:

```
public void init()
{
  resize(320, 240);
  frame = new menuframe("menu test");
  frame.resize(100, 100);

  menu = new menuclass(frame);
→ menu.CreateMenu();
    .
    .
    .
```

Our menu is now installed in the frame window. All that remains in the `init()` method is to add the buttons we'll need to display or hide the frame window:

```
public void init()
{
  resize(320, 240);
  frame = new menuframe("menu test");
  frame.resize(100, 100);

  menu = new menuclass(frame);
  menu.CreateMenu();

→ button1 = new Button("Make window visible");
→ add(button1);
→ button2 = new Button("Make window invisible");
→ add(button2);
}
```

In addition, set up the applet's `action()` method right after the `init()` function in the menus class:

```
public boolean action (Event e, Object o){
    .
    .
    .
}
```

In this case, we'll just show or hide the frame window we've named frame, and you saw how to do that in the last example:

```
public boolean action (Event e, Object o){
→   if(e.target.equals(button1)){
→      frame.show();
→   }
→   if(e.target.equals(button2)){
→      frame.hide();
→   }
    return true;
}
```

Our menu is installed and ready to go—except for one thing. None of the menu items actually do anything! Let's change that now. When the user selects a menu item, we want to report the item selected in our frame window. We do that by adding an `action()` method to our frame window's class like this:

```
class menuframe extends Frame
{
   menuframe(String title)
   {
      super(title);
      resize(200, 200);
   }

→   public boolean action(Event e, Object o)
      { .

        .

        .

      }
}
```

The object that caused the `action()` method to be called is passed as `e.target`, and you can check if that is a menu item by seeing if it is of the Java type `MenuItem` this way:

```
class menuframe extends Frame
{
   menuframe(String title)
   {
```

```
      super(title);
      resize(200, 200);
   }

   public boolean action(Event e, Object o)
   {
→     if (e.target instanceof MenuItem){
            .
            .
            .
      }
   }
}
```

If so, you want to display the caption of the menu item the user selected, and as you have seen, the caption of the control that caused the event is stored as (String)o, where o is the object of class Object passed to us. But there's a problem—we know that we need a graphics object corresponding to our window to draw in it, but how do we get that? You'll see more about that when I discuss graphics handling, but one way to get a graphics object is to store the display string and have it placed on the screen during the window's paint event. You can trigger a paint event with the repaint() method. First, store the string in the global String object displaytext and then trigger the paint event with repaint():

```
class menuframe extends Frame
{
→  String displaytext = new String();

   menuframe(String title)
   {
      super(title);
      resize(200, 200);
   }

   public boolean action(Event e, Object o)
   {
      if (e.target instanceof MenuItem){
→        displaytext = (String)o;
```

```
→        repaint();
      }
      return true;
   }
}
```

Now, add the code for the `paint()` method in the frame window this way:

```
class menuframe extends Frame
{
   String displaytext = new String();

   menuframe(String title)
   {
     super(title);
     resize(200, 200);
   }

   public boolean action(Event e, Object o)
   {
     if (e.target instanceof MenuItem){
       displaytext = (String)o;
       repaint();
     }
     return true;
   }

→  public void paint(Graphics g)
→  {
→    g.drawString(displaytext, 15, 15);
→  }
   }
```

And that's it—our menus applet is ready to run. When you run it and click on the Make Window Visible button, the frame window with the menu appears, as in Figure 7.8.

FIGURE 7.8:

Our menus applet
supports menus.

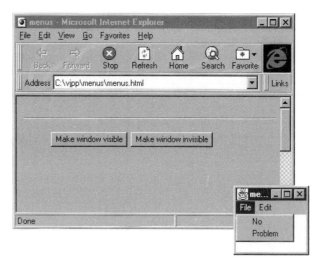

When the user selects a menu item, the caption of that item appears
in the frame window, as shown in Figure 7.9. Our menu applet is a
success—now we're using menus. As you can see, the Visual J++
Menu Editor makes the process easy. The code for this applet
appears in menus.java.

FIGURE 7.9:

When the user makes
a menu selection, we
report it in our window.

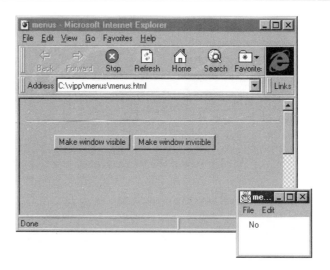

menus.java

```
//*********************************************************************************
// menus.java:  Applet
//
//*********************************************************************************
import java.applet.*;
import java.awt.*;
import menuclass;


//=================================================================================
// Main Class for applet menus
//
//=================================================================================
public class menus extends Applet implements Runnable
{
  // THREAD SUPPORT:
  //   m_menus  is the Thread object for the applet
  //-------------------------------------------------------------------------------
  Thread  m_menus = null;
  Button button1, button2;
  menuclass menu;
  menuframe frame;

  // menus Class Constructor
  //-------------------------------------------------------------------------------
  public menus()
  {
    // TODO: Add constructor code here
  }


  // APPLET INFO SUPPORT:
  //   The getAppletInfo() method returns a string describing the applet's
  // author, copyright date, or miscellaneous information.
```

```
//-------------------------------------------------------------------
public String getAppletInfo()
{
   return "Name: menus\r\n" +
         "Author: Steven Holzner\r\n" +
         "Created with Microsoft Visual J++ Version 1.0";
}


// The init() method is called by the AWT when an applet is first loaded or
// reloaded.  Override this method to perform whatever initialization your
// applet needs, such as initializing data structures, loading images or
// fonts, creating frame windows, setting the layout manager, or adding UI
// components.
//-------------------------------------------------------------------
public void init()
{
   // If you use a ResourceWizard-generated "control creator" class to
   // arrange controls in your applet, you may want to call its
   // CreateControls() method from within this method. Remove the following
   // call to resize() before adding the call to CreateControls();
   // CreateControls() does its own resizing.
   //-------------------------------------------------------------------
   resize(320, 240);
   frame = new menuframe("menu test");
   frame.resize(100, 100);
   menu = new menuclass(frame);
   menu.CreateMenu();

   button1 = new Button("Make window visible");
   add(button1);
   button2 = new Button("Make window invisible");
   add(button2);
}

public boolean action (Event e, Object o){
   if(e.target.equals(button1)){
      frame.show();
   }
   if(e.target.equals(button2)){
      frame.hide();
   }
```

```
   return true;
}

// Place additional applet clean up code here.  destroy() is called
// when your applet is terminating and being unloaded.
//-----------------------------------------------------------------------
public void destroy()
{
   // TODO: Place applet cleanup code here
}

// menus Paint Handler
//-----------------------------------------------------------------------
public void paint(Graphics g)
{
   // TODO: Place applet paint code here
   //g.drawString("Running: " + Math.random(), 10, 20);
}

//   The start() method is called when the page containing the applet
// first appears on the screen. The AppletWizard's initial implementation
// of this method starts execution of the applet's thread.
//-----------------------------------------------------------------------
public void start()
{
   if (m_menus == null)
   {
     m_menus = new Thread(this);
     m_menus.start();
   }
   // TODO: Place additional applet start code here
}

//   The stop() method is called when the page containing the applet is
// no longer on the screen. The AppletWizard's initial implementation of
// this method stops execution of the applet's thread.
//-----------------------------------------------------------------------
public void stop()
{
   if (m_menus != null)
   {
     m_menus.stop();
```

```
        m_menus = null;
    }

    // TODO: Place additional applet stop code here
}

// THREAD SUPPORT
// The run() method is called when the applet's thread is started. If
// your applet performs any ongoing activities without waiting for user
// input, the code for implementing that behavior typically goes here. For
// example, for an applet that performs animation, the run() method controls
// the display of images.
//---------------------------------------------------------------------------
public void run()
{
  while (true)
  {
    try
    {
      repaint();
      // TODO:  Add additional thread-specific code here
      Thread.sleep(50);
    }
    catch (InterruptedException e)
    {
      // TODO: Place exception-handling code here in case an
      //    InterruptedException is thrown by Thread.sleep(),
      //    meaning that another thread has interrupted this one
      stop();
    }
  }
}


  // TODO: Place additional applet code here

}

class menuframe extends Frame
{
```

```
String displaytext = new String();

menuframe(String title)
{
   super(title);
   resize(200, 200);
}

public boolean action(Event e, Object o)
{
   if (e.target instanceof MenuItem){
     displaytext = (String)o;
     repaint();
   }
   return true;
}

public void paint(Graphics g)
{
   g.drawString(displaytext, 15, 15);
}
}
```

What's Next?

That completes our exploration of Java menus and pop-up windows for the moment. As you can see, Visual J++ offers us considerable help here with these powerful techniques. Now, we will continue by turning to dialog boxes in the next chapter.

CHAPTER
EIGHT

8

Dialog Boxes and
Visual J++ Layouts

- ■ Placing dialog boxes on the screen

- ■ Designing a layout with the Dialog Editor

- ■ Using the Resource Wizard to create a dialog box

- ■ Using ActiveX objects in Java

In this chapter, we'll examine dialog boxes and new layouts in Java. Using the methods in this chapter, you will be able to support dialog boxes that can take input from the user and even—as you'll see—use the Visual J++ Dialog Editor to design the appearance of applets (not just dialog boxes) by creating a new and customized layout for those applets. In addition, you'll see a powerful technique in this chapter—how to integrate ActiveX controls into Java programs. Doing so turns out to be remarkably similar to developing resources such as menus and dialog boxes, so that will fit right in with our other topics. Let's get started by seeing how to support dialog boxes in Java.

Placing Dialog Boxes on the Screen

Like menus, dialog classes need to be attached to a frame window. For that reason, we can start our dialog box example as we started our menu example in the last chapter—with an applet that pops a frame window on the screen:

```
-----------------------------------------------------------
|                                                         |
|                                                         |
|      -------------------        -------------------     |
|      |Make window visible|      |Make window invisible|   |
|      -------------------        -------------------     |
|                                                         |
|                                                         |
|                                                         |
|                                                         |
|                                                         |
|                                                         |
-----------------------------------------------------------
```

When the user clicks on the Make Window Visible button, we can pop a frame window on the screen. Because we want to let the user pop up a dialog box from this frame window, we'll put a Click Me button in this frame window:

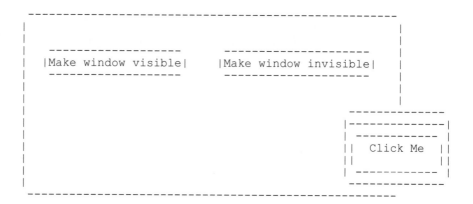

When the user clicks on the Click Me button, we can pop the dialog box on the screen, giving it an OK button:

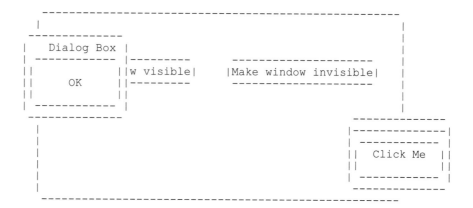

To remove the dialog box from the screen, the user simply clicks on the OK button.

Let's start this new applet now. Create a new applet named dialogs with the Applet Wizard. Next, open the dialogs class:

```
public class dialogs extends Applet
{       .

        .

        .
```

We will need the Make Window Visible button and the Make Window Invisible button, as well as the frame window. We will create a new frame window class called dialogframe and declare a new object of that class named frame this way:

```
public class dialogs extends Applet
{
→       Button button1, button2;
→       dialogframe frame;

        .

        .

        .
```

Now let's create our new frame class, dialogframe. This is the frame window that will have a Click Me button in it and that will pop the dialog box on the screen when the user clicks on that button. We start by deriving the dialogframe class from the Java Frame class:

```
class dialogframe extends Frame {

}
```

Next, add the new class's constructor. The Frame class has a constructor that takes one argument—a string holding the window's title—so we give our constructor one argument too and pass that on to the base class's constructor this way:

```
class dialogframe extends Frame {

→           dialogframe(String title){
```

```
➜              super(title);
                  .

                  .

                  .

               }
        }
```

Next, set the layout to a new GridLayout—recall that windows and dialog boxes need a layout manager if you're going to place controls in them:

```
class dialogframe extends Frame {

     dialogframe(String title){
        super(title);
➜       setLayout(new GridLayout(1, 1));
                  .

                  .

                  .

     }
}
```

At this point, we're ready to add the Click Me button, which we do like this:

```
class dialogframe extends Frame {

     Button button1;

     dialogframe(String title){
        super(title);
        setLayout(new GridLayout(1, 1));
➜       button1 = new Button("Click Me");
➜       add(button1);
                  .

                  .

                  .

     }

}
```

We can also create a new dialog box object here to place on the screen when the user clicks on the Click Me button. This dialog box object will be from a new class that we derive from the Java `Dialog` class, and we can call that new class `OKDialog` (because the dialog box has one button in it—the OK button). The object of this class that we'll create will be called `dialogbox1`:

```
class dialogframe extends Frame {

    Button button1;
→   OKDialog dialogbox1;

    dialogframe(String title){
      super(title);
      setLayout(new GridLayout(1, 1));
      button1 = new Button("Click Me");
      add(button1);
    }

}
```

Let's create the `dialogbox1` object now. The constructor for the `Dialog` class takes three arguments: a reference to a frame window, the title string for the dialog box, and a boolean argument indicating whether the dialog box should be modal (if a dialog box is modal, the user cannot do anything else in the applet until he or she deals with the dialog box—the dialog box keeps the input focus until it is dismissed from the screen). The frame window we connect this dialog box to will be the current window—but how do we reference the current window? What can we call it so that we can pass it to the dialog box's constructor? Java has the `this` keyword for just such a purpose, and we can make our constructor call look like this (where the third parameter, set to `FALSE`, means that our dialog box will be nonmodal):

```
class dialogframe extends Frame {

    Button button1;
    OKDialog dialogbox1;

    dialogframe(String title){
```

```
          super(title);
          setLayout(new GridLayout(1, 1));
          button1 = new Button("Click Me");
          add(button1);
➜         dialogbox1 = new OKDialog(this, "Dialog Box", false);
      }
  }
```

The this keyword functions much as it does in C++, and it refers
to the current object. It's used in cases like this—where you need to
refer to the current object in which you are working.

Now, we can connect our Click Me button in the frame window
so that it displays the new dialog box when the user clicks on it.
We do that in the action() method, which we add to the
dialogframe class now:

```
class dialogframe extends Frame {

    Button button1;
    OKDialog dialogbox1;

    dialogframe(String title){
        super(title);
        setLayout(new GridLayout(1, 1));
        button1 = new Button("Click Me");
        add(button1);
        dialogbox1 = new OKDialog(this, "Dialog Box", false);
    }

➜   public boolean action (Event e, Object o){

    }
}
```

Here, we simply check to see if the Click Me button was clicked:

```
class dialogframe extends Frame {

    Button button1;
```

```
        OKDialog dialogbox1;

        dialogframe(String title){
            super(title);
            setLayout(new GridLayout(1, 1));
            button1 = new Button("Click Me");
            add(button1);
            dialogbox1 = new OKDialog(this, "Dialog Box", false);
        }

        public boolean action (Event e, Object o){
→           if(e.target.equals(button1)){

            }
        }
    }
```

If so, we want to display our new dialog box, which is represented by the object named `dialogbox1`. To make the dialog box appear on the screen, we do just as we did with our frame window object—we use its `show()` method:

```
class dialogframe extends Frame {

    Button button1;
    OKDialog dialogbox1;

    dialogframe(String title){
        super(title);
        setLayout(new GridLayout(1, 1));
        button1 = new Button("Click Me");
        add(button1);
        dialogbox1 = new OKDialog(this, "Dialog Box", false);
    }

    public boolean action (Event e, Object o){
        if(e.target.equals(button1)){
→           dialogbox1.show();
        }
        return true;
    }
}
```

At this point, all that remains is to design our dialog box class, OKDialog. We will look into that now.

The OKDialog class is derived from the Java Dialog class, and we can add its declaration to the end of our dialogs.java file now:

```
class OKDialog extends Dialog {
    .
    .
    .
}
```

The Java Dialog class's methods appear in Table 8.1.

TABLE 8.1: The Java Dialog Class's Methods

Method	Does This
Dialog(Frame, boolean)	Constructs Dialog, modal if boolean is true
Dialog(Frame, String, boolean)	Constructs Dialog with given title, modal if boolean is true
addNotify()	Creates object's peer
getTitle()	Returns title of object
isModal()	Returns true if object is modal
isResizable()	Returns true if Dialog is resizable
paramString()	Gets parameter string of Dialog
setResizable(boolean)	Sets object's resizable flag
setTitle(String)	Sets object's title

We begin by setting up the `OKDialog` class's constructor. This constructor will take the same arguments as the `Dialog` class itself, so we pass those arguments back to the `Dialog` class's constructor:

```
class OKDialog extends Dialog {

➜     OKDialog(Frame hostFrame, String title, boolean dModal){
           .
           .
           .

       }
}
```

We pass back the parameters to the base class's constructor this way using the `super()` method:

```
class OKDialog extends Dialog {

       OKDialog(Frame hostFrame, String title, boolean dModal){
         super(hostFrame, title, dModal);
           .
           .
           .

       }
}
```

NOTE If you include a call to `super()` in a constructor, it should be the first line in that constructor. If it is not, Visual J++ considers it an error. This is because `super()` calls the base class's constructor, and the rule in Java is that if you call constructor A from constructor B, that call should be the first line of code in constructor B.

Next, we set up a size for our new dialog box of, say, 100 x 100 pixels:

```
class OKDialog extends Dialog {

       OKDialog(Frame hostFrame, String title, boolean dModal){
         super(hostFrame, title, dModal);
```

```
→        resize(100, 100);

             .

             .

             .

         }
}
```

Microsoft Internet Explorer requires you to give an initial size to dialog boxes (or they won't appear) with the `resize()` **method before displaying them, although Netscape Navigator will give them a default size if you don't specify one.**

The next step is to place the OK button in the dialog box. That means we have to set up a new layout, and we'll use a simple GridLayout this way:

```
class OKDialog extends Dialog {

    OKDialog(Frame hostFrame, String title, boolean dModal){
        super(hostFrame, title, dModal);
        resize(100, 100);
→       setLayout(new GridLayout(1, 1));

            .

            .

            .

    }
}
```

Now we add our button, calling it OKButton:

```
class OKDialog extends Dialog {

→    Button OKButton;

    OKDialog(Frame hostFrame, String title, boolean dModal){
        super(hostFrame, title, dModal);
        resize(100, 100);
        setLayout(new GridLayout(1, 1));
→       OKButton = new Button("OK");
```

→
```
        add(OKButton);
    }
}
```

And we're almost done. All that remains is to make our OK button do something when the user clicks on it. In this case, we'll hide the dialog box when the user clicks on the OK button. As you might expect, we can handle the button clicks with an `action()` method like this in our `dialog box` class:

```
class OKDialog extends Dialog {

    Button OKButton;

    OKDialog(Frame hostFrame, String title, boolean dModal){
        super(hostFrame, title, dModal);
        resize(100, 100);
        setLayout(new GridLayout(1, 1));
        OKButton = new Button("OK");
        add(OKButton);
    }
```

→
```
    public boolean action (Event e, Object o){
        .
        .
        .
    }
}
```

All we do in this `action()` method is to determine if the OK button was clicked, and if so, we hide the dialog box using its `hide()` method:

```
class OKDialog extends Dialog {

    Button OKButton;

    OKDialog(Frame hostFrame, String title, boolean dModal){
        super(hostFrame, title, dModal);
        resize(100, 100);
        setLayout(new GridLayout(1, 1));
```

```
                    OKButton = new Button("OK");
                    add(OKButton);
                }

                public boolean action (Event e, Object o){
→                   if(e.target.equals(OKButton)){
→                       hide();
→                   }
                    return true;
                }
            }
```

That's it for our dialog box class, OKDialog. We've also finished our frame window class, dialogframe. All that remains is to connect the Make Window Visible and Make Window Invisible buttons in the applet so that it displays the frame window. The dialog box is part of the frame window, so we don't have to handle displaying that.

Back in the applet's init() method, we create the buttons we've declared, button1 (caption: "Make window visible") and button2 (caption: "Make window invisible"):

```
public void init()
{
    // If you use a ResourceWizard-generated "control creator" class to
    // arrange controls in your applet, you may want to call its
    // CreateControls() method from within this method. Remove the following
    // call to resize() before adding the call to CreateControls();
    // CreateControls() does its own resizing.
    //----------------------------------------------------------------------
    resize(320, 240);
→   button1 = new Button("Make window visible");
→   add(button1);
→   button2 = new Button("Make window invisible");
→   add(button2);
            .
            .
            .
}
```

Next, we create a new frame window of the `dialogframe` class, giving it the title "Hello World!" and a size like this:

```
public void init()
{
   resize(320, 240);
   button1 = new Button("Make window visible");
   add(button1);
   button2 = new Button("Make window invisible");
   add(button2);

   frame = new dialogframe("Hello World!");
   frame.resize(100, 100);

}
```

At this point, all that is left to do is to make the Make Window Visible and Make Window Invisible buttons functional. We do that by showing or hiding the frame window with the `show()` and `hide()` methods in an `action()` method we add to the main applet's class:

```
public boolean action (Event e, Object o){
   if(e.target.equals(button1)){
      frame.show();
   }
   if(e.target.equals(button2)){
      frame.hide();
   }
   return true;
}
```

Now the dialogs applet is ready to go. When you run this applet and click on the Make Window Visible button, you see our frame window with its Click Me button, as in Figure 8.1.

FIGURE 8.1:

Our dialog box's frame window

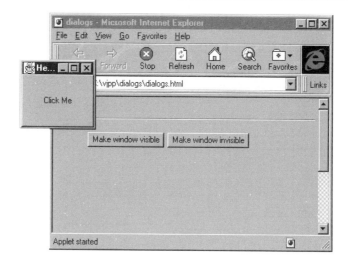

When you click on the Click Me button in the frame window, the dialog box pops up, as shown in Figure 8.2. Clicking on the OK button in the dialog box makes it disappear. Our new dialogs applet is a success. The code for this applet appears in `dialogs.java`.

FIGURE 8.2:

Our new Java dialog box

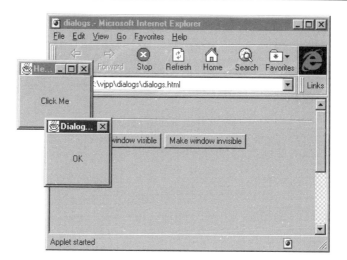

dialogs.java

```
//********************************************************************
// dialogs.java:  Applet
//
//********************************************************************
import java.applet.*;
import java.awt.*;

//===================================================================
// Main Class for applet dialogs
//
//===================================================================
public class dialogs extends Applet
{
  Button button1, button2;
  dialogframe frame;

  // dialogs Class Constructor
  //-----------------------------------------------------------------
  public dialogs()
  {
    // TODO: Add constructor code here
  }

  // APPLET INFO SUPPORT:
  //   The getAppletInfo() method returns a string describing the applet's
  // author, copyright date, or miscellaneous information.
  //-----------------------------------------------------------------
  public String getAppletInfo()
  {
    return "Name: dialogs\r\n" +
         "Author: Steven Holzner\r\n" +
         "Created with Microsoft Visual J++ Version 1.0";
  }


  // The init() method is called by the AWT when an applet is first loaded or
  // reloaded.  Override this method to perform whatever initialization your
  // applet needs, such as initializing data structures, loading images or
  // fonts, creating frame windows, setting the layout manager, or adding UI
  // components.
```

```
//-------------------------------------------------------------------
public void init()
{
   // If you use a ResourceWizard-generated "control creator" class to
   // arrange controls in your applet, you may want to call its
   // CreateControls() method from within this method. Remove the following
   // call to resize() before adding the call to CreateControls();
   // CreateControls() does its own resizing.
   //-------------------------------------------------------------------
   resize(320, 240);
   button1 = new Button("Make window visible");
   add(button1);
   button2 = new Button("Make window invisible");
   add(button2);

   frame = new dialogframe("Hello World!");
   frame.resize(100, 100);

}

public boolean action (Event e, Object o){
   if(e.target.equals(button1)){
       frame.show();
   }
   if(e.target.equals(button2)){
       frame.hide();
   }
   return true;
}

// Place additional applet clean up code here.  destroy() is called
// when your applet is terminating and being unloaded.
//-------------------------------------------------------------------
public void destroy()
{
   // TODO: Place applet cleanup code here
}

// dialogs Paint Handler
//-------------------------------------------------------------------
public void paint(Graphics g)
{
```

```
    //g.drawString("Created with Microsoft Visual J++ Version 1.0", 10, 20);
  }

  //   The start() method is called when the page containing the applet
  // first appears on the screen. The AppletWizard's initial implementation
  // of this method starts execution of the applet's thread.
  //--------------------------------------------------------------------------
  public void start()
  {
     // TODO: Place additional applet start code here
  }

  //   The stop() method is called when the page containing the applet is
  // no longer on the screen. The AppletWizard's initial implementation of
  // this method stops execution of the applet's thread.
  //--------------------------------------------------------------------------
  public void stop()
  {
  }



  // TODO: Place additional applet code here

}

class dialogframe extends Frame {

    Button button1;
    OKDialog dialogbox1;

    dialogframe(String title){
    super(title);
    setLayout(new GridLayout(1, 1));
    button1 = new Button("Click Me");
    add(button1);
    dialogbox1 = new OKDialog(this, "Dialog Box", false);
  }

  public boolean action (Event e, Object o){
      if(e.target.equals(button1)){
```

```
        dialogbox1.show();
    }
    return true;
  }
}

class OKDialog extends Dialog {

    Button OKButton;

    OKDialog(Frame hostFrame, String title, boolean dModal){
        super(hostFrame, title, dModal);
        resize(100, 100);
        setLayout(new GridLayout(1, 1));
        OKButton = new Button("OK");
        add(OKButton);
    }

    public boolean action (Event e, Object o){
        if(e.target.equals(OKButton)){
            hide();
        }
        return true;
    }
  }
}
```

In the last chapter, you saw that Visual J++ has a Menu Editor to design menus, so it will probably not be a surprise to learn that Visual J++ also includes a Dialog Editor that you can use to design dialog boxes. That tool offers us a lot of power, and we're going to explore it next.

Designing an Applet's Layout with the Visual J++ Dialog Editor

The Visual J++ Dialog Editor actually does much more than create dialog boxes, and it may surprise you to learn that the Dialog Editor has nothing at all to do with the Java `Dialog` class. What it really does is create a customized layout for the controls you want to add to a dialog box—but it's not limited to dialog boxes. You can use this layout with any Java *container*—that is, any object derived from the Java `Container` class, such as dialog boxes, panels, applets, windows, and so on.

For this reason, the Dialog Editor can help with a frequently tiring problem—arranging the controls in the applet itself. You'll see how the Dialog Editor can lay out the controls in an applet (which can save a lot of time struggling with the GridBagLayout manager). For Java programmers, this is a great boon. In this example, we'll place a Click Me button and a text field in our applet like this:

```
 --------------------------------------------------------------------
|                                                                    |
|                                                                    |
|     ---------------------        ---------------------             |
|    |       Click Me      |      |                     |            |
|     ---------------------        ---------------------             |
|                                                                    |
|                                                                    |
|                                                                    |
|                                                                    |
|                                                                    |
|                                                                    |
 --------------------------------------------------------------------
```

When the user clicks on the Click Me button, we can display the No Problem message in the text field like this:

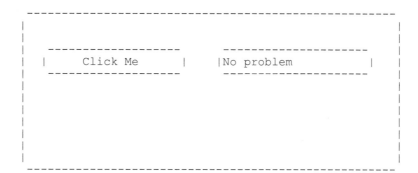

Although we use only two controls here, we can place and position as many as we like in our applet with the Dialog Editor. Let's see how this works.

Create a new applet with the Applet Wizard and name it dlgapplet (do not include multitasking or animation support). After the applet files have been created, we will use the Dialog Editor to lay out the controls we want. Create the project files now with the Visual J++ Applet Wizard.

Using the Dialog Editor

You start the Dialog Editor much the same way as you start the Menu Editor. Choose File ➤ New ➤ Resource Template, and then choose Insert ➤ Resource Item to open the Insert Resource dialog box. Select the Dialog icon, and click on OK. This creates the file Templ1.rct, opens it in a window, and opens the Dialog Editor, as shown in Figure 8.3.

FIGURE 8.3:

The Visual J++ Dialog Editor

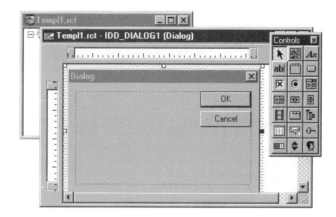

As you can see in Figure 8.3, the dialog box we are editing comes with two buttons, OK and Cancel, but we won't need these buttons for our applet. Simply click on each button and press Delete to remove them.

Now we will add the Click Me button. To do that, select the Button tool in the tool box at the right of the Dialog Editor, as shown in Figure 8.4—it's the one on the right in the second row. Using this tool, you can "draw" a new button (by dragging the mouse), creating this new control, as shown in Figure 8.4.

FIGURE 8.4:

Creating a button control

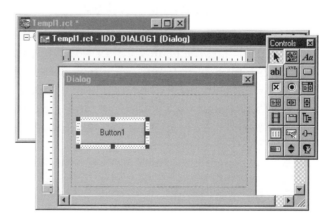

To change the button's label from Button1 to Click Me, double-click on the button now to open its Properties window, as shown in Figure 8.5. Give this button the caption Click Me, as also shown in Figure 8.5.

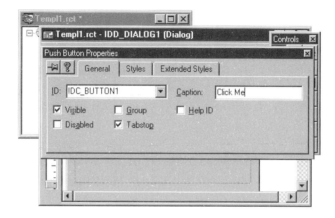

In the same way, draw a new text field control, using the Edit control, which is at the left in the second row in the Dialog Editor tool box. So far, the Dialog Editor has created for us a dialog box with the name IDD_DIALOG1, a button with the name IDC_BUTTON1, and a text field with name ID IDC_EDIT1. We can accept these default names. Close the Dialog Editor now and save the Temp11.rct file by choosing Save As from the Visual J++ File menu. This file holds the specification of our new dialog box. The next step is to turn the Temp11.rct file into a .java file that we can include in our dlgapplet applet.

Using the Visual J++ Resource Wizard to Create a Dialog Box

We will turn the Temp11.rct file into a .java file with the Visual J++ Resource Wizard. To start the Resource Wizard, choose Tools ➤ Java Resource Wizard. Next, in the File Name text box, type Temp11.rct and click on Finish. This creates two files: the specification for our dialog box, IDD_DIALOG1.java, and DialogLayout.java, which is the Visual J++ specialized layout manager that places the controls as we want them.

IDD_DIALOG1.java

```
//----------------------------------------------------------------------
// IDD_DIALOG1.java:
//   Implementation of "control creator" class IDD_DIALOG1
//----------------------------------------------------------------------
import java.awt.*;
import DialogLayout;

public class IDD_DIALOG1
{
  Container  m_Parent    = null;
  boolean    m_fInitialized = false;
  DialogLayout m_Layout;

  // Control definitions
  //--------------------------------------------------------------------
  Button    IDC_BUTTON1;
  TextField   IDC_EDIT1;


  // Constructor
  //--------------------------------------------------------------------
  public IDD_DIALOG1 (Container parent)
  {
    m_Parent = parent;
  }

  // Initialization.
  //--------------------------------------------------------------------
  public boolean CreateControls()
  {
    // CreateControls should be called only once
    //------------------------------------------------------------------
    if (m_fInitialized || m_Parent == null)
      return false;

    // m_Parent must be extended from the Container class
```

```
//--------------------------------------------------------------------
if (!(m_Parent instanceof Container))
  return false;

// Since a given font may not be supported across all platforms, it
// is safe to modify only the size of the font, not the typeface.
//--------------------------------------------------------------------
Font OldFnt = m_Parent.getFont();
if (OldFnt != null)
{
  Font NewFnt = new Font(OldFnt.getName(), OldFnt.getStyle(), 8);

  m_Parent.setFont(NewFnt);
}

// All position and sizes are in dialog logical units, so we use a
// DialogLayout as our layout manager.
//--------------------------------------------------------------------
m_Layout = new DialogLayout(m_Parent, 186, 95);
m_Parent.setLayout(m_Layout);
m_Parent.addNotify();

Dimension size  = m_Layout.getDialogSize();
Insets insets = m_Parent.insets();

m_Parent.resize(insets.left + size.width  + insets.right,
        insets.top  + size.height + insets.bottom);

// Control creation
//--------------------------------------------------------------------
IDC_BUTTON1 = new Button ("Click Me");
m_Parent.add(IDC_BUTTON1);
m_Layout.setShape(IDC_BUTTON1, 13, 32, 67, 18);

IDC_EDIT1 = new TextField ("");
m_Parent.add(IDC_EDIT1);
m_Layout.setShape(IDC_EDIT1, 99, 30, 70, 21);

m_fInitialized = true;
return true;
  }
}
```

Next, we add these two new files, IDD_DIALOG1.java and DialogLayout.java, to our applet's project. To do that, choose Insert ➤ Files into Project, select these two files, and click on the Add button. Now we're ready to write the Java code we'll need for our dlgapplet applet.

Start by importing the new dialog class IDD_DIALOG1 this way in the dlgapplet applet:

```
//****************************************************************
// dlgapplet.java:     Applet
//
//****************************************************************
import java.applet.*;
import java.awt.*;
➜ import IDD_DIALOG1;
       .
       .
       .
```

Next, create an object of this new class called dlg. You do that at the beginning of our applet's class definition:

```
public class dlgapplet extends Applet
{
➜      IDD_DIALOG1 dlg;
       .
       .
       .
```

The next step is to create the new dlg object, and you do that in the init() method. You have to pass a reference to an object based on the Java Container class to IDD_DIALOG1's class constructor, and since we want to install the new dialog layout in the applet itself (although you can pass dialog objects, frame window objects, and other objects to this constructor—anything derived from the Java Container class), we will pass a this keyword:

```
public void init()
{
    // If you use a ResourceWizard-generated "control creator" class to
    // arrange controls in your applet, you may want to call its
    // CreateControls() method from within this method. Remove the following
    // call to resize() before adding the call to CreateControls();
    // CreateControls() does its own resizing.
    //------------------------------------------------------------------
    resize(320, 240);
➜   dlg = new IDD_DIALOG1(this);
        .
        .
        .
}
```

You may have noticed the warning placed in the init() method by Visual J++ (in the comment lines), which says that if you use a Resource Wizard layout in your applet, you should call CreateControls() in the init() method and comment out the resize() line. That's exactly what we do now:

```
public void init()
{
    // If you use a ResourceWizard-generated "control creator" class to
    // arrange controls in your applet, you may want to call its
    // CreateControls() method from within this method. Remove the following
    // call to resize() before adding the call to CreateControls();
    // CreateControls() does its own resizing.
    //------------------------------------------------------------------
➜   //resize(320, 240);
    dlg = new IDD_DIALOG1(this);
➜   dlg.CreateControls();
}
```

That installs our new layout in the applet:

```
---------------------------------------------------------
|                                                       |
|                                                       |
|     -----------------------     ---------------------- |
|     |       Click Me      |     |                    | |
|     -----------------------     ---------------------- |
|                                                       |
|                                                       |
|                                                       |
|                                                       |
|                                                       |
|                                                       |
---------------------------------------------------------
```

The only thing left to do is to connect the Click Me button to the text field so that when the user clicks on the button, the No Problem message appears in the text field. We can do that in an `action()` method, so add that to our applet now:

```
public boolean action(Event e, Object o)
{   .
        .
        .
        .
}
```

We check to see if the button was clicked on like this:

```
    public boolean action(Event e, Object o)
    {
➜       if (e.target instanceof Button)
        {   .
            .
            .
        }
    }
```

And if so, we place the No Problem message in the text field, which is an object named IDC_EDIT1 embedded in the dlg class. Since we can reach that object like this:

```
dlg.IDC_EDIT1
```

we place our message in the text field like this:

```
public boolean action(Event e, Object o)
{
  if (e.target instanceof Button)
  {
→    dlg.IDC_EDIT1.setText("No problem");
     return true;
  }
  return false;
}
```

Our dlgapplet is ready to go. Run the applet now, as shown in Figure 8.6. As you can see, our controls are set up as we want them. We've been able to use the Visual J++ Dialog Editor to design the layout of our applet. For Java programmers who don't like to struggle with the various layout managers in Java, this is a terrific asset of Visual J++. That's it for this example—the code for this applet appears in `dlgapplet.java`.

FIGURE 8.6:

Our applet designed using the Dialog Editor

dlgapplet.java

```
//*************************************************************************
// dlgapplet.java:Applet
//
//*************************************************************************
import java.applet.*;
import java.awt.*;
import IDD_DIALOG1;
//=========================================================================
// Main Class for applet dlgapplet
//
//=========================================================================
public class dlgapplet extends Applet
{
   IDD_DIALOG1 dlg;

   // dlgapplet Class Constructor
   //----------------------------------------------------------------------
   public dlgapplet()
   {
     // TODO: Add constructor code here
   }

   // APPLET INFO SUPPORT:
   //   The getAppletInfo() method returns a string describing the applet's
   // author, copyright date, or miscellaneous information.
   //----------------------------------------------------------------------
   public String getAppletInfo()
   {
     return "Name: dlgapplet\r\n" +
         "Author: Steven Holzner\r\n" +
         "Created with Microsoft Visual J++ Version 1.0";
   }


   // The init() method is called by the AWT when an applet is first loaded or
   // reloaded.  Override this method to perform whatever initialization your
   // applet needs, such as initializing data structures, loading images or
   // fonts, creating frame windows, setting the layout manager, or adding UI
   // components.
   //----------------------------------------------------------------------
```

```
public void init()
{
  // If you use a ResourceWizard-generated "control creator" class to
  // arrange controls in your applet, you may want to call its
  // CreateControls() method from within this method. Remove the following
  // call to resize() before adding the call to CreateControls();
  // CreateControls() does its own resizing.
  //------------------------------------------------------------------------
  //resize(320, 240);
  dlg = new IDD_DIALOG1(this);
  dlg.CreateControls();

}


public boolean action(Event e, Object o)
{
  if (e.target instanceof Button)
  {
    dlg.IDC_EDIT1.setText("No problem");
    return true;
  }
  return false;
}

// Place additional applet clean up code here.  destroy() is called
// when your applet is terminating and being unloaded.
//--------------------------------------------------------------------------
public void destroy()
{
  // TODO: Place applet cleanup code here
}

// dlgapplet Paint Handler
//--------------------------------------------------------------------------
public void paint(Graphics g)
{
  //g.drawString("Created with Microsoft Visual J++ Version 1.0", 10, 20);
}

//   The start() method is called when the page containing the applet
// first appears on the screen. The AppletWizard's initial implementation
```

```
// of this method starts execution of the applet's thread.
//-----------------------------------------------------------------
public void start()
{
   // TODO: Place additional applet start code here
}


//   The stop() method is called when the page containing the applet is
// no longer on the screen. The AppletWizard's initial implementation of
// this method stops execution of the applet's thread.
//-----------------------------------------------------------------
public void stop()
{
}




   // TODO: Place additional applet code here


}
```

In this chapter, you've seen that the Visual J++ Resource Wizard can help us by creating a "wrapper" Java class for our resource templates. Another popular Wizard creates wrapper classes for us—the Microsoft Java Type Library Wizard. This Wizard takes ActiveX Internet controls and creates Java .class wrappers for you so that you can incorporate them into your Java programs. This is a powerful technique, and we'll take a look at it next.

> **NOTE** ActiveX controls are the special Internet-oriented controls that Web browsers such as the Internet Explorer let you embed in a Web page. Examples include pop-up menu controls, pop-up window controls, and many more. You can download many such controls free from Microsoft's Web site at http://www.microsoft.com.

Using ActiveX Objects in Java

After you create Java wrapper classes for an ActiveX control, you can use it in code just as you would use any other Java class. As you can imagine, being able to import ActiveX controls into Java can add a lot of power to an applet. (The Visual J++ professional edition from Microsoft comes with a number of ready-to-use ActiveX controls.)

We'll use the Java Type Library Wizard to create the Java wrapper classes we'll need from ActiveX controls. The Type Library Wizard works on type library files with the extension `.tlb`. A type library contains all the information about the objects and interfaces in an ActiveX control. This information also appears in `.dll`, `.ocx`, or even `.exe` files, so you can also run the Type Library Wizard on files of those types (ActiveX controls usually have the extension `.ocx`).

To create a wrapper for an ActiveX control so that you can use it in an applet, you run the Microsoft Java Type Library Wizard on the control. The Type Library Wizard creates wrapper `.class` files and stores them in a new directory under the directory `c:\windows\java\trustlib`. To create wrapper `.class` files for an ActiveX control, choose Tools ➤ Java Type Library Wizard to open the Type Library Wizard. The ActiveX controls registered in your system are listed in the Select Items to Be Converted box. (If you don't see the ActiveX control you want there, it may not be registered, in which case you can run the `regsvr32.exe` tool by choosing Tools ➤ Register Control.) After selecting the ActiveX control you want, click on OK. This creates a directory in `c:\windows\java\trustlib` and places the correct wrapper `.class` files in it.

> **TIP**
> ActiveX controls downloaded from the Internet are usually stored in the directory `c:\windows\occache` and will usually have the extension `.ocx`.

For example, if you are working with an ActiveX control named `calculatorcontrol.ocx`, the Type Library Wizard creates the directory `c:\windows\java\trustlib\calculatorcontrol`. You'll find a Java `.class` file for each of the classes and interfaces in the ActiveX control in this new directory. If your ActiveX control contains an object named `calculator` and an interface named `Icalculator`, you'll find that the Type Library Wizard has placed the files `calculator.class` and `Icalculator.class` in the directory named `c:\windows\java\trustlib\calculatorcontrol`. These are the wrapper classes we'll use in our Java code. In addition, the Type Library Wizard creates a file named `summary.txt`, which tells you about the methods in the ActiveX control that you can now reach from Java. For example, here is the `summary.txt` file for the ActiveX `iemenu.ocx` control, Microsoft's pop-up menu control:

```
public class iemenu/IEPOP extends java.lang.Object
{
}
public interface iemenu/DIEPOPEvents extends com.ms.com.IUnknown
{
    public abstract void Click(int);
}
public interface iemenu/IIEPOP extends com.ms.com.IUnknown
{
    public abstract void RemoveItem(int);
    public abstract java.lang.String getMenuitem();
    public abstract void putMenuitem(java.lang.String);
    public abstract void AboutBox();
    public abstract void PopUp(com.ms.com.Variant, com.ms.com.Variant);
    public abstract short getItemcount();
    public abstract void Clear();
    public abstract void AddItem(java.lang.String, com.ms.com.Variant);
}
```

TIP

The names of the classes and methods in an ActiveX control are usually available from the control's manufacturer. For example, Microsoft lists this information for all the ActiveX controls you can download from its Web site. However, if you don't know the names of the methods and classes in your ActiveX control or don't know which parameters the methods take, you can either look at the `summary.txt` file or run the OLE 2 Object Viewer tool, `ole2vw32.exe`, which comes with Visual J++ (choose Tools ➤ OLE Object View). To read in your ActiveX control, choose File ➤ View Type Library, and you will see all the classes in the ActiveX control, as well as the methods in those classes and the parameters they take. In addition, choose Tools ➤ OLE Control Test Container to test out the ActiveX control, sending it data and/or user interface events.

The Type Library Wizard also displays the `import` statement you should use in Java to import the new wrapper classes—this statement appears in Visual J++'s output window (at the bottom of the Developer Studio's display). In our calculator example, the Type Library Wizard creates a package of classes (like a normal Java package) named `calculatorcontrol` and gives us this statement to use when importing our `.ocx` control:

```
import calculatorcontrol.*;
```

TIP

As with any other Java package, you can load in only a part of the package. For example, if you want only the `calculator` class in the `calculatorcontrol` package, you would use this `import` statement: `import calculatorcontrol.calculator;`.

Once you include this line in your applet's code, you are free to use the classes in the `calculatorcontrol` package, the `Icalculator` and `calculator` classes. For example, here we create a new object of the `calculator` class named `number_cruncher`:

```
→ import calculatorcontrol.*;

   public class calcapplet extends Applet
   {
→      Icalculator number_cruncher;


       public void init()
       {
→          number_cruncher = (Icalculator) new calculator();
          .
          .
          .
```

If the `calculator` class has a method named `add()` that takes two integers and returns a long value, we can use the `number_cruncher` object's `add()` method like this:

```
   import calculatorcontrol.*;

   public class calcapplet extends Applet
   {
       Icalculator number_cruncher;


       public void init()
       {
→          ing int1 = 1001, int2 = 2001;
           number_cruncher = (Icalculator) new calculator();
→          long result = number_cruncher.add(int1, int2);
          .
          .
          .
```

In this way, you can reach and execute the ActiveX control's methods. You can use most standard Java data types in calls to an ActiveX control's methods, but for some data types you have to make special

provisions. Table 8.2 shows the Java data types to use when an
ActiveX control requires a particular data type.

TABLE 8.2:   ActiveX to Java Data Type Conversions

ActiveX Type	Java Type
boolean	boolean
char	char
double	double
int	int
float	float
long	int
short	short
unsigned char	byte
wchar_t	short
BSTR	class java.lang.String
CURRENCY	long
DATE	double
SCODE/HRESULT	int
VARIANT	class com.ms.com.Variant
IDispatch *	class java.lang.Object
IUnknown *	class java.lang.Object
SAFEARRAY(<typename>)	array of <typename>
<typename> *	one-element array of <typename>
void	void
LPSTR	class java.lang.String

Note in particular the Variant type in Table 8.3. There is no
Variant type in Java, but some ActiveX controls require Variant
parameters, so Microsoft has added the class com.ms.com.Variant
to Visual J++. You simply include this class like this:

```
import com.ms.com.Variant;
```

in your applet. You create a new `Variant` this way:

```
variant1 = new Variant();
```

This class's constructor takes no parameters. You then get or set the value in this `Variant` with the `Variant` class's `get` and `put` methods, as shown in Table 8.3. For example, to place an integer with the value of 5 into a `Variant` object, you would use this statement:

```
variant1.putInt(5);
```

TABLE 8.3: Microsoft `Variant` Class's `Get` and `Put` Methods

Method	Does This
`getShort()`	Gets short integer
`getInt()`	Gets integer
`getFloat()`	Gets float
`getDouble()`	Gets double
`getCurrency()`	Gets currency value
`getDate()`	Gets date value
`getString()`	Gets string
`getError()`	Gets integer error value
`getBoolean()`	Gets boolean
`getObject()`	Gets object
`getByte()`	Gets byte
`putEmpty()`	Puts empty value
`putNull()`	Puts null value
`putShort()`	Puts short integer
`putInt()`	Puts integer
`putFloat()`	Puts float
`putDouble()`	Puts double
`putCurrency()`	Puts currency value
`putDate()`	Puts date value
`putString()`	Puts string

TABLE 8.3: Microsoft `Variant` Class's `Get` and `Put` Methods (continued)

Method	Does This
putDispatch()	Puts dispatch object
putError()	Puts integer error value
putBoolean()	Puts boolean
putObject()	Puts object
putByte()	Puts byte
putEmptyRef()	Puts empty reference
putNullRef()	Puts null reference

In this way, then, you can supply the ActiveX control's methods with the data they require in the format they require, and you can read the data they return. It's that easy to use an ActiveX control in Visual J++—create a wrapper package and classes, import them into your applet, create an object of the class you want, and call its methods as you would normally. As you can imagine, this is a powerful technique, because it gives you the power to use the dozens of available ActiveX controls.

What's Next?

That's all for our coverage of ActiveX at the moment. We've come far in this chapter—from dialog boxes to using the Dialog Editor to laying out a whole applet to using ActiveX. We've added a considerable amount of power to our Visual J++ arsenal already. In the next chapter, we continue that process as we turn to another favorite with Java programmers everywhere—graphics programming.

CHAPTER
NINE

9

Graphics!

In this chapter, we're going to start exploring a popular topic among Java programmers—graphics. You'll see how to work with the elementary graphics methods in Java—drawing lines, rectangles, circles, and ovals. We'll even design and run a graphics applet named artist, which will allow the user to draw graphics with the mouse. Let's begin by seeing how to use the mouse so that we can add mouse support to our artist applet (not to mention the fact that using the mouse is by itself a powerful Java technique).

Using the Mouse in Java

To see how to use the mouse, let's set up a new applet named mousedemo. Create that applet now with the Applet Wizard. The Visual J++ Applet Wizard can provide mouse support, and we'll take advantage of that now. In Step 3 of the Applet Wizard, you'll see the question, "Which mouse event handlers would you like added?" as shown in Figure 9.1. Our mousedemo applet will explore all Java mouse events, so check the `mouseDown()`, `mouseUp()` checkbox, the `mouseDrag()`, `mouseMove()` checkbox, and the `mouseEnter()`, `mouseExit()` checkbox as shown in Figure 9.1. Then click on the Finish button, and let the Applet Wizard finish creating the applet (as usual—unless otherwise specified—omit animation and multithreading support).

FIGURE 9.1:

Adding mouse support
in the Applet Wizard

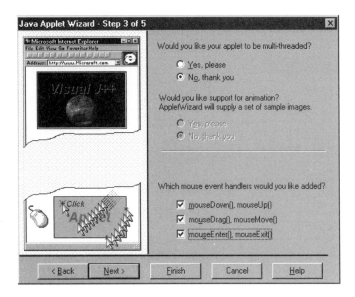

We can add two labels to our mousedemo applet like this:

Then, when a mouse event—such as a mouse button going down
or a mouse click—occurs, we can report that. For example, if the
`mouseEnter()` method is called in our applet, we know that the
mouse has entered the applet's boundaries, and we can report that
like this:

```
 -------------------------------------------------
|                                                 |
|                                                 |
|         This is our Java Mouse Applet           |
|                                                 |
|         The mouse entered the applet            |
|                                                 |
|                                                 |
|                                                 |
|                                                 |
|                                                 |
|                                                 |
 -------------------------------------------------
```

As the mouse moves around in our applet, we can report continuously on its position (in pixels):

```
 -------------------------------------------------
|                                                 |
|                                                 |
|         This is our Java Mouse Applet           |
|                                                 |
|        x position: 258 y position: 121          |
|                                                 |
|                                                 |
|                                                 |
|                                                 |
|                                                 |
|                                                 |
 -------------------------------------------------
```

When the user clicks the mouse, we can report that as well:

```
 -------------------------------------------------
|                                                 |
|                                                 |
|         This is our Java Mouse Applet           |
|                                                 |
|        The left mouse button went down          |
|                                                 |
|                                                 |
|                                                 |
|                                                 |
|                                                 |
|                                                 |
 -------------------------------------------------
```

And when the mouse leaves the boundaries of our applet, we can report that too:

```
-------------------------------------------------
|                                               |
|                                               |
|          This is our Java Mouse Applet        |
|                                               |
|            The mouse left the applet          |
|                                               |
|                                               |
|                                               |
|                                               |
|                                               |
|                                               |
-------------------------------------------------
```

Let's start writing our Java code now. We can give our two labels the names `headerlabel` and `displaylabel` like this:

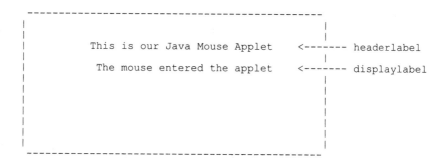

We add the declaration of these two labels to our applet like this:

```
public class mousedemo extends Applet
{
    Label headerlabel, displaylabel;
    .
    .
    .
```

Next, we create these two labels in the init() method:

```
public void init()
{
   // If you use a ResourceWizard-generated "control creator" class to
   // arrange controls in your applet, you may want to call its
   // CreateControls() method from within this method. Remove the following
   // call to resize() before adding the call to CreateControls();
   // CreateControls() does its own resizing.
   //------------------------------------------------------------------------
   resize(320, 240);
➡  headerlabel = new Label("This is our Java Mouse Applet");
➡  add(headerlabel);
➡  displaylabel = new Label("Welcome to the mouse demo applet");
➡  displaylabel.setAlignment(Label.CENTER);
➡  add(displaylabel);
}
```

Let's add one more refinement. Since we'll be placing strings of various lengths in the displaylabel label, we can set that label's *alignment* to CENTER so that all text appears centered in the displaylabel control:

```
public void init()
{
   resize(320, 240);
   headerlabel = new Label("This is our Java Mouse Applet");
   add(headerlabel);
   displaylabel = new Label("Welcome to the mouse demo applet");
➡  displaylabel.setAlignment(Label.CENTER);
   add(displaylabel);
}
```

TIP   Besides setting a label's alignment to Label.CENTER, you can also set it to Label.RIGHT or Label.LEFT. Unfortunately, this does not work for other controls such as text fields.

Now our two labels, `headerlabel` and `displaylabel`, are ready to go. It's time to examine the Applet Wizard's mouse support.

Mouse activities such as mouse clicks or the user moving the mouse are handled in `mouse` event handlers. The first `mouse` event handler we'll take a look at is the `mouseDown` event handler. If we have defined a `mouseDown()` method in our applet, that method will be called when a mouse button is pressed while the mouse is in the boundaries of our applet. The Applet Wizard has added a `mouseDown()` method to our applet for us, so find that now in `mousedemo.java` and open it.

The *mouseDown()* Method

The `mouseDown()` event handler that the Applet Wizard has added to our code looks like this:

```
// MOUSE SUPPORT:
//   The mouseDown() method is called if the mouse button is pressed
// while the mouse cursor is over the applet's portion of the screen.
//-------------------------------------------------------------------
public boolean mouseDown(Event evt, int x, int y)
{
    // TODO: Place applet mouseDown code here
    return true;
}
```

This is the method that will be called when the mouse button is pressed while the mouse is in our applet. The x and y parameters give the x and y location of the mouse when the button is pressed, and the `evt` event object holds more information about the event, such as which mouse button was clicked. In particular, the `Event` class data member named `modifiers` (that is, `evt.modifiers`) will be zero if the left mouse button went down and otherwise will be non-zero. We can use that information to display which button was clicked now.

NOTE Java currently handles only one or two mouse buttons, the left or right button, even though some mice have three buttons.

We first check to see if `evt.modifiers` is zero, which means the left mouse button was clicked:

```
// MOUSE SUPPORT:
//     The mouseDown() method is called if the mouse button is pressed
// while the mouse cursor is over the applet's portion of the screen.
//-------------------------------------------------------------------------
public boolean mouseDown(Event evt, int x, int y)
{
→   if(evt.modifiers == 0){
        .
        .
        .

    }
```

If so, we report that the left mouse button was pressed, like this, placing the text "The left mouse button went down" in our `displaylabel` label:

```
// MOUSE SUPPORT:
//     The mouseDown() method is called if the mouse button is pressed
// while the mouse cursor is over the applet's portion of the screen.
//-------------------------------------------------------------------------
public boolean mouseDown(Event evt, int x, int y)
{
    if(evt.modifiers == 0){
→       displaylabel.setText("The left mouse button went down");
    } .
        .
        .
```

Otherwise, there's only one other possibility, and we indicate that the right mouse button went down in an `else` clause:

```
// MOUSE SUPPORT:
//   The mouseDown() method is called if the mouse button is pressed
```

```
// while the mouse cursor is over the applet's portion of the screen.
//-------------------------------------------------------------------------
public boolean mouseDown(Event evt, int x, int y)
{
   if(evt.modifiers == 0){
      displaylabel.setText("The left mouse button went down");
   }
   else{
      displaylabel.setText("The right mouse button went down");
   }
   return true;
}
```

The general form of the Java `if` statement is:

```
if(conditional){
[code block 1]
}
else{
[code block 2]
}
```

where the code in code block 1 is executed if the conditional expression evaluates to TRUE, and the code in code block 2 is executed otherwise.

And that's it—we've handled the `mouseDown` event. The corresponding event is the `mouseUp` event, which we'll take a look at now.

The *mouseUp()* Method

The `mouseUp` event is handled in the `mouseUp()` method, which the Applet Wizard has added to our applet like this:

```
// MOUSE SUPPORT:
//The mouseUp() method is called if the mouse button is released
// while the mouse cursor is over the applet's portion of the screen.
//-------------------------------------------------------------------------
```

```
public boolean mouseUp(Event evt, int x, int y)
{
   // TODO: Place applet mouseUp code here
   return true;
}
```

Here, we can also check the `evt.modifiers` data member to see if the left or right mouse button went up and report on that this way:

```
// MOUSE SUPPORT:
//    The mouseUp() method is called if the mouse button is released
// while the mouse cursor is over the applet's portion of the screen.
//---------------------------------------------------------------------
public boolean mouseUp(Event evt, int x, int y)
{
→   if(evt.modifiers == 0){
→      displaylabel.setText("The left mouse button went up");
→   }
→   else{
→      displaylabel.setText("The right mouse button went up");
→   }
→   return true;
}
```

And that's it—we've reported what happened by placing text in our `displaylabel` label: either "The left mouse button went up" or "The right mouse button went up." That takes care of `mouseDown()` and `mouseUp()`. The next event pair is the `mouseDrag()` and `mouseMove()` methods. We'll explore them now.

The *mouseDrag()* Method

The `mouseDrag()` event handler is called when the user is dragging the mouse (holding a mouse button down and moving the mouse). The Applet Wizard has added this code to our applet to handle the `mouseDrag` event:

```
// MOUSE SUPPORT:
//The mouseDrag() method is called if the mouse cursor moves over the
```

```
// applet's portion of the screen while the mouse button is held down.
//------------------------------------------------------------------------
public boolean mouseDrag(Event evt, int x, int y)
{
   // TODO: Place applet mouseDrag code here
   return true;
}
```

In this case, we can indicate that the mouse is being dragged by placing a text message, "The mouse is being dragged," into the `displaylabel`:

```
// MOUSE SUPPORT:
// The mouseDrag() method is called if the mouse cursor moves over the
// applet's portion of the screen while the mouse button is being held down.
//------------------------------------------------------------------------
public boolean mouseDrag(Event evt, int x, int y)
{
➔   displaylabel.setText("The mouse is being dragged");
   return true;
}
```

The `mouseMove` event is similar to the `mouseDrag` event, except that `mouseMove` occurs when the mouse is moved while no buttons are being pressed.

The *mouseMove()* Method

The Applet Wizard has added the `mouseMove()` method to our applet like this:

```
// MOUSE SUPPORT:
//The mouseMove() method is called if the mouse cursor moves over the
// applet's portion of the screen and the mouse isn't being held down.
//------------------------------------------------------------------------
public boolean mouseMove(Event evt, int x, int y)
{
   // TODO: Place applet mouseMove code here
   return true;
}
```

The current location of the mouse is passed to us in the x and y parameters, and we can display both coordinates with code like this:

```
// MOUSE SUPPORT:
// The mouseMove() method is called if the mouse cursor moves over the
// applet's portion of the screen and the mouse isn't being held down.
//-------------------------------------------------------------------
public boolean mouseMove(Event evt, int x, int y)
{
    displaylabel.setText("x position: " + x + " y position: " + y);
    return true;
}
```

Now, when the user moves the mouse, we can report the new mouse position with the string x position: 258 y position: 121 in our displaylabel.

That takes care of the mouseMove and mouseDrag pair. The next pair of mouse events are the mouseEnter and mouseExit events, and they finish off our mouse-handling exploration.

The *mouseEnter()* Method

The mouseEnter event occurs when the mouse enters the boundaries of our applet on the screen. The Applet Wizard has placed this code in our applet to handle this event:

```
// MOUSE SUPPORT:
//The mouseEnter() method is called if the mouse cursor enters the
// applet's portion of the screen.
//-------------------------------------------------------------------
public boolean mouseEnter(Event evt, int x, int y)
{
    // TODO: Place applet mouseEnter code here
    return true;
}
```

Using this method, we can report that the mouse has entered our applet by placing the message, "The mouse entered the applet," in the `displaylabel`:

```
// MOUSE SUPPORT:
//   The mouseEnter() method is called if the mouse cursor enters the
// applet's portion of the screen.
//--------------------------------------------------------------------
public boolean mouseEnter(Event evt, int x, int y)
{
➜    displaylabel.setText("The mouse entered the applet");
    return true;
}
```

TIP

If you take advantage of the `mouseEnter` event in a Java frame window, you can change the mouse cursor to whatever you want with the `Frame` class `setCursor()` method when the mouse is in your window.

The last of the mouse events is the `mouseExit` event; we will take a look at that now.

The *mouseExit()* Method

As you might expect—having seen the `mouseEnter` event—the `mouseExit` event occurs when the mouse leaves the applet. The Applet Wizard has placed this code in our applet to handle the `mouseExit` event:

```
// MOUSE SUPPORT:
//The mouseExit() method is called if the mouse cursor leaves the
// applet's portion of the screen.
//--------------------------------------------------------------------
public boolean mouseExit(Event evt, int x, int y)
{
    // TODO: Place applet mouseExit code here
    return true;
}
```

In our case, we'll simply report that the mouse left the applet with a message like this:

```
// MOUSE SUPPORT:
//The mouseExit() method is called if the mouse cursor leaves the
// applet's portion of the screen.
//---------------------------------------------------------------------
public boolean mouseExit(Event evt, int x, int y)
{
    displaylabel.setText("The mouse left the applet");
    return true;
}
```

Our mousedemo applet is ready to use. Run it now. As you can see in Figure 9.2, our mousedemo applet is reporting the current location of the mouse in our applet.

FIGURE 9.2:

The mousedemo applet reports the current position of the mouse.

If the user presses the left mouse button, we report that as well in our mousedemo applet, as shown in Figure 9.3. As you can tell by playing around with this applet, all the other mouse events are active as well, which means that our mousedemo applet is a success. We're using the mouse now. The code for this applet appears in `mousedemo.java`.

FIGURE 9.3:

The mousedemo applet indicates that the left mouse button was clicked.

mousedemo.java

```
//***************************************************************************
// mousedemo.java:  Applet
//
//***************************************************************************
import java.applet.*;
import java.awt.*;


//===========================================================================
// Main Class for applet mousedemo
//
//===========================================================================
public class mousedemo extends Applet
{
   Label headerlabel, displaylabel;

   // mousedemo Class Constructor
   //-----------------------------------------------------------------------
   public mousedemo()
   {
      // TODO: Add constructor code here
   }

   // APPLET INFO SUPPORT:
```

```
//   The getAppletInfo() method returns a string describing the applet's
// author, copyright date, or miscellaneous information.
//-------------------------------------------------------------------------
public String getAppletInfo()
{
   return "Name: mousedemo\r\n" +
         "Author: Steven Holzner\r\n" +
         "Created with Microsoft Visual J++ Version 1.0";
}



// The init() method is called by the AWT when an applet is first loaded or
// reloaded.  Override this method to perform whatever initialization your
// applet needs, such as initializing data structures, loading images or
// fonts, creating frame windows, setting the layout manager, or adding UI
// components.
//-------------------------------------------------------------------------
public void init()
{
   // If you use a ResourceWizard-generated "control creator" class to
   // arrange controls in your applet, you may want to call its
   // CreateControls() method from within this method. Remove the following
   // call to resize() before adding the call to CreateControls();
   // CreateControls() does its own resizing.
   //----------------------------------------------------------------------
   resize(320, 240);
   headerlabel = new Label("This is our Java Mouse Applet");
   add(headerlabel);
   displaylabel = new Label("Welcome to the mouse demo applet");
   displaylabel.setAlignment(Label.CENTER);
   add(displaylabel);

   // TODO: Place additional initialization code here
}

// Place additional applet clean up code here.  destroy() is called
// when your applet is terminating and being unloaded.
//-------------------------------------------------------------------------
public void destroy()
{
```

```
     // TODO: Place applet cleanup code here
}


// mousedemo Paint Handler
//--------------------------------------------------------------------------
public void paint(Graphics g)
{
   //g.drawString("Created with Microsoft Visual J++ Version 1.0", 10, 20);
}


//   The start() method is called when the page containing the applet
// first appears on the screen. The AppletWizard's initial implementation
// of this method starts execution of the applet's thread.
//--------------------------------------------------------------------------
public void start()
{
   // TODO: Place additional applet start code here
}


//   The stop() method is called when the page containing the applet is
// no longer on the screen. The AppletWizard's initial implementation of
// this method stops execution of the applet's thread.
//--------------------------------------------------------------------------
public void stop()
{
}



// MOUSE SUPPORT:
//   The mouseDown() method is called if the mouse button is pressed
// while the mouse cursor is over the applet's portion of the screen.
//--------------------------------------------------------------------------
public boolean mouseDown(Event evt, int x, int y)
{
   if(evt.modifiers == 0){
     displaylabel.setText("The left mouse button went down");
   }
   else{
     displaylabel.setText("The right mouse button went down");
   }
```

```
      return true;
   }

   // MOUSE SUPPORT:
   //   The mouseUp() method is called if the mouse button is released
   // while the mouse cursor is over the applet's portion of the screen.
   //-------------------------------------------------------------------------
   public boolean mouseUp(Event evt, int x, int y)
   {
      if(evt.modifiers == 0){
         displaylabel.setText("The left mouse button went up");
      }
      else{
         displaylabel.setText("The right mouse button went up");
      }
      return true;
   }

   // MOUSE SUPPORT:
   //   The mouseDrag() method is called if the mouse cursor moves over the
   // applet's portion of the screen while the mouse button is being held down.
   //-------------------------------------------------------------------------
   public boolean mouseDrag(Event evt, int x, int y)
   {
      displaylabel.setText("The mouse is being dragged");
      return true;
   }

   // MOUSE SUPPORT:
   //   The mouseMove() method is called if the mouse cursor moves over the
   // applet's portion of the screen and the mouse button isn't being held down.
   //-------------------------------------------------------------------------
   public boolean mouseMove(Event evt, int x, int y)
   {
      displaylabel.setText("x position: " + x + " y position: " + y);
      return true;
   }

   // MOUSE SUPPORT:
   //   The mouseEnter() method is called if the mouse cursor enters the
   // applet's portion of the screen.
   //-------------------------------------------------------------------------
```

```
public boolean mouseEnter(Event evt, int x, int y)
{
   displaylabel.setText("The mouse entered the applet");
   return true;
}

// MOUSE SUPPORT:
//   The mouseExit() method is called if the mouse cursor leaves the
// applet's portion of the screen.
//-------------------------------------------------------------------------
public boolean mouseExit(Event evt, int x, int y)
{
   displaylabel.setText("The mouse left the applet");
   return true;
}


// TODO: Place additional applet code here

}
```

Now that we've seen how to use the mouse in a Java applet, we're ready to create our artist applet, which will let the user use the mouse to create graphics such as lines, rectangles, and circles. We'll turn to that now.

The Artist Applet

To explore how graphics works in Java, we'll create the artist applet. We can present the user with a collection of drawing "tools" (buttons) from which the user can select:

```
-------------------------------------------------------------------------
|                                                                       |
|   -----------   -----------   -----------   -----------   -----------  |
|   | Draw tool |  | Line tool |  | Oval tool |  | Rect tool |  | Round tool | |
|   -----------   -----------   -----------   -----------   -----------  |
|                                                                       |
|                                                                       |
|                                                                       |
|                                                                       |
|                                                                       |
|                                                                       |
|                                                                       |
|                                                                       |
-------------------------------------------------------------------------
```

After the user selects a drawing tool (by clicking on a drawing tool button) for example, the rectangle tool, he or she can draw the figure with the mouse:

```
---------------------------------------------------------------------
|                                                                   |
|  ------------   ------------   ------------   -----------   ------------  |
|  | Draw tool |  | Line tool |  | Oval tool |  | Rect tool |  | Round tool |  |
|  ------------   ------------   ------------   -----------   ------------  |
|                                                                   |
|                       ---------------------                       |
|                       |                   |                       |
|                       |                   |                       |
|                       |                   |                       |
|                       ---------------------                       |
|                                                                   |
|                                                                   |
---------------------------------------------------------------------
```

To do this, the user simply clicks on the Rect button, moves the mouse to the beginning of the new graphics figure, drags the mouse to the other end of the graphics figure, and releases the mouse button. When the mouse button goes up, we can draw the selected figure.

Let's see this in action. Create a new applet named artist now. In Step 3 of the Applet Wizard, add support for the `mouseUp` and `mouseDown` events, as well as the `mouseMove` event. This creates our new applet's outline; it's up to us to flesh it out. Open the new `artist` class now:

```
public class artist extends Applet
{      .
       .
       .
```

Setting Up Artist's Drawing Tools

We can add our drawing tools now as buttons. We will examine five types of graphics here—lines, ovals (and circles), rectangles, rounded rectangles, and freehand drawing—so we need five buttons to match. We set those up like this:

```
public class artist extends Applet
{
```
→   `Button drawbutton, linebutton, ovalbutton, rectbutton, roundedbutton;`

    .
    .
    .

Next, we create those buttons in the `init()` method:

```
public void init()
{
    // If you use a ResourceWizard-generated "control creator" class to
    // arrange controls in your applet, you may want to call its
    // CreateControls() method from within this method. Remove the following
    // call to resize() before adding the call to CreateControls();
    // CreateControls() does its own resizing.
    //-----------------------------------------------------------------------
    resize(320, 240);
```
→   `drawbutton = new Button("Draw tool");`
→   `linebutton = new Button("Line tool");`
→   `ovalbutton = new Button("Oval tool");`
→   `rectbutton = new Button("Rect tool");`
→   `roundedbutton = new Button("Round tool");`

    .
    .
    .

We'll use the default FlowLayout manager here, so we just add the buttons to that layout now:

```
public void init()
{
    // If you use a ResourceWizard-generated "control creator" class to
    // arrange controls in your applet, you may want to call its
    // CreateControls() method from within this method. Remove the following
    // call to resize() before adding the call to CreateControls();
    // CreateControls() does its own resizing.
    //-----------------------------------------------------------------------
    resize(320, 240);
    drawbutton = new Button("Draw tool");
    linebutton = new Button("Line tool");
    ovalbutton = new Button("Oval tool");
```

```
        rectbutton = new Button("Rect tool");
        roundedbutton = new Button("Round tool");

→       add(drawbutton);
→       add(linebutton);
→       add(ovalbutton);
→       add(rectbutton);
→       add(roundedbutton);

    }
```

Now our buttons are installed, and we can make them active. But note that the drawing does not take place when the user clicks on a drawing tool; it takes place when the user releases the mouse button. That is, we'll draw the required figure in the `mouseUp()` method.

But how will we know which figure to draw? We'll have to know which button the user clicked, so we can set some *boolean* flags, one for each drawing tool, when the user clicks on one of the drawing tools.

NOTE A boolean flag is simply a boolean variable (which can take the values TRUE or FALSE) used to indicate the state (TRUE or FALSE) of some option in a program. For example, `windowvisibleboolean` may be a boolean flag, which, if TRUE, indicates that a particular window is visible.

Setting Artist's Internal Boolean Flags

We will create and initialize our boolean flags now. If the user clicks on the Line drawing tool, we will set the flag named `lineboolean` to TRUE; if the user clicks on the Rect drawing tool, we will set the flag named `rectboolean` to TRUE, and so on. Our flags will be `drawboolean`, `lineboolean`, `ovalboolean`, `rectboolean`, and `roundedboolean`, and we'll start out with all of them set to FALSE:

```
public class artist extends Applet
{
    Button drawbutton, linebutton, ovalbutton, rectbutton, roundedbutton;
```
→   `boolean drawboolean = false;`
→   `boolean lineboolean = false;`
→   `boolean ovalboolean = false;`
→   `boolean rectboolean = false;`
→   `boolean roundedboolean = false;`

.
.
.

We will keep track of the mouse as well in our artist applet, because we draw our graphics figures after the mouse button goes up. Therefore, we add two new flags, mousedownboolean and mouseupboolean, like this:

```
public class artist extends Applet
{
    Button drawbutton, linebutton, ovalbutton, rectbutton, roundedbutton;
```
→   `boolean mousedownboolean = false;`
→   `boolean mouseupboolean = false;`
     `boolean drawboolean = false;`
     `boolean lineboolean = false;`
     `boolean ovalboolean = false;`
     `boolean rectboolean = false;`
     `boolean roundedboolean = false;`

.
.
.

After we make these flags active, we'll know in any method of the applet which drawing tool the user has selected and the mouse state. That's important to us—knowing what we're being asked to draw and when we can draw it. We will connect the buttons we've installed to these flags, and then we won't need to worry about the buttons any more.

> **TIP**
>
> We are dividing our program into a user interface part (which has buttons) and a drawing part (which uses flags). The artist applet is not a long program, but dividing the parts of a program into self-contained (and, therefore, easily debugged) parts is usually a good programming practice. Long, monolithic programs quickly get to be unwieldy.

We make the drawing tool buttons active in an `action()` method that we can add to our applet now:

```
public boolean action(Event e, Object o){

}
```

First, we can check if the user clicked on the Draw button to start freehand drawing. The name of this button is `drawbutton`, and we check whether it was clicked this way:

```
    public boolean action(Event e, Object o){
➜      if(e.target.equals(drawbutton)){
            .
            .
            .

        }
    }
```

If this button was clicked, we want to set the `drawboolean` flag to TRUE, and all the other flags to FALSE. Since we'll be setting one flag to TRUE and all others to FALSE whenever the user clicks on a drawing tool, we can set up a small method to set all our flags to FALSE and save many lines of code. Simply add this function, which we will call `setallfalse()`, to the end of the applet class's code this way:

```
    void setallfalse()
    {
        mousedownboolean = false;
        mouseupboolean = false;
        drawboolean = false;
        lineboolean = false;
```

```
      ovalboolean = false;
      rectboolean = false;
      roundedboolean = false;
   }
```

That means that if the user clicked on the freehand drawing tool, we set all flags to FALSE with a call to our new method setallfalse():

```
public boolean action(Event e, Object o){
   if(e.target.equals(drawbutton)){
→     setallfalse();
          .
          .
          .
      }
   }
```

And then we set the drawboolean flag to TRUE:

```
public boolean action(Event e, Object o){
   if(e.target.equals(drawbutton)){
      setallfalse();
      drawboolean = true;
      }
   }
```

We can connect the other buttons to their boolean flags this way:

```
public boolean action(Event e, Object o){
   if(e.target.equals(drawbutton)){
      setallfalse();
      drawboolean = true;
      }
→  if(e.target.equals(linebutton)){
→     setallfalse();
→     lineboolean = true;
→     }
→  if(e.target.equals(ovalbutton)){
→     setallfalse();
→     ovalboolean = true;
→     }
→  if(e.target.equals(rectbutton)){
```

```
→          setallfalse();
→          rectboolean = true;
→        }
→        if(e.target.equals(roundedbutton)){
→          setallfalse();
→          roundedboolean = true;
→        }
         return true;
     }
```

And we're done. We don't have to worry about the buttons any more, since from now on, we can simply check the boolean flags we set up.

Drawing Graphics Figures in the Artist Applet

Now the user turns from the drawing tool buttons to using the mouse to outline the graphics figure. The user will press the mouse button at some location in our applet that we can call the *anchor point*:

```
anchor point   x
```

The user then moves the mouse to a new location, which we might call the *drawto point*:

```
anchor point   x



                            x drawto point
```

When the user releases the mouse button, we are expected to draw the graphics figure, as bounded by the anchor and drawto points:

```
anchor point   x---------------
                |             |
                |             |
                |             |
                ---------------x drawto point
```

That's how we'll proceed. We'll record the location at which the mouse went down in the mouseDown() method, and we'll start the drawing process in the mouseUp() method. Let's look at the mouseDown() method now.

Handling the *mouseDown* Event

In the mouseDown event, we want to record the beginning point of the graphics figure, the point we have called the anchor point. We can store points in Java using the Java Point class, which has two data members: x and y. We'll declare two Point objects, anchorpoint and drawtopoint, in our applet like this:

```
public class artist extends Applet
{
    Button drawbutton, linebutton, ovalbutton, rectbutton, roundedbutton;

➔    Point anchorpoint, drawtopoint;

    boolean mousedownboolean = false;
    boolean mouseupboolean = false;
    boolean drawboolean = false;
    boolean lineboolean = false;
    boolean ovalboolean = false;
    boolean rectboolean = false;
    boolean roundedboolean = false;
         .
         .
         .
```

The x-coordinate of a point such as anchorpoint can be reached as: anchorpoint.x and the y-coordinate as anchorpoint.y. Now find the `mouseDown()` method so that we can place the correct data in the `anchorpoint` variable:

```
// MOUSE SUPPORT:
//   The mouseDown() method is called if the mouse button is pressed
// while the mouse cursor is over the applet's portion of the screen.
//------------------------------------------------------------------------
public boolean mouseDown(Event evt, int x, int y)
{
    // TODO: Place applet mouseDown code here
    return true;
}
```

The location at which the mouse went down is passed to us in the x and y parameters, and we want to store that location in the anchor point object, `anchorpoint`. We do that by creating a new object of the `Point` class, passing the x,y coordinates as arguments to the `Point` class's constructor:

```
// MOUSE SUPPORT:
//   The mouseDown() method is called if the mouse button is pressed
// while the mouse cursor is over the applet's portion of the screen.
//------------------------------------------------------------------------
public boolean mouseDown(Event evt, int x, int y)
{
→    anchorpoint = new Point(x, y);
        .

        .

        .

    return true;
}
```

> **TIP**
>
> Memory-frugal C++ programmers may worry about lines of code such as `anchorpoint = new Point(x, y);` because the user might click the mouse button several times while using our applet and so execute this line each time. What happens to the old anchor points? Do those objects remain in memory, taking up space? Should we delete them? It turns out there is no delete operator in Java as there is in C++, but it's not such a big problem. When no object variables refer to a particular object, Java deallocates that object's memory automatically (a process called *automatic garbage collection*). Thus, if you want to save memory space by getting rid of objects that are no longer needed, you can simply set their variables to `null` (for example, `framewindow = null;`).

In addition, now that the mouse button is down, we set the mouse boolean flags, `mousedownboolean` and `mouseupboolean`, to indicate that:

```
// MOUSE SUPPORT:
//   The mouseDown() method is called if the mouse button is pressed
// while the mouse cursor is over the applet's portion of the screen.
//-------------------------------------------------------------------
public boolean mouseDown(Event evt, int x, int y)
{
   anchorpoint = new Point(x, y);
→  mousedownboolean = true;
→  mouseupboolean = false;
   return true;
}
```

And we can set the same flags when the mouse button goes back up in the `mouseUp()` method to show that the mouse is up.

Handling the *mouseUp* Event

We set the mouse boolean flags like this in the `mouseUp()` method:

```
// MOUSE SUPPORT:
//   The mouseUp() method is called if the mouse button is released
// while the mouse cursor is over the applet's portion of the screen.
```

```
//-------------------------------------------------------------------
public boolean mouseUp(Event evt, int x, int y)
{
➜      mousedownboolean = false;
➜      mouseupboolean = true;
        .
        .
        .

}
```

Note that when the mouse button goes up, the user is indicating the end point of the graphics figure—the drawto point:

```
                  anchor point  x---------------
                                |              |
                                |              |
                                |              |
                                 ---------------x  drawto point
```

We can record the drawto point like this, using the parameters x and y passed to us in mouseUp():

```
// MOUSE SUPPORT:
//   The mouseUp() method is called if the mouse button is released
// while the mouse cursor is over the applet's portion of the screen.
//-------------------------------------------------------------------
public boolean mouseUp(Event evt, int x, int y)
{
  mousedownboolean = false;
  mouseupboolean = true;

➜      drawtopoint = new Point(x, y);
        .
        .
        .

  return true;
}
```

Now we have the two points, anchorpoint and drawtopoint, that we'll need to draw our figure. The actual drawing should be done in the paint() method, which is where we are passed an object of the

Graphics class to use in painting in our applet. To force the paint event to occur, we call repaint() in the mouseUp() method like this:

```
// MOUSE SUPPORT:
//   The mouseUp() method is called if the mouse button is released
// while the mouse cursor is over the applet's portion of the screen.
//----------------------------------------------------------------------
public boolean mouseUp(Event evt, int x, int y)
{
   mousedownboolean = false;
   mouseupboolean = true;

   drawtopoint = new Point(x, y);
   repaint();
      .
      .
      .
   return true;
}
```

Now we're ready to draw. We will start with one of the most common graphics figures—lines.

Creating Lines

When the user clicks on the Line tool button, he or she can draw lines in our applet, stretching from the point we have called anchorpoint to the point we have called drawtopoint:

```
-----------------------------------------------------------------------
|                                                                     |
|   -----------   -----------   -----------   -----------   ----------- |
|   | Draw tool || Line tool || Oval tool || Rect tool || Round tool | |
|   -----------   -----------   -----------   -----------   ----------- |
|                                                                     |
|                                                                     |
|         anchorpoint ------------------- drawtopoint                  |
|                                                                     |
|                                                                     |
|                                                                     |
|                                                                     |
-----------------------------------------------------------------------
```

Now that the user has released the mouse button, the `paint()` method is called, and we can draw the line. Open the `paint()` method now:

```
// artist Paint Handler
//-------------------------------------------------------------
public void paint(Graphics g)
{    .

         .

         .
```

Since there can be many causes for the `paint` event, we first check to make sure that the mouse button went up (by checking the variable `mouseupboolean`). If so, we should draw our figure:

```
// artist Paint Handler
//-------------------------------------------------------------
public void paint(Graphics g)
{
   if(mouseupboolean){
       .

       .

       .

}
```

If the mouse indeed went up, we next check to see if we should be drawing a line—that is, we check the boolean flag `lineboolean`:

```
// artist Paint Handler
//-------------------------------------------------------------
public void paint(Graphics g)
{
   if(mouseupboolean){
       if(lineboolean){
         .

         .

         .

       }
```

If we are expected to draw a line, the line is to stretch from the anchor point to the drawto point. We can use the `Graphics` class's drawLine() method to draw this line, and we pass it the start and end coordinates of the line like this:

```
// artist Paint Handler
//-------------------------------------------------------------
public void paint(Graphics g)
{
  if(mouseupboolean){
    if(lineboolean){
→       g.drawLine(anchorpoint.x, anchorpoint.y,
➥ drawtopoint.x, drawtopoint.y);
    } .
      .
      .
```

Our line now appears in the applet, as shown in Figure 9.4. The drawLine() method is only one of the methods of the Graphics class—that class's methods appear in Table 9.1.

FIGURE 9.4:

Drawing lines in the artist applet

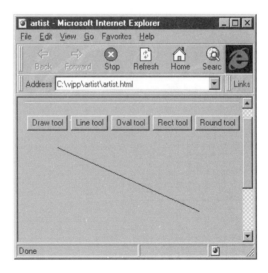

TABLE 9.1: The `Graphics` Class's Methods

Method	Does This
`Graphics()`	Constructs the `Graphics` object
`clearRect(int, int, int, int)`	Clears given rectangle
`clipRect(int, int, int, int)`	Clips to given rectangle
`copyArea` `(int, int, int, int, int, int)`	Copies area of screen
`create()`	Creates new `Graphics` copy of original object
`dispose()`	Disposes of `Graphics`
`draw3DRect` `(int, int, int, int, boolean)`	Draws 3-D rectangle
`drawArc` `(int, int, int, int, int, int)`	Draws arc bounded by given rectangle
`drawBytes` `(byte[], int, int, int, int)`	Draws given bytes using the current color
`drawChars` `(char[], int, int, int, int)`	Draws given characters using the current font and color
`drawImage` `(Image, int, int, ImageObserver)`	Draws given image

`drawImage`
`(Image, int, int, int, int,`
`ImageObserver)`
	Draws given image inside rectangle

`drawImage`
`(Image, int, int, Color,`
`ImageObserver)`
	Draws given image at (x, y) location

`drawImage`
`(Image, int, int, int, int,`
`Color, ImageObserver)`
	Draws image inside given rectangle, with indicated background color

`drawLine(int, int, int, int)`	Draws a line from beginning to ending coordinates
`drawOval(int, int, int, int)`	Draws oval inside the given rectangle

TABLE 9.1: The Graphics Class's Methods (continued)

Method	Does This
drawPolygon(int[], int[], int)	Draws a polygon defined by array of x points and y points
drawPolygon(Polygon)	Draws polygon defined by given points
drawRect(int, int, int, int)	Draws outline of given rectangle
drawRoundRect (int, int, int, int, int, int)	Draws rounded rectangle
drawString(String, int, int)	Draws a string
fill3DRect (int, int, int, int, boolean)	Fills a 3-D rectangle
fillArc (int, int, int, int, int, int)	Fills arc using current color
fillOval(int, int, int, int)	Fills oval inside given rectangle with current color
fillPolygon(Polygon)	Fills polygon with current color
fillRect(int, int, int, int)	Fills given rectangle with the current color
fillRoundRect (int, int, int, int, int, int)	Draws rounded rectangle filled with current color
finalize()	Disposes of graphic when it is not referenced
getClipRect()	Gets clipping area
getColor()	Gets current color
getFont()	Gets current font
getFontMetrics()	Gets current font metrics
getFontMetrics(Font)	Gets current font metrics for given font
setColor(Color)	Sets current color to given color
setFont(Font)	Sets font for all text operations

TABLE 9.1: The `Graphics` Class's Methods (continued)

Method	Does This
`setPaintMode()`	Sets paint mode to overwrite destination with current color
`setXORMode(Color)`	Sets painting mode to XOR
`toString()`	Gets string representing `Graphic`'s value
`translate(int, int)`	Translates given parameters to origin

Now that we've seen how to create lines, we'll move on to creating circles and ovals.

Creating Circles and Ovals

The user clicks on the Oval tool button to draw circles and ovals:

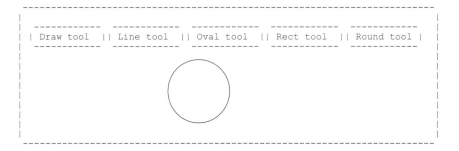

Let's work on creating circles now. We can do that with the `Graphics` class's `drawOval()` method (with which you can draw both ovals and circles). This method—like the other graphics methods you'll see in this chapter—works a bit differently from the `drawLine()` method we just used. In `drawLine()`, we only needed to pass the x,y coordinates of the beginning and end of the line. With other graphics methods such as `drawOval()` and `drawRect()`, we need to pass the upper left corner of the figure's bounding rectangle and its width and height:

```
anchorpoint  x---------------------         ^
             |                      |  |      |
             |                      |  |      |
             |                      |  |   height
             |                      |  |      |
             |                      |  |      |
             |                      |  |      V
             ---------------------
             <------- width --------->
```

It looks as if we can pass the anchor point as the upper left corner of the figure's bounding rectangle. However, there is no special reason that the user should haved place the anchor point at upper left—in fact, the anchor point may even be at lower right. We will, therefore, reorder the anchor point and the drawto point to make sure that the anchor point is at upper left and that the drawto point is at lower right.

We can reorder these points in the `mouseUp()` method, just before we paint the graphics figure the user has requested in our applet. As mentioned, we won't need to rearrange the two bounding points for the `drawLine()` method, but we will need to do so for the other graphics methods. For that reason, we first make sure we are not drawing a line by checking the `lineboolean` variable in an `if...else` statement:

```
// MOUSE SUPPORT:
//   The mouseUp() method is called if the mouse button is released
// while the mouse cursor is over the applet's portion of the screen.
//-------------------------------------------------------------------
public boolean mouseUp(Event evt, int x, int y)
{
   mousedownboolean = false;
```

```
   mouseupboolean = true;

➡   if(lineboolean){
       drawtopoint = new Point(x, y);
   }
➡  else{
       .

       .

       .

   }
 }
```

If we are not drawing a line, we can continue, rearranging the `anchorpoint` point to be the top left of our figure's bounding rectangle and rearranging the `drawtopoint` point to be the bottom right of the bounding rectangle. We do that simply by comparing values in each of these points, since the Java applet coordinate system looks like this:

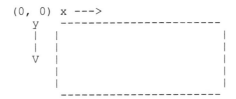

We can use the Java `Math` class's `min()` and `max()` methods to compare values. The `min()` method takes two values and returns the lesser; the `max()` method takes two values and returns the greater. We can, therefore, sort the anchor and drawto points like this:

```
// MOUSE SUPPORT:
//  The mouseUp() method is called if the mouse button is released
// while the mouse cursor is over the applet's portion of the screen.
//-------------------------------------------------------------------
public boolean mouseUp(Event evt, int x, int y)
{
   mousedownboolean = false;
```

```
      mouseupboolean = true;

      if(lineboolean){
         drawtopoint = new Point(x, y);
      }
      else{
→         drawtopoint = new Point(Math.max(x, anchorpoint.x),
↳      Math.max(y, anchorpoint.y));
→         anchorpoint = new Point(Math.min(x, anchorpoint.x),
↳      Math.min(y, anchorpoint.y));
                  .
                  .
                  .

      }
   }
```

Here we are using the Java `Math` class, and that class is part of the `java.lang` package. We need to import that class in the beginning of our applet so that Visual J++ can find the `min()` and `max()` methods:

```
//****************************************************************************
// artist.java: Applet
//
//****************************************************************************
import java.applet.*;
import java.awt.*;
→ import java.lang.Math;
         .
         .
         .
```

We'll also need the width and height of our figure's bounding rectangle:

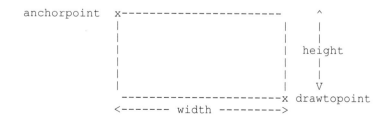

```
anchorpoint  x------------------------             ^
             |                        |   |         |
             |                        |   |         |
             |                        |   |      height
             |                        |   |         |
             |                        |   |         |
             |                        |   |         V
             ------------------------x drawtopoint
             <------- width --------->
```

Now that we've ordered the anchor point to be the upper left and the drawto point to be the lower right, we can find the height and the width of our bounding rectangle through simple subtraction, like this:

```
// MOUSE SUPPORT:
//The mouseUp() method is called if the mouse button is released
// while the mouse cursor is over the applet's portion of the screen.
//-----------------------------------------------------------------
public boolean mouseUp(Event evt, int x, int y)
{
   mousedownboolean = false;
   mouseupboolean = true;

   if(lineboolean){
      drawtopoint = new Point(x, y);
   }
   else{
      drawtopoint = new Point(Math.max(x, anchorpoint.x),
   Math.max(y,anchorpoint.y));
      anchorpoint = new Point(Math.min(x, anchorpoint.x),
   Math.min(y, anchorpoint.y));
         width = drawtopoint.x - anchorpoint.x;
         height = drawtopoint.y - anchorpoint.y;
   }
   repaint();
   return true;
}
```

To pass these values on to the `paint()` method, we make them classwide variables, declaring them at the beginning of the class:

```
//================================================================
// Main Class for applet artist
//
//================================================================
public class artist extends Applet
{
   Button drawbutton, linebutton, ovalbutton, rectbutton, roundedbutton;

   Point anchorpoint, drawtopoint;
   int width, height;

      .
      .
      .
```

Now we're ready to draw ovals and circles with the drawOval()
method. We place the code to draw these figures in the paint()
method, which currently looks like this:

```
// artist Paint Handler
//------------------------------------------------------------------
public void paint(Graphics g)
{
   if(mouseupboolean){

     if(lineboolean){
        g.drawLine(anchorpoint.x, anchorpoint.y, drawtopoint.x, drawtopoint.y);
     }    .
              .
              .
```

Here, we check to make sure the user has released the mouse button, and we should draw the oval or circle by examining the boolean
flag mouseupboolean. If that is set, we are supposed to draw a figure. Next, we check the ovalboolean boolean flag to see if we are
supposed to be drawing an oval or a circle:

```
// artist Paint Handler
//------------------------------------------------------------------
public void paint(Graphics g)
{
    if(mouseupboolean){

      if(lineboolean){
         g.drawLine(anchorpoint.x, anchorpoint.y, drawtopoint.x,
            drawtopoint.y);
      }
➜       if(ovalboolean){
                .
      }         .
                .
```

If so, we use the Graphics class drawOval() method to draw the
oval or circle. We pass it the coordinates of the upper left point of the
figure's bounding rectangle—that is, our anchor point—and the

figure's width and height, which we have just stored in the applet-wide variables *width* and *height*:

```
// artist Paint Handler
//--------------------------------------------------------------------
public void paint(Graphics g)
{
   if(mouseupboolean){

     if(lineboolean){
        g.drawLine(anchorpoint.x, anchorpoint.y, drawtopoint.x,
 ➥ drawtopoint.y);
     }
     if(ovalboolean){
 ➔       g.drawOval(anchorpoint.x, anchorpoint.y, width, height);
     }     .
              .
              .
```

Our circles and ovals now appear on the screen, as shown in Figure 9.5.

FIGURE 9.5:

Our artist applet can draw ovals.

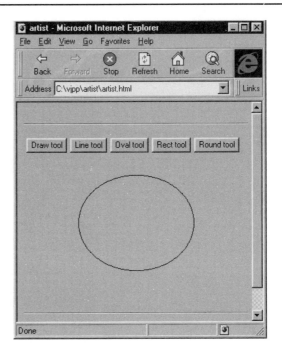

Now that we've set up a rectangle to bound our graphics figure, it will be easy to draw rectangles, and we'll turn to that next.

Creating Rectangles

Our next step is to draw rectangles. The user can draw rectangles by clicking on the Rect tool button and using the mouse:

```
----------------------------------------------------------------------
|                                                                    |
|   -----------   -----------   -----------   -----------   ----------- |
|  | Draw tool  || Line tool  || Oval tool  || Rect tool  || Round tool | |
|   -----------   -----------   -----------   -----------   ----------- |
|                                                                    |
|                    -------------------------                       |
|                   |                         |                      |
|                   |                         |                      |
|                   |                         |                      |
|                    -------------------------                       |
|                                                                    |
----------------------------------------------------------------------
```

We've already included all the mouse support that we'll need to draw rectangles. The `Graphics` method we'll use to draw rectangles is `drawRect()`, and we'll use that method in our applet's `paint()` method. We'll need to pass the upper left point of our rectangle and its width and height, but we've already calculated those variables in the `mouseUp()` method—so all we really have to do is to draw our rectangle.

First, we make sure that we are supposed to be drawing rectangles by checking the `rectboolean` boolean flag (set when the user clicks on the Rect tool button):

```
// artist Paint Handler
//-----------------------------------------------------------------
public void paint(Graphics g)
{
   if(mouseupboolean){

      if(lineboolean){
```

```
        g.drawLine(anchorpoint.x, anchorpoint.y, drawtopoint.x,
          drawtopoint.y);
      }
      if(ovalboolean){
        g.drawOval(anchorpoint.x, anchorpoint.y, width, height);
      }
➜     if(rectboolean){
           .
      }   .
           .
```

If we are indeed drawing rectangles, we use the `drawRect()` method, passing it the four parameters it needs—the upper left point of the rectangle's x,y coordinates, as well as the rectangle's width and height:

```
// artist Paint Handler
//-------------------------------------------------------------------
public void paint(Graphics g)
{
if(mouseupboolean){

    if(lineboolean){
      g.drawLine(anchorpoint.x, anchorpoint.y,
        drawtopoint.x, drawtopoint.y);
    }
    if(ovalboolean){
      g.drawOval(anchorpoint.x, anchorpoint.y, width, height);
    }
    if(rectboolean){
➜       g.drawRect(anchorpoint.x, anchorpoint.y, width, height);
    }   .
        .
        .
```

And that's all we need—now the user can draw rectangles in our artist applet, as shown in Figure 9.6.

FIGURE 9.6:

Our artist applet can draw rectangles.

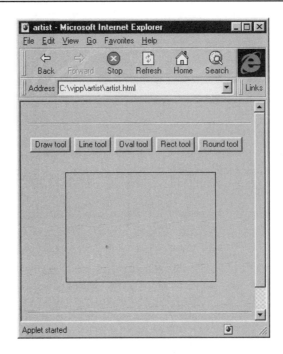

TIP

The `Graphics` class actually has a method called `draw3DRect()`, which is supposed to draw 3-D rectangles. At this time, however, it only draws the same rectangles as the `drawRect()` method; perhaps some future version of Java will rectify that.

Now that we are able to draw straight rectangles, it turns out that we can draw rectangles with rounded corners just as easily. Let's examine this process now.

Creating Rounded Rectangles

When the user clicks the Round tool button, he or she can use the mouse to draw rounded rectangles, like this:

As before, all the mouse handling has already been done—we know the rectangle's width and height, as well as the location of its upper left corner. All we have to do in the `paint()` method is to check if we are supposed to draw a rounded rectangle by examining the `roundedboolean` boolean flag:

```
// artist Paint Handler
//---------------------------------------------------------------------
public void paint(Graphics g)
{
   if(mouseupboolean){

      if(lineboolean){
         g.drawLine(anchorpoint.x, anchorpoint.y, drawtopoint.x,
            drawtopoint.y);
      }
      if(ovalboolean){
         g.drawOval(anchorpoint.x, anchorpoint.y, width, height);
      }
      if(rectboolean){
         g.drawRect(anchorpoint.x, anchorpoint.y, width, height);
      }
      if(roundedboolean){

      }        .
   }            .
             .
```

If so, we can call the Graphics method drawRoundRect(). This takes the usual parameters—the coordinates of the upper left of the rectangle, as well as its height and width—and two new parameters. These new parameters control the rounding of the corners. The first parameter is the width of the rounding arc (in pixels), and the second parameter is the height of the rounding arc. In this case, we will give both parameters the value of 10:

```
// artist Paint Handler
//-------------------------------------------------------------------
public void paint(Graphics g)
{
   if(mouseupboolean){

      if(lineboolean){
         g.drawLine(anchorpoint.x, anchorpoint.y, drawtopoint.x,
            drawtopoint.y);
      }
      if(ovalboolean){
         g.drawOval(anchorpoint.x, anchorpoint.y, width, height);
      }
      if(rectboolean){
         g.drawRect(anchorpoint.x, anchorpoint.y, width, height);
      }
      if(roundedboolean){
         g.drawRoundRect(anchorpoint.x, anchorpoint.y, width, height, 10, 10);
      }          .
   }          .
             .
```

And that's it—now the user can draw rounded rectangles, as shown in Figure 9.7.

Our artist applet
can draw rounded
rectangles.

That's it for the standard graphics figures: lines, circles, ovals, rectangles, and rounded rectangles. However, we can go one better—we can support freehand drawing in our artist applet, letting the user draw with the mouse. We'll take a look at that next.

Freehand Drawing

When the user clicks on the Draw tool button, he or she can create a freehand drawing with the mouse, like this:

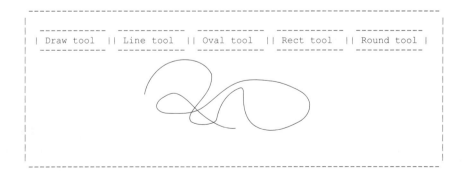

The user presses the mouse button at some starting location in our applet and then drags the mouse. To handle this new capability, we can use the `mouseDrag()` method, which the Applet Wizard has added to our applet:

```
// MOUSE SUPPORT:
//The mouseDrag() method is called if the mouse cursor moves over the
// applet's portion of the screen while the mouse button is held down.
//-------------------------------------------------------------------
public boolean mouseDrag(Event evt, int x, int y)
{
   // TODO: Place applet mouseDrag code here
   return true;
}
```

This method is called when the user drags the mouse. We can check whether the Draw tool is selected (and so we should be drawing on the screen) by looking at the `drawboolean` boolean flag:

```
// MOUSE SUPPORT:
//The mouseDrag() method is called if the mouse cursor moves over the
// applet's portion of the screen while the button is being held down.
//-------------------------------------------------------------------
public boolean mouseDrag(Event evt, int x, int y)
{
      if(drawboolean){

      }
   return true;
}
```

One way of drawing freehand with the mouse is to record the mouse locations as it is dragged around in the applet and then "connect the dots." That is, we store each point we get in the `mouseDrag` event and then draw from point to point in the `paint()` method.

We start that process by storing the points we get in the `mouseDrag` event in an array of `Point` objects named `points[]`. We can declare an array of, say, 300 `Point` objects. The syntax for declaring an array in Java is:

```
Type name[] = new Type[number]
```

We can, therefore, declare our array of points this way:

```
//===========================================================================
// Main Class for applet artist
//
//===========================================================================
public class artist extends Applet
{
    Button drawbutton, linebutton, ovalbutton, rectbutton, roundedbutton;
```

➜
```
    Point points[] = new Point[300];
    Point anchorpoint, drawtopoint;
    int width, height;
            .
            .
            .
```

Technically, Java supports only one-dimesional arrays. Two dimensional arrays are really arrays of one-dimensional arrays. For example, here is how you declare and initialize a 3×3 two-dimensional array of `String` objects:

```
String stringarray[][] =
{
    {"Hello", "there", "USA"},
    {"Hello", "there", "Europe"},
    {"Hello", "there", "World!"},
};
```

In addition, we will need an index value in that array so that we will be able to tell where to add the next point and how many points to draw. We can call that array index `currentpoint`:

```
//===========================================================================
// Main Class for applet artist
//
//===========================================================================
```

```
public class artist extends Applet
{
   Button drawbutton, linebutton, ovalbutton, rectbutton, roundedbutton;

   Point points[] = new Point[300];
   Point anchorpoint, drawtopoint;
→  int currentpoint = 0;
   int width, height;
      .
      .
      .
```

Now our point array is set up, and we can add points to it in the `mouseDrag()` method. The point passed to us is the current location of the mouse, so we add that to our `points[]` array this way:

```
// MOUSE SUPPORT:
//The mouseDrag() method is called if the mouse cursor moves over the
// applet's portion of the screen while the button is being held down.
//-----------------------------------------------------------------------
public boolean mouseDrag(Event evt, int x, int y)
{
   if(drawboolean){
→     points[currentpoint++] = new Point(x, y);
         .
         .
   }
   return true;
}
```

NOTE If you're not familiar with the C++ operator ++, all it does is to increment a variable. Used this way, as a postfix operator, `points[currentpoint++] = new Point(x, y);`, it adds 1 to the variable *currentpoint* after the whole statement is executed. Used as a prefix operator, `points[++currentpoint] = new Point(x, y);`, it adds 1 to *currentpoint* before the rest of the statement is executed. We, therefore, use that new, incremented value as the array index. Note that ++ is an operator that may be overloaded, so you should not assume that it always adds 1 each time it's used. It may have been redefined for a certain class to add, say, 1000, or even the characters *abc*.

That is, we add a new point made from the x and y parameters passed to us, store it in the `points[]` array, and then increment the `currentpoint` array index. After we store the point, we call `repaint()` to draw the points in the array on the screen:

```
// MOUSE SUPPORT:
//The mouseDrag() method is called if the mouse cursor moves over the
// applet's portion of the screen while the button is being held down.
//---------------------------------------------------------------------
public boolean mouseDrag(Event evt, int x, int y)
{
   if(drawboolean){
      points[currentpoint++] = new Point(x, y);
➜     repaint();
   }
   return true;
}
```

All that remains is to add code to the `paint()` method to draw the points in the `points[]` array. First, in the `paint()` method, we check to make sure we are supposed to be drawing freehand by examining the `drawboolean` boolean flag:

```
// artist Paint Handler
//---------------------------------------------------------------------
public void paint(Graphics g)
{
   if(mouseupboolean){

      if(lineboolean){
         g.drawLine(anchorpoint.x, anchorpoint.y, drawtopoint.x,
➥ drawtopoint.y);
      }
      if(ovalboolean){
         g.drawOval(anchorpoint.x, anchorpoint.y, width, height);
      }
      if(rectboolean){
         g.drawRect(anchorpoint.x, anchorpoint.y, width, height);
      }
      if(roundedboolean){
```

```
            g.drawRoundRect(anchorpoint.x, anchorpoint.y, width, height, 10, 10);
        }
    }
➜   if(drawboolean){
        .
        .
        .
➜   }
    }
```

If we are to draw freehand, we will draw the points in the points[] array. We can loop over all those points, from 0 to the value in *currentpoint* this way with a for loop. This loop looks like this in general, just as it would in C or C++:

```
for(initial statement; conditional test; increment statement){
    loop body
}
```

You use the initial statement to set up a loop index, the conditional test to see if you have looped enough, and the increment statement to increment (or decrement) your loop index. In our case, we can loop over all the points in the points[] array this way:

```
// artist Paint Handler
//------------------------------------------------------------------------
public void paint(Graphics g)
{
    int loop_index;

    if(mouseupboolean){
        .
        .
        .
    }
    if(drawboolean){
➜       for(loop_index = 0; loop_index < currentpoint; loop_index++){
            .
            .
            .
        }
    }
}
```

There are three types of loops in Java—for, while, and do loops. Their syntax looks like this:

```
for(initial statement; conditional test; increment statement){
    loop body
}



while(conditional test){
    loop body
}



do{
    loop body
}while(conditional test)
```

We will then "connect-the-dots," that is, draw a line from one point to the next, which will display a continuous freehand drawing on the screen. We will draw all these line segments with the Graphics drawLine() method:

```
// artist Paint Handler
//---------------------------------------------------------------------
public void paint(Graphics g)
{
    int loop_index;

    if(mouseupboolean){
        .
        .
        .

    }
    if(drawboolean){
        for(loop_index = 0; loop_index < currentpoint; loop_index++){
            g.drawLine(points[loop_index].x, points[loop_index].y,
        points[loop_index + 1].x, points[loop_index + 1].y);
        }
    }
}
```

NOTE
You may wonder why we used lines to connect the points we stored when the mouse moved across our applet instead of drawing the points themselves. The reason is that the `mouseDrag()` method is not called for each pixel the mouse moves over. Only a limited number of mouse events are generated each second, and if we simply drew the individual points, we'd end up with a series of uncoordinated points trailing over the screen.

That's all there is to it. Now run the artist applet and click on the Draw tool button. When you do, you can draw freehand with the mouse, as shown in Figure 9.8.

FIGURE 9.8:

Our artist applet can draw freehand.

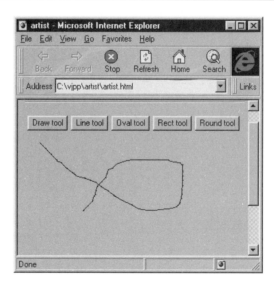

That's it for freehand drawing, and that's it for our artist applet. We've come far in this applet—from handling the mouse to drawing graphics such as lines, circles, ovals, rectangles, and more. We've gotten a good start in graphics handling. You can find the code for this applet in `artist.java`.

artist.java

```
//*************************************************************************
// artist.java: Applet
//
//*************************************************************************
import java.applet.*;
import java.awt.*;
import java.lang.Math;


//=========================================================================
// Main Class for applet artist
//
//=========================================================================
public class artist extends Applet
{
   Button drawbutton, linebutton, ovalbutton, rectbutton, roundedbutton;

     Point points[] = new Point[300];
     Point anchorpoint, drawtopoint;
     int currentpoint = 0;
     int width, height;

     boolean mousedownboolean = false;
     boolean mouseupboolean = false;
     boolean drawboolean = false;
     boolean lineboolean = false;
     boolean ovalboolean = false;
     boolean rectboolean = false;
     boolean roundedboolean = false;

   // artist Class Constructor
   //----------------------------------------------------------------------
   public artist()
   {
      // TODO: Add constructor code here
   }

   // APPLET INFO SUPPORT:
   //   The getAppletInfo() method returns a string describing the applet's
   // author, copyright date, or miscellaneous information.
   //----------------------------------------------------------------------
```

```
public String getAppletInfo()
{
    return "Name: artist\r\n" +
          "Author: Steven Holzner\r\n" +
          "Created with Microsoft Visual J++ Version 1.0";
}


// The init() method is called by the AWT when an applet is first loaded or
// reloaded.  Override this method to perform whatever initialization your
// applet needs, such as initializing data structures, loading images or
// fonts, creating frame windows, setting the layout manager, or adding UI
// components.
//-------------------------------------------------------------------------
public void init()
{
    // If you use a ResourceWizard-generated "control creator" class to
    // arrange controls in your applet, you may want to call its
    // CreateControls() method from within this method. Remove the following
    // call to resize() before adding the call to CreateControls();
    // CreateControls() does its own resizing.
    //---------------------------------------------------------------------
    resize(320, 240);
    drawbutton = new Button("Draw tool");
    linebutton = new Button("Line tool");
    ovalbutton = new Button("Oval tool");
    rectbutton = new Button("Rect tool");
    roundedbutton = new Button("Round tool");

    add(drawbutton);
    add(linebutton);
    add(ovalbutton);
    add(rectbutton);
    add(roundedbutton);

    // TODO: Place additional initialization code here
}

public boolean action(Event e, Object o){
    if(e.target.equals(drawbutton)){
        setallfalse();
        drawboolean = true;
    }
```

```
  if(e.target.equals(linebutton)){
    setallfalse();
    lineboolean = true;
  }
  if(e.target.equals(ovalbutton)){
    setallfalse();
    ovalboolean = true;
  }
  if(e.target.equals(rectbutton)){
    setallfalse();
    rectboolean = true;
  }
  if(e.target.equals(roundedbutton)){
    setallfalse();
    roundedboolean = true;
  }
  return true;
}


// Place additional applet clean up code here.  destroy() is called
// when your applet is terminating and being unloaded.
//-------------------------------------------------------------------------
public void destroy()
{
  // TODO: Place applet cleanup code here
}


// artist Paint Handler
//-------------------------------------------------------------------------
public void paint(Graphics g)
{
  if(mouseupboolean){

    if(lineboolean){
      g.drawLine(anchorpoint.x, anchorpoint.y, drawtopoint.x, drawtopoint.y);
    }
    if(ovalboolean){
      g.drawOval(anchorpoint.x, anchorpoint.y, width, height);
    }
    if(rectboolean){
      g.drawRect(anchorpoint.x, anchorpoint.y, width, height);
    }
```

```
      if(roundedboolean){
        g.drawRoundRect(anchorpoint.x, anchorpoint.y, width, height, 10, 10);
      }
    }
    if(drawboolean){
      for(int loop_index = 0; loop_index < currentpoint; loop_index++){
      g.drawLine(points[loop_index].x, points[loop_index].y,
  points[loop_index + 1].x, points[loop_index + 1].y);
      }
    }
  }


  //   The start() method is called when the page containing the applet
  // first appears on the screen. The AppletWizard's initial implementation
  // of this method starts execution of the applet's thread.
  //-----------------------------------------------------------------------
  public void start()
  {
    // TODO: Place additional applet start code here
  }


  //   The stop() method is called when the page containing the applet is
  // no longer on the screen. The AppletWizard's initial implementation of
  // this method stops execution of the applet's thread.
  //-----------------------------------------------------------------------
  public void stop()
  {
  }



  // MOUSE SUPPORT:
  //   The mouseDown() method is called if the mouse button is pressed
  // while the mouse cursor is over the applet's portion of the screen.
  //-----------------------------------------------------------------------
  public boolean mouseDown(Event evt, int x, int y)
  {
    mousedownboolean = true;
    mouseupboolean = false;
    anchorpoint = new Point(x, y);
    return true;
  }


  // MOUSE SUPPORT:
```

```
//   The mouseUp() method is called if the mouse button is released
// while the mouse cursor is over the applet's portion of the screen.
//-------------------------------------------------------------------------
public boolean mouseUp(Event evt, int x, int y)
{
   mousedownboolean = false;
   mouseupboolean = true;

   if(lineboolean){
      drawtopoint = new Point(x, y);
   }
   else{
      drawtopoint = new Point(Math.max(x, anchorpoint.x),
Math.max(y, anchorpoint.y));
      anchorpoint = new Point(Math.min(x, anchorpoint.x),
Math.min(y, anchorpoint.y));
      width = drawtopoint.x - anchorpoint.x;
      height = drawtopoint.y - anchorpoint.y;
   }
   repaint();
   return true;
}


// MOUSE SUPPORT:
// The mouseDrag() method is called if the mouse cursor moves over the
// applet's portion of the screen while the mouse button is being held down.
//-------------------------------------------------------------------------
public boolean mouseDrag(Event evt, int x, int y)
{
   if(drawboolean){
      points[currentpoint++] = new Point(x, y);
      repaint();
   }
   return true;
}


// MOUSE SUPPORT:
// The mouseMove() method is called if the mouse cursor moves over the
// applet's portion of the screen and the mouse button isn't being held down.
//-------------------------------------------------------------------------
public boolean mouseMove(Event evt, int x, int y)
{
```

```
    // TODO: Place applet mouseMove code here
    return true;
}


// TODO: Place additional applet code here

void setallfalse()
{
    mousedownboolean = false;
    mouseupboolean = false;
    drawboolean = false;
    lineboolean = false;
    ovalboolean = false;
    rectboolean = false;
    roundedboolean = false;
}
}
```

What's Next?

That's it for our coverage of the basics of graphics handling in Java. We've come far in this chapter, from using the mouse to drawing circles, lines, ovals, rounded rectangles, and even drawing freehand. Let's turn now to another powerful graphics topic—handling images.

CHAPTER
TEN

10

Image Handling

- ■ Creating the image doubler applet

- ■ Using image maps

- ■ Handling fonts

- ■ Reading from the keyboard

- ■ Selecting fonts and font types

- ■ Using the `FontMetrics` class

- ■ Working with pixel arrays

In this chapter, we're going to examine the ins and outs of Java image handling. As you can imagine, with so much of Java being targeted at Web browsers, image handling is a popular topic. In this chapter, you'll see how to read images into an applet, display them, and stretch them to new shapes. You'll also see how to support *image* maps—those clickable images you see on the Web—how to handle fonts, and even how to load images into an array of pixels so that you can work pixel by pixel if you want. Let's start with our first example, which will read in an image and stretch it as we direct.

The Image Doubler Applet

We'll start our image-handling discussion with a simple applet that reads in an image and displays it:

When the user clicks in the applet, we can double the x and y dimensions of the image, stretching it to four times its original area:

And this process can continue as we double the horizontal and vertical size of the image each time the user clicks in the applet:

Let's see how this works now. Create a new applet with the Applet Wizard named doubler, and give this applet support for the mouseDown event. In this applet, we'll read in a graphics figure and double it in horizontal and vertical dimensions each time the user clicks in the applet. We'll use the image that appears in Figure 10.1, which we'll name figure.jpg.

FIGURE 10.1:

This image will be stretched by the doubler applet.

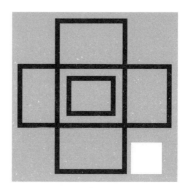

TIP   Although we are using a `.jpg` image file here, you can read both `.jpg`, and `.gif` files into Java applets.

Create this applet now and open the `doubler` class:

```
public class doubler extends Applet
{   .
        .
        .
```

We'll need some way to store the image after we read it in, and we can do that in a Java `Image` object that we will name `doublerimage`:

```
public class doubler extends Applet
{
➜    Image doublerimage;
        .
        .
        .
```

We'll use this class throughout this chapter, because it provides Java's support for image handling. The `Image` class's methods appear in Table 10.1.

TABLE 10.1: The `Image` Class's Methods

Method	Does This
`Image()`	Constructs a new `Image` object
`flush()`	Flushes resources of this `Image` object
`getGraphics()`	Gets a `Graphics` object for this image
`getHeight(ImageObserver)`	Gets the height of the image in pixels
`getProperty(String, ImageObserver)`	Gets a property of the image
`getSource()`	Gets the object that actually produces the image's pixels
`getWidth(ImageObserver)`	Gets the width of the image in pixels

Now we have the file we want to read in, `figure.jpg`, and we've declared the `Image` object we'll store that image in, `doublerimage`. The next step is to read in that image, and you do that with the Java Applet class method `getImage()`. One way to use `getImage()` is to pass an object of the Java `URL` class to `getImage()`, which specifies the URL (Uniform Resource Locator) of the image to read in. The `URL` class holds only URLs, and its methods appear in Table 10.2. If you know the URL of an image, you can create a `URL` object like this:

```
url = new URL("http://www.sybex.com");
```

Another way of using the `getImage()` method is to pass the URL of the directory containing the image and the name of the image file like this:

```
getImage(url, "figure.jpg");
```

TABLE 10.2: The URL Class's Methods

Method	Does This
`URL(String, String, int, String)`	Create URL from given protocol, host, port, and file
`URL(String, String, String)`	Creates absolute URL from given protocol, host, and file
`URL(String)`	Creates URL from this URL string
`equals(Object)`	Compares two URL objects and returns TRUE if they are the same
`getContent()`	Gets contents from connection
`getFile()`	Gets filename from URL
`getHost()`	Gets host name from URL
`getPort()`	Gets port number from URL
`getProtocol()`	Gets protocol name of this URL
`hashCode()`	Gets hash table indexing
`openConnection()`	Creates a URLConnection object (contains a connection to the URL)
`openStream()`	Opens an input stream for this URL
`sameFile(URL)`	Compares two URLs
`set(String, String, int, String, String)`	Sets fields of the object
`toExternalForm()`	Reverses the parsing of URL object
`toString()`	Converts the URL to a string

In our case, we'll assume that the figure is in the same directory as the file `doubler.class`, and we'll use the handy Applet method `getCodeBase()`. This method returns the URL of the `.class` file we are executing, and that means we can read in our image this way in the applet's `init()` method:

```
public void init()
{
    // If you use a ResourceWizard-generated "control creator" class to
    // arrange controls in your applet, you may want to call its
    // CreateControls() method from within this method. Remove the following
    // call to resize() before adding the call to CreateControls();
    // CreateControls() does its own resizing.
    //--------------------------------------------------------------------
    resize(320, 240);

    doublerimage = getImage(getCodeBase(), "figure.jpg");
            .
            .
            .
```

This code reads the image into our applet and stores it in the `Image` object `doublerimage`.

> **NOTE**
> It usually takes a while to read in an image, so you shouldn't assume that it is available as soon as you've executed the `getImage()` method. If it's important that the image be present before you continue with your applet (for example, if your code depends on finding the width and height of images the user specifies by filename), you can use the Java `MediaTracker` class to wait until the image is read in. We'll use the `MediaTracker` class later in this chapter.

We will display this image starting at a certain location (10, 10) in the applet, and we can refer to this location as the anchor point, because it won't change even when the image is stretched:

```
                        ---------------------------------------------
   anchorpoint ----> --------                                       |
                    |  |        |                                   |
                    |  |        |                                   |
                    |  |        |                                   |
                    |   --------                                    |
                    |                                               |
                    |                                               |
                    |                                               |
                    |                                               |
                    |                                               |
                    |                                               |
                        ---------------------------------------------
```

We set up the anchor point like this:

```
public class doubler extends Applet
{
    Image doublerimage;
→   Point anchorpoint;
        .

        .

        .
```

And we create that new point in the init() method:

```
public void init()
{
    // If you use a ResourceWizard-generated "control creator" class to
    // arrange controls in your applet, you may want to call its
    // CreateControls() method from within this method. Remove the following
    // call to resize() before adding the call to CreateControls();
    // CreateControls() does its own resizing.
    //------------------------------------------------------------------------
    resize(320, 240);

    doublerimage = getImage(getCodeBase(), "figure.jpg");
→   anchorpoint = new Point(10, 10);
        .

        .

        .

}
```

In addition, we'll need to track the image's new height and width as we stretch it, so we add two new integers, `height` and `width`:

```
public class doubler extends Applet
{
    Image doublerimage;
    Point anchorpoint;
→   int width, height;
        .
        .
        .
```

We give our image an initial size of 30×30 pixels this way:

```
public void init()
{
  // If you use a ResourceWizard-generated "control creator" class to
  // arrange controls in your applet, you may want to call its
  // CreateControls() method from within this method. Remove the following
  // call to resize() before adding the call to CreateControls();
  // CreateControls() does its own resizing.
  //-------------------------------------------------------------------
  resize(320, 240);

  doublerimage = getImage(getCodeBase(), "figure.jpg");
  anchorpoint = new Point(10, 10);
→ width = 30;
→ height = 30;
}
```

Next, we display the image. To do this, we use the `Graphics` class `drawImage()` method. We'll need a `Graphics` object corresponding to our applet's display, so we'll add this code to the `paint()` method. First, we draw a rectangle to frame the image with the `drawRect()` method. We pass the coordinates of the upper left of the rectangle we want—the anchor point—and the width and height of the bounding rectangle this way:

```
public void paint(Graphics g)
{
```

→ `g.drawRect(anchorpoint.x, anchorpoint.y, width, height);`

.

.

.

}

Now we display the image itself from the `doublerimage` object with the `drawImage()` method. We pass this method the following parameters: the image object `doublerimage`, the coordinates at which our image is supposed to be drawn in the applet, with width and height of the image, and a `this` keyword. The last argument is actually supposed to be an object of the Java `ImageObserver` class, which is how Java oversees the process of loading in images (if the image is not found, an error is generated, and we can inform the user), and by passing a `this` pointer, we use the default `ImageObserver` object for our applet:

```
public void paint(Graphics g)
{
    g.drawRect(anchorpoint.x, anchorpoint.y, width, height);
→   g.drawImage(doublerimage, anchorpoint.x, anchorpoint.y,
➥   width, height, this);
}
```

At this point, then, our applet draws the `figure.jpg` image on the screen, making it 30 pixels × 30 pixels:

A small version of our image is now on the screen. We can stretch it easily, just by specifying a new width and height for the image in the `drawImage()` method:

```java
public void paint(Graphics g)
{
    g.drawRect(anchorpoint.x, anchorpoint.y, width, height);
    g.drawImage(doublerimage, anchorpoint.x, anchorpoint.y,
    width, height, this);
}
```

We'll double the height and width of the image when the user clicks in the applet. Open the `mouseDown()` method now:

```java
// MOUSE SUPPORT:
//   The mouseDown() method is called if the mouse button is pressed
// while the mouse cursor is over the applet's portion of the screen.
//-----------------------------------------------------------------------
public boolean mouseDown(Event evt, int x, int y)
{
    // TODO: Place applet mouseDown code here
    return true;
}
```

When the user clicks in the applet, we simply multiply the values in the *width* and *height* variables by 2 and repaint the applet this way:

```java
// MOUSE SUPPORT:
//   The mouseDown() method is called if the mouse button is pressed
// while the mouse cursor is over the applet's portion of the screen.
//-----------------------------------------------------------------------
public boolean mouseDown(Event evt, int x, int y)
{
    width *= 2;
    height *= 2;
    repaint();

    return true;
}
```

> **NOTE**
>
> We use the C++ syntax here to double a value: `width *= 2;`. If you're not familiar with this usage, it is just the same as `width = width * 2;`. Java allows you to use this C++ shortcut with most numeric operators, for example, `*=`, `+=`, `-=`, and `/=`.

When we repaint the image, its height and width will both have doubled to 60 pixels. Run this applet now, as shown in Figure 10.2. You can see our image in the applet, although that image is quite small.

FIGURE 10.2:

Our doubler applet will double this image in size.

Double-click on the applet now, multiplying the width and height of the image by four. The results appear in Figure 10.3. Our doubler applet is a success. We've been able to read in an image, display it, and stretch it. The code for this applet appears in `doubler.java`.

FIGURE 10.3:

Our doubler applet has quadrupled this image's height and width.

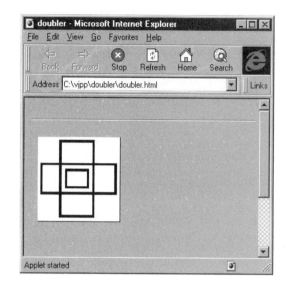

doubler.java

```
//****************************************************************************
// doubler.java:  Applet
//
//****************************************************************************
import java.applet.*;
import java.awt.*;
import java.lang.Math;


//============================================================================
// Main Class for applet doubler
//
//============================================================================
public class doubler extends Applet
{
   Image doublerimage;
   Point anchorpoint;
   int width, height;

   // doubler Class Constructor
   //-------------------------------------------------------------------------
```

```
public doubler()
{
  // TODO: Add constructor code here
}

// APPLET INFO SUPPORT:
//   The getAppletInfo() method returns a string describing the applet's
// author, copyright date, or miscellaneous information.
//-------------------------------------------------------------------
public String getAppletInfo()
{
  return "Name: doubler\r\n" +
       "Author: Steven Holzner\r\n" +
       "Created with Microsoft Visual J++ Version 1.0";
}


// The init() method is called by the AWT when an applet is first loaded or
// reloaded.  Override this method to perform whatever initialization your
// applet needs, such as initializing data structures, loading images or
// fonts, creating frame windows, setting the layout manager, or adding UI
// components.
//-------------------------------------------------------------------
public void init()
{
  // If you use a ResourceWizard-generated "control creator" class to
  // arrange controls in your applet, you may want to call its
  // CreateControls() method from within this method. Remove the following
  // call to resize() before adding the call to CreateControls();
  // CreateControls() does its own resizing.
  //-------------------------------------------------------------------
  resize(320, 240);

  doublerimage = getImage(getCodeBase(), "figure.jpg");
  anchorpoint = new Point(10, 10);
  width = 30;
  height = 30;
}

// Place additional applet clean up code here.  destroy() is called
// when your applet is terminating and being unloaded.
//-------------------------------------------------------------------
```

```
public void destroy()
{
  // TODO: Place applet cleanup code here
}

// doubler Paint Handler
//--------------------------------------------------------------------------
public void paint(Graphics g)
{
  g.drawRect(anchorpoint.x, anchorpoint.y, width, height);
  g.drawImage(doublerimage, anchorpoint.x, anchorpoint.y, width, height,
    ➥ this);
}

//   The start() method is called when the page containing the applet
// first appears on the screen. The AppletWizard's initial implementation
// of this method starts execution of the applet's thread.
//--------------------------------------------------------------------------
public void start()
{
  // TODO: Place additional applet start code here
}

//   The stop() method is called when the page containing the applet is
// no longer on the screen. The AppletWizard's initial implementation of
// this method stops execution of the applet's thread.
//--------------------------------------------------------------------------
public void stop()
{
}


// MOUSE SUPPORT:
//   The mouseDown() method is called if the mouse button is pressed
// while the mouse cursor is over the applet's portion of the screen.
//--------------------------------------------------------------------------
public boolean mouseDown(Event evt, int x, int y)
{
  width *= 2;
  height *= 2;
  repaint();

  return true;
```

```
    }

    // MOUSE SUPPORT:
    //   The mouseUp() method is called if the mouse button is released
    // while the mouse cursor is over the applet's portion of the screen.
    //----------------------------------------------------------------------
    public boolean mouseUp(Event evt, int x, int y)
    {

        return true;
    }


    // TODO: Place additional applet code here

}
```

Now that you've seen how to load an image in, let's take a look at how to "interact" with an image. In this case, you'll see how to support image maps, those clickable maps you see on the World Wide Web.

Image Maps

An image map is an image on which you can click to cause the Web browser to move to a new URL. An image map might have several active areas:

```
----------------------------------------------------
|                                                   |
|                                   ---------       |
|               ---------          | Click Me |     |
|              | Click Me |         ---------        |
|               ---------                           |
|                                                   |
|                                                   |
|                                   ---------        |
|                                  | Click Me |      |
|                                   ---------        |
|                                                   |
|                                                   |
----------------------------------------------------
```

When the user clicks on one of these areas, the Web browser displays the home page of a new URL. The image map we will use in this example, named `map.jpg`, appears in Figure 10.4, and has hyperlinks to Sybex, Sun, and Microsoft. When the user clicks on one of those labeled rectangles, the Web browser opens the appropriate URL.

FIGURE 10.4:

Our image map

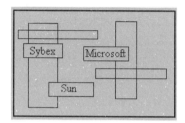

Let's begin this example now. Create a new applet with the Visual J++ Applet Wizard and call it imagemap. Be sure this applet has `mouseDown()` support. We'll need a place to store our image after we load it in and before displaying it, so we create a new `Image` object named `image`:

```
public class imagemap extends Applet
{
➜   Image image;
        .
        .
        .
```

We load our image map from the file `map.jpg` and store it in the object named `image` in the `init()` method:

```
public void init()
{
    // If you use a ResourceWizard-generated "control creator" class to
    // arrange controls in your applet, you may want to call its
    // CreateControls() method from within this method. Remove the following
    // call to resize() before adding the call to CreateControls();
    // CreateControls() does its own resizing.
    //------------------------------------------------------------------------
```

```
   resize(320, 240);

→  image = getImage(getCodeBase(), "map.jpg");
}
```

Next, we display the image in our applet:

```
// imagemap Paint Handler
//--------------------------------------------------------------------------
public void paint(Graphics g)
{
→  g.drawImage(image, 10, 10, 240, 155, this);
}
```

Although the image is displayed, it's still just a part of our applet, so the normal `mouseDown` and `mouseUp` events will occur even when we click on the image. That's the key to Java image maps—you simply find the location that the user clicked in an applet to see if the click occurred in an active area.

To add mouse support to our applet, open the `mouseDown()` method now:

```
// MOUSE SUPPORT:
//   The mouseDown() method is called if the mouse button is pressed
// while the mouse cursor is over the applet's portion of the screen.
//--------------------------------------------------------------------------
public boolean mouseDown(Event evt, int x, int y)
{
   // TODO: Place applet mouseDown code here
   return true;
}
```

To add mouse support, you have to know which regions of the image map to make active. You can do that with the Visual J++ Bitmap Editor.

To edit `map.jpg` in the Visual J++ Bitmap Editor, add `map.jpg` to the imagemap applet now. Choose Insert ➤ Files into Project, and then double-click on the `map.jpg` entry in the Project Workspace window to open `map.jpg`, as shown in Figure 10.5.

FIGURE 10.5:

Mapping out our
image map

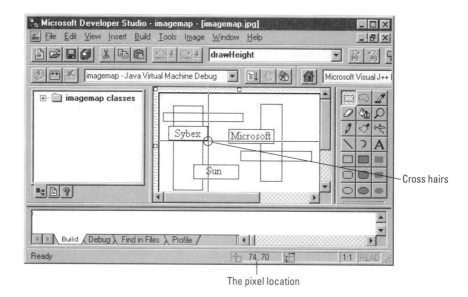

When you move the mouse over the image, the Bitmap Editor shows
you where you are with a set of cross hairs, as shown in Figure 10.5.
You can read the pixel location of the mouse at the lower right, as also
shown in Figure 10.5. In this way, you can find the pixel coordinates of
each area you want to make active in the image map.

You can check to see if the mouse was clicked in the first of these
areas, the Sybex hyperlink, in the mouseDown() method, where we
compare the mouse location passed to us in the x and y parameters
with the Sybex hyperlink's coordinates:

```
// MOUSE SUPPORT:
//   The mouseDown() method is called if the mouse button is pressed
// while the mouse cursor is over the applet's portion of the screen.
//----------------------------------------------------------------------
public boolean mouseDown(Event evt, int x, int y)
{

    if(x > 17 && x < 72 && y > 50 && y < 70){
        .
        .
        .
    }
}
```

Here, && is the Java logical AND operator, which means that we are requiring x > 17 AND x < 72 AND y > 50 AND y < 70 to be TRUE.

> **TIP**
>
> Java has other logical operators. The || operator ORs a number of boolean values together, and the result is TRUE if any of the values are true. There are also the binary (bit-by-bit numeric) operators &, |, and ^ (XOR). The other common boolean operator is the NOT operator, !, which toggles a boolean: if booleanvalue is TRUE, then !booleanvalue is FALSE.

In fact, this is not quite right, because these are the coordinates of the Sybex hyperlink in the image map, but we started the image map at the location (10, 10) in the paint method:

```
// imagemap Paint Handler
//-------------------------------------------------------------
public void paint(Graphics g)
{
➡    g.drawImage(image, 10, 10, 240, 155, this);
}
```

We must therefore add 10 to each coordinate measurement like this:

```
// MOUSE SUPPORT:
//  The mouseDown() method is called if the mouse button is pressed
// while the mouse cursor is over the applet's portion of the screen.
//-------------------------------------------------------------
public boolean mouseDown(Event evt, int x, int y)
{

➡    if(x > 17 + 10 && x < 72 + 10 && y > 50 + 10 && y < 70 + 10){
         .
         .
         .
```

When the user clicks on the Sybex hyperlink, we want the Web browser to navigate to the Sybex web site, http://www.sybex.com. To do that, we'll need a new URL class object representing this URL.

We can declare a new URL object named `url` and set it to `http://www.sybex.com` like this (import `java.net.*` to get the URL class):

```
// MOUSE SUPPORT:
//   The mouseDown() method is called if the mouse button is pressed
// while the mouse cursor is over the applet's portion of the screen.
//-------------------------------------------------------------------
public boolean mouseDown(Event evt, int x, int y)
{
➜   URL url = null;

    if(x > 17 + 10 && x < 72 + 10 && y > 50 + 10 && y < 70 + 10){
➜   try {url = new URL("http://www.sybex.com");}
➜   catch (MalformedURLException exp1) {}
        .
        .
        .
```

Note the `try` and `catch` keywords here. These keywords catch Java *exceptions*, which represent error conditions (you'll see more about Java exceptions in Chapter 13, *Java Exceptions and Visual J++ Debugging*). Because loading a new URL is an operation that is subject to many errors, Visual J++ requires that you enclose this operation in a `try...catch` block.

Now that we have our new URL object, we can use the Web browser to navigate to that URL. To do so, you work with the Web browser itself, which is called the applet's *context*. Here, we'll use the Applet class's `getAppletContext()` method to reach the Web browser, and we'll use the context's `showDocument()` method to open the new URL:

```
// MOUSE SUPPORT:
//   The mouseDown() method is called if the mouse button is pressed
// while the mouse cursor is over the applet's portion of the screen.
//-------------------------------------------------------------------
public boolean mouseDown(Event evt, int x, int y)
{
    URL url = null;

    if(x > 17 + 10 && x < 72 + 10 && y > 50 + 10 && y < 70 + 10){
```

```
    try {url = new URL("http://www.sybex.com");}
    catch (MalformedURLException exp1) {}
→   getAppletContext().showDocument(url);
  }     .
        .
        .
```

Now that we've opened the new URL, we can check for the other active spots in our image map, adding them to our applet like this:

```
// MOUSE SUPPORT:
//   The mouseDown() method is called if the mouse button is pressed
// while the mouse cursor is over the applet's portion of the screen.
//------------------------------------------------------------------------
public boolean mouseDown(Event evt, int x, int y)
{
    URL url = null;

    if(x > 17 + 10 && x < 72 + 10 && y > 50 + 10 && y < 70 + 10){
        try {url = new URL("http://www.sybex.com");}
        catch (MalformedURLException exp1) {}
        getAppletContext().showDocument(url);
    }

→   if(x > 53 + 10 && x < 120 + 10 && y > 104 + 10 && y < 125 + 10){
→       try {url = new URL("http://www.sun.com");}
→       catch (MalformedURLException exp2) {}
→       getAppletContext().showDocument(url);
→   }

→   if(x > 105 + 10 && x < 171 + 10 && y > 54 + 10 && y < 74 + 10){
→       try {url = new URL("http://www.microsoft.com");}
→       catch (MalformedURLException exp3) {}
→   getAppletContext().showDocument(url);
→   }
    return true;
  }
```

The imagemap applet is ready to go. Run it now, as shown in Figure 10.6, and click on one of the active areas. Your Web browser navigates to the corresponding URL. The imagemap applet is a success. The code for this applet appears in `imagemap.java`.

FIGURE 10.6:

Our image map at work

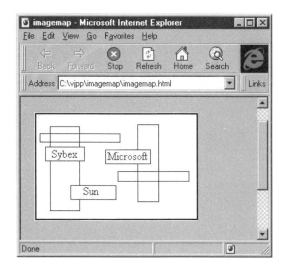

TIP

If you want to show the user which hyperlink the mouse cursor is over in your image map, you can use the `mouseMove()` method to track the mouse movements, reporting back to the user in a `Label` control.

imagemap.java

```
//*****************************************************************************
// imagemap.java: Applet
//
//*****************************************************************************
import java.applet.*;
import java.awt.*;
import java.net.*;


//=============================================================================
// Main Class for applet imagemap
//
```

```
//==============================================================================
public class imagemap extends Applet
{

   Image image;

   // imagemap Class Constructor
   //--------------------------------------------------------------------------
   public imagemap()
   {
      // TODO: Add constructor code here
   }

   // APPLET INFO SUPPORT:
   //   The getAppletInfo() method returns a string describing the applet's
   // author, copyright date, or miscellaneous information.
   //--------------------------------------------------------------------------
   public String getAppletInfo()
   {
      return "Name: imagemap\r\n" +
            "Author: Steven Holzner\r\n" +
            "Created with Microsoft Visual J++ Version 1.0";
   }


   // The init() method is called by the AWT when an applet is first loaded or
   // reloaded.  Override this method to perform whatever initialization your
   // applet needs, such as initializing data structures, loading images or
   // fonts, creating frame windows, setting the layout manager, or adding UI
   // components.
   //--------------------------------------------------------------------------
   public void init()
   {
      // If you use a ResourceWizard-generated "control creator" class to
      // arrange controls in your applet, you may want to call its
      // CreateControls() method from within this method. Remove the following
      // call to resize() before adding the call to CreateControls();
      // CreateControls() does its own resizing.
      //-----------------------------------------------------------------------

      resize(320, 240);

      image = getImage(getCodeBase(), "map.jpg");
```

```
}

// Place additional applet clean up code here.  destroy() is called
// when your applet is terminating and being unloaded.
//-------------------------------------------------------------------------
public void destroy()
{
   // TODO: Place applet cleanup code here
}

// imagemap Paint Handler
//-------------------------------------------------------------------------
public void paint(Graphics g)
{
   g.drawImage(image, 10, 10, 240, 155, this);
}

//   The start() method is called when the page containing the applet
// first appears on the screen. The AppletWizard's initial implementation
// of this method starts execution of the applet's thread.
//-------------------------------------------------------------------------
public void start()
{
   // TODO: Place additional applet start code here
}

//   The stop() method is called when the page containing the applet is
// no longer on the screen. The AppletWizard's initial implementation of
// this method stops execution of the applet's thread.
//-------------------------------------------------------------------------
public void stop()
{
}


// MOUSE SUPPORT:
//   The mouseDown() method is called if the mouse button is pressed
// while the mouse cursor is over the applet's portion of the screen.
//-------------------------------------------------------------------------
public boolean mouseDown(Event evt, int x, int y)
{
```

```
  URL url = null;

    if(x > 17 + 10 && x < 72 + 10 && y > 50 + 10 && y < 70 + 10){
      try {url = new URL("http://www.sybex.com");}
      catch (MalformedURLException exp1) {}
      getAppletContext().showDocument(url);
    }

     if(x > 53 + 10 && x < 120 + 10 && y > 104 + 10 && y < 125 + 10){
      try {url = new URL("http://www.sun.com");}
      catch (MalformedURLException exp2) {}
      getAppletContext().showDocument(url);
    }

    if(x > 105 + 10 && x < 171 + 10 && y > 54 + 10 && y < 74 + 10){
      try {url = new URL("http://www.microsoft.com");}
      catch (MalformedURLException exp3) {}
      getAppletContext().showDocument(url);
    }
    return true;
}

// MOUSE SUPPORT:
//   The mouseUp() method is called if the mouse button is released
// while the mouse cursor is over the applet's portion of the screen.
//---------------------------------------------------------------------------
public boolean mouseUp(Event evt, int x, int y)
{
  // TODO: Place applet mouseUp code here
  return true;
}

// MOUSE SUPPORT:
//   The mouseDrag() method is called if the mouse cursor moves over the
// applet's portion of the screen while the mouse button is being held down.
//---------------------------------------------------------------------------
public boolean mouseDrag(Event evt, int x, int y)
{
  // TODO: Place applet mouseDrag code here
  return true;
}

// MOUSE SUPPORT:
```

```
//   The mouseMove() method is called if the mouse cursor moves over the
// applet's portion of the screen and the mouse button isn't being held down.
//-------------------------------------------------------------------------
public boolean mouseMove(Event evt, int x, int y)
{
   // TODO: Place applet mouseMove code here
   return true;
}


// MOUSE SUPPORT:
//   The mouseEnter() method is called if the mouse cursor enters the
// applet's portion of the screen.
//-------------------------------------------------------------------------
public boolean mouseEnter(Event evt, int x, int y)
{
   // TODO: Place applet mouseEnter code here
   return true;
}


// MOUSE SUPPORT:
//   The mouseExit() method is called if the mouse cursor leaves the
// applet's portion of the screen.
//-------------------------------------------------------------------------
public boolean mouseExit(Event evt, int x, int y)
{
   // TODO: Place applet mouseExit code here
   return true;
}



// TODO: Place additional applet code here

}
```

Handling Fonts

You may be surprised to find font handling in a graphics chapter, but characters are graphics too, although we don't usually think of them that way. You haven't yet seen how to handle fonts in Java, and this is an appropriate time. For example, you might write an applet, called fonts, that presents the user with a series of buttons representing various formatting options, such as italics and bold, and even font choices, such as Roman or Courier:

```
---------------------------------------------------------------
|                                                             |
|  ------     --------    -------    -------    ---------    -------  |
| | bold |   | italic |  | large |  | roman |  | courier |  | clear | |
|  ------     --------    -------    -------    ---------    -------  |
|                                                             |
|                                                             |
|                                                             |
|                                                             |
|                                                             |
|                                                             |
|                                                             |
---------------------------------------------------------------
```

After the user selects font options, he or she can type text. We'll read it directly from the keyboard (in the keyDown() method), displaying it in our applet as a centered string of text in the font and with the formatting options the user wants:

```
---------------------------------------------------------------
|                                                             |
|  ------     --------    -------    -------    ---------    -------  |
| | bold |   | italic |  | large |  | roman |  | courier |  | clear | |
|  ------     --------    -------    -------    ---------    -------  |
|                                                             |
|                                                             |
|                This is centered text                        |
|                                                             |
|                                                             |
|                                                             |
|                                                             |
---------------------------------------------------------------
```

Let's start this applet now. Create the new applet named fonts with the Applet Wizard, and open the new fonts class. We'll start by setting up the buttons in our applet. There are six buttons, and we name them after their function: boldbutton (makes the text bold), italicbutton (makes the text italic), buttonlarge (sets the font to a large type size), romanbutton (switches to the Roman font), courierbutton (switches to the Courier font), and clearbutton (clears the text string). We add those buttons now:

```
public class fonts extends Applet
{
➜   Button boldbutton, italicbutton, buttonlarge;
➜   Button romanbutton, courierbutton, clearbutton;
         .
         .
         .
```

Next, we create those buttons in the init() function and add them to our applet's layout:

```
public void init()
{
    // If you use a ResourceWizard-generated "control creator" class to
    // arrange controls in your applet, you may want to call its
    // CreateControls() method from within this method. Remove the following
    // call to resize() before adding the call to CreateControls();
    // CreateControls() does its own resizing.
    //-----------------------------------------------------------------------
    resize(320, 240);

➜   boldbutton = new Button("bold");
➜   italicbutton = new Button("italic");
➜   buttonlarge = new Button("large");
➜   romanbutton = new Button("roman");
➜   courierbutton = new Button("courier");
➜   clearbutton = new Button("clear");

➜   add(boldbutton);
➜   add(italicbutton);
➜   add(buttonlarge);
➜   add(romanbutton);
➜   add(courierbutton);
➜   add(clearbutton);
}
```

As in our artist applet, we set up a boolean flag for each button except the clear button (the clear button can clear the text string as soon as it is clicked; we do not have to wait for the `paint()` method to execute, as we do for the font settings):

```
public class fonts extends Applet
{
.  Button boldbutton, italicbutton, buttonlarge;
   Button romanbutton, courierbutton, clearbutton;
➜  boolean boldboolean = false;
➜  boolean italicboolean = false;
➜  boolean largeboolean = false;
➜  boolean romanboolean = true;
➜  boolean courierboolean = false;
      .
      .
      .
```

All our boolean flags are set to FALSE initially, except the flag `romanboolean`, since we will use Roman as our default font. To make these boolean flags active, we set up an `action()` method in the `fonts` class:

```
   public boolean action(Event e, Object o){
      .
      .
      .
   }
```

Let's handle the Bold button now. When the user clicks on this button, he or she wants the entered text to be boldface; so we could set the boolean flag `boldboolean` to TRUE. But if we do so, how will the user turn off boldface? It's better to *toggle* the bold setting on and off, and we do that with the negation operator (!). We simply reverse the setting of the `boldboolean` flag, like this:

```
public boolean action(Event e, Object o){
➜  if(e.target.equals(boldbutton)){
```

```
→    boldboolean = !boldboolean;
→  } .
     .
     .
```

The first three font settings—boldface, italics, and large— can be toggled on and off, and we set them up this way:

```
public boolean action(Event e, Object o){
  if(e.target.equals(boldbutton)){
    boldboolean = !boldboolean;
  }
→  if(e.target.equals(italicbutton)){
→    italicboolean = !italicboolean;
→  }
→  if(e.target.equals(buttonlarge)){
→    largeboolean = !largeboolean;
→  }
     .
     .
     .
```

If the user clicks on a Roman button or a Courier button, however, we can't simply toggle a boolean flag. There are two fontname flags: romanboolean and courierboolean. Since only one can be true at a time, when we set one to TRUE, we must set the other to FALSE:

```
public boolean action(Event e, Object o){
if(e.target.equals(boldbutton)){
  boldboolean = !boldboolean;
}    .
     .
     .

→  if(e.target.equals(romanbutton)){
→    romanboolean = true;
→    courierboolean = false;
→  }
→  if(e.target.equals(courierbutton)){
→    courierboolean = true;
```

```
→      romanboolean = false;
→   }      .
              .
              .
              .
    }
```

And that's almost it. All that remains is to activate the Clear button, on which the user clicks to clear text. We can store that text in a String object named text:

```
public class fonts extends Applet
{
→   String text = "";
    Button boldbutton, italicbutton, buttonlarge;
    Button romanbutton, courierbutton, clearbutton;
    boolean boldboolean = false;
    boolean italicboolean = false;
    boolean largeboolean = false;
    boolean romanboolean = true;
    boolean courierboolean = false;
       .
       .
       .
```

And we clear that object simply by setting it to a null or empty string (using "") when the user clicks on the Clear button:

```
public boolean action(Event e, Object o){
   if(e.target.equals(boldbutton)){
     boldboolean = !boldboolean;
   }    .
           .
           .
→   if(e.target.equals(clearbutton)){
→      text = "";
→   }

    repaint();
    return true;
}
```

We also include a call to `repaint()` at the end of the `action` method so that the user can immediately see the result of clicking on a button, without having to wait for the new key to be pressed. And that brings us to the question: How do you read direct keyboard input in Java?

Reading from the Keyboard in Java

So far, we've used text fields to handle keyboard input. It is possible, however, to read keys directly in Java using a `keyDown()` method. Add that method to our `fonts` class now:

```
public boolean keyDown(Event e, int k){

}
```

TIP Besides `keyDown`, Java also has a `keyUp` event. The `keyUp()` method has the same arguments as `keyDown()`.

We are passed two parameters in `keyDown()`—an `Event` object and an integer. The integer represents the key itself, and we can add that new key to our `String` object `text` like this, where we use a cast of the character type, `char`:

```
public boolean keyDown(Event e, int k){
   text = text + (char)k;
     .
     .
     .
}
```

> **NOTE**
>
> Unless you are familiar with C++, you may be surprised to see a line like `text = text + (char)k;`, because text is an object of the Java `String` class. In Java, as in C++, operators such as the + operator can be overloaded to work with objects of various classes, and the + operator is overloaded to work with `String` objects.

Now that we've stored the newly pressed character, we can display it on the screen by calling `repaint()`, because all the graphics, as usual, are in the `paint()` method:

```
public boolean keyDown(Event e, int k){
   text = text + (char)k;
➜   repaint();
   return true;
}
```

Let's write our `paint()` method now, because that's where the guts of this applet are.

Selecting Fonts and Font Types

When we enter the `paint()` method, we already have a string of text—that is, the `String` object named text—to display. Our goal is to display that text using the font settings the user has indicated—which are now mirrored in the settings of our boolean flags—so that it appears centered in our applet:

```
-------------------------------------------------------------
|                                                           |
|  ------    --------    -------    -------   ---------   -------   |
| | bold |  | italic |  | large |  | roman | | courier | | clear | |
|  ------    --------    -------    -------   ---------   -------   |
|                                                           |
|                                                           |
|               This is centered text                       |
|                                                           |
|                                                           |
|                                                           |
|                                                           |
|                                                           |
-------------------------------------------------------------
```

In the `paint()` method, then, we'll set up the type, size, and actual typeface of the font we will use to display the characters in the text object, and we'll set up an object of class `Font` with this information. We then simply install that `Font` object in the `Graphics` object passed to us in `paint()` and draw our string.

We start our `paint()` method by setting up the variables we'll need and setting their default values. For example, the name of the font we'll use is stored as a string, and our default will be Roman:

```
     public void paint(Graphics g)
     {
→        String fontname = "Roman";
            .
            .
            .
```

The type of font—plain, bold, or italic—is set up in an integer variable that can take one of the following predefined `Font` class constants: `Font.PLAIN`, `Font.BOLD`, `Font.ITALIC`. Our default will be plain text, `Font.PLAIN`:

```
public void paint(Graphics g)
{
   String fontname = "Roman";
→  int type = Font.PLAIN;
      .
      .
      .
```

The point size of the font is also stored as an integer. Our default will be 24 point:

```
public void paint(Graphics g)
{
   String fontname = "Roman";
   int type = Font.PLAIN;
→  int size = 24;
      .
      .
      .
```

We've set up the default values for our font. Next, we create the `font` object itself that we will load into the `Graphics` object we get passed to us in the `paint()` method:

```
public void paint(Graphics g)
{
   String fontname = "Roman";
   int type = Font.PLAIN;
   int size = 24;
→  Font font;
      .
      .
      .
```

The methods of the Java `Font` class appear in Table 10.3.

TABLE 10.3: The Font Class's Methods

Method	Does This
Font(String, int, int)	Creates font object with given name, style (Font.BOLD, Font.PLAIN, or Font.ITALIC), and point size
equals(Object)	Compares font to specified font
getFamily()	Gets family name of font
getFont(String)	Gets a font from the system properties list
getFont(String, Font)	Gets given font from system properties list
getName()	Gets logical name of font
getSize()	Gets point size of font
getStyle()	Gets font style
hashCode()	Gets the font hashcode
isBold()	Returns TRUE if font is bold
isItalic()	Returns TRUE if font is italic
isPlain()	Returns TRUE if font is plain
toString()	Converts font to a string

The next step is to set up the three variables *fontname*, *type*, and *size* according to how the user wants them so that they can be used to set up the Font object. To do that, we check the various boolean flags we have set up and set these three variables accordingly:

```
public void paint(Graphics g)
{
    String fontname = "Roman";
    int type = Font.PLAIN;
    int size = 24;
    Font font;

➜   if(boldboolean){
➜       type = type | Font.BOLD;
➜   }
```

```
→   if(italicboolean){
→       type = type | Font.ITALIC;
→   }
→   if(largeboolean){
→       size = 48;
→   }
→   if(romanboolean){
→       fontname = "Roman";
→   }
→   if(courierboolean){
→       fontname = "Courier";
→   }      .
                .
                .
```

> **TIP**
>
> Since text can be italic and bold at the same time, you can use the OR operator, |, to combine font types. For example, valid font types include: `Font.PLAIN` | `Font.ITALIC` or `Font.BOLD` | `Font.ITALIC`.

At this point, then, we have the font's name, its size, and its type (that is, plain or bold, italic or not). We create the `Font` object now and install it in our `Graphics` object using the `setFont()` method:

```
public void paint(Graphics g)
{
    String fontname = "Roman";
    int type = Font.PLAIN;
    int size = 24;
    Font font;

    if(boldboolean){
        type = type | Font.BOLD;
    }    .
             .
             .
→   font = new Font(fontname, type, size);
→   g.setFont(font);
}
```

And that's it—the font the user selected, in the font style selected is now installed. When we draw text in the `Graphics` object with `drawString()`, the text will appear in this new font.

However, we wanted to do more—we wanted to make sure the text appears centered in the applet. We do that with a `FontMetrics` object.

The *FontMetrics* Class

To make sure our text string is centered in the applet, we have to know how much space the string will take up on the screen, both horizontally and vertically. We do that with a `FontMetrics` object (in addition, we'll have to find out how wide and tall our applet is in pixels, and you'll see how to do that here). First, we add a new `FontMetrics` object called `fontmetrics` to our applet:

```
public class fonts extends Applet
{
   String text = "";
   Button boldbutton, italicbutton, buttonlarge;
   Button romanbutton, courierbutton, clearbutton;
   boolean boldboolean = false;
   boolean italicboolean = false;
   boolean largeboolean = false;
   boolean romanboolean = true;
   boolean courierboolean = false;
→  FontMetrics fontmetrics;
      .
      .
      .
```

We then create this `FontMetrics` object, passing it the `font` object we have set up so that it will be able to return information about strings displayed in that font:

```
public void paint(Graphics g)
{
```

```
String fontname = "Roman";
int type = Font.PLAIN;
int size = 24;
Font font;
   .
   .
   .

font = new Font(fontname, type, size);
g.setFont(font);

➜   fontmetrics = getFontMetrics(font);
   .
   .
   .

}
```

The FontMetrics class's methods appear in Table 10.4.

TABLE 10.4: The FontMetrics Class's Methods

Method	Does This
FontMetrics(Font)	Creates a FontMetrics object using given font
bytesWidth(byte[], int, int)	Returns width of byte array
charWidth(int)	Gets width of given character
charWidth(char)	Gets width of given character
charsWidth(char[], int, int)	Gets width of character array
getAscent()	Gets font ascent
getDescent()	Gets font descent
getFont()	Gets the font
getHeight()	Gets total height of this font
getLeading()	Gets standard line spacing for font
getMaxAdvance()	Gets maximum advance width of any character
getMaxAscent()	Gets maximum ascent of characters
getMaxDescent()	Gets maximum descent of characters
getWidths()	Gets widths of first 256 characters
stringWidth(String)	Gets width of given String
toString()	Gets String representation for object

Now we can retrieve the width of the text this way:

```
width = fontmetrics.stringWidth(text);
```

and we can retrieve its height this way:

```
height = fontmetrics.getHeight();
```

(Note that the height of the line of text is a constant—not depending on string length—so we don't have to pass the line of text itself to the `getHeight()` method.)

We'll also need the height and width of our applet, and we'll find that with the Applet method `size()`, which returns an object of the Java `Dimension` class. The `width` and `height` members of this `Dimension` object will give us the width and height of our applet.

The last thing to keep in mind is that when we pass the location of a string to `drawString()` so that it can appear on the screen, the location we pass is actually the bottom left of the string on the screen—*not* the top left as many Windows programmers expect.

Putting all this together, we find the x and y location at which to print our string, making sure it is centered in the applet's display:

```
public void paint(Graphics g)
{
   String fontname = "Roman";
   int type = Font.PLAIN;
   int size = 24;
   Font font;
        .

        .

        .

   font = new Font(fontname, type, size);
   g.setFont(font);

   fontmetrics = getFontMetrics(font);
```

```
→   x = (size().width - fontmetrics.stringWidth(text)) / 2;
→   y = (size().height + fontmetrics.getHeight()) / 2;
            .
            .
            .

    }
```

We also need to declare the new integer variables *x* and *y*, which hold the location of the text string in the applet:

```
public class fonts extends Applet
{
    String text = "";
→   int x = 0;
→   int y = 0;
    Button boldbutton, italicbutton, buttonlarge;
    Button romanbutton, courierbutton, clearbutton;
    boolean boldboolean = false;
    boolean italicboolean = false;
    boolean largeboolean = false;
    boolean romanboolean = true;
    boolean courierboolean = false;
        .
        .
        .
```

All that remains now is to display the text string itself, and we do that with `drawString()`:

```
public void paint(Graphics g)
{
    String fontname = "Roman";
    int type = Font.PLAIN;
    int size = 24;
    Font font;
        .
        .
        .

    font = new Font(fontname, type, size);
    g.setFont(font);

    fontmetrics = getFontMetrics(font);
```

```
    x = (size().width - fontmetrics.stringWidth(text)) / 2;
    y = (size().height + fontmetrics.getHeight()) / 2;

➔   g.drawString(text, x, y);
    }
```

Run the applet now as shown in Figure 10.7. Select a few font options—in Figure 10.7, we've selected bold large italic font and typed a few characters. As you can see, our fonts applet is a success. The code for this applet appears in `fonts.java`.

FIGURE 10.7:

The fonts applet lets the user specify various font options.

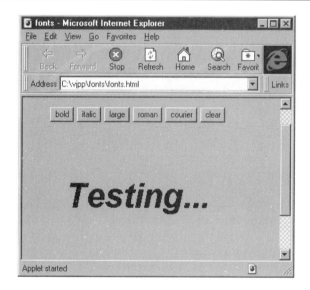

fonts.java

```
//*****************************************************************************
// fonts.java:  Applet
//
//*****************************************************************************
import java.applet.*;
import java.awt.*;


//=============================================================================
// Main Class for applet fonts
```

```
//
//==============================================================================
public class fonts extends Applet
{
   String text = "";
   int x = 0;
   int y = 0;
   Button boldbutton, italicbutton, buttonlarge;
   Button romanbutton, courierbutton, clearbutton;
   boolean boldboolean = false;
   boolean italicboolean = false;
   boolean largeboolean = false;
   boolean romanboolean = true;
   boolean courierboolean = false;
   FontMetrics fontmetrics;

   // fonts Class Constructor
   //--------------------------------------------------------------------
   public fonts()
   {
      // TODO: Add constructor code here
   }

   // APPLET INFO SUPPORT:
   //    The getAppletInfo() method returns a string describing the applet's
   // author, copyright date, or miscellaneous information.
   //--------------------------------------------------------------------
   public String getAppletInfo()
   {
      return "Name: fonts\r\n" +
            "Author: Steven Holzner\r\n" +
            "Created with Microsoft Visual J++ Version 1.0";
   }


   // The init() method is called by the AWT when an applet is first loaded or
   // reloaded.  Override this method to perform whatever initialization your
   // applet needs, such as initializing data structures, loading images or
   // fonts, creating frame windows, setting the layout manager, or adding UI
   // components.
   //--------------------------------------------------------------------
   public void init()
   {
```

```
    // If you use a ResourceWizard-generated "control creator" class to
    // arrange controls in your applet, you may want to call its
    // CreateControls() method from within this method. Remove the following
    // call to resize() before adding the call to CreateControls();
    // CreateControls() does its own resizing.
    //----------------------------------------------------------------------
    resize(320, 240);

    boldbutton = new Button("bold");
    italicbutton = new Button("italic");
    buttonlarge = new Button("large");
    romanbutton = new Button("roman");
    courierbutton = new Button("courier");
    clearbutton = new Button("clear");

    add(boldbutton);
    add(italicbutton);
    add(buttonlarge);
    add(romanbutton);
    add(courierbutton);
    add(clearbutton);
  }

  public boolean action(Event e, Object o){
  if(e.target.equals(boldbutton)){
     boldboolean = !boldboolean;
  }
  if(e.target.equals(italicbutton)){
     italicboolean = !italicboolean;
  }
  if(e.target.equals(buttonlarge)){
     largeboolean = !largeboolean;
  }
  if(e.target.equals(romanbutton)){
     romanboolean = true;
     courierboolean = false;
  }
  if(e.target.equals(courierbutton)){
     courierboolean = true;
     romanboolean = false;
  }
  if(e.target.equals(clearbutton)){
```

```
      text = "";
    }
    repaint();
    return true;
}

// Place additional applet clean up code here.  destroy() is called
// when your applet is terminating and being unloaded.
//-------------------------------------------------------------------------
public void destroy()
{
    // TODO: Place applet cleanup code here
}

// fonts Paint Handler
//-------------------------------------------------------------------------
public void paint(Graphics g)
{
    String fontname = "Roman";
    int type = Font.PLAIN;
    int size = 24;
    Font font;

    if(boldboolean){
       type = type | Font.BOLD;
    }
    if(italicboolean){
       type = type | Font.ITALIC;
    }
       if(largeboolean){
       size = 48;
    }
    if(romanboolean){
       fontname = "Roman";
    }
    if(courierboolean){
       fontname = "Courier";
    }

    font = new Font(fontname, type, size);
    g.setFont(font);

    fontmetrics = getFontMetrics(font);
```

```
    x = (size().width - fontmetrics.stringWidth(text)) / 2;
    y = (size().height + fontmetrics.getHeight()) / 2;

    g.drawString(text, x, y);
}


//   The start() method is called when the page containing the applet
// first appears on the screen. The AppletWizard's initial implementation
// of this method starts execution of the applet's thread.
//-------------------------------------------------------------------------
public void start()
{
    // TODO: Place additional applet start code here
}


//   The stop() method is called when the page containing the applet is
// no longer on the screen. The AppletWizard's initial implementation of
// this method stops execution of the applet's thread.
//-------------------------------------------------------------------------
public void stop()
{
}



// MOUSE SUPPORT:
//   The mouseDown() method is called if the mouse button is pressed
// while the mouse cursor is over the applet's portion of the screen.
//-------------------------------------------------------------------------
public boolean mouseDown(Event evt, int x, int y)
{
    // TODO: Place applet mouseDown code here
    return true;
}

// MOUSE SUPPORT:
//   The mouseUp() method is called if the mouse button is released
// while the mouse cursor is over the applet's portion of the screen.
//-------------------------------------------------------------------------
public boolean mouseUp(Event evt, int x, int y)
{
    // TODO: Place applet mouseUp code here
```

```
    return true;
  }

  public boolean keyDown(Event e, int k){
    text = text + (char)k;
    repaint();
    return true;
  }



  // MOUSE SUPPORT:
  //   The mouseDrag() method is called if the mouse cursor moves over the
  //   applet's portion of the screen while the mouse button is being held down.
  //-------------------------------------------------------------------------
  public boolean mouseDrag(Event evt, int x, int y)
  {
    // TODO: Place applet mouseDrag code here
    return true;
  }

  // MOUSE SUPPORT:
  //   The mouseMove() method is called if the mouse cursor moves over the
  //   applet's portion of the screen and the mouse button isn't being held down.
  //-------------------------------------------------------------------------
  public boolean mouseMove(Event evt, int x, int y)
  {
    // TODO: Place applet mouseMove code here
    return true;
  }

  // MOUSE SUPPORT:
  //   The mouseEnter() method is called if the mouse cursor enters the
  //   applet's portion of the screen.
  //-------------------------------------------------------------------------
  public boolean mouseEnter(Event evt, int x, int y)
  {
    // TODO: Place applet mouseEnter code here
    return true;
  }

  // MOUSE SUPPORT:
  //   The mouseExit() method is called if the mouse cursor leaves the
```

```
// applet's portion of the screen.
//---------------------------------------------------------------
public boolean mouseExit(Event evt, int x, int y)
{
   // TODO: Place applet mouseExit code here
   return true;
}


// TODO: Place additional applet code here

}
```

Our last example on image handling will show us how to work with *pixel arrays*. We'll load an image into a pixel array and then create a copy of the original image using this pixel array.

Working with Pixel Arrays: The Copier Applet

Being able to work quickly pixel by pixel is the foundation of all real graphics manipulation. In this example, you'll see how to load an image into an array of pixels and then use that array to create a new image—copying the original image—and display the result. Our new applet will be called copier, and with it, we'll be able to copy images pixel by pixel:

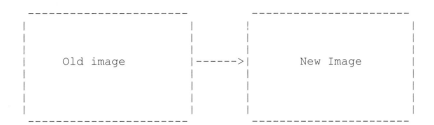

Create the copier applet now using the Applet Wizard. We'll need two Image objects, one for the original image, which we might call copierimage, and one for the copy of that image, which we can call copiedimage:

```
public class copier extends Applet
{
→   Image copierimage, copiedimage;
        .
        .
        .
```

Begin by loading in the figure we used in the doubler applet at the beginning of this chapter and which appears in Figure 10.1. We will make a copy of this image:

```
public void init()
{
   // If you use a ResourceWizard-generated "control creator" class to
   // arrange controls in your applet, you may want to call its
   // CreateControls() method from within this method. Remove the following
   // call to resize() before adding the call to CreateControls();
   // CreateControls() does its own resizing.
   //-----------------------------------------------------------------
   resize(320, 240);

→  copierimage = getImage(getCodeBase(), "figure.jpg");
       .
       .
       .
```

Using MediaTrackers to Handle Images

Although it might seem as though we have loaded in our image at this point, in fact it takes a good amount of time for this process to finish (although getImage() returns at once). However, we'll need the dimensions of the image we're loading in before much longer, so we should wait for the image to be fully loaded. We do that with a `MediaTracker` object. This object oversees the image-loading process for us. We'll call its `waitForID()` method, which won't return until the image is loaded, and we can continue with our code. We can pass the `MediaTracker` constructor a reference to our applet this way to create a new `MediaTracker` object named `mediatracker`:

```
public void init()
{
   resize(320, 240);

   copierimage = getImage(getCodeBase(), "figure.jpg");

➔  MediaTracker mediatracker = new MediaTracker(this);
           .
           .
           .
```

Next, we request the `mediatracker` object to watch our image named `copierimage` this way:

```
public void init()
{
   resize(320, 240);

   copierimage = getImage(getCodeBase(), "figure.jpg");

   MediaTracker mediatracker = new MediaTracker(this);
➔  mediatracker.addImage(copierimage, 0);
           .
           .
           .
```

Now we simply call the `MediaTracker` method `waitForID()`. Visual J++ requires us to call this method in a `try...catch` block, so we do that like this (you'll see all about `try...catch` blocks in the next chapter):

```
public void init()
{
```

```
          resize(320, 240);

          copierimage = getImage(getCodeBase(), "figure.jpg");

          MediaTracker mediatracker = new MediaTracker(this);
          mediatracker.addImage(copierimage, 0);

➜    try{mediatracker.waitForID(0);}
➜    catch(Exception e){}
               .
               .
               .
```

When we return from waitForID(), our image is loaded, and we can proceed. We'll need the height and width of the image so that we can set up our pixel array, and we get that with the Image class's getWidth() and getHeight() methods, storing that data in our *height* and *width* variables:

```
public void init()
{
   resize(320, 240);
        .
        .
        .
   try{mediatracker.waitForID(0);}
   catch(Exception e){}

➜    width = copierimage.getWidth(null);
➜    height = copierimage.getHeight(null);
          .
          .
          .
```

We can place the image in the copierimage object into a pixel array as soon as we set up that array. We first declare that array like this (as well as the width and height variables we just used), naming it pixelarray[]:

```
public class copier extends Applet
{

   Image copierimage, copiedimage;
```

```
→   int width, height;
→   int pixelarray[];
        .
        .
        .
```

Arrays in Java are really one-dimensional, so we dimension our array with the `new` keyword like this, where we set up as many integer elements as we'll need for an image that is made up of `width` × `height` pixels:

```
public void init()
{
   resize(320, 240);
        .
        .
        .

   try{mediatracker.waitForID(0);}
   catch(Exception e){}

   width = copierimage.getWidth(null);
   height = copierimage.getHeight(null);
→  pixelarray = new int[width * height];
        .
        .
        .
```

Now our pixel array is ready to store the image. The next step, then, is to "grab" the pixels from the image and store them in the pixel array. We do that with a `PixelGrabber` object.

Grabbing Pixels from an Image with *PixelGrabber*

To transfer pixel values from the `copierimage` object to the array named `pixelarray[]`, we need an object of the Java `PixelGrabber` class. We declare that object, calling it `pixelgrabber`, like this:

```
public class copier extends Applet
{

   Image copierimage, copiedimage;
```

```
          int pixelarray[];
     →    PixelGrabber pixelgrabber;
          int width, height;
                .
                .
                .
```

Now we can create the `PixelGrabber` object. To do that, we need to pass to the `PixelGrabber` constructor the following values: the actual object that "produces" the pixels in the `Image` object, the four coordinates of the image to grab from the source image, the target array for the pixels, the offset into the array at which to start storing pixels, and the number of pixels in a row of the image. That looks like this:

```
public void init()
{
   resize(320, 240);
        .
        .
        .

   width = copierimage.getWidth(null);
   height = copierimage.getHeight(null);
   pixelarray = new int[width * height];

→  pixelgrabber = new PixelGrabber(copierimage.getSource(), 0, 0, width,
↪  height, pixelarray, 0, width);
        .
        .
        .
```

That's all there is to it. This sets up the `PixelGrabber` object, but does not actually "grab" the pixels. We do that with the `PixelGrabber` `grabPixels()` method, which Visual J++ also requires us to place in a `try...catch` block:

```
public void init()
{
    resize(320, 240);
        .
        .
        .

    pixelgrabber = new PixelGrabber(copierimage.getSource(), 0, 0, width,
➠  height, pixelarray, 0, width);
➡  try{pixelgrabber.grabPixels();}
➡  catch (Exception e){}
        .
        .
        .
```

The pixels are now stored in the `pixelarray[]` array. The data for pixel (x, y) in the image is now stored in the array at location `pixelarray[x + (y * rowsize)]`. We've stored an image in an array of pixels. This is a powerful technique; you can work on the pixels individually.

In this example, however, we want to execute the reverse process—creating a copy of the original image by creating an image from the array of pixels. We do that with the `MemoryImageSource` class.

The *MemoryImageSource* Class

Just as the `PixelGrabber` class lets you convert an image to a pixel array, the `MemoryImageSource` class lets you convert a pixel array to an image. We can create a new `MemoryImageSource` object named `memimagesource` now; declare that object in our main class. The `MemoryImageSource` class's constructor takes these parameters: the width and height of the image, the array of pixels, the offset in the array at which to start reading pixels, and the number of pixels in a row. That looks like this:

```
public void init()
{
```

```
   resize(320, 240);

        .

        .

        .

   pixelgrabber = new PixelGrabber(copierimage.getSource(), 0, 0, width,
➥  height, pixelarray, 0, width);
   try{pixelgrabber.grabPixels();}
   catch (Exception e){}

➜  memimagesource = new MemoryImageSource(width, height, pixelarray, 0,
➥  width);

        .

        .

        .
```

Now we've created a `MemoryImageSource` object. This object functions just as its name indicates—as a source in memory for this image. We can use the applet's `createImage()` method to turn this into the copy of the original image, which we store in the `copiedimage` object, and then force a `paint` event with `repaint()` to display the copied image:

```
public void init()
{
   resize(320, 240);

        .

        .

        .

   pixelgrabber = new PixelGrabber(copierimage.getSource(), 0, 0, width,
➥  height, pixelarray, 0, width);
   try{pixelgrabber.grabPixels();}
   catch (Exception e){}

   memimagesource = new MemoryImageSource(width, height, pixelarray, 0,
➥  width);
➜  copiedimage = createImage(memimagesource);
➜  repaint();
}
```

And that's almost it—we've read the image into a pixel array and made a copy of it. All that remains is to display the image now that the `init()` method is complete, and we do that in the `paint()` method:

```
// copier Paint Handler
//---------------------------------------------------------------------
public void paint(Graphics g)
{
    g.drawImage(copiedimage, 0, 0, copiedimage.getWidth(null),
    copiedimage.getHeight(null), this);
}
```

Finally, import `java.awt.image.*` to our applet and run the copier applet now (making sure the `figure.jpg` file is in the same directory as the `copier.class` file). The result appears in Figure 10.8. We have read in the original image, placed it into a pixel array, transferred that to a new image, and displayed the result. The copier applet is a success. The code for this applet appears in `copier.java`.

FIGURE 10.8:

Our copier applet reads an image into a pixel array and makes a copy of it for display.

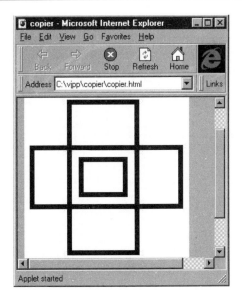

copier.java

```
//****************************************************************************
// copier.java: Applet
//
//****************************************************************************
import java.applet.*;
import java.awt.*;
import java.awt.image.*;


//============================================================================
// Main Class for applet copier
//
//============================================================================
public class copier extends Applet
{

   Image copierimage, copiedimage;
   int pixelarray[];
   PixelGrabber pixelgrabber;
   MemoryImageSource memimagesource;
   int width, height;

   // copier Class Constructor
   //--------------------------------------------------------------------------
   public copier()
   {
     // TODO: Add constructor code here
   }

   // APPLET INFO SUPPORT:
   //   The getAppletInfo() method returns a string describing the applet's
   // author, copyright date, or miscellaneous information.
   //--------------------------------------------------------------------------
   public String getAppletInfo()
   {
     return "Name: copier\r\n" +
          "Author: Steven Holzner\r\n" +
          "Created with Microsoft Visual J++ Version 1.0";
   }


   // The init() method is called by the AWT when an applet is first loaded or
```

```
// reloaded.  Override this method to perform whatever initialization your
// applet needs, such as initializing data structures, loading images or
// fonts, creating frame windows, setting the layout manager, or adding UI
// components.
//----------------------------------------------------------------------------
public void init()
{
   // If you use a ResourceWizard-generated "control creator" class to
   // arrange controls in your applet, you may want to call its
   // CreateControls() method from within this method. Remove the following
   // call to resize() before adding the call to CreateControls();
   // CreateControls() does its own resizing.
   //-------------------------------------------------------------------------
   resize(320, 240);

   copierimage = getImage(getCodeBase(), "figure.jpg");

   MediaTracker mediatracker = new MediaTracker(this);
   mediatracker.addImage(copierimage, 0);

   try{mediatracker.waitForID(0);}
   catch(Exception e){}

   width = copierimage.getWidth(null);
   height = copierimage.getHeight(null);
   pixelarray = new int[width * height];

   pixelgrabber = new PixelGrabber(copierimage.getSource(), 0, 0, width,
   height, pixelarray, 0, width);
   try{pixelgrabber.grabPixels();}
   catch (Exception e){}

   memimagesource = new MemoryImageSource(width, height, pixelarray, 0,
   width);
   copiedimage = createImage(memimagesource);
   repaint();
}

// Place additional applet clean up code here.  destroy() is called
// when your applet is terminating and being unloaded.
//----------------------------------------------------------------------------
public void destroy()
{
```

```
    // TODO: Place applet cleanup code here
  }

  // copier Paint Handler
  //-------------------------------------------------------------------
  public void paint(Graphics g)
  {
    g.drawImage(copiedimage, 0, 0, copiedimage.getWidth(null),
➥ copiedimage.getHeight(null), this);
  }

  //   The start() method is called when the page containing the applet
  // first appears on the screen. The AppletWizard's initial implementation
  // of this method starts execution of the applet's thread.
  //-------------------------------------------------------------------
  public void start()
  {
    // TODO: Place additional applet start code here
  }

  //   The stop() method is called when the page containing the applet is
  // no longer on the screen. The AppletWizard's initial implementation of
  // this method stops execution of the applet's thread.
  //-------------------------------------------------------------------
  public void stop()
  {
  }



  // TODO: Place additional applet code here

}
```

What's Next?

That's it for our coverage of image handling—as far as static images go, anyway. We've come far in this chapter, from handling images, to working with image maps, fonts, the keyboard, and converting an image into an array and an array into an image. In the next chapter, we're going to explore one of the most popular of all Java topics—graphics animation.

Graphics Animation

- Exploring the `run()` method

- Customizing animation applets

- Using `update()` to remove animation flicker

- Using double buffering

- Using the Card layout manager

In this chapter, we'll take a guided tour of a popular Java topic: graphics animation. For a long time, Web pages contained static images and text, but Java introduced animation to Web pages, and that is one of the primary reasons for its popularity. You can animate Web pages without using Java, for example, by embedding video files such .avi files, by using looping .gif images (which hold a number of internal images), or by using other packages such as VB Script. Java remains the animation tool of choice for most Web programmers, however, especially now that the Internet Explorer supports Java.

The fundamentals of animation are, of course, simply placing a series of images on the screen in rapid succession to give the impression of movement. We start with one image:

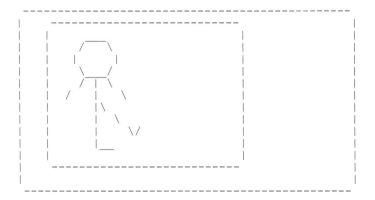

and then rapidly move on to the next:

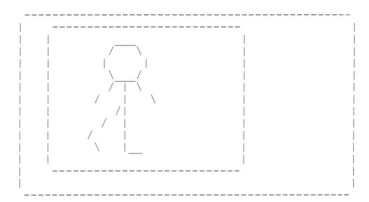

Flipping images in this way creates the animation. Java applets and applications can be multithreaded, and, in fact, a separate thread handles the animation, as you'll see. Besides seeing how the Visual J++ Applet Wizard handles animation, we'll use the Sun Animator class in this chapter and work on reducing screen flicker through methods such as clipping, update overriding, and double buffering. Let's start now with our first animation applet.

The Globe Applet

The Visual J++ Applet Wizard does a tremendous amount of work in adding animation support to applets. We will make our first animation example the default animation applet that the Applet Wizard creates—the little globe that spins around, as shown in Figure 11.1.

FIGURE 11.1:

Our animated globe
spins around.

FIGURE 11.1:

Our animated globe
spins around.

Creating this example will be no problem—we'll simply let the
Applet Wizard do all the work. It's in dissecting this example that
we'll put our effort, seeing how the animation actually works. After
you understand thoroughly what the Applet Wizard has done, you'll
be able to modify it to handle your own animations.

Create this new applet named `globe` now. Simply start the Applet
Wizard, type **globe** in the Name box, click on Create, and then click
on Finish. By default, the Applet Wizard creates the applet we want.

Dissecting the Globe Applet

We'll dissect the code for this applet, `globe.java`. As we take apart
the animation support the Applet Wizard has given us, you'll see
how to create your own animations.

At the beginning of the `globe` class, the Applet Wizard has added a
number of new variables to the applet and includes comments
explaining all the variables:

```
public class globe extends Applet implements Runnable
{
  // THREAD SUPPORT:
  //   m_globe  is the Thread object for the applet
  //-------------------------------------------------------------------------
  Thread  m_globe = null;

  // ANIMATION SUPPORT:
  //   m_Graphics      used for storing the applet's Graphics context
  //   m_Images[]      the array of Image objects for the animation
  //   m_nCurrImage    the index of the next image to be displayed
  //   m_ImgWidth      width of each image
  //   m_ImgHeight     height of each image
  //   m_fAllLoaded    indicates whether all images have been loaded
  //   NUM_IMAGES      number of images used in the animation
  //-------------------------------------------------------------------------
  private Graphics m_Graphics;
  private Image  m_Images[];
  private int    m_nCurrImage;
  private int    m_nImgWidth  = 0;
  private int    m_nImgHeight = 0;
  private boolean  m_fAllLoaded = false;
  private final int NUM_IMAGES = 18;
       .
       .
       .
```

Let's see how these variables are used. The first variable is *m_globe*, which represents a new *thread*. You'll see how threads work in the next chapter, but for now, note that threads are the foundation of multitasking. A thread is simply a separate stream of execution within the applet or application, and a Java applet or application can have many threads going at once. In this case, the m_globe thread is the thread that handles the animation in our applet. Like any other thread (including the main thread that runs the applet), this thread can force paint events by calling repaint() and so can draw the animation images we'll need on the screen.

The m_globe thread is started with this code in the start()
method:

```
// The start() method is called when the page containing the applet
// first appears on the screen. The AppletWizard's initial implementation
// of this method starts execution of the applet's thread.
//----------------------------------   ------------------------------------
public void start()
{
   if (m_globe == null)
   {
      m_globe = new Thread(this);
      m_globe.start();
   }
   // TODO: Place additional applet start code here
}
```

You can stop the m_globe thread by executing its stop() method.
In this case, we stop the thread when we exit the applet. The stop()
method is called, and the Applet Wizard stops the animation thread
there:

```
// The stop() method is called when the page containing the applet is
// no longer on the screen. The AppletWizard's initial implementation of
// this method stops execution of the applet's thread.
//--------------------------------------------------------------------
public void stop()
{
   if (m_globe != null)
   {
      m_globe.stop();
      m_globe = null;
   }

   // TODO: Place additional applet stop code here
}
```

> If you want to pause your animation, you can use the `Thread` class's `suspend()` method, as you'll see in the next chapter. In this case, that would look like this: `m_globe.suspend()`. To restart the animation, you would use the `resume()` method like this: `m_globe.resume()`.

Now that the `m_globe` thread has been started, the applet's `run()` method is called. This is where the main code for the thread goes. Bear in mind that this execution stream is independent of the rest of the applet—while we are working in the `run()` method, the rest of the applet may be doing other things.

Exploring the *run()* Method

We load in the images and handle the animation in the `run()` method. We'll dissect this important method piece by piece. The Applet Wizard begins by setting the index of the current image to zero. There are 18 images in the globe animation, and our applet tracks the number of the currently displayed image in the integer `m_nCurrImage`:

```
// THREAD SUPPORT
//   The run() method is called when the applet's thread is started. If
// your applet performs any ongoing activities without waiting for user
// input, the code for implementing that behavior typically goes here.
// For example, for an applet that performs animation, the run() method
// controls the display of images.
//-------------------------------------------------------------------
public void run()
{
    m_nCurrImage = 0;
        .
        .
        .
```

Next, we load the images into an array of images called `m_Images[]`. The applet tracks whether the images have all been loaded with the boolean variable *m_fAllLoaded*, and first it verifies that variable is set to `FALSE`. If so, it's time to create the `m_Images[]` array and load in the images:

```
public void run()
{
   m_nCurrImage = 0;

   // If re-entering the page, then the images have already been loaded.
   // m_fAllLoaded == TRUE.
   //--------------------------------------------------------------------
   if (!m_fAllLoaded)
   {
      repaint();
      m_Graphics = getGraphics();
      m_Images   = new Image[NUM_IMAGES];
            .
            .
            .
```

There are a few things to notice here. The `repaint()` call calls the `paint()` method, but since the images aren't loaded in yet, that simply places a "Loading images..." message on the screen.

Next, note the creation of the `Graphics` object `m_Graphics` with the applet's `getGraphics()` method. This is how we get a `graphics` object for our applet that we can draw in (without waiting for a `paint` event), and this is where the applet will display our images. Also, note that the `m_Images[]` array is dimensioned with the constant value `NUM_IMAGES`. The Applet Wizard sets this constant to 18 because there are 18 images:

```
public class globe extends Applet implements Runnable
{
   private Graphics m_Graphics;
   private Image    m_Images[];
   private int   m_nCurrImage;
   private int   m_nImgWidth  = 0;
   private int   m_nImgHeight = 0;
   private boolean  m_fAllLoaded = false;
```

➜   private final int NUM_IMAGES = 18;
            .
            .
            .
            .

NOTE	When you customize an animation applet for your own animation, NUM_IMAGES is one of the numbers you have to change (our customized animation applet, for example, will use only four images).

Now the applet loads in the images. It does so by assembling the name of the current image to load in into the String object named strImage (that is, the images are stored in the files img0001.gif to img00111.gif) and by loading that image in with getImage(), as we did in the last chapter. As we also did in the last chapter, the Applet uses a MediaTracker object to make sure all the images are read in:

```
public void run()
{
   m_nCurrImage = 0;

   if (!m_fAllLoaded)
   {
      repaint();
      m_Graphics = getGraphics();
      m_Images   = new Image[NUM_IMAGES];

      // Load in all the images
      //-------------------------------------------------------------------
      MediaTracker tracker = new MediaTracker(this);
      String strImage;

      // For each image in the animation, this method first constructs a
      // string containing the path to the image file; then it begins
      // loading the image into the m_Images array.  Note that the call to
      // getImage will return before the image is completely loaded.
      //-------------------------------------------------------------------
      for (int i = 1; i <= NUM_IMAGES; i++)
      {
```

➜ (MediaTracker tracker line)
➜ (String strImage line)
➜ (for loop line)
➜ (opening brace line)

```
        // Build path to next image
        //-----------------------------------------------------------------
➡       strImage = "images/img00" + ((i < 10) ? "0" : "") + i + ".gif";
➡       m_Images[i-1] = getImage(getDocumentBase(), strImage);
➡       tracker.addImage(m_Images[i-1], 0);
      }     .
              .
              .
```

The applet uses the return value from the `MediaTracker` object's `isErrorAny()` method to set the `m_fAllLoaded` boolean flag, indicating whether the images were all safely loaded:

```
public void run()
{
  m_nCurrImage = 0;

  if (!m_fAllLoaded)
  {  .
       .
       .
    for (int i = 1; i <= NUM_IMAGES; i++)
    {
      // Build path to next image
      //-----------------------------------------------------------------
      strImage = "images/img00" + ((i < 10) ? "0" : "") + i + ".gif";
      m_Images[i-1] = getImage(getDocumentBase(), strImage);

      tracker.addImage(m_Images[i-1], 0);
    }

    // Wait until all images are fully loaded
    //-----------------------------------------------------------------
➡     try
➡     {
➡       tracker.waitForAll();
➡       m_fAllLoaded = !tracker.isErrorAny();
➡     }
➡     catch (InterruptedException e)
➡     {
        // TODO: Place exception-handling code here in case an
        //    InterruptedException is thrown by Thread.sleep(),
```

```
    //    meaning that another thread has interrupted this one
  } .
          .
          .
          .
```

If the images were not loaded correctly, m_fAllLoaded will be FALSE, and the Applet informs the user that an error occurred:

```
public void run()
{
   m_nCurrImage = 0;
           .
           .
           .
     try
     {
       tracker.waitForAll();
       m_fAllLoaded = !tracker.isErrorAny();
     }
     catch (InterruptedException e)
     {
     }

➔    if (!m_fAllLoaded)
➔    {
➔      stop();
➔      m_Graphics.drawString("Error loading images!", 10, 40);
➔      return;
➔    } .
           .
           .
           .
```

At this point, then, the images are loaded into the m_Images[] array. The applet now places the first image on the screen. It first finds the image's width and height and places that data in the m_nImgWidth and m_nImgHeight integers; then it calls repaint() to display this image (note that since the image index, m_nCurrImage, is still set to zero, we'll display the first image here):

```
public void run()
{
```

```
m_nCurrImage = 0;
         .
         .
         .

   if (!m_fAllLoaded)
   {
     stop();
     m_Graphics.drawString("Error loading images!", 10, 40);
     return;
   }

   // Assuming all images are same width and height.
   //------------------------------------------------------------
➜   m_nImgWidth  = m_Images[0].getWidth(this);
➜   m_nImgHeight = m_Images[0].getHeight(this);
➜ }
➜ repaint();
      .
      .
      .
```

The actual animation is handled by something you don't see too often in programming—an infinite loop. This loop keeps going and going with no built-in method of termination, drawing images forever (recall that this thread is terminated in the stop() method, so this is not really a problem). In this case, the infinite loop is a while loop, where the loop condition is set to TRUE. The actual drawing process is enclosed in a try...catch block in case problems cause exceptions:

```
public void run()
{
  if (!m_fAllLoaded)
      .
      .
      .
      m_nImgWidth  = m_Images[0].getWidth(this);
      m_nImgHeight = m_Images[0].getHeight(this);
  }
```

```
        repaint();

→       while (true)
→       {
→         try
→         {

        [Draw next image]

→         }
→         catch (InterruptedException e)
→         {

        [Error in case we can't draw the image]

→         }
→       }
        }
```

All the applet does is draw the image by calling the `displayImage()` method (you'll see that method in a moment), incrementing the index in the image array (that is, in `m_nCurrImage`), setting that index back to zero, if the end of the image array is reached, and then putting the thread to *sleep* for 50 milliseconds. Putting a thread to sleep suspends its execution. Here, with the call `Thread.sleep(50);`, the applet puts the thread to sleep for 50 milliseconds, making that the time between successive animation frames. This, then, is how the animation works in our applet:

```
public void run()
{
  if (!m_fAllLoaded)
  {
    repaint();
    m_Graphics = getGraphics();
    m_Images   = new Image[NUM_IMAGES];
      .
      .
      .
    m_nImgWidth  = m_Images[0].getWidth(this);
    m_nImgHeight = m_Images[0].getHeight(this);
```

```
      }
      repaint();

      while (true)
      {
        try
        {
          // Draw next image in animation
          //-------------------------------------------------------------------
→         displayImage(m_Graphics);
→         m_nCurrImage++;
→         if (m_nCurrImage == NUM_IMAGES)
→           m_nCurrImage = 0;

          // TODO:  Add additional thread-specific code here
→         Thread.sleep(50);
        }
        catch (InterruptedException e)
        {
          // TODO: Place exception-handling code here in case an
          //    InterruptedException is thrown by Thread.sleep(),
          //    meaning that another thread has interrupted this one
→         stop();
        }
      }
    }
```

This loop calls the method `displayImage()` to do the actual drawing on the screen. As you may recall, the applet set up a new `graphics` object representing our applet named `m_Graphics`, and it passes that object to `displayImage()`. The code in the `displayImage()` method first checks to see if the images are all loaded by examining the *m_fAllLoaded* variable:

```
      private void displayImage(Graphics g)
      {
→       if (!m_fAllLoaded)
→         return;
          .
          .
          .
      }
```

If the images are all loaded, the applet draws the image centered in the middle of the applet, just as we did with text in the last chapter (although we had to set up a `FontMetrics` object in the last chapter to find out the length of our text string on the screen, we already know the height and width of our image in this applet):

```
private void displayImage(Graphics g)
{
   if (!m_fAllLoaded)
      return;

   // Draw Image in center of applet
   //-----------------------------------------------------------------
   g.drawImage(m_Images[m_nCurrImage],(size().width - m_nImgWidth)   / 2,
(size().height - m_nImgHeight) / 2, null);
}
```

The only additional code is in the `paint()` method. In the `paint()` method, the code clears the applet's display by copying the applet's *clipping rectangle* into a Java `Rectangle` object called r and clearing it. You'll see more about clipping rectangles in the next example. If you want to limit graphics operations to a specific rectangle on the screen, you set up a clipping rectangle bounding that area. In this case, the clipping rectangle is the whole applet's display. In the `paint()` method, then, the applet first checks if all images were loaded, gets the clipping rectangle and clears it with the `clearRect()` method, and then displays the new image by calling `displayImage()`:

```
public void paint(Graphics g)
{
   // ANIMATION SUPPORT:
   //   The following code displays a status message until all the
   //   images are loaded. Then it calls displayImage to display the current
   //   image.
   //-----------------------------------------------------------------
   if(m_fAllLoaded)
   {
      Rectangle r = g.getClipRect();

      g.clearRect(r.x, r.y, r.width, r.height);
```

➡   ```
     displayImage(g);
     ```
➡    ```
     }  .
     ```
```
     .
     .
     .

   }
```

If, on the other hand, the images were not loaded, the `paint()` method just places the string "Loading images..." on the screen:

```java
public void paint(Graphics g)
{
  if (m_fAllLoaded)
  {
    Rectangle r = g.getClipRect();

    g.clearRect(r.x, r.y, r.width, r.height);
    displayImage(g);
  }
  else
    g.drawString("Loading images...", 10, 20);

    // TODO: Place additional applet Paint code here
}
```

(The ➡ arrows point to the `else` and `g.drawString("Loading images...", 10, 20);` lines.)

And that's it—we've created and run our first animation applet without writing one line of code, thanks to the Applet Wizard. The code for this applet appears in `globe.java`.

globe.java

```java
//*****************************************************************************
// globe.java:  Applet
//
//*****************************************************************************
import java.applet.*;
import java.awt.*;


//=============================================================================
// Main Class for applet globe
//
//=============================================================================
```

```
public class globe extends Applet implements Runnable
{
  // THREAD SUPPORT:
  //   m_globe is the Thread object for the applet
  //----------------------------------------------------------------------------
  Thread  m_globe = null;

  // ANIMATION SUPPORT:
  //   m_Graphics    used for storing the applet's Graphics context
  //   m_Images[]    the array of Image objects for the animation
  //   m_nCurrImage  the index of the next image to be displayed
  //   m_ImgWidth    width of each image
  //   m_ImgHeight   height of each image
  //   m_fAllLoaded  indicates whether all images have been loaded
  //   NUM_IMAGES    number of images used in the animation
  //----------------------------------------------------------------------------
  private Graphics m_Graphics;
  private Image m_Images[];
  private int   m_nCurrImage;
  private int   m_nImgWidth  = 0;
  private int   m_nImgHeight = 0;
  private boolean  m_fAllLoaded = false;
  private final int NUM_IMAGES = 18;


  // globe Class Constructor
  //----------------------------------------------------------------------------
  public globe()
  {
    // TODO: Add constructor code here
  }

  // APPLET INFO SUPPORT:
  //   The getAppletInfo() method returns a string describing the applet's
  // author, copyright date, or miscellaneous information.
  //----------------------------------------------------------------------------
  public String getAppletInfo()
  {
    return "Name: globe\r\n" +
         "Author: Steven Holzner\r\n" +
```

```
                "Created with Microsoft Visual J++ Version 1.0";
}


// The init() method is called by the AWT when an applet is first loaded or
// reloaded.  Override this method to perform whatever initialization your
// applet needs, such as initializing data structures, loading images or
// fonts, creating frame windows, setting the layout manager, or adding UI
// components.
//-----------------------------------------------------------------------------
public void init()
{
  // If you use a ResourceWizard-generated "control creator" class to
  // arrange controls in your applet, you may want to call its
  // CreateControls() method from within this method. Remove the following
  // call to resize() before adding the call to CreateControls();
  // CreateControls() does its own resizing.
  //---------------------------------------------------------------------------
  resize(320, 240);

  // TODO: Place additional initialization code here
}


// Place additional applet clean up code here.  destroy() is called
// when your applet is terminating and being unloaded.
//-----------------------------------------------------------------------------
public void destroy()
{
  // TODO: Place applet cleanup code here
}


// ANIMATION SUPPORT:
//   Draws the next image, if all images are currently loaded
//-----------------------------------------------------------------------------
private void displayImage(Graphics g)
{
  if (!m_fAllLoaded)
    return;

  // Draw Image in center of applet
  //---------------------------------------------------------------------------
  g.drawImage(m_Images[m_nCurrImage],
```

```
                    (size().width - m_nImgWidth)   / 2,
                    (size().height - m_nImgHeight) / 2, null);
}

// globe Paint Handler
//--------------------------------------------------------------------------
public void paint(Graphics g)
{
   // ANIMATION SUPPORT:
   //   The following code displays a status message until all the
   // images are loaded. Then it calls displayImage to display the current
   // image.
   //--------------------------------------------------------------------------
   if (m_fAllLoaded)
   {
      Rectangle r = g.getClipRect();

      g.clearRect(r.x, r.y, r.width, r.height);
      displayImage(g);
   }
   else
      g.drawString("Loading images...", 10, 20);

   // TODO: Place additional applet Paint code here
}

//   The start() method is called when the page containing the applet
// first appears on the screen. The AppletWizard's initial implementation
// of this method starts execution of the applet's thread.
//--------------------------------------------------------------------------
public void start()
{
   if (m_globe == null)
   {
      m_globe = new Thread(this);
      m_globe.start();
   }
   // TODO: Place additional applet start code here
}

//   The stop() method is called when the page containing the applet is
// no longer on the screen. The AppletWizard's initial implementation of
```

```
// this method stops execution of the applet's thread.
//----------------------------------------------------------------------
public void stop()
{
  if (m_globe != null)
  {
    m_globe.stop();
    m_globe = null;
  }

  // TODO: Place additional applet stop code here
}


// THREAD SUPPORT
//   The run() method is called when the applet's thread is started. If
// your applet performs any ongoing activities without waiting for user
// input, the code for implementing that behavior typically goes here. For
// example, for an applet that performs animation, the run() method controls
// the display of images.
//----------------------------------------------------------------------
public void run()
{
  m_nCurrImage = 0;

  // If re-entering the page, then the images have already been loaded.
  // m_fAllLoaded == TRUE.
  //----------------------------------------------------------------------
  if (!m_fAllLoaded)
  {
    repaint();
    m_Graphics = getGraphics();
    m_Images   = new Image[NUM_IMAGES];

    // Load in all the images
    //----------------------------------------------------------------------
    MediaTracker tracker = new MediaTracker(this);
    String strImage;

    // For each image in the animation, this method first constructs a
    // string containing the path to the image file; then it begins
    // loading the image into the m_Images array.  Note that the call to
    // getImage will return before the image is completely loaded.
```

```
    //---------------------------------------------------------------------
    for (int i = 1; i <= NUM_IMAGES; i++)
    {
        // Build path to next image
        //-----------------------------------------------------------------
        strImage = "images/img00" + ((i < 10) ? "0" : "") + i + ".gif";
        m_Images[i-1] = getImage(getDocumentBase(), strImage);

        tracker.addImage(m_Images[i-1], 0);
    }

    // Wait until all images are fully loaded
    //---------------------------------------------------------------------
    try
    {
        tracker.waitForAll();
        m_fAllLoaded = !tracker.isErrorAny();
    }
    catch (InterruptedException e)
    {
        // TODO: Place exception-handling code here in case an
        //    InterruptedException is thrown by Thread.sleep(),
        //    meaning that another thread has interrupted this one
    }

    if (!m_fAllLoaded)
    {
        stop();
        m_Graphics.drawString("Error loading images!", 10, 40);
        return;
    }


    // Assuming all images are same width and height.
    //---------------------------------------------------------------------
    m_nImgWidth  = m_Images[0].getWidth(this);
    m_nImgHeight = m_Images[0].getHeight(this);
}
repaint();

while (true)
{
```

```
      try
      {
        // Draw next image in animation
        //-------------------------------------------------------------------
        displayImage(m_Graphics);
        m_nCurrImage++;
        if (m_nCurrImage == NUM_IMAGES)
          m_nCurrImage = 0;

        // TODO:  Add additional thread-specific code here
        Thread.sleep(50);
      }
      catch (InterruptedException e)
      {
        // TODO: Place exception-handling code here in case an
        //    InterruptedException is thrown by Thread.sleep(),
        //    meaning that another thread has interrupted this one
        stop();
      }
    }
  }
}



  // TODO: Place additional applet code here

}
```

The next logical step is to customize the animation applets that the Applet Wizard creates for us, and we'll do that now.

Customizing Animation Applets

We'll now customize an animation applet. For example, we might have a figure that looks like this:

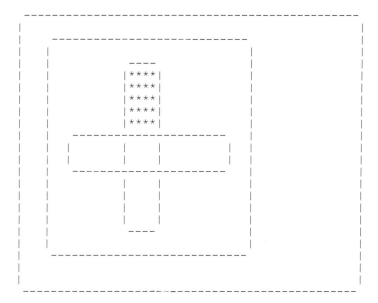

After a short time, we can place the next image on the screen:

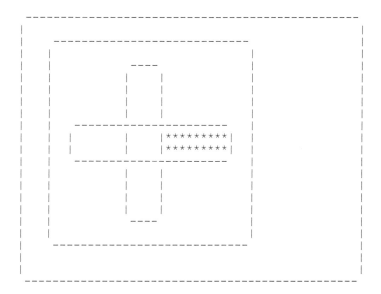

And so on until we get back to the first figure and keep going, making this image appear to twirl. We will use the images in Figure 11.2, which, when played in succession, give the impression of a twirling figure. Let's call this applet `twirler`. Create this applet with the Applet Wizard now, and be sure to include animation support.

FIGURE 11.2:

The frames of our twirler animation applet

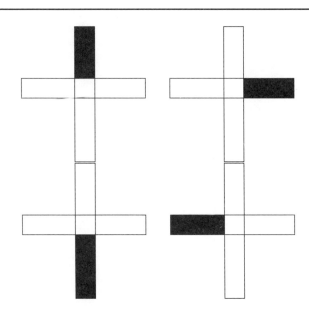

Customizing this new applet is easy. All we have to do is store our images in the image directory that is right under the directory that contains our `.java` and `.class` files, give them the names `IMG0001.GIF`, `IMG0002.GIF`, `IMG0003.GIF`, and `IMG0004.GIF`, and change the applet so that it works with 4 images, not 111. To change the number of images, we change the constant `NUM_IMAGES` at the beginning of our applet like this:

```
// ANIMATION SUPPORT:
//   m_Graphics    used for storing the applet's Graphics context
//   m_Images[]    the array of Image objects for the animation
//   m_nCurrImage  the index of the next image to be displayed
```

```
//   m_ImgWidth    width of each image
//   m_ImgHeight   height of each image
//   m_fAllLoaded  indicates whether all images have been loaded
//   NUM_IMAGES    number of images used in the animation
//-----------------------------------------------------------------------
private Graphics m_Graphics;
private Image m_Images[];
private int  m_nCurrImage;
private int  m_nImgWidth  = 0;
private int  m_nImgHeight = 0;
private boolean  m_fAllLoaded = false;
private final int NUM_IMAGES = 4; //18;
         .
         .
         .
```

And, amazingly, that's all there is to it. Run the applet now, as shown in Figure 11.3. The figure twirls—our applet is a success.

FIGURE 11.3:

Our customized twirler animation applet

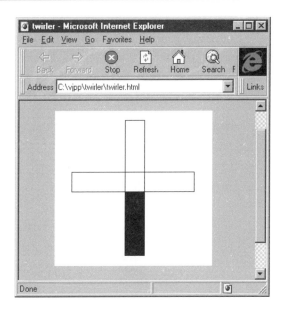

> **TIP**
>
> If you want to change the time between successive frames, modify `Thread.sleep(50);` in the `run()` method. If you want the image to appear somewhere other than in the center of the applet, modify the following line in the `displayImage()` method: `g.drawImage(m_Images[m_nCurrImage], (size().width - m_nImgWidth) / 2, (size().height - m_nImgHeight) / 2, null);`.

However, there is more going on in our twirler applet. One of the major problems of graphics animation is flicker on the screen, and we'll take a look at fixing that now.

Using *update()* to Remove Animation Flicker

Flicker occurs when you ask the applet to do too much work to display a frame. Of course, the amount of flicker always depends on the speed of the user's machine, but we can do several things to reduce and often eliminate it ourselves.

The Applet Wizard has already taken the first step toward eliminating flicker: The applet avoids using the `paint()` method. Instead, the Applet Wizard creates its own graphics object, `m_Graphics`, in the `run()` method:

```
public void run()
{
  if (!m_fAllLoaded)
  {
    m_Graphics = getGraphics();
    m_Images   = new Image[NUM_IMAGES];
      .
      .
      .
```

And the Applet Wizard calls the `displayImage()` method with
that `graphics` object instead of setting up the drawing code and calling `repaint()`:

```
public void run()
{
  if (!m_fAllLoaded)
  {
    m_Graphics = getGraphics();
    m_Images   = new Image[NUM_IMAGES];
         .

         .

         .
    while (true)
    {
      try
      {
        // Draw next image in animation
        //-----------------------------------------------------
        displayImage(m_Graphics);
        m_nCurrImage++;
        if (m_nCurrImage == NUM_IMAGES)
          m_nCurrImage = 0;
            .

            .

            .
      }
    }
  }
}
```

In the `displayImage()` method, the figure is actually drawn on the
screen using that new `Graphics` object:

```
private void displayImage(Graphics g)
{
  if (!m_fAllLoaded)
    return;

  // Draw Image in center of applet
  //-------------------------------------------------------------------------
```

```
→   g.drawImage(m_Images[m_nCurrImage], (size().width - m_nImgWidth)
↪ / 2,(size().height - m_nImgHeight) / 2, null);

}
```

One reason our applet avoids the `paint()` method is the large amount of overhead in the `paint()` method. When you call `repaint()`, and before the `paint()` method is called, Java clears the entire applet's display in the `update()` method, and that is a major cause of flicker. That is, the applet shows a frame of animation, clears entirely, shows a new frame of animation, and so on—you can see how that would cause flicker.

If you do want to use the `paint()` method, however, you can override the `update()` method, creating your own version:

```
public void update(Graphics g){
      .
      .
      .
}
```

Rather than clearing the applet's window, you simply call the `paint()` method directly here:

```
public void update(Graphics g){
→     paint(g);
}
```

You can even do better: You can limit the repainting (and hence the time to update the animated image) in the `paint()` method to only the rectangle that surrounds the animation frame. Such a rectangle is called a *clipping rectangle,* and you can set the clipping rectangle with the `Graphics clipRect()` method. For our current animation example, that would look like this:

```
public void update(Graphics g){
→   g.clipRect((size().width - m_nImgWidth) / 2, (size().height -
↪ m_nImgHeight) / 2, m_nImgWidth, m_nImgHeight);
    paint(g);
}
```

And that's it for our twirler example. In this example, you've seen how to customize the animation applets that the Applet Wizard creates, and you've seen how to minimize or eliminate screen flicker, a basic problem in Java. The code for this applet appears in `twirler.java`

twirler.java

```
//*************************************************************************
// twirler.java:  Applet
//
//*************************************************************************
import java.applet.*;
import java.awt.*;

//=========================================================================
// Main Class for applet twirler
//
//=========================================================================
public class twirler extends Applet implements Runnable
{
   // THREAD SUPPORT:
   //   m_twirler  is the Thread object for the applet
   //-----------------------------------------------------------------------
   Thread  m_twirler = null;

   // ANIMATION SUPPORT:
   //   m_Graphics     used for storing the applet's Graphics context
   //   m_Images[]     the array of Image objects for the animation
   //   m_nCurrImage   the index of the next image to be displayed
   //   m_ImgWidth     width of each image
   //   m_ImgHeight    height of each image
   //   m_fAllLoaded   indicates whether all images have been loaded
   //   NUM_IMAGES     number of images used in the animation
   //-----------------------------------------------------------------------
   private Graphics m_Graphics;
   private Image m_Images[];
   private int   m_nCurrImage;
   private int   m_nImgWidth  = 0;
   private int   m_nImgHeight = 0;
   private boolean m_fAllLoaded = false;
```

```java
private final int NUM_IMAGES = 4; //18;


// twirler Class Constructor
//-------------------------------------------------------------------------
public twirler()
{
  // TODO: Add constructor code here
}


// APPLET INFO SUPPORT:
//   The getAppletInfo() method returns a string describing the applet's
// author, copyright date, or miscellaneous information.
//-------------------------------------------------------------------------
public String getAppletInfo()
{
  return "Name: twirler\r\n" +
       "Author: Steven Holzner\r\n" +
       "Created with Microsoft Visual J++ Version 1.0";
}



// The init() method is called by the AWT when an applet is first loaded or
// reloaded.  Override this method to perform whatever initialization your
// applet needs, such as initializing data structures, loading images or
// fonts, creating frame windows, setting the layout manager, or adding UI
// components.
//-------------------------------------------------------------------------
public void init()
{
  // If you use a ResourceWizard-generated "control creator" class to
  // arrange controls in your applet, you may want to call its
  // CreateControls() method from within this method. Remove the following
  // call to resize() before adding the call to CreateControls();
  // CreateControls() does its own resizing.
  //-----------------------------------------------------------------------
  resize(320, 240);

  // TODO: Place additional initialization code here
}


// Place additional applet clean up code here.  destroy() is called
```

```
// when your applet is terminating and being unloaded.
//-----------------------------------------------------------------------------
public void destroy()
{
   // TODO: Place applet cleanup code here
}

// ANIMATION SUPPORT:
//   Draws the next image, if all images are currently loaded
//-----------------------------------------------------------------------------
private void displayImage(Graphics g)
{
   if (!m_fAllLoaded)
      return;

   // Draw Image in center of applet
   //--------------------------------------------------------------------------
   g.drawImage(m_Images[m_nCurrImage],
         (size().width - m_nImgWidth)  / 2,
         (size().height - m_nImgHeight) / 2, null);
}

// twirler Paint Handler
//-----------------------------------------------------------------------------
public void paint(Graphics g)
{
   // ANIMATION SUPPORT:
   //   The following code displays a status message until all the
   //   images are loaded. Then it calls displayImage to display the current
   //   image.
   //--------------------------------------------------------------------------
   if (m_fAllLoaded)
   {
      Rectangle r = g.getClipRect();

      g.clearRect(r.x, r.y, r.width, r.height);
      displayImage(g);
   }
   else
```

```
         g.drawString("Loading images...", 10, 20);

    // TODO: Place additional applet Paint code here
}

//   The start() method is called when the page containing the applet
// first appears on the screen. The AppletWizard's initial implementation
// of this method starts execution of the applet's thread.
//-------------------------------------------------------------------------
public void start()
{
    if (m_twirler == null)
    {
        m_twirler = new Thread(this);
        m_twirler.start();
    }
    // TODO: Place additional applet start code here
}

//   The stop() method is called when the page containing the applet is
// no longer on the screen. The AppletWizard's initial implementation of
// this method stops execution of the applet's thread.
//-------------------------------------------------------------------------
public void stop()
{
    if (m_twirler != null)
    {
        m_twirler.stop();
        m_twirler = null;
    }

    // TODO: Place additional applet stop code here
}

// THREAD SUPPORT
//   The run() method is called when the applet's thread is started. If
// your applet performs any ongoing activities without waiting for user
// input, the code for implementing that behavior typically goes here. For
// example, for an applet that performs animation, the run() method controls
// the display of images.
//-------------------------------------------------------------------------
public void run()
{
```

```
m_nCurrImage = 0;

// If re-entering the page, then the images have already been loaded.
// m_fAllLoaded == TRUE.
//---------------------------------------------------------------------------
if (!m_fAllLoaded)
{
   repaint();
   m_Graphics = getGraphics();
   m_Images   = new Image[NUM_IMAGES];

   // Load in all the images
   //------------------------------------------------------------------------
   MediaTracker tracker = new MediaTracker(this);
   String strImage;

   // For each image in the animation, this method first constructs a
   // string containing the path to the image file; then it begins
   // loading the image into the m_Images array.  Note that the call to
   // getImage will return before the image is completely loaded.
   //------------------------------------------------------------------------
   for (int i = 1; i <= NUM_IMAGES; i++)
   {
      // Build path to next image
      //---------------------------------------------------------------------
      strImage = "images/img00" + ((i < 10) ? "0" : "") + i + ".gif";
      m_Images[i-1] = getImage(getDocumentBase(), strImage);

      tracker.addImage(m_Images[i-1], 0);
   }

   // Wait until all images are fully loaded
   //------------------------------------------------------------------------
   try
   {
      tracker.waitForAll();
      m_fAllLoaded = !tracker.isErrorAny();
   }
   catch (InterruptedException e)
   {
      // TODO: Place exception-handling code here in case an
      //    InterruptedException is thrown by Thread.sleep(),
```

```
      //    meaning that another thread has interrupted this one
    }

    if (!m_fAllLoaded)
    {
      stop();
      m_Graphics.drawString("Error loading images!", 10, 40);
      return;
    }


    // Assuming all images are same width and height.
    //------------------------------------------------------------------
    m_nImgWidth  = m_Images[0].getWidth(this);
    m_nImgHeight = m_Images[0].getHeight(this);
  }
  repaint();

  while (true)
  {
    try
    {
      // Draw next image in animation
      //--------------------------------------------------------------
      displayImage(m_Graphics);
      m_nCurrImage++;
      if (m_nCurrImage == NUM_IMAGES)
        m_nCurrImage = 0;

      // TODO:  Add additional thread-specific code here
      Thread.sleep(100);
    }
    catch (InterruptedException e)
    {
      // TODO: Place exception-handling code here in case an
      //    InterruptedException is thrown by Thread.sleep(),
      //    meaning that another thread has interrupted this one
      stop();
    }
```

```
    }
  }

// TODO: Place additional applet code here

}
```

There are more animation techniques available in Java. One of them is *double buffering*. This technique lets us handle complex animation images, and we'll explore that technique now.

Double Buffering

Double buffering allows us to develop complex graphics images off-screen and then flash them on the screen when they are ready. That is, we wouldn't want to create the graphics we want to animate on the screen, in front of the user, frame by frame, as the user watches. Instead, it is far better to create each image in memory and then display it only when ready.

For this example, our graphics images won't actually be all that complex. We'll simply develop a series of white boxes that contain a rectangle in the upper left corner:

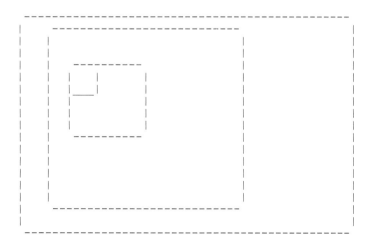

In succeeding frames, the rectangle becomes larger. As we work through all 20 images in an animation example, it looks as though the rectangle is growing from upper left to the lower right:

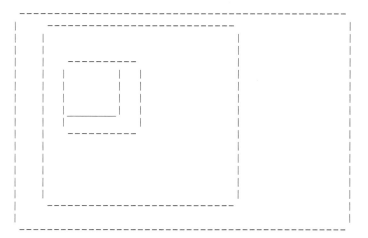

None of these images will exist on disk. We'll create them in memory and then display them on the screen. In the previous chapter, we developed an image in memory from a pixel array. Here you'll see how to use Graphics class methods with a memory image. Developing graphics off-screen and then displaying them is a powerful Java technique.

Create this new applet named doublebuffer now, and give it animation support. We will need an image object in memory that we can draw in—this will be our "buffer" image. We create this object of the Image class, which we'll call image, with the applet's createImage() method in the init() method:

```
public void init()
{
    // If you use a ResourceWizard-generated "control creator" class to
    // arrange controls in your applet, you may want to call its
    // CreateControls() method from within this method. Remove the following
    // call to resize() before adding the call to CreateControls();
```

```
    // CreateControls() does its own resizing.
    //----------------------------------------------------------------
    resize(320, 240);
➜   image = createImage(101, 101);
        .
        .
        .

    }
```

We can connect a Graphics object to that new image, and that will be the basis of all our graphics work—that is, we'll draw in this new Graphics object, using its methods, such as drawRect(). To create this object, named graphics, we use the Image object's getGraphics() method:

```
public void init()
{
    // If you use a ResourceWizard-generated "control creator" class to
    // arrange controls in your applet, you may want to call its
    // CreateControls() method from within this method. Remove the following
    // call to resize() before adding the call to CreateControls();
    // CreateControls() does its own resizing.
    //----------------------------------------------------------------
    resize(320, 240);
    image = createImage(101, 101);
➜   graphics = image.getGraphics();

}
```

We also declare these two new objects at the beginning of our applet:

```
public class doublebuffer extends Applet implements Runnable
{
    // THREAD SUPPORT:
    //   m_doublebuffer  is the Thread object for the applet
    //------------------------------------------------------------
    Thread  m_doublebuffer = null;

➜   Image image;
```

```
→   Graphics graphics;
        .
        .
        .
```

The graphics work in an Applet Wizard–designed animation applet goes on in the `displayImage()` method, so open that now:

```
// ANIMATION SUPPORT:
//   Draws the next image, if all images are currently loaded
//------------------------------------------------------------
private void displayImage(Graphics g)
{   .
      .
      .
```

We are passed a `graphics` object, named `g`, in the `displayImage()` method, and we are supposed to display our image using that object. First, however, we have to create our images—a white box with rectangles marching from upper left to lower right. We can create 20 such frames, using an integer loop index named `loop_index` to keep the images straight:

```
public class doublebuffer extends Applet implements Runnable
{
    // THREAD SUPPORT:
    //   m_doublebuffer  is the Thread object for the applet
    //------------------------------------------------------------
    Thread  m_doublebuffer = null;

    Image image;
    Graphics graphics;
→   int loop_index = 0;
      .
      .
      .
```

We can use the value of `loop_index` as both the x and y dimensions of the current rectangle (in pixels). First, in the `displayImage()` method, delete the code that the Applet Wizard has placed there. Now, we increment `loop_index` by a value of 5, which will make each rectangle 5 pixels larger horizontally and vertically than the preceding one. If the `loop_index` gets too big, we set it back to zero:

```
// ANIMATION SUPPORT:
//   Draws the next image, if all images are currently loaded
//-----------------------------------------------------------------
private void displayImage(Graphics g)
{
    loop_index += 5;
    if(loop_index >= 100) loop_index = 0;
        .
        .
        .
```

Next, we need to construct our graphics image—a white box with a rectangle in it of dimensions `loop_index` × `loop_index`. We can simply draw in memory the `Graphics` object—named `graphics`—which we've already set up. We start by setting the drawing color in our memory image with the `setColor()` method. Here we set the drawing color to white so that we can draw the white box itself:

```
// ANIMATION SUPPORT:
//   Draws the next image, if all images are currently loaded
//-----------------------------------------------------------
private void displayImage(Graphics g)
{
    loop_index += 5;
    if(loop_index >= 100) loop_index = 0;
    graphics.setColor(new Color(255, 255, 255));
        .
        .
        .
```

We pass the `setColor()` method a new Java `Color` object that has been set to white. You set the color of a `Color` object by passing red, green, and blue color values to its constructor, and those values range from 0 to 255. The color white has all these values set to 255.

TIP It takes a little practice to get the color values you want in your applet just right, but several color values are easy to set. For example, pure red is Color(255, 0, 0), pure green is Color(0, 255, 0), and pure blue is Color(0, 0, 255). White is the combination of all these, so it is Color(255, 255, 255). Black is Color(0, 0, 0), and gray is Color(128, 128, 128).

Now that we've installed white as the drawing color, we color the whole rectangle white with a call to the Graphics fillRect() method:

```
// ANIMATION SUPPORT:
//   Draws the next image, if all images are currently loaded
//------------------------------------------------------------
private void displayImage(Graphics g)
{
    loop_index += 5;
    if(loop_index >= 100) loop_index = 0;
    graphics.setColor(new Color(255, 255, 255));
→   graphics.fillRect(0, 0, 100, 100);
        .
        .
        .
```

After drawing the white background, we set the drawing color to black (Color(0, 0, 0)) to draw a black rectangle of dimensions loop_index × loop_index (which will get larger in the next image as we loop progressively):

```
// ANIMATION SUPPORT:
//   Draws the next image, if all images are currently loaded
//------------------------------------------------------------
private void displayImage(Graphics g)
{
    loop_index += 5;
    if(loop_index >= 100) loop_index = 0;
    graphics.setColor(new Color(255, 255, 255));
    graphics.fillRect(0, 0, 100, 100);
→   graphics.setColor(new Color(0, 0, 0));
```

➡️ ```
graphics.drawRect(0, 0, loop_index, loop_index);
```
    .

    .

    .

Now that we've drawn the graphics image we want in the `Graphics` object corresponding to our `Image` object, the last step is to place that now-prepared `Image` object on the screen, and we do that in `drawImage()`:

```
// ANIMATION SUPPORT:
//   Draws the next image, if all images are currently loaded
//---
private void displayImage(Graphics g)
{
    loop_index += 5;
    if(loop_index >= 100) loop_index = 0;
    graphics.setColor(new Color(255, 255, 255));
    graphics.fillRect(0, 0, 100, 100);
    graphics.setColor(new Color(0, 0, 0));
    graphics.drawRect(0, 0, loop_index, loop_index);
    g.drawImage(image, 10, 10, this);
}
```
(➡️ marks the line `g.drawImage(image, 10, 10, this);`)

Now that the `drawImage()` method is set up correctly, we have to make sure that this method is called. The Applet Wizard has set up the `run()` method to load in images and display them, but, of course, we have no images to load in from disk here. We, therefore, replace that code with this, which repeatedly calls `displayImage()`:

```
// THREAD SUPPORT
//   The run() method is called when the applet's thread is started. If
// your applet performs any ongoing activities without waiting for user
// input, the code for implementing that behavior typically goes here. For
// example, for an applet that performs animation, the run() method controls
// the display of images.
//---
public void run()
{
    m_Graphics = getGraphics();
    while(true){
```
(➡️ marks the line `while(true){`)
```

```
➜        displayImage(m_Graphics);
➜        try {Thread.sleep(100);}
➜        catch(InterruptedException e) { }
➜     }
    }
```

In addition, we remove the part of the code that has to do with loading images in from disk in the `paint()` method:

```
public void paint(Graphics g)
{
  // ANIMATION SUPPORT:
  //   The following code displays a status message until all the
  //   images are loaded. Then it calls displayImage to display the current
  //   image.
  //------------------------------------------------------------------------
➜  //if (m_fAllLoaded)
➜  //{
      Rectangle r = g.getClipRect();

      g.clearRect(r.x, r.y, r.width, r.height);
      displayImage(g);
➜  //}
➜  //else
➜     //g.drawString("Loading images...", 10, 20);

    // TODO: Place additional applet Paint code here
  }
```

Our doublebuffer applet is ready to go. Run it now, as shown in Figure 11.4. The rectangle in the applet appears to grow from upper left to lower right continuously, and we are creating the images off screen and then displaying them when they are ready. Our doublebuffer applet is a success. The code for this applet appears in `doublebuffer.java`.

FIGURE 11.4:

Our double-buffering animation example develops graphics off screen.

doublebuffer.java

```
//**********************************************************************************
// doublebuffer.java: Applet
//
//**********************************************************************************
import java.applet.*;
import java.awt.*;
//import java.util.Random;


//================================================================================
// Main Class for applet doublebuffer
//
//================================================================================
public class doublebuffer extends Applet implements Runnable
{
    // THREAD SUPPORT:
    //   m_doublebuffer  is the Thread object for the applet
    //--------------------------------------------------------------------------
    Thread  m_doublebuffer = null;

    // ANIMATION SUPPORT:
```

```
//   m_Graphics    used for storing the applet's Graphics context
//   m_Images[]    the array of Image objects for the animation
//   m_nCurrImage  the index of the next image to be displayed
//   m_ImgWidth    width of each image
//   m_ImgHeight   height of each image
//   m_fAllLoaded  indicates whether all images have been loaded
//   NUM_IMAGES    number of images used in the animation
//-------------------------------------------------------------------------
private Graphics m_Graphics;
//private Image  m_Images[];
//private int    m_nCurrImage;
//private int    m_nImgWidth  = 0;
//private int    m_nImgHeight = 0;
//private boolean  m_fAllLoaded = false;
//private final int NUM_IMAGES = 18;

Image image;
Graphics graphics;
int loop_index = 0;

// doublebuffer Class Constructor
//-------------------------------------------------------------------------
public doublebuffer()
{
  // TODO: Add constructor code here
}

// APPLET INFO SUPPORT:
//   The getAppletInfo() method returns a string describing the applet's
// author, copyright date, or miscellaneous information.
//-------------------------------------------------------------------------
public String getAppletInfo()
{
  return "Name: doublebuffer\r\n" +
      "Author: Steven Holzner\r\n" +
      "Created with Microsoft Visual J++ Version 1.0";
}


// The init() method is called by the AWT when an applet is first loaded or
// reloaded.  Override this method to perform whatever initialization your
// applet needs, such as initializing data structures, loading images or
```

```
// fonts, creating frame windows, setting the layout manager, or adding UI
// components.
//-----------------------------------------------------------------------
public void init()
{
  // If you use a ResourceWizard-generated "control creator" class to
  // arrange controls in your applet, you may want to call its
  // CreateControls() method from within this method. Remove the following
  // call to resize() before adding the call to CreateControls();
  // CreateControls() does its own resizing.
  //---------------------------------------------------------------------
  resize(320, 240);
  image = createImage(101, 101);
  graphics = image.getGraphics();

  // TODO: Place additional initialization code here
}

// Place additional applet clean up code here.  destroy() is called
// when your applet is terminating and being unloaded.
//-----------------------------------------------------------------------
public void destroy()
{
  // TODO: Place applet cleanup code here
}

// ANIMATION SUPPORT:
//   Draws the next image, if all images are currently loaded
//-----------------------------------------------------------------------
private void displayImage(Graphics g)
{
  loop_index += 5;
  if(loop_index >= 100) loop_index = 0;
  graphics.setColor(new Color(255, 255, 255));
  graphics.fillRect(0, 0, 100, 100);
  graphics.setColor(new Color(0, 0, 0));
  graphics.drawRect(0, 0, loop_index, loop_index);
  g.drawImage(image, 10, 10, this);

//if (!m_fAllLoaded)
//   return;

  // Draw Image in center of applet
```

```
   //-------------------------------------------------------------------------
   //g.drawImage(m_Images[m_nCurrImage],
   //         (size().width - m_nImgWidth)   / 2,
   //         (size().height - m_nImgHeight) / 2, null);
   }


   // doublebuffer Paint Handler
   //-------------------------------------------------------------------------
   public void paint(Graphics g)
   {
     // ANIMATION SUPPORT:
     //   The following code displays a status message until all the
     // images are loaded. Then it calls displayImage to display the current
     // image.
     //-------------------------------------------------------------------------
     //if (m_fAllLoaded)
     //{
       Rectangle r = g.getClipRect();

       g.clearRect(r.x, r.y, r.width, r.height);
       displayImage(g);
     //}
     //else
       //g.drawString("Loading images...", 10, 20);

     // TODO: Place additional applet Paint code here
   }


   //   The start() method is called when the page containing the applet
   // first appears on the screen. The AppletWizard's initial implementation
   // of this method starts execution of the applet's thread.
   //-------------------------------------------------------------------------
   public void start()
   {
     if (m_doublebuffer == null)
     {
       m_doublebuffer = new Thread(this);
       m_doublebuffer.start();
     }
     // TODO: Place additional applet start code here
   }


   //   The stop() method is called when the page containing the applet is
```

```
// no longer on the screen. The AppletWizard's initial implementation of
// this method stops execution of the applet's thread.
//----------------------------------------------------------------------
public void stop()
{
   if (m_doublebuffer != null)
   {
     m_doublebuffer.stop();
     m_doublebuffer = null;
   }

   // TODO: Place additional applet stop code here
}


// THREAD SUPPORT
//    The run() method is called when the applet's thread is started. If
// your applet performs any ongoing activities without waiting for user
// input, the code for implementing that behavior typically goes here. For
// example, for an applet that performs animation, the run() method controls
// the display of images.
//----------------------------------------------------------------------
public void run()
{

   m_Graphics = getGraphics();
   while(true){
     displayImage(m_Graphics);
     try {Thread.sleep(100);}
     catch(InterruptedException e) { }
   }
   // If re-entering the page, then the images have already been loaded.
   // m_fAllLoaded == TRUE.
   //--------------------------------------------------------------------
   //if (!m_fAllLoaded)
   //{
   //   m_nCurrImage = 0;
   //     m_Graphics = getGraphics();
   //     m_Images   = new Image[NUM_IMAGES];

       // Load in all the images
       //--------------------------------------------------------------
     //MediaTracker tracker = new MediaTracker(this);
```

```
//String strImage;

   // For each image in the animation, this method first constructs a
   // string containing the path to the image file; then it begins
   // loading the image into the m_Images array.  Note that the call to
   // getImage will return before the image is completely loaded.
   //-------------------------------------------------------------------
//for (int i = 1; i <= NUM_IMAGES; i++)
//{
   // Build path to next image
   //-------------------------------------------------------------------
// strImage = "images/img00" + ((i < 10) ? "0" : "") + i + ".gif";
// m_Images[i-1] = getImage(getDocumentBase(), strImage);

//   tracker.addImage(m_Images[i-1], 0);
//}

   // Wait until all images are fully loaded
   //-------------------------------------------------------------------
//try
//{
// tracker.waitForAll();
// m_fAllLoaded = !tracker.isErrorAny();
//}
//catch (InterruptedException e)
//{
   // TODO: Place exception-handling code here in case an
   //    InterruptedException is thrown by Thread.sleep(),
   //    meaning that another thread has interrupted this one
//}

//if (!m_fAllLoaded)
//{
// stop();
// m_Graphics.drawString("Error loading images!", 10, 40);
// return;
//}

   // Assuming all images are same width and height.
   //-------------------------------------------------------------------
//m_nImgWidth  = m_Images[0].getWidth(this);
```

```
    //m_nImgHeight = m_Images[0].getHeight(this);
  //}
  //repaint();

  //while (true)
  //{
  //try
  //{
      // Draw next image in animation
      //------------------------------------------------------------------
        //displayImage(m_Graphics);
        //m_nCurrImage++;
      //if (m_nCurrImage == NUM_IMAGES)
          //m_nCurrImage = 0;

      // TODO:  Add additional thread-specific code here
      //Thread.sleep(50);
    //}
    //catch (InterruptedException e)
    //{
      // TODO: Place exception-handling code here in case an
      //    InterruptedException is thrown by Thread.sleep(),
      //    meaning that another thread has interrupted this one
      //stop();
    //}
  //}
}



// TODO: Place additional applet code here

}
```

Sun has produced an `animator` class that can perform animation
for you, and we'll take a look at that now.

The Sun Animator

The built-in support for sound and video in Java is not so good—although it can handle .au sound files, it cannot yet handle video files. Even so, you can use Sun's `animator` class to create motion in your applets. The Sun `animator` class comes with Visual J++ as an example. To use this class, you pass various parameters to the `animator` class as parameters in your Web page. Here is Sun's own documentation for that:

`<APPLET CODE="animator.class"WIDTH = "aNumber"`	the width (in pixels) of the widest frame
`HEIGHT = "aNumber">`	the height (in pixels) of the tallest frame
`<PARAM NAME="IMAGESOURCE"VALUE="aDirectory">`	the directory that has the animationframes (a series of pictures in GIF or JPEG format, by default named T1.gif, T2.gif, ...)
`<PARAM NAME="STARTUP"VALUE="aFile">`	an image to display at load time
`<PARAM NAME="BACKGROUND"VALUE="aFile">`	an image to paint the frames against
`<PARAM NAME="STARTIMAGE"VALUE="aNumber">`	number of the starting frame (1..n)
`<PARAM NAME="ENDIMAGE"VALUE="aNumber">`	number of the end frame (1..n)
`<PARAM NAME="NAMEPATTERN"VALUE="dir/prefix%N.suffix">`	a pattern to use for generating names based on STARTIMAGE and ENDIMAGE (See below.)
`<PARAM NAME="PAUSE"VALUE="100">`	milliseconds to pause between images default (can be overriden by PAUSES)
`<PARAM NAME="PAUSES"VALUE="300|200||400|200">`	millisecond delay per frame. Blank uses default PAUSE value
`<PARAM NAME="REPEAT"VALUE="true">`	repeat the sequence?
`<PARAM NAME="POSITIONS" VALUE="100@200||200@100||200@200|100@100|105@105">`	positions (X@Y) for each frame. Blank means use previous frame's position

```
<PARAM NAME="IMAGES"VALUE="3|3|2|1|2|3|17">          explicit order for frames (see
                                                      below)

<PARAM NAME="SOUNDSOURCE"VALUE="aDirectory">         the directory that has the
                                                      audio files

<PARAM NAME="SOUNDTRACK"VALUE="aFile">               an audio file to play throughout

<PARAM NAME="SOUNDS"SOUNDS="aFile.au|||||bFile.au">  audio files keyed to individual
                                                      frames

</APPLET>
```

To use the `animator` class, all you really have to do is to name your images `T1.gif`, `T2.gif`, `T3.gif`, and so on and then set the `endimage` parameter to the number of images you have. For example, here's how you would set up our twirler images with the `animator` class:

```
<HTML>
<BODY>

<CENTER>
<H1>Our animation example</H1>
<APPLET CODE = animator.class WIDTH = 300 HEIGHT = 200>
<PARAM NAME = endimage VALUE = 4>
<PARAM NAME = pause VALUE = 200>
<PARAM NAME = repeat VALUE = true>
</APPLET>
</CENTER>

</HTML>
</BODY>
```

This displays our twirler on the screen.

That's it for our coverage of the animator class. Next, we'll look at the last of the Java layout managers. Although technically not an animation topic, the Card layout manager can mimic animation in many ways that the image-handling techniques we've been covering so far cannot.

The Card Layout Manager

If you want to animate things other than images in Java, a Java layout manager can handle many of the details. For example, if you have a panel filled with label controls:

you can use the Card layout manager to flash another panel on the screen:

In this way, the Card layout manager supports animation—not animation of images, but of controls and panels. For that reason, we'll take a look at this layout manager now, developing the example above.

Create a new applet named cards now, omitting animation and multithreading support in the Applet Wizard. We'll need a panel class that contains four labels for the four text strings: This, is, card,

and one. We can call the panel class `cardlayoutpanel` this way (add
this class to the end of the `cards.java` file):

```
class cardlayoutpanel extends Panel {

}
```

We set the layout in the panel to a grid layout for our four labels:

```
class cardlayoutpanel extends Panel {

➡   cardlayoutpanel(){
➡       setLayout(new GridLayout(4, 1));
            .
            .
            .

    }
}
```

Now we add our four labels, leaving the last one blank (so that we
can fill in the card number there—"one" or "two" and so on):

```
class cardlayoutpanel extends Panel {
    Label label1, label2, label3, label4;

    cardlayoutpanel(){
        setLayout(new GridLayout(4, 1));
➡       label1 = new Label("This");
➡       add(label1);
➡       label2 = new Label("is");
➡       add(label2);
➡       label3 = new Label("panel");
➡       add(label3);
➡       label4 = new Label("");
➡       add(label4);
    }
}
```

We've designed the panels that will make up the "cards" in the card layout, and now we add four of those panels to our applet:

```
public class cards extends Applet
{
→    cardlayoutpanel panel1, panel2, panel3, panel4;
     .
     .
     .
```

After declaring our four cards, we set up the Card layout manager in the init() method:

```
public void init()
{
  // If you use a ResourceWizard-generated "control creator" class to
  // arrange controls in your applet, you may want to call its
  // CreateControls() method from within this method. Remove the following
  // call to resize() before adding the call to CreateControls();
  // CreateControls() does its own resizing.
  //---------------------------------------------------------------------
  resize(320, 240);

→  CardLayout cardlayout = new CardLayout();
→  setLayout(cardlayout);
     .
     .
     .
}
```

We then add the four panels we have created to this layout. In order, the cards in a Card layout are referred to with the strings "first", "second", and so on. We cadd our new panels this way:

```
public void init()
{
   resize(320, 240);

   CardLayout cardlayout = new CardLayout();
   setLayout(cardlayout);
→  panel1 = new cardlayoutpanel();
→  panel1.label4.setText("one.");
```

```
→        panel2 = new cardlayoutpanel();
→        panel2.label4.setText("two.");
→        panel3 = new cardlayoutpanel();
→        panel3.label4.setText("three.");
→        panel4 = new cardlayoutpanel();
→        panel4.label4.setText("four.");
→        add("first", panel1);
→        add("second", panel2);
→        add("third", panel3);
→        add("fourth", panel4);
                 .
                 .
                 .


     }
```

None of these cards appear on the screen yet. We can flash the cards we want on the screen with the Card layout method show(). In this case, we'll display the second card using the string "second":

```
public void init()
{
  resize(320, 240);

  CardLayout cardlayout = new CardLayout();
  setLayout(cardlayout);
  panel1 = new cardlayoutpanel();
  panel1.label4.setText("one.");
  panel2 = new cardlayoutpanel();
  panel2.label4.setText("two.");
  panel3 = new cardlayoutpanel();
  panel3.label4.setText("three.");
  panel4 = new cardlayoutpanel();
  panel4.label4.setText("four.");
  add("first", panel1);
  add("second", panel2);
  add("third", panel3);
  add("fourth", panel4);
→  cardlayout.show(this, "second");

  }
```

Whenever we want to flash a new card onto the screen, we can use the show() method. In this way, we are able to "animate" whole panels. Run this applet now. The result appears in Figure 11.5, and the code for this applet appears in cards.java. Our card layout applet is a success—using this new layout, you can animate not only images, but also controls and panels.

FIGURE 11.5:

The Card layout manager animates panels.

cards.java

```
//*************************************************************************
// cards.java:  Applet
//
//*************************************************************************
import java.applet.*;
import java.awt.*;

//=========================================================================
// Main Class for applet cards
//
//=========================================================================
public class cards extends Applet
```

```
{
   cardlayoutpanel panel1, panel2, panel3, panel4;

   // cards Class Constructor
   //-------------------------------------------------------------------------
   public cards()
   {
      // TODO: Add constructor code here
   }

   // APPLET INFO SUPPORT:
   //   The getAppletInfo() method returns a string describing the applet's
   // author, copyright date, or miscellaneous information.
   //-------------------------------------------------------------------------
   public String getAppletInfo()
   {
      return "Name: cards\r\n" +
             "Author: Steven Holzner\r\n" +
             "Created with Microsoft Visual J++ Version 1.0";
   }


   // The init() method is called by the AWT when an applet is first loaded or
   // reloaded.  Override this method to perform whatever initialization your
   // applet needs, such as initializing data structures, loading images or
   // fonts, creating frame windows, setting the layout manager, or adding UI
   // components.
   //-------------------------------------------------------------------------
   public void init()
   {
      // If you use a ResourceWizard-generated "control creator" class to
      // arrange controls in your applet, you may want to call its
      // CreateControls() method from within this method. Remove the following
      // call to resize() before adding the call to CreateControls();
      // CreateControls() does its own resizing.
      //-------------------------------------------------------------------------
      resize(320, 240);

      CardLayout cardlayout = new CardLayout();
      setLayout(cardlayout);
      panel1 = new cardlayoutpanel();
      panel1.label4.setText("one.");
```

```
   panel2 = new cardlayoutpanel();
   panel2.label4.setText("two.");
   panel3 = new cardlayoutpanel();
   panel3.label4.setText("three.");
   panel4 = new cardlayoutpanel();
   panel4.label4.setText("four.");
   add("first", panel1);
   add("second", panel2);
   add("third", panel3);
   add("fourth", panel4);
   cardlayout.show(this, "second");

}


// Place additional applet clean up code here.  destroy() is called
// when your applet is terminating and being unloaded.
//-------------------------------------------------------------------------
public void destroy()
{
   // TODO: Place applet cleanup code here
}


// cards Paint Handler
//-------------------------------------------------------------------------
public void paint(Graphics g)
{
   g.drawString("Created with Microsoft Visual J++ Version 1.0", 10, 20);
}


//   The start() method is called when the page containing the applet
// first appears on the screen. The AppletWizard's initial implementation
// of this method starts execution of the applet's thread.
//-------------------------------------------------------------------------
public void start()
{
   // TODO: Place additional applet start code here
}


//   The stop() method is called when the page containing the applet is
// no longer on the screen. The AppletWizard's initial implementation of
// this method stops execution of the applet's thread.
//-------------------------------------------------------------------------
```

```
public void stop()
{
}




// TODO: Place additional applet code here

}

class cardlayoutpanel extends Panel {
  Label label1, label2, label3, label4;

  cardlayoutpanel(){
    setLayout(new GridLayout(4, 1));
    label1 = new Label("This");
    add(label1);
    label2 = new Label("is");
    add(label2);
    label3 = new Label("panel");
    add(label3);
    label4 = new Label("");
    add(label4);
  }
}
```

What's Next?

That's it for our animation coverage for the moment. In the next chapter, we'll turn to a topic we already have some experience with—multithreading. You've seen a little about multithreading in this chapter already, because multithreading is the basis of animation in Java. However, there is much more to examine—using multiple threads and coordinating multiple threads, for example—and we'll look at how to do that and more in the next chapter.

CHAPTER
TWELVE

12

Multithreaded Applets

- Using the `start()` and `stop()` methods

- Using the `run()` method

- Controlling threads and setting priority

- Loading images in the background

- Using multiple threads

- Coordinating multiple threads

- Synchronizing threads

- Synchronizing functions

In this chapter, we're going to explore an aspect of Java that we first saw in the previous chapter—multithreading. Animation provided a good introduction to this topic. In Java, a thread (that is, an independent stream of execution) endlessly places animation frames in an applet while the applet's main thread does other work. That's a good overview of the usefulness of multithreading in applets—while we do other work, a thread can be hard at work on a background task.

For example, in this chapter, you'll see how a thread can load an applet's graphics (which is often a time-consuming business) in the background while we do other things in the applet's main thread. You'll also see how to set a thread's priority, how to coordinate threads at work, and how to use multiple threads. We'll start by examining the support for multithreading that Visual J++ creates for us with the Applet Wizard.

What Makes a Multithreaded Applet Tick?

You already know one easy way to create a multithreaded applet—you can let the Visual J++ Applet Wizard do it for you. When you ask the Wizard to create a multithreaded applet (without animation support), the Applet Wizard creates an applet that uses a new thread to display random numbers.

Use the Applet Wizard now to create a new applet that displays random numbers, and name the applet random. To do that, be sure you answer the question, "Would you like your applet to be multi-threaded?" in Step 3 of the Applet Wizard by clicking on the Yes,

Please button. Omit animation support by answering the question, "Would you like support for animation?" by clicking on the No, Thank You button. This creates the random applet, which displays random numbers, and you can run it right away, as shown in Figure 12.1.

FIGURE 12.1:

The random applet uses a thread to display random numbers.

Now that we have a working multithreaded applet, our next step is to take it apart and see what makes it tick.

Dissecting *random.java*

The Applet Wizard has started out our new applet by declaring the random class and a thread named m_random, which it sets to null (that is, to zero):

```
public class random extends Applet implements Runnable
{
  // THREAD SUPPORT:
  //   m_random  is the Thread object for the applet
  //-----------------------------------------------------------
```

➜   `Thread  m_random = null;`

         .

         .

         .

The `random` class uses the keywords `implements Runnable`—you'll find those keywords in the declaration of the `random` class above. `Runable` is a special Java interface that all multithreaded applets must use, and including the keywords `implements Runnable` in this way adds Java support for multithreading to our applet. You'll see more about the `Runnable` interface later in this chapter. An interface is as close as Java comes to allowing multiple inheritance; it's a set of method and constant declarations that allow you to avoid inheriting data members and inherit only common functionality.

The *start()* and *stop()* Methods

The Applet Wizard has also added a `start()` method to our applet:

```
//   The start() method is called when the page containing the applet
// first appears on the screen. The AppletWizard's initial implementation
// of this method starts execution of the applet's thread.
//--------------------------------------------------------------------------
public void start()
{
➜  if (m_random == null)
➜  {
➜     m_random = new Thread(this);
➜     m_random.start();
➜  }
   // TODO: Place additional applet start code here
}
```

This method is called when the applet is first loaded, and it's where you create and start a new thread. Here, the applet first checks to see if the `Thread` object `m_random` is set to `null` and, if so, creates the new thread, passing the `Thread` class's constructor a reference to our applet with the `this` keyword, and then starts the new thread by calling its `start()` method. This begins the execution of the new thread, which means that it starts executing the code in the `run()` method that you'll see in a minute.

If we did not shut down the thread when the applet was dismissed from the screen, the thread would keep going until the Web browser closes. The Applet Wizard, therefore, adds this code to the applet's `stop()` method, which is called when the applet is finished:

```
//  The stop() method is called when the page containing the applet is
//  no longer on the screen. The AppletWizard's initial implementation of
//  this method stops execution of the applet's thread.
//-------------------------------------------------------------------------
public void stop()
{
➜   if (m_random != null)
➜   {
➜      m_random.stop();
➜      m_random = null;
➜   }

    // TODO: Place additional applet stop code here
}
```

Here, we simply use the `Thread` class's `stop()` method to stop the `m_random` thread, and we set that variable to `null`. Doing so ends the thread and deallocates its memory (when the Java garbage is collected).

The *run()* Method

The real work of a multithreaded applet takes place in the `run()` method. This is the method in which we place the code that we want the new thread (or threads) to execute. The main thread of the applet will not enter here, but the new threads we create and start will come here automatically. Here's what the `run()` method in the random applet looks like:

```
// THREAD SUPPORT
//   The run() method is called when the applet's thread is started. If
// your applet performs any ongoing activities without waiting for user
// input, the code for implementing that behavior typically goes here. For
// example, for an applet that performs animation, the run() method
// controls the display of images.
//------------------------------------------------------------------------
public void run()
{
  while (true)
  {
    try
    {
      repaint();
      // TODO:  Add additional thread-specific code here
      Thread.sleep(50);
    }
    catch (InterruptedException e)
    {
      // TODO: Place exception-handling code here in case an
      //    InterruptedException is thrown by Thread.sleep(),
      //    meaning that another thread has interrupted this one
      stop();
    }
  }
}
```

In this case, the thread calls `repaint()`, which repaints the applet's display (note that threads such as `m_random` can call any method in the applet, just as we can ourselves in the main thread) and then "sleeps" for 50 milliseconds using the `Thread` class's `sleep()` method. Note also that the Applet Wizard has enclosed these operations in a `try...catch` block in case something goes wrong (for example, in case another thread interrupts `m_random`).

> **NOTE**
>
> We have only one new thread executing code in our random applet, but if you have more than one, things get a little more complex. One thread might be executing code in the `run()` method at the same time as another one; the first thread might even be temporarily suspended by Windows so that the threads execute at different rates. Each thread gets its own separate copy of the `run()` method to run, but when you start using or accessing system resources, using a number of threads can get complex. I'll talk about this later.

The way the random numbers actually get on the screen is through the code in the `paint()` method, which the `m_random` thread calls every 50 milliseconds. Here, the applet simply uses the Java `Math` package's `random()` method to draw random numbers on the screen:

```
public void paint(Graphics g)
{
  // TODO: Place applet paint code here
  g.drawString("Running: " + Math.random(), 10, 20);
}
```

And that's it—we've created and run our random multithreaded applet without writing a single line of code, thanks to the Visual J++ Applet Wizard. The code for this example appears in `random.java`.

random.java

```
//*****************************************************************************
// random.java: Applet
//
//*****************************************************************************
import java.applet.*;
import java.awt.*;


//=============================================================================
// Main Class for applet random
//
//=============================================================================
```

```
public class random extends Applet implements Runnable
{
  // THREAD SUPPORT:
  //   m_random is the Thread object for the applet
  //-----------------------------------------------------------------------------
  Thread  m_random = null;


  // random Class Constructor
  //-----------------------------------------------------------------------------
  public random()
  {
    // TODO: Add constructor code here
  }


  // APPLET INFO SUPPORT:
  //   The getAppletInfo() method returns a string describing the applet's
  // author, copyright date, or miscellaneous information.
  //-----------------------------------------------------------------------------
  public String getAppletInfo()
  {
    return "Name: random\r\n" +
         "Author: Steven Holzner\r\n" +
         "Created with Microsoft Visual J++ Version 1.0";
  }

  // The init() method is called by the AWT when an applet is first loaded or
  // reloaded.  Override this method to perform whatever initialization your
  // applet needs, such as initializing data structures, loading images or
  // fonts, creating frame windows, setting the layout manager, or adding UI
  // components.
  //-----------------------------------------------------------------------------
  public void init()
  {
    // If you use a ResourceWizard-generated "control creator" class to
    // arrange controls in your applet, you may want to call its
    // CreateControls() method from within this method. Remove the following
    // call to resize() before adding the call to CreateControls();
    // CreateControls() does its own resizing.
    //-----------------------------------------------------------------------------
```

```
    resize(320, 240);

    // TODO: Place additional initialization code here
}

// Place additional applet clean up code here.  destroy() is called
// when your applet is terminating and being unloaded.
//--------------------------------------------------------------------------
public void destroy()
{
    // TODO: Place applet cleanup code here
}

// random Paint Handler
//--------------------------------------------------------------------------
public void paint(Graphics g)
{
    // TODO: Place applet paint code here
    g.drawString("Running: " + Math.random(), 10, 20);
}

//   The start() method is called when the page containing the applet
// first appears on the screen. The AppletWizard's initial implementation
// of this method starts execution of the applet's thread.
//--------------------------------------------------------------------------
public void start()
{
    if (m_random == null)
    {
        m_random = new Thread(this);
        m_random.start();
    }
    // TODO: Place additional applet start code here
}

//   The stop() method is called when the page containing the applet is
// no longer on the screen. The AppletWizard's initial implementation of
// this method stops execution of the applet's thread.
//--------------------------------------------------------------------------
public void stop()
{
```

```
   if (m_random != null)
   {
     m_random.stop();
     m_random = null;
   }

   // TODO: Place additional applet stop code here
}

// THREAD SUPPORT
//   The run() method is called when the applet's thread is started. If
// your applet performs any ongoing activities without waiting for user
// input, the code for implementing that behavior typically goes here. For
// example, for an applet that performs animation, the run() method controls
// the display of images.
//----------------------------------------------------------------------
public void run()
{
   while (true)
   {
     try
     {
       repaint();
       // TODO:  Add additional thread-specific code here
       Thread.sleep(50);
     }
     catch (InterruptedException e)
     {
       // TODO: Place exception-handling code here in case an
       //    InterruptedException is thrown by Thread.sleep(),
       //    meaning that another thread has interrupted this one
       stop();
     }
   }
}


   // TODO: Place additional applet code here

}
```

Now that we've got a new thread running, let's see a little about controlling threads in general—pausing and resuming them in code, as well as setting their priority.

Controlling Threads and Setting Priority

So far, then, we've set up a new thread and let it run, but we can get far more control over threads than that. For example, we can set the *priority* of a thread with the Thread class's setPriority() method. We can give three priorities to threads, using the predefined constants in the Thread class: Thread.MIN_PRIORITY, Thread.NORM_PRIORITY (this is the default), and Thread.MAX_PRIORITY. A minimum-priority thread is used to execute tasks in the background, and maximum priority threads are used for urgent tasks. For example, if we wanted to give our m_random thread in the last example the maximum priority, we would do so like this:

```
//  The start() method is called when the page containing the applet
// first appears on the screen. The AppletWizard's initial implementation
// of this method starts execution of the applet's thread.
//-------------------------------------------------------------------------
public void start()
{
   if (m_random == null)
   {
     m_random = new Thread(this);
     m_random.setPriority(Thread.MAX_PRIORITY);
     m_random.start();
   }
   // TODO: Place additional applet start code here
}
```

TIP Although we've set the m_random thread's priority when it was first created here, you can set a thread's priority at any time.

Setting a thread's priority gives you considerably more control in working with threads. Now we can relegate background tasks to the background and give important tasks the highest priority.

Suspending and Resuming Thread Execution

You can also suspend and resume threads at any time, using the Thread class's suspend() and resume() methods. For example, in the last chapter, we created a multithreaded example named twirler, which whirled a graphics figure around and around. We can modify that applet now with two buttons, Pause Thread and Restart Thread, like this:

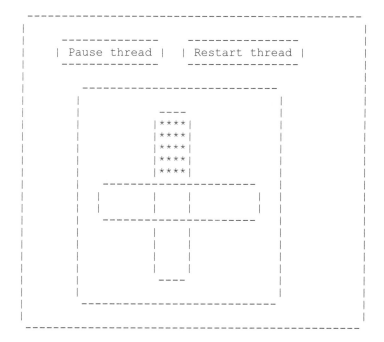

When the user clicks on the Pause Thread button, we can suspend the thread responsible for the animation, freezing the figure and giving us a graphic demonstration of thread control. When the user clicks on the Restart Thread button, the twirling starts again.

Let's name this new applet onoff. Create it now—give it multi-threading and animation support—and add the code we used in the twirler example in the last chapter to support the animation. Don't forget to copy the files img001.jpg to img004.jpg in a subdirectory called images to the new onoff directory. (If you don't want to go through all that work, you can simply refer to the onoff.java file listing.) Next, we add the two buttons we'll need to the onoff applet this way (the name of the animation thread that we'll pause and resume is m_onoff):

```
public class onoff extends Applet implements Runnable
{
    Thread  m_onoff = null;

    private Graphics m_Graphics;
    private Image  m_Images[];
    private int   m_nCurrImage;
    private int   m_nImgWidth  = 0;
    private int   m_nImgHeight = 0;
    private boolean  m_fAllLoaded = false;
    private final int NUM_IMAGES = 4; //18;
➜   Button button1, button2;
        .
        .
        .
```

We next add the Pause Thread and Restart Thread buttons to our applet:

```
// The init() method is called by the AWT when an applet is first loaded or
// reloaded.  Override this method to perform whatever initialization your
// applet needs, such as initializing data structures, loading images or
// fonts, creating frame windows, setting the layout manager, or adding UI
// components.
//------------------------------------------------------------------------
```

```
public void init()
{
    // If you use a ResourceWizard-generated "control creator" class to
    // arrange controls in your applet, you may want to call its
    // CreateControls() method from within this method. Remove the following
    // call to resize() before adding the call to CreateControls();
    // CreateControls() does its own resizing.
    //---------------------------------------------------------------------
    resize(320, 240);
```
→ `    button1 = new Button("Pause thread");`
→ `    add(button1);`
→ `    button2 = new Button("Restart thread");`
→ `    add(button2);`

```
}
```

Note that we should also move the animated figure down somewhat to allow room for our new buttons. Here, we simply move the figure down by 20 pixels:

```
// ANIMATION SUPPORT:
//   Draws the next image, if all images are currently loaded
//---------------------------------------------------------------------
private void displayImage(Graphics g)
{
    if (!m_fAllLoaded)
        return;

    // Draw Image in center of applet
    //---------------------------------------------------------------------
```
→ `g.drawImage(m_Images[m_nCurrImage], (size().width - m_nImgWidth) / 2,`
↪ `(size().height - m_nImgHeight) / 2 + 20, null);`

```
}
```

> **TIP** If you ever need the exact screen size of a Java control, you can use its `size()` method, `button1.size()`, which returns a Java object of class `Dimension`. We've used `size()` with whole applets, but it also works with controls.

We then connect the buttons to an `action` method:

```
public boolean action (Event e, Object o){
   if(e.target.equals(button1)){
          .
          .
          .

   }
   if(e.target.equals(button2)){
          .
          .
          .

   }
   return true;
}
```

The user clicks on the Pause Thread button (`button1`) to suspend the animation thread. Our animation thread is named `m_onoff`, and we suspend that thread like this:

```
public boolean action (Event e, Object o){
   if(e.target.equals(button1)){
➔       m_onoff.suspend();
   }
   if(e.target.equals(button2)){
          .
          .
          .

   }
   return true;
}
```

The user clicks on the Restart Thread button (`button2`) to resume the animation, so we call the `m_onoff` thread's `resume()` method:

```
public boolean action (Event e, Object o){
   if(e.target.equals(button1)){
     m_onoff.suspend();
   }
   if(e.target.equals(button2)){
➔     m_onoff.resume();
   }
```

```
        return true;
    }
```

Now the user can start and stop the animation thread in our applet by simply clicking on a button, which freezes and restarts the animation. Run the applet now as shown in Figure 12.2, and click on the Pause Thread button to pause the thread. The whirling figure will stop until you click on the Restart Thread button. Our onoff applet is a success, and the code for this applet appears in `onoff.java`.

FIGURE 12.2:

We can start and stop the animation thread in our onoff applet.

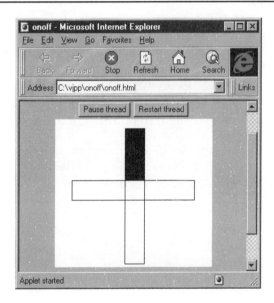

onoff.java

```
//***************************************************************************
// onoff.java:  Applet
//
//***************************************************************************
import java.applet.*;
import java.awt.*;


//===========================================================================
// Main Class for applet onoff
//
```

```
//===========================================================================
public class onoff extends Applet implements Runnable
{
   // THREAD SUPPORT:
   //   m_onoff  is the Thread object for the applet
   //---------------------------------------------------------------------------
   Thread  m_onoff = null;

   // ANIMATION SUPPORT:
   //   m_Graphics     used for storing the applet's Graphics context
   //   m_Images[]     the array of Image objects for the animation
   //   m_nCurrImage   the index of the next image to be displayed
   //   m_ImgWidth     width of each image
   //   m_ImgHeight    height of each image
   //   m_fAllLoaded   indicates whether all images have been loaded
   //   NUM_IMAGES     number of images used in the animation
   //---------------------------------------------------------------------------
   private Graphics m_Graphics;
   private Image m_Images[];
   private int  m_nCurrImage;
   private int  m_nImgWidth  = 0;
   private int  m_nImgHeight = 0;
   private boolean  m_fAllLoaded = false;
   private final int NUM_IMAGES = 4; //18;
   Button button1, button2;


   // onoff Class Constructor
   //---------------------------------------------------------------------------
   public onoff()
   {
      // TODO: Add constructor code here
   }

   // APPLET INFO SUPPORT:
   //   The getAppletInfo() method returns a string describing the applet's
   // author, copyright date, or miscellaneous information.
   //---------------------------------------------------------------------------
   public String getAppletInfo()
   {
      return "Name: onoff\r\n" +
           "Author: Steven Holzner\r\n" +
```

```
            "Created with Microsoft Visual J++ Version 1.0";
}


// The init() method is called by the AWT when an applet is first loaded or
// reloaded.  Override this method to perform whatever initialization your
// applet needs, such as initializing data structures, loading images or
// fonts, creating frame windows, setting the layout manager, or adding UI
// components.
//-------------------------------------------------------------------- -----
public void init()
{
  // If you use a ResourceWizard-generated "control creator" class to
  // arrange controls in your applet, you may want to call its
  // CreateControls() method from within this method. Remove the following
  // call to resize() before adding the call to CreateControls();
  // CreateControls() does its own resizing.
  //-------------------------------------------------------------------
  resize(320, 240);
  button1 = new Button("Pause thread");
  add(button1);
  button2 = new Button("Restart thread");
  add(button2);

  // TODO: Place additional initialization code here
}



public boolean action (Event e, Object o){
  if(e.target.equals(button1)){
    m_onoff.suspend();
  }
  if(e.target.equals(button2)){
    m_onoff.resume();
  }
  return true;
}

// Place additional applet clean up code here.  destroy() is called
// when your applet is terminating and being unloaded.
//-------------------------------------------------------------------------
```

```
public void destroy()
{
   // TODO: Place applet cleanup code here
}


// ANIMATION SUPPORT:
//   Draws the next image, if all images are currently loaded
//--------------------------------------------------------------------------
private void displayImage(Graphics g)
{
   if (!m_fAllLoaded)
      return;

   // Draw Image in center of applet
   //-----------------------------------------------------------------------
   g.drawImage(m_Images[m_nCurrImage],
         (size().width - m_nImgWidth) / 2,
         (size().height - m_nImgHeight) / 2 + 20, null);
}


// onoff Paint Handler
//--------------------------------------------------------------------------
public void paint(Graphics g)
{
   // ANIMATION SUPPORT:
   //   The following code displays a status message until all the
   //   images are loaded. Then it calls displayImage to display the current
   //   image.
   //-----------------------------------------------------------------------
   if (m_fAllLoaded)
   {
      Rectangle r = g.getClipRect();

      g.clearRect(r.x, r.y, r.width, r.height);
      displayImage(g);
   }
   else
      g.drawString("Loading images...", 10, 20);

   // TODO: Place additional applet Paint code here
}


//   The start() method is called when the page containing the applet
```

```
// first appears on the screen. The AppletWizard's initial implementation
// of this method starts execution of the applet's thread.
//--------------------------------------------------------------------------
public void start()
{
   if (m_onoff == null)
   {
     m onoff = new Thread(this);
     m_onoff.start();
   }
   // TODO: Place additional applet start code here
}


//   The stop() method is called when the page containing the applet is
// no longer on the screen. The AppletWizard's initial implementation of
// this method stops execution of the applet's thread.
//--------------------------------------------------------------------------
public void stop()
{
   if (m_onoff != null)
   {
     m_onoff.stop();
     m_onoff = null;
   }

   // TODO: Place additional applet stop code here
}


// THREAD SUPPORT
//   The run() method is called when the applet's thread is started. If
// your applet performs any ongoing activities without waiting for user
// input, the code for implementing that behavior typically goes here. For
// example, for an applet that performs animation, the run() method controls
// the display of images.
//--------------------------------------------------------------------------
public void run()
{
   m_nCurrImage = 0;

   // If re-entering the page, then the images have already been loaded.
   // m_fAllLoaded == TRUE.
   //--------------------------------------------------------------------------
```

```
if (!m_fAllLoaded)
{
   repaint();
   m_Graphics = getGraphics();
   m_Images  = new Image[NUM_IMAGES];

   // Load in all the images
   //-----------------------------------------------------------------------
   MediaTracker tracker = new MediaTracker(this);
   String strImage;

   // For each image in the animation, this method first constructs a
   // string containing the path to the image file; then it begins
   // loading the image into the m_Images array.  Note that the call to
   // getImage will return before the image is completely loaded.
   //-----------------------------------------------------------------------
   for (int i = 1; i <= NUM_IMAGES; i++)
   {
      // Build path to next image
      //--------------------------------------------------------------------
      strImage = "images/img00" + ((i < 10) ? "0" : "") + i + ".gif";
      m_Images[i-1] = getImage(getDocumentBase(), strImage);

      tracker.addImage(m_Images[i-1], 0);
   }

   // Wait until all images are fully loaded
   //-----------------------------------------------------------------------
   try
   {
      tracker.waitForAll();
      m_fAllLoaded = !tracker.isErrorAny();
   }
   catch (InterruptedException e)
   {
      // TODO: Place exception-handling code here in case an
      //    InterruptedException is thrown by Thread.sleep(),
      //    meaning that another thread has interrupted this one
   }

   if (!m_fAllLoaded)
   {
```

```
            stop();
            m_Graphics.drawString("Error loading images!", 10, 40);
            return;
        }


        // Assuming all images are same width and height.
        //----------------------------------------------------------------------
        m_nImgWidth  = m_Images[0].getWidth(this);
        m_nImgHeight = m_Images[0].getHeight(this);
    }
    repaint();

    while (true)
    {
        try
        {
            // Draw next image in animation
            //--------------------------------------------------------------
            displayImage(m_Graphics);
            m_nCurrImage++;
            if (m_nCurrImage == NUM_IMAGES)
                m_nCurrImage = 0;

            // TODO:  Add additional thread-specific code here
            Thread.sleep(50);
        }
        catch (InterruptedException e)
        {
            // TODO: Place exception-handling code here in case an
            //    InterruptedException is thrown by Thread.sleep(),
            //    meaning that another thread has interrupted this one
            stop();
        }
    }
}


    // TODO: Place additional applet code here

}
```

Next, we're going to use threads for something they are often used for in practice—handling a time-consuming task in the background.

Loading Images in the Background

One time-consuming aspect of Java programming is loading in images. This process can take a great deal of time, and we could be doing other things with that time—such as responding to the user's requests in other areas of the applet.

> **TIP**
>
> In reality, the loading of images in Java is rather well multithreaded already with the `loadImage()` method, but we'll still use this task as an example of a time-consuming process.

One of the examples you saw in Chapter 10 is the doubler applet, which reads in a graphics file named `figure.jpg` and displays it. When the user clicks in the applet, we double the x and y dimensions of the figure, stretching it. We can modify this applet so that the image, `figure.jpg`, is loaded in the background as an example of a slow process that we can perform in the background. Let's call this new applet `slow`. Create it now, adding multithreading support, which the original doubler applet did not have.

In this applet, we loaded the image `figure.jpg` during the `init()` method, displayed it in the `paint()` method, and doubled its dimensions—that is, the values in the variables *width* and *height*—when the user clicked the mouse. Here's how we displayed the image in the `paint()` method:

```
// slow Paint Handler
//------------------------------------------------------------
public void paint(Graphics g)
{
```

```
➜    g.drawRect(anchorpoint.x, anchorpoint.y, width, height);
➜    g.drawImage(doublerimage, anchorpoint.x, anchorpoint.y,
   ➥ width, height, this);
    }
```

Obviously we won't be able to display the image until it's loaded by the background thread, so let's add a boolean flag, loadedboolean, to tell us when the background thread is finished loading the image. We declare that boolean at the beginning of the applet, setting it to FALSE initially:

```
public class slow extends Applet implements Runnable
{
    Image doublerimage;
    Point anchorpoint;
    int width, height;
➜   boolean loadedboolean = false;
       .
       .
       .
```

We then straddle the image-displaying code with an if statement, which executes the image-displaying code only if the image has actually been loaded:

```
// slow Paint Handler
//-------------------------------------------------------------
public void paint(Graphics g)
{
➜   if(loadedboolean){
       g.drawRect(anchorpoint.x, anchorpoint.y, width, height);
       g.drawImage(doublerimage, anchorpoint.x, anchorpoint.y, width,
    ➥ height, this);
➜   }
   }
```

Now we will add the code for the background thread. The Applet Wizard has already added the required `start()` and `stop()` methods for this thread object, `m_slow`, as well as the `run()` method. Our goal is to read in the `figure.jpg` image in this thread and to set the `loadedboolean` flag when we are done. We start the process of loading the image with `getImage()`:

```
// THREAD SUPPORT
//     The run() method is called when the applet's thread is started. If
// your applet performs any ongoing activities without waiting for user
// input, the code for implementing that behavior typically goes here. For
// example, for an applet that performs animation, the run() method controls
// the display of images.
//-------------------------------------------------------------------------
public void run()
{
    doublerimage = getImage(getCodeBase(), "figure.jpg");
        .
        .
        .

}
```

Because this process will take some time, we add it to a `MediaTracker` object named `mediatracker` this way:

```
public void run()
{
    doublerimage = getImage(getCodeBase(), "figure.jpg");
    MediaTracker mediatracker = new MediaTracker(this);
    mediatracker.addImage(doublerimage, 0);
        .
        .
        .

}
```

We then wait for the image to be loaded in fully this way in our run() method:

```
public void run()
{
   doublerimage = getImage(getCodeBase(), "figure.jpg");
   MediaTracker mediatracker = new MediaTracker(this);
   mediatracker.addImage(doublerimage, 0);

   try{mediatracker.waitForID(0);}
   catch(Exception e){}
        .

        .

        .

}
```

After this code executes, our image is loaded, and we set the loadedboolean flag to TRUE, indicating that the image is ready to use, and we force a paint event by calling repaint():

```
public void run()
{
   doublerimage = getImage(getCodeBase(), "figure.jpg");
   MediaTracker mediatracker = new MediaTracker(this);
   mediatracker.addImage(doublerimage, 0);

   try{mediatracker.waitForID(0);}
   catch(Exception e){}

   loadedboolean = true;
   repaint();
        .

        .

        .

}
```

We won't need the m_slow thread any more, so we stop it now. We also set the m_slow variable to null so that other parts of the applet (such as the Applet Wizard–supplied code in the `stop()` method) won't try to stop a now nonexistent thread:

```
public void run()
{
    doublerimage = getImage(getCodeBase(), "figure.jpg");
    MediaTracker mediatracker = new MediaTracker(this);
    mediatracker.addImage(doublerimage, 0);

    try{mediatracker.waitForID(0);}
    catch(Exception e){}

    loadedboolean = true;
    repaint();

    m_slow.stop();
    m_slow = null;
}
```

Now run the applet, as shown in Figure 12.3. When you do, the new thread `m_slow` opens the graphics image and reads it in. Our new applet is a success. The code for this applet appears in `slow.java`.

FIGURE 12.3:

This applet uses a new thread to load in its graphics.

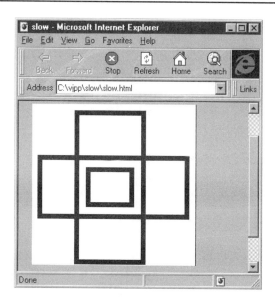

slow.java

```
//**************************************************************************
// slow.java: Applet
//
//**************************************************************************
import java.applet.*;
import java.awt.*;


//==========================================================================
// Main Class for applet slow
//
//==========================================================================
public class slow extends Applet implements Runnable
{
   Image doublerimage;
   Point anchorpoint;
   int width, height;
   boolean loadedboolean = false;

   // THREAD SUPPORT:
   //    m_slow  is the Thread object for the applet
   //--------------------------------------------------------------------
   Thread  m_slow = null;


   // slow Class Constructor
   //--------------------------------------------------------------------
   public slow()
   {
      // TODO: Add constructor code here
   }

   // APPLET INFO SUPPORT:
   //    The getAppletInfo() method returns a string describing the applet's
   // author, copyright date, or miscellaneous information.
   //--------------------------------------------------------------------
   public String getAppletInfo()
   {
      return "Name: slow\r\n" +
            "Author: Steven Holzner\r\n" +
```

```
            "Created with Microsoft Visual J++ Version 1.0";
}


// The init() method is called by the AWT when an applet is first loaded or
// reloaded.  Override this method to perform whatever initialization your
// applet needs, such as initializing data structures, loading images or
// fonts, creating frame windows, setting the layout manager, or adding UI
// components.
//--------------------------------------------------------------------------
public void init()
{
  // If you use a ResourceWizard-generated "control creator" class to
  // arrange controls in your applet, you may want to call its
  // CreateControls() method from within this method. Remove the following
  // call to resize() before adding the call to CreateControls();
  // CreateControls() does its own resizing.
  //------------------------------------------------------------------------
  resize(320, 240);

  anchorpoint = new Point(10, 10);
  width = 30;
  height = 30;

  // TODO: Place additional initialization code here
}


// Place additional applet clean up code here.  destroy() is called
// when your applet is terminating and being unloaded.
//--------------------------------------------------------------------------
public void destroy()
{
  // TODO: Place applet cleanup code here
}


// slow Paint Handler
//--------------------------------------------------------------------------
public void paint(Graphics g)
{
  // TODO: Place applet paint code here
  if(loadedboolean){
    g.drawRect(anchorpoint.x, anchorpoint.y, width, height);
```

```
        g.drawImage(doublerimage, anchorpoint.x, anchorpoint.y, width,
 height, this);
    }
  }

  //   The start() method is called when the page containing the applet
  // first appears on the screen. The AppletWizard's initial implementation
  // of this method starts execution of the applet's thread.
  //-----------------------------------------------------------------------
  public void start()
  {
    if (m_slow == null)
    {
      m_slow = new Thread(this);
      m_slow.start();
    }
    // TODO: Place additional applet start code here
  }

  //   The stop() method is called when the page containing the applet is
  // no longer on the screen. The AppletWizard's initial implementation of
  // this method stops execution of the applet's thread.
  //-----------------------------------------------------------------------
  public void stop()
  {
    if (m_slow != null)
    {
      m_slow.stop();
      m_slow = null;
    }

    // TODO: Place additional applet stop code here
  }

  // THREAD SUPPORT
  //   The run() method is called when the applet's thread is started. If
  // your applet performs any ongoing activities without waiting for user
  // input, the code for implementing that behavior typically goes here. For
  // example, for an applet that performs animation, the run() method controls
  // the display of images.
  //-----------------------------------------------------------------------
  public void run()
  {
```

```
   doublerimage = getImage(getCodeBase(), "figure.jpg");
   MediaTracker mediatracker = new MediaTracker(this);
   mediatracker.addImage(doublerimage, 0);

   try{mediatracker.waitForID(0);}
   catch(Exception e){}

   loadedboolean = true;
   repaint();

   m_slow.stop();
   m_slow = null;
}


// MOUSE SUPPORT:
//   The mouseDown() method is called if the mouse button is pressed
// while the mouse cursor is over the applet's portion of the screen.
//--------------------------------------------------------------------------
public boolean mouseDown(Event evt, int x, int y)
{
   width *= 2;
   height *= 2;
   repaint();

   return true;
}


// MOUSE SUPPORT:
//   The mouseUp() method is called if the mouse button is released
// while the mouse cursor is over the applet's portion of the screen.
//--------------------------------------------------------------------------
public boolean mouseUp(Event evt, int x, int y)
{
   // TODO: Place applet mouseUp code here
   return true;
}


   // TODO: Place additional applet code here


}
```

We've gotten a good start in handling threads, but there is much more to this topic. For example, we've only used one new thread in our applets so far, but what if we need two?

Using Multiple Threads

You may have noticed that there is only one `run()` method in our multithreaded applets. But what if a number of new threads are supposed to be doing different tasks? If there's only one `run` method, that is a problem. One way out of that difficulty is to distinguish among threads by giving them *names*. For example, let's say we had an applet with two text fields and two threads:

```
-----------------------------------------------------
|                                                   |
|     -------------------   ------------------      |
|    | Start the threads | | Stop the threads |     |
|     -------------------   ------------------      |
|                                                   |
|         ---------------------------               |
|        |---------------------------|              |
|         ---------------------------               |
|                                                   |
|         ---------------------------               |
|        |                           |              |
|         ---------------------------               |
|                                                   |
-----------------------------------------------------
```

When the user starts the threads, `thread1` and `thread2`, we might want `thread1` to successively count integers in the first text field and `thread2` to count integers in the second text box:

```
----------------------------------------------------------
|                                                        |
|     --------------------   --------------------        |
|     | Start the threads |  | Stop the threads  |       |
|     --------------------   --------------------        |
|                                                        |
|       ----------------------------                     |
|       |100                       |   <-- from thread 1 |
|       ----------------------------                     |
|                                                        |
|       ----------------------------                     |
|       |104                       |   <-- from thread 2 |
|       ----------------------------                     |
|                                                        |
----------------------------------------------------------
```

But how do we tell them apart so that they can accomplish their separate tasks? Let's put together an example to see how this works. Create this new applet now, giving it multithreaded support and calling it integers. Remove the code that the Applet Wizard has placed in start(), because we will start our own threads. Because the user needs a button to start the thread and a button to stop the thread, we add these new controls to our integers class:

```
public class integers extends Applet implements Runnable
{
➜   Button button1, button2;
➜   TextField text1, text2;
        .
        .
        .
```

We'll use two threads in this example, thread1 and thread2, so we add these threads now:

```
public class integers extends Applet implements Runnable
{
    Button button1, button2;
➜   Thread thread1 = null;
➜   Thread thread2 = null;
    TextField text1, text2;
        .
        .
        .
```

Because we will not use the default thread given to us by the Applet Wizard, m_integers, in this example, we remove all the support for this thread, substituting our own support for thread1 and thread2 as you'll see. Next, we give the the first button, button1, the label "Start the threads" and the second one, the label "Stop the threads," as well as add our two text fields to the applet's layout in the init() method:

```java
public void init()
{
   // If you use a ResourceWizard-generated "control creator" class to
   // arrange controls in your applet, you may want to call its
   // CreateControls() method from within this method. Remove the following
   // call to resize() before adding the call to CreateControls();
   // CreateControls() does its own resizing.
   //------------------------------------------------------------------------
   resize(320, 240);

   button1 = new Button("Start the threads");
   button2 = new Button("Stop the threads");
   add(button1);
   add(button2);

   text1 = new TextField(25);
   text2 = new TextField(25);
   add(text1);
   add(text2);

   // TODO: Place additional initialization code here
}
```

Because we will start the two new threads, thread1 and thread2, when the user clicks on the Start the Threads button, button1, we add that to an action() method now. In this case, however, we will need some way to differentiate the two threads so that they can perform their separate tasks. We make that possible by giving each thread a name when we create it. A thread name is simply a string, and it's used for only this purpose—to keep multiple threads straight. We pass the name of each thread—"thread1" or "thread2"—to the `Thread` class's constructor this way:

```
public boolean action (Event e, Object o){

    if(e.target.equals(button1)){
➜       thread1 = new Thread(this, "thread1");
➜       thread2 = new Thread(this, "thread2");
    }   .
            .
            .
            .

}
```

And we start each thread at the same time:

```
public boolean action (Event e, Object o){

    if(e.target.equals(button1)){
        thread1 = new Thread(this, "thread1");
➜       thread1.start();
        thread2 = new Thread(this, "thread2");
➜       thread2.start();
    } .
        .
        .
        .

}
```

That starts our two named threads. The next step is to enable the Stop the Threads button, `button2`. The user clicks on that button to stop the threads, and we stop the two threads, setting the thread objects to `null`, this way:

```
public boolean action (Event e, Object o){

    if(e.target.equals(button1)){
        thread1 = new Thread(this, "thread1");
        thread1.start();
        thread2 = new Thread(this, "thread2");
        thread2.start();
    }
➜   if(e.target.equals(button2)){
➜       if(thread1 != null && thread2 != null);
```

```
→        thread1.stop();
→        thread2.stop();
→        thread1 = null;
→        thread2 = null;
→    }
         return true;
     }
```

In addition, replace the code in the `stop()` method with `thread1.stop();` and `thread1.stop();`. Now we turn to the `run()` method, where all the action will take place. Clear all the code in this method that the Applet Wizard has set up for us, because that code deals with the (unused) Applet Wizard–supplied `m_integers` thread:

```
// THREAD SUPPORT
//   The run() method is called when the applet's thread is started. If
// your applet performs any ongoing activities without waiting for user
// input, the code for implementing that behavior typically goes here. For
// example, for an applet that performs animation, the run() method controls
// the display of images.
//------------------------------------------------------------------------
public void run()
{     .

      .

      .

}
```

Our goal in the `run` method is for `thread1` to place successive integers in the text field `text1` and for `thread2` to place successive integers in the text field `text2`. To do that, we set up a loop with an index named `loop_index` that loops from 1 to the maximum possible integer value, which is held in the `Integer` class constant, `Integer.MAX_VALUE`:

```
public void run()
{
   for(int loop_index = 1; loop_index < Integer.MAX_VALUE; loop_index++){
      .

      .

      .

   }
}
```

> **TIP**
>
> Besides `Integer.MAX_VALUE`, the minimum value an integer can have is stored in the constant `Integer.MIN_VALUE`. These constants are also available for other numeric classes such as `Float` and `Double`.

Both `thread1` *and* `thread2` will execute this loop, each as a separate thread. Each thread, therefore, will have its own copy of this method to execute. How do we make sure that the output from `thread1` goes into `text1` and that the output from `thread2` goes into `text2`? We do that with the `Thread` class's `getName()` method, which returns the name we've assigned to each thread. For example, to find out whether this copy of the `run()` method is being executed by `thread1`, we perform this check:

```
public void run()
{
    String displaystring = new String("");
    for(int loop_index = 1; loop_index < Integer.MAX_VALUE; loop_index++){
➜       if(((Thread.currentThread()).getName()).equals("thread1")){
            .
            .
            .
➜       }
    }
```

If the name of the current thread is indeed `thread1`, we can display the current integer—that is, the current value of the `loop_index` variable—in the `text1` text field this way:

```
public void run()
{
    String displaystring = new String("");
    for(int loop_index = 1; loop_index < Integer.MAX_VALUE; loop_index++){
        if(((Thread.currentThread()).getName()).equals("thread1")){
➜          text1.setText(displaystring.valueOf(loop_index));
        } .
            .
            .
            .
    }
}
```

And we do the same for `thread2`, checking its name and directing its output to `text2` this way:

```
public void run()
{
   String displaystring = new String("");
   for(int loop_index = 1; loop_index < Integer.MAX_VALUE; loop_index++){
      if(((Thread.currentThread()).getName()).equals("thread1")){
         text1.setText(displaystring.valueOf(loop_index));
      }
      if(((Thread.currentThread()).getName()).equals("thread2")){
         text2.setText(displaystring.valueOf(loop_index));
      }
   }
}
```

That's it—now you know how to keep multiple new threads separate, even though you only use one `run()` method (you'll see another way to do this at the end of the chapter). Run the applet now, as shown in Figure 12.4, and click on the Start the Threads button. You'll see the integers appear in both text fields as the two threads perform their task. Our integers applet is a success—now we're working with multiple threads. The code for this applet appears in `integers.java`.

FIGURE 12.4:

This example supports
two new threads.

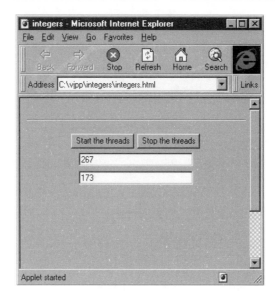

integers.java

```java
//****************************************************************************
// integers.java: Applet
//
//****************************************************************************
import java.applet.*;
import java.awt.*;


//============================================================================
// Main Class for applet integers
//
//============================================================================
public class integers extends Applet implements Runnable
{
    Button button1, button2;
    Thread thread1 = null;
    Thread thread2 = null;
    TextField text1, text2;

  // THREAD SUPPORT:
  //   m_integers is the Thread object for the applet
```

```
//------------------------------------------------------------------------
//Thread  m_integers = null;


// integers Class Constructor
//------------------------------------------------------------------------
public integers()
{
  // TODO: Add constructor code here
}

// APPLET INFO SUPPORT:
//   The getAppletInfo() method returns a string describing the applet's
// author, copyright date, or miscellaneous information.
//------------------------------------------------------------------------
public String getAppletInfo()
{
  return "Name: integers\r\n" +
       "Author: Steven Holzner\r\n" +
       "Created with Microsoft Visual J++ Version 1.0";
}


// The init() method is called by the AWT when an applet is first loaded or
// reloaded.  Override this method to perform whatever initialization your
// applet needs, such as initializing data structures, loading images or
// fonts, creating frame windows, setting the layout manager, or adding UI
// components.
//------------------------------------------------------------------------
public void init()
{
  // If you use a ResourceWizard-generated "control creator" class to
  // arrange controls in your applet, you may want to call its
  // CreateControls() method from within this method. Remove the following
  // call to resize() before adding the call to CreateControls();
  // CreateControls() does its own resizing.
  //------------------------------------------------------------------------
  resize(320, 240);

  button1 = new Button("Start the threads");
  button2 = new Button("Stop the threads");
```

```
  add(button1);
  add(button2);

  text1 = new TextField(25);
  text2 = new TextField(25);
  add(text1);
  add(text2);

  // TODO: Place additional initialization code here
}

public boolean action (Event e, Object o){

  if(e.target.equals(button1)){
    thread1 = new Thread(this, "thread1");
    thread1.start();
    thread2 = new Thread(this, "thread2");
    thread2.start();
  }
  if(e.target.equals(button2)){
    if(thread1 != null && thread2 != null);
    thread1.stop();
    thread2.stop();
    thread1 = null;
    thread2 = null;
  }
  return true;
}

// Place additional applet clean up code here.  destroy() is called
// when your applet is terminating and being unloaded.
//---------------------------------------------------------------------------
public void destroy()
{
  // TODO: Place applet cleanup code here
}

// integers Paint Handler
//---------------------------------------------------------------------------
```

```
public void paint(Graphics g)
{
  // TODO: Place applet paint code here
  //g.drawString("Running: " + Math.random(), 10, 20);
}


//   The start() method is called when the page containing the applet
// first appears on the screen. The AppletWizard's initial implementation
// of this method starts execution of the applet's thread.
//--------------------------------------------------------------------------
public void start()
{
  // TODO: Place additional applet start code here
}


//   The stop() method is called when the page containing the applet is
// no longer on the screen. The AppletWizard's initial implementation of
// this method stops execution of the applet's thread.
//--------------------------------------------------------------------------
public void stop()
{

  thread1.stop();
  thread2.stop();
  // TODO: Place additional applet stop code here
}


// THREAD SUPPORT
//   The run() method is called when the applet's thread is started. If
// your applet performs any ongoing activities without waiting for user
// input, the code for implementing that behavior typically goes here. For
// example, for an applet that performs animation, the run() method controls
// the display of images.
//--------------------------------------------------------------------------
public void run()
{
  String displaystring = new String("");
  for(int loop_index = 1; loop_index < Integer.MAX_VALUE; loop_index++){
    if(((Thread.currentThread()).getName()).equals("thread1")){
      text1.setText(displaystring.valueOf(loop_index));
    }
    if(((Thread.currentThread()).getName()).equals("thread2")){
```

```
        text2.setText(displaystring.valueOf(loop_index));
      }
    }
  }



// TODO: Place additional applet code here

}
```

You now have a good start on working with multiple threads. However, if instead of working independently, what if two threads want access to the same resource in our applet? For example, what if the two threads are supposed to write alternate lines in one file? Thread execution can vary dramatically between threads, because the operating system, not us, schedules time for each thread. How can we coordinate the work of two threads so that they will take turns with the same resource?

Coordinating Multiple Threads

To see how Java allows multiple threads to share access to a single resource, let's set up an example in which two separate threads take turns writing to the same file. As we did in the previous example, we'll use multiple thread. In the previous example, two threads shared the same `run()` method. There is, however, a more elegant way of handling this. We can create our own new `Runnable` class with its own `start()`, `stop()`, and `run()` methods. This way, the two thread objects won't share the same copy of the `run()` method. (You can even give the two threads entirely different `run()` methods by setting up two different `runnable` classes.) Let's see how this works now by coordinating our two new threads in an applet named coordinate. We might have two buttons in this applet like this:

```
-------------------------------------------------------------------------------
|                                                                             |
|    ------------------------------------    ------------------------------   |
|    | Start the file-writing threads |    | Stop the file-writing threads |  |
|    ------------------------------------    ------------------------------   |
|                                                                             |
|                                                                             |
|                                                                             |
-------------------------------------------------------------------------------
```

When the user clicks on the Start the File-Writing Threads button, the two threads begin writing to the same file. When the user clicks on the Stop the File-Writing Threads button, the process stops. Create the coordinate applet now. Do *not* give this applet multithreaded support with the Applet Wizard. Our main applet class is not going to be multithreaded here; we will add multithreading support to the applet ourselves. We begin by adding the two buttons we'll need, which we can call button1 and button2:

```
public class coordinate extends Applet
{
➜   Button button1, button2;
        .
        .
        .
```

Because two threads will write to the same file in this applet, we add those two threads, thread1 and thread2, now:

```
public class coordinate extends Applet
{
    Button button1, button2;
➜   Thread thread1 = null, thread2 = null;
        .
        .
        .
```

In addition, we'll need two new Java Runnable objects, one for each of these new threads, so that they will have their own run()

methods. We will call our new `Runnable` class `demorunnable`, and we will call the two objects of that class `runnable1` and `runnable2`:

```
public class coordinate extends Applet
{
    Button button1, button2;
    Thread thread1 = null, thread2 = null;
→   demorunnable runnable1, runnable2;
         .
         .
         .
```

Each of these objects—`runnable1` and `runnable2`—will have its own `run()` method. Let's set up the `demorunnable` class now. This class `implements Runnable` so that it can be multithreaded and support a `run()` method:

```
→ class demorunnable implements Runnable{

}
```

Next, we add the new `runnable` class's `run()` method:

```
class demorunnable implements Runnable{

→   public void run(){
          .
          .
          .
→   }
}
```

Here, let's print out 1000 strings to the file. Set up a `for` loop for 1000 iterations:

```
class demorunnable implements Runnable{

    public void run(){
```

```
➜        for(int loop_index = 1; loop_index < 1000; loop_index++){
             .
             .
             .
➜        }
      }
   }
```

The next step is to write out a string to a file. How do we do that?

The System Object

In this case, we'll write to the *standard output stream*. This data is handled differently by different Web browsers—some browsers display this data in a window, some in a file. Microsoft Internet Explorer 3.0 writes data sent to this stream to the file `javalog.txt`, which it places in the directory `c:\windows\java`. First, however, you have to enable Java-logging in Internet Explorer. In Internet Explorer, choose View ➤ Options to open the Options dialog box, and then select the Advanced tab, as shown in Figure 12.5. Check the Enable Java Logging checkbox.

FIGURE 12.5:

Enable Java logging in Internet Explorer.

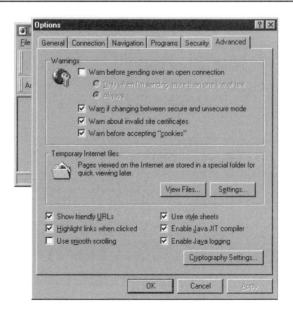

To print to this file, we use the Java System object. For example, to print out the string "No problem," you execute this line of code:

```
System.out.println("No problem");
```

Here, we can simply give our two threads different names—such as "No" and "problem"—and print out their names in the log file with the `System.out.println()` method:

```
class demorunnable implements Runnable{

  public void run(){
    for(int loop_index = 1; loop_index < 1000; loop_index++){
➜     System.out.println((Thread.currentThread()).getName());
            .
            .
            .
    }
  }
}
```

At this point, then, our two threads are printing out to the log file. How do we get them to take turns?

Using *yield()* to Make Threads Take Turns

We get our threads to take turns with the `Thread` class `yield()` method, which causes the thread to yield control to another thread, which then yields control back, and so on:

```
class demorunnable implements Runnable{

  public void run(){
    for(int loop_index = 1; loop_index < 1000; loop_index++){
      System.out.println((Thread.currentThread()).getName());
➜     Thread.yield();
    }
  }
}
```

And that's it—now the threads take turns writing to the log file. Java does the rest of the work, coordinating these threads for us. We have yet to write the `init()` method for this applet, however. There we add the new buttons we'll need to the applet's layout:

```
public void init()
{
   // If you use a ResourceWizard-generated "control creator" class to
   // arrange controls in your applet, you may want to call its
   // CreateControls() method from within this method. Remove the following
   // call to resize() before adding the call to CreateControls();
   // CreateControls() does its own resizing.
   //--------------------------------------------------------------------------
   resize(320, 240);

→  button1 = new Button("Start the file-writing threads");
→  button2 = new Button("Stop the file-writing threads");
→  add(button1);
→  add(button2);
         .
         .
         .

}
```

We then create the two new `runnable` objects we'll use, `runnable1` and `runnable2`:

```
public void init()
{
   resize(320, 240);

   button1 = new Button("Start the file-writing threads");
   button2 = new Button("Stop the file-writing threads");
   add(button1);
   add(button2);

→  runnable1 = new demorunnable();
→  runnable2 = new demorunnable();
         .
         .
         .

}
```

Finally, we create the two new threads themselves, placing one thread in `runnable1` and one in `runnable2`, as well as giving them the names "No" and "problem":

```
public void init()
{
   resize(320, 240);

   button1 = new Button("Start the file-writing threads");
   button2 = new Button("Stop the file-writing threads");
   add(button1);
   add(button2);

   runnable1 = new demorunnable();
   runnable2 = new demorunnable();
→  thread1 = new Thread(runnable1, "No");
→  thread2 = new Thread(runnable2, "problem");

}
```

Finally, we connect the buttons to start and stop the threads in an `action()` method (note that we're just expecting to click the Start button once and the Stop button once in this example; if you want to click the buttons more than once each, you should remove the null assignments below):

```
→ public boolean action (Event e, Object o){
→
→    if(e.target.equals(button1)){
→       thread1.start();
→       thread2.start();
→
→    }
→    if(e.target.equals(button2)){
→       thread1.stop();
→       thread2.stop();
→       thread1 = null;
→       thread2 = null;
→    }
→    return true;
→ }
```

Run the applet now, as shown in Figure 12.6. Click on the Start the File-Writing Threads button, and then click on the Stop the File-Writing Threads button.

FIGURE 12.6:

Our coordinate applet coordinates two new threads.

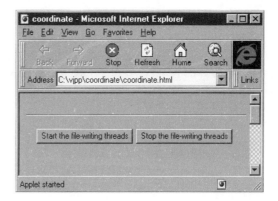

The result of this appears in the log file, where you can see the two threads are taking turns:

```
No
problem
No
problem
No
problem
No
problem
No
problem
No
problem
No
problem
    .
    .
    .
```

And that's it—our multiple thread coordinate applet is a success. The code for this applet appears in `coordinate.java`.

coordinate.java

```
//**************************************************************************
// coordinate.java: Applet
//
//**************************************************************************
import java.applet.*;
import java.awt.*;

//==========================================================================
// Main Class for applet coordinate
//
//==========================================================================
public class coordinate extends Applet
{
   Button button1, button2;
   demorunnable runnable1, runnable2;
   Thread thread1 = null, thread2 = null;


   // coordinate Class Constructor
   //------------------------------------------------------------------------
   public coordinate()
   {
      // TODO: Add constructor code here
   }

   // APPLET INFO SUPPORT:
   //   The getAppletInfo() method returns a string describing the applet's
   // author, copyright date, or miscellaneous information.
   //------------------------------------------------------------------------
   public String getAppletInfo()
   {
      return "Name: coordinate\r\n" +
           "Author: Steven Holzner\r\n" +
           "Created with Microsoft Visual J++ Version 1.0";
   }


   // The init() method is called by the AWT when an applet is first loaded or
   // reloaded.  Override this method to perform whatever initialization your
   // applet needs, such as initializing data structures, loading images or
```

```
// fonts, creating frame windows, setting the layout manager, or adding UI
// components.
//-----------------------------------------------------------------------
public void init()
{
  // If you use a ResourceWizard-generated "control creator" class to
  // arrange controls in your applet, you may want to call its
  // CreateControls() method from within this method. Remove the following
  // call to resize() before adding the call to CreateControls();
  // CreateControls() does its own resizing.
  //-----------------------------------------------------------------------
  resize(320, 240);

  button1 = new Button("Start the file-writing threads");
  button2 = new Button("Stop the file-writing threads");
  add(button1);
  add(button2);

  runnable1 = new demorunnable();
  runnable2 = new demorunnable();
  thread1 = new Thread(runnable1, "No");
  thread2 = new Thread(runnable2, "problem");

}


public boolean action (Event e, Object o){

  if(e.target.equals(button1)){
    thread1.start();
    thread2.start();

  }
  if(e.target.equals(button2)){
    thread1.stop();
    thread2.stop();
    thread1 = null;
    thread2 = null;
  }
  return true;
}


// Place additional applet clean up code here.  destroy() is called
```

```java
// when your applet is terminating and being unloaded.
//-------------------------------------------------------------------------
public void destroy()
{
    // TODO: Place applet cleanup code here
}


// coordinate Paint Handler
//-------------------------------------------------------------------------
public void paint(Graphics g)
{
    //g.drawString("Created with Microsoft Visual J++ Version 1.0", 10, 20);
}


//   The start() method is called when the page containing the applet
// first appears on the screen. The AppletWizard's initial implementation
// of this method starts execution of the applet's thread.
//-------------------------------------------------------------------------
public void start()
{
    // TODO: Place additional applet start code here
}


//   The stop() method is called when the page containing the applet is
// no longer on the screen. The AppletWizard's initial implementation of
// this method stops execution of the applet's thread.
//-------------------------------------------------------------------------
public void stop()
{
}




    // TODO: Place additional applet code here

}


class demorunnable implements Runnable{

  public void run(){
```

```
for(int loop_index = 1; loop_index < 1000; loop_index++){
    System.out.println((Thread.currentThread()).getName());
    Thread.yield();
    }
  }
}
```

You've seen quite a bit about thread handling at this point, but there is more to come—let's look into some issues concerning thread synchronization.

Thread Synchronization

Let's set up an applet that counts integers steadily from 0 to the maximum possible integer value and displays them as it does so:

```
-----------------------------------------------------
|                                                   |
|         ------------------------------            |
|        |1531                        |     |        |
|         ------------------------------            |
|                                                   |
|                                                   |
|                                                   |
|                                                   |
 -----------------------------------------------------
```

That's fine as long as we only have one thread in the applet. But if we have two threads that do the counting—incrementing and displaying the value in the same variable—it could be a problem. For example, it is possible that thread1 will be interrupted by thread2 after incrementing our counter from 1000 to 1001. Then, thread2 will increment our counter from 1001 to 1002, and at this point, control might go back to thread1, which reads the new value in the counter and prints out 1002, skipping 1001 entirely. This means our series of integers would run 1000, 1002, 1002..., which is obviously a problem. Let's see how to protect the variable that holds the current counter value so that only one thread at a time has access until the incrementing and displaying operation is completely finished.

Let's create a new applet named counter now. Give this applet multithreading support. We add our two threads, thread1 and thread2, to our applet now, and we also add the text field we'll need, as well as the *counter* variable:

```
public class counter extends Applet implements Runnable
{
    // THREAD SUPPORT:
    //   m_counter   is the Thread object for the applet
    //-----------------------------------------------------------
➜   Thread thread1 = null, thread2 = null;
➜   TextField text1;
➜   int counter = 0;
        .
        .
        .
```

Now we can add the text field to our applet's layout:

```
public void init()
{
    // If you use a ResourceWizard-generated "control creator" class to
    // arrange controls in your applet, you may want to call its
    // CreateControls() method from within this method. Remove the following
    // call to resize() before adding the call to CreateControls();
    // CreateControls() does its own resizing.
    //-----------------------------------------------------------------------
    resize(320, 240);
➜   text1 = new TextField(20);
➜   add(text1);

}
```

And we also start both threads in the start() method and stop them in the stop() method:

```
public void start()
{
```

```
→   if (thread1 == null && thread2 == null)
→   {
→       thread1 = new Thread(this);
→       thread1.start();
→       thread2 = new Thread(this);
→       thread2.start();
→   }
    }

    public void stop()
    {
→   if (thread1 != null && thread2 != null)
→   {
→       thread1.stop();
→       thread1 = null;
→
→       thread2.stop();
→       thread2 = null;
    }

    }
```

Now open the run() method. First, we'll do this the wrong way, simply incrementing the *counter* variable and displaying the result. That looks like this:

```
public void run()
{
→  String displaystring = new String("");
→  for(int loop_index = 0; loop_index < Integer.MAX_VALUE; loop_index++){
→      counter++;
→      text1.setText(displaystring.valueOf(counter));
    }
}
```

This looks like it should work, but our previous problem remains. That is, if both thread1 and thread2 are working with the same *counter* variable, we're in danger of having one thread being interrupted between the time it increments the counter and the time it reads the value back from the counter to display it. In that case, the other thread could have incremented the counter again by that time, and we'd end up displaying the wrong value. This is a general problem, and it's solved by denying multiple accesses to the same resource in a program until the currently accessing thread is finished with its work. One way to deny multiple access to the same resource—our *counter* variable—is to put all the operations having to do with the counter into a *synchronized* function.

Synchronized Functions

We can put all the code having to do with the *counter* variable into a new function named `displaycounter()`:

```
public void displaycounter()
{
➜   String displaystring = new String("");
➜   counter++;
➜   text1.setText(displaystring.valueOf(counter));
}
```

Now, every time we want to increment the counter and display the result, we can call `displaycounter()` in our `run()` method like this:

```
public void run()
{
   for(int loop_index = 0; loop_index < Integer.MAX_VALUE; loop_index++){
➜     displaycounter();
   }
}
```

It seems, however, that we have the same problem as before, because both threads could call this new function and be operating in it at the same time. However, we can use the keyword `synchronized` to make sure that only one thread can enter the `displaycounter()` method at a time:

```
➜ public synchronized void displaycounter()
   {
       String displaystring = new String("");
```

```
        counter++;
        text1.setText(displaystring.valueOf(counter));
    }
```

That's it—we have fixed the problem, and the integers count up steadily with no omissions. Our counter applet is a success; restricting access to a function or method is a powerful Java technique in multithreading. The code for this applet appears in counter.java.

counter.java

```
//**********************************************************************
// counter.java:  Applet
//
//**********************************************************************
import java.applet.*;
import java.awt.*;


//======================================================================
// Main Class for applet counter
//
//======================================================================
public class counter extends Applet implements Runnable
{
  // THREAD SUPPORT:
  //   m_counter  is the Thread object for the applet
  //--------------------------------------------------------------------
  Thread thread1 = null, thread2 = null;
  TextField text1;
  int counter = 0;

  // counter Class Constructor
  //--------------------------------------------------------------------
  public counter()
  {
    // TODO: Add constructor code here
  }

  // APPLET INFO SUPPORT:
  //   The getAppletInfo() method returns a string describing the applet's
  // author, copyright date, or miscellaneous information.
```

```
//----------------------------------------------------------------------------
public String getAppletInfo()
{
    return "Name: counter\r\n" +
           "Author: Steven Holzner\r\n" +
           "Created with Microsoft Visual J++ Version 1.0";
}


// The init() method is called by the AWT when an applet is first loaded or
// reloaded.  Override this method to perform whatever initialization your
// applet needs, such as initializing data structures, loading images or
// fonts, creating frame windows, setting the layout manager, or adding UI
// components.
//----------------------------------------------------------------------------
public void init()
{
    // If you use a ResourceWizard-generated "control creator" class to
    // arrange controls in your applet, you may want to call its
    // CreateControls() method from within this method. Remove the following
    // call to resize() before adding the call to CreateControls();
    // CreateControls() does its own resizing.
    //------------------------------------------------------------------------
    resize(320, 240);
    text1 = new TextField(20);
    add(text1);

    // TODO: Place additional initialization code here
}


// Place additional applet clean up code here.  destroy() is called
// when your applet is terminating and being unloaded.
//----------------------------------------------------------------------------
public void destroy()
{
    // TODO: Place applet cleanup code here
}


// counter Paint Handler
//----------------------------------------------------------------------------
public void paint(Graphics g)
{
```

```
   // TODO: Place applet paint code here
   //g.drawString("Running: " + Math.random(), 10, 20);
}

//   The start() method is called when the page containing the applet
// first appears on the screen. The AppletWizard's initial implementation
// of this method starts execution of the applet's thread.
//-------------------------------------------------------------------------
public void start()
{
   if (thread1 == null && thread2 == null)
   {
      thread1 = new Thread(this);
      thread1.start();
      thread2 = new Thread(this);
      thread2.start();
   }
   // TODO: Place additional applet start code here
}

//   The stop() method is called when the page containing the applet is
// no longer on the screen. The AppletWizard's initial implementation of
// this method stops execution of the applet's thread.
//-------------------------------------------------------------------------
public void stop()
{
   if (thread1 != null && thread2 != null)
   {
      thread1.stop();
      thread1 = null;

      thread2.stop();
      thread2 = null;
   }

   // TODO: Place additional applet stop code here
}

// THREAD SUPPORT
//   The run() method is called when the applet's thread is started. If
// your applet performs any ongoing activities without waiting for user
// input, the code for implementing that behavior typically goes here. For
```

```
// example, for an applet that performs animation, the run() method controls
// the display of images.
//--------------------------------------------------------------------------
public void run()
{
   for(int loop_index = 0; loop_index < Integer.MAX_VALUE; loop_index++){
      displaycounter();
   }
}

public synchronized void displaycounter()
{
   String displaystring = new String("");
   counter++;
   text1.setText(displaystring.valueOf(counter));
}



   // TODO: Place additional applet code here

}
```

There's another way to do the same thing—instead of restricting access to a function, we can restrict access to the data itself. We'll examine this next.

Synchronizing Data Objects

We can restrict access to data if it is embedded in a Java object. For example, we might set up a new class to hold our counter data named counterclass:

```
➡ class counterclass{

   }
```

We declare our counter's data as an `integer` in this class named `internal_data` (making it public so that we can reach it from other classes):

```
class counterclass{
➜ public int internal_data;
            .
            .
            .

}
```

We also set up a constructor for this class to set the value in the `internal_data` variable to 0:

```
class counterclass{
    public int internal_data;
➜   public counterclass(){
➜       internal_data = 0;
➜   }
  }
```

Now, instead of an integer named counter, we use an object of the `counterclass` class in our counter applet:

```
public class counter extends Applet implements Runnable
{
    // THREAD SUPPORT:
    //   m_counter   is the Thread object for the applet
    //-----------------------------------------------------------
    Thread thread1 = null, thread2 = null;
    TextField text1;
➜   counterclass counter = new counterclass();
            .
            .
            .

```

To reach the counter value in the `counter` object, we can refer to it in the `run()` method as `counter.internal_data`, and we increment and display that value this way:

```
public void run()
{
```

```
   String displaystring = new String("");
   for(int loop_index = 0; loop_index < Integer.MAX_VALUE; loop_index++){
➜     counter.internal_data++;
➜     text1.setText(displaystring.valueOf(counter.internal_data));
   }
 }
```

We can restrict access to the `counter` object using a `synchronized` block. Another way to use the `synchronized` keyword defines a code block, and after we indicate which object we want to restrict access to, only one thread at a time will have access to it:

```
public void run()
{
   String displaystring = new String("");
   for(int loop_index = 0; loop_index < Integer.MAX_VALUE; loop_index++){
➜     synchronized(counter){
         counter.internal_data++;
         text1.setText(displaystring.valueOf(counter.internal_data));
➜     }
   }
 }
```

That's it—once again we have restricted access to our counter data, making sure one thread has to wait until the other is finished with our *counter* variable. The new version of counter.java appears in counter.java, version 2.

counter.java, version 2

```
//***********************************************************************************
// counter.java:  Applet
//
//***********************************************************************************
import java.applet.*;
import java.awt.*;


//===================================================================================
// Main Class for applet counter
//
//===================================================================================
```

```java
public class counter extends Applet implements Runnable
{
  // THREAD SUPPORT:
  //   m_counter  is the Thread object for the applet
  //---------------------------------------------------------------------------
  Thread thread1 = null, thread2 = null;
  TextField text1;
  counterclass counter = new counterclass();

  // counter Class Constructor
  //---------------------------------------------------------------------------
  public counter()
  {
    // TODO: Add constructor code here
  }


  // APPLET INFO SUPPORT:
  //   The getAppletInfo() method returns a string describing the applet's
  // author, copyright date, or miscellaneous information.
  //---------------------------------------------------------------------------
  public String getAppletInfo()
  {
    return "Name: counter\r\n" +
         "Author: Steven Holzner\r\n" +
         "Created with Microsoft Visual J++ Version 1.0";
  }



  // The init() method is called by the AWT when an applet is first loaded or
  // reloaded.  Override this method to perform whatever initialization your
  // applet needs, such as initializing data structures, loading images or
  // fonts, creating frame windows, setting the layout manager, or adding UI
  // components.
  //---------------------------------------------------------------------------
  public void init()
  {
    // If you use a ResourceWizard-generated "control creator" class to
    // arrange controls in your applet, you may want to call its
    // CreateControls() method from within this method. Remove the following
    // call to resize() before adding the call to CreateControls();
    // CreateControls() does its own resizing.
    //-------------------------------------------------------------------------
```

```
   resize(320, 240);
   text1 = new TextField(20);
   add(text1);

   // TODO: Place additional initialization code here
}


// Place additional applet clean up code here.  destroy() is called
// when your applet is terminating and being unloaded.
//-----------------------------------------------------------------------------
public void destroy()
{
   // TODO: Place applet cleanup code here
}


// counter Paint Handler
//-----------------------------------------------------------------------------
public void paint(Graphics g)
{
   // TODO: Place applet paint code here
   //g.drawString("Running: " + Math.random(), 10, 20);
}


//  The start() method is called when the page containing the applet
// first appears on the screen. The AppletWizard's initial implementation
// of this method starts execution of the applet's thread.
//-----------------------------------------------------------------------------
public void start()
{
   if (thread1 == null && thread2 == null)
   {
     thread1 = new Thread(this);
     thread1.start();
     thread2 = new Thread(this);
     thread2.start();
   }
   // TODO: Place additional applet start code here
}


//  The stop() method is called when the page containing the applet is
// no longer on the screen. The AppletWizard's initial implementation of
// this method stops execution of the applet's thread.
```

```
//-------------------------------------------------------------------
public void stop()
{
   if (thread1 != null && thread2 != null)
   {
      thread1.stop();
      thread1 = null;

      thread2.stop();
      thread2 = null;
   }

   // TODO: Place additional applet stop code here
}


// THREAD SUPPORT
//   The run() method is called when the applet's thread is started. If
// your applet performs any ongoing activities without waiting for user
// input, the code for implementing that behavior typically goes here. For
// example, for an applet that performs animation, the run() method controls
// the display of images.
//-------------------------------------------------------------------
public void run()
{
   String displaystring = new String("");
   for(int loop_index = 0; loop_index < Integer.MAX_VALUE; loop_index++){
      synchronized(counter){
         counter.internal_data++;
         text1.setText(displaystring.valueOf(counter.internal_data));
      }
   }
}



   // TODO: Place additional applet code here

}

class counterclass{
   public int internal_data;
   public counterclass(){
```

```
    internal_data = 0;
  }
}
```

What's Next?

That's it for our guided tour of Java multithreading. We've come far in this chapter: from starting off with threads to setting their priority, suspending and resuming them, using multiple threads, coordinating multiple threads, and restricting access to shared resources. In the next chapter, we'll examine how to debug Visual J++ code and how to handle Java exceptions.

CHAPTER
THIRTEEN

13

Java Exceptions and Visual J++ Debugging

- ■ Using exception handling

- ■ Defining your own exceptions

- ■ Nesting exceptions

- ■ Debugging with Visual J++

- ■ Using Java with databases

In this chapter, we're going to examine how to handle Java exceptions and how to debug Visual J++ programs. Java exceptions usually occur when there has been some unforeseen problem in program execution, such as trying to read past the end of an array. These errors can stop an applet completely. You'll see how to handle many such exceptions yourself in this chapter.

Of course, it's best to try to make your applet bullet-proof, and that's what debugging is all about. If your applet isn't working as it should, you can use the Visual J++ debugger to work through it line by line if need be. You'll see how that works in this chapter.

In addition, since this is the last chapter, I'll talk some about the future of Java when we examine client-server and database-handling issues.

Let's begin now with Java exception handling.

Using Exception Handling

You saw exception handling as far back as Chapter 10, in which we used a `MediaTracker` object. We loaded a graphics image file in our copier applet, and we had to make sure the image was loaded before trying to get its dimensions. For that reason, we used the `MediaTracker` class, and Visual J++ insists that we use a `try...catch` block like this:

```
public void init()
{
    resize(320, 240);

    copierimage = getImage(getCodeBase(), "figure.jpg");

    MediaTracker mediatracker = new MediaTracker(this);
```

```
    mediatracker.addImage(copierimage, 0);

➜   try{mediatracker.waitForID(0);}
➜   catch(Exception e){}

    width = copierimage.getWidth(null);
    height = copierimage.getHeight(null);
    pixelarray = new int[width * height];

    pixelgrabber = new PixelGrabber(copierimage.getSource(), 0,0, width,
➦height, pixelarray, 0, width);
    try{pixelgrabber.grabPixels();}
    catch (Exception e){}

    memimagesource = new MemoryImageSource(width, height,
➦pixelarray, 0, width);
    copiedimage = createImage(memimagesource);
}
```

This `try...catch` block handles exceptions. So what are exceptions? *Exceptions* are objects of the Java `Exception` class that are usually used (the technical verb is *thrown*) when a problem in program flow occurs at run time. How do `try...catch` blocks work? The idea is to place sensitive code that can cause exceptions in a `try{}` block and to handle the exceptions that occur in a `catch{}` block or in a series of `catch{}` blocks, usually one for each type of exception that might occur:

```
try{
    .
    .
[sensitive code]
    .
    .
}

catch(expclass1 e1){
    .
    .
```

```
[handle exception_class1]
    .
    .
    .
}

catch(expclass2 e2){
    .
    .
[handle exception_class2]
    .
    .
}

finally{
    .
    .
[exit code]
    .
    .
}
```

TIP

Notice the `finally{}` block at the end of our `try...catch` statement outline above. This block surrounds code that you want to execute for sure in the event of a serious error. For example, you might want to stop certain threads before quitting the program, and you can do that by putting code in a `finally{}` clause.

Let's see this in more detail. You may recall that in our artist applet, we stored the successive locations of the mouse as it was dragged over the screen in an array called `points[]`:

```
// MOUSE SUPPORT:
// The mouseDrag() method is called if the mouse cursor moves over the
// applet's portion of the screen while the mouse button is being held down.
//-----------------------------------------------------------------------
public boolean mouseDrag(Event evt, int x, int y)
{
    if(drawboolean){
```

```
➜      points[currentpoint++] = new Point(x, y);
       currentpoint = 0;
       repaint();
   }
   return true;
 }
```

But this array could hold only 300 points, and that's not very good programming. What if the user wants to draw a great deal and drags the mouse so much that we need more than 300 points? In that case, we can generate an exception and handle the problem in a `catch{}` block. First, we enclose the sensitive code line in which we fill the array inside a `try{}` block:

```
// MOUSE SUPPORT:
// The mouseDrag() method is called if the mouse cursor moves over the
// applet's portion of the screen while the mouse button is being held down.
//--------------------------------------------------------------------------
public boolean mouseDrag(Event evt, int x, int y)
{
   if(drawboolean){
➜    try{
       points[currentpoint++] = new Point(x, y);
➜    }    .

           .

     repaint();
   }
   return true;
 }
```

Next, we set up a `catch` block. Because we expect the Java `ArrayIndexOutOfBoundsException` exception, we handle that in our code this way:

```
// MOUSE SUPPORT:
// The mouseDrag() method is called if the mouse cursor moves over the
// applet's portion of the screen while the mouse button is being held down.
//--------------------------------------------------------------------------
public boolean mouseDrag(Event evt, int x, int y)
{
   if(drawboolean){
```

```
      try{
        points[currentpoint++] = new Point(x, y);
      }
➜     catch(ArrayIndexOutOfBoundsException e){
           .
           .
           .
      }
      repaint();
   }
   return true;
}
```

Here are the Java predefined exceptions:

- `ArithmeticException`

- `ArrayIndexOutOfBoundsException`

- `ArrayStoreException`

- `AWTException`

- `ClassCastException`

- `ClassNotFoundException`

- `CloneNotSupportedException`

- `EmptyStackException`

- `EOFException`

- `FileNotFoundException`

- `IllegalAccessException`

- `IllegalArgumentException`

- `IllegalMonitorStateException`

- `IllegalThreadStateException`

- `IndexOutOfBoundsException`

- `InstantiationException`

- `InterruptedException`
- `InterruptedIOException`
- `IOException`
- `MalformedURLException`
- `NegativeArraySizeException`
- `NoSuchElementException`
- `NoSuchMethodException`
- `NullPointerException`
- `NumberFormatException`
- `ProtocolException`
- `RuntimeException`
- `SecurityException`
- `SocketException`
- `StringIndexOutOfBoundsException`
- `uncaughtException`
- `UnknownHostException`
- `UnknownServiceException`
- `UTFDataFormatException`

In Java, there are `Error` objects as well as `Exception` objects, and errors are handled in much the same way as exceptions. Here are the Java errors:

- `AbstractMethodError`
- `AWTError`
- `ClassCircularityError`
- `ClassFormatError`

- IllegalAccessError

- IncompatibleClassChangeError

- InstantiationError

- InternalError

- LinkageError

- NoClassDefFoundError

- NoSuchFieldError

- NoSuchMethodError

- OutOfMemoryError

- StackOverflowError

- ThreadDeath

- UnknownError

- UnsatisfiedLinkError

- VerifyError

- VirtualMachineError

If the ArrayIndexOutOfBounds exception does occur, the code in our catch block is executed. Here, we can set the array index back to 0 and print out a message with System.out.println(), the call we saw in the last chapter that writes to a log file:

```
// MOUSE SUPPORT:
// The mouseDrag() method is called if the mouse cursor moves over the
// applet's portion of the screen while the mouse button is being held down.
//-------------------------------------------------------------------
public boolean mouseDrag(Event evt, int x, int y)
{
   if(drawboolean){
     try{
       points[currentpoint++] = new Point(x, y);
     }
     catch(ArrayIndexOutOfBoundsException e){
```

```
→        currentpoint = 0;
→        System.out.println(e.getMessage());
      }
    repaint();
  }
  return true;
}
```

Note that we print out the message we get from `e.getMessage()`, where `e` is the object of the Java class `ArrayIndexOutOfBounds Exception`. Exceptions are derived from the Java `Throwable` class (when we generate an exception, we say an exception was thrown), and `getMessage()` is a method of that class. This method simply returns a string explaining the cause of the exception—such as an array overflow. The Java `Throwable` class methods appear in Table 13.1.

TABLE 13.1: The Java `Throwable` Class's Methods

Method	Does This
`Throwable()`	Constructs a `Throwable` with no message
`Throwable(String)`	Constructs a `Throwable` with a message
`fillInStackTrace()`	Fills in object's stack trace
`getMessage()`	Returns message of `Throwable`
`printStackTrace()`	Prints `Throwable` and `Throwable`'s stack trace
`printStackTrace(PrintStream)`	Prints `Throwable` and `Throwable`'s stack trace to `PrintStream`
`toString()`	Returns a description of the object

And that's it—if the array in our artist applet is filled to overflowing, an exception is thrown. We handle this exception by resetting the array index to zero and printing out a string to the log file. Our first exception-handling applet is a success. The code for this applet appears in `artist.java`.

artist.java (with Exception Handling)

```
//*********************************************************************************
// artist.java: Applet
//
//*********************************************************************************
import java.applet.*;
import java.awt.*;
import java.lang.Math;


//===============================================================================
// Main Class for applet artist
//
//===============================================================================
public class artist extends Applet
{
   Button drawbutton, linebutton, ovalbutton, rectbutton, roundedbutton;

      Point points[] = new Point[300];
      Point anchorpoint, drawtopoint;
      int currentpoint = 0;
      int width, height;

      boolean mousedownboolean = false;
      boolean mouseupboolean = false;
      boolean drawboolean = false;
      boolean lineboolean = false;
      boolean ovalboolean = false;
      boolean rectboolean = false;
      boolean roundedboolean = false;

   // artist Class Constructor
   //----------------------------------------------------------------------------
   public artist()
   {
      // TODO: Add constructor code here
   }


   // APPLET INFO SUPPORT:
   //    The getAppletInfo() method returns a string describing the applet's
   // author, copyright date, or miscellaneous information.
   //----------------------------------------------------------------------------
```

```
public String getAppletInfo()
{
   return "Name: artist\r\n" +
       "Author: Steven Holzner\r\n" +
       "Created with Microsoft Visual J++ Version 1.0";
}


// The init() method is called by the AWT when an applet is first loaded or
// reloaded.  Override this method to perform whatever initialization your
// applet needs, such as initializing data structures, loading images or
// fonts, creating frame windows, setting the layout manager, or adding UI
// components.
//-------------------------------------------------------------------------
public void init()
{
   // If you use a ResourceWizard-generated "control creator" class to
   // arrange controls in your applet, you may want to call its
   // CreateControls() method from within this method. Remove the following
   // call to resize() before adding the call to CreateControls();
   // CreateControls() does its own resizing.
   //----------------------------------------------------------------------
   resize(320, 240);
   drawbutton = new Button("Draw tool");
   linebutton = new Button("Line tool");
   ovalbutton = new Button("Oval tool");
   rectbutton = new Button("Rect tool");
   roundedbutton = new Button("Round tool");

   add(drawbutton);
   add(linebutton);
   add(ovalbutton);
   add(rectbutton);
   add(roundedbutton);

   // TODO: Place additional initialization code here
}



public boolean action(Event e, Object o){
   if(e.target.equals(drawbutton)){
```

```
     setallfalse();
     drawboolean = true;
   }
   if(e.target.equals(linebutton)){
     setallfalse();
     lineboolean = true;
   }
   if(e.target.equals(ovalbutton)){
     setallfalse();
     ovalboolean = true;
   }
   if(e.target.equals(rectbutton)){
     setallfalse();
     rectboolean = true;
   }
   if(e.target.equals(roundedbutton)){
     setallfalse();
     roundedboolean = true;
   }
   return true;
   }


// Place additional applet clean up code here.  destroy() is called
// when your applet is terminating and being unloaded.
//-------------------------------------------------------------------------
public void destroy()
{
   // TODO: Place applet cleanup code here
}


// artist Paint Handler
//-------------------------------------------------------------------------
public void paint(Graphics g)
{
   if(mouseupboolean){

     if(lineboolean){
        g.drawLine(anchorpoint.x, anchorpoint.y, drawtopoint.x,
➥ drawtopoint.y);
     }
     if(ovalboolean){
```

```
         g.drawOval(anchorpoint.x, anchorpoint.y, width, height);
      }
      if(rectboolean){
         g.drawRect(anchorpoint.x, anchorpoint.y, width, height);
      }
      if(roundedboolean){
         g.drawRoundRect(anchorpoint.x, anchorpoint.y, width, height, 10, 10);
      }
   }
   if(drawboolean){
      for(int loop_index = 0; loop_index < currentpoint; loop_index++){
         g.drawLine(points[loop_index].x, points[loop_index].y,
➥ points[loop_index + 1].x, points[loop_index + 1].y);
      }
   }
}


// The start() method is called when the page containing the applet
// first appears on the screen. The AppletWizard's initial implementation
// of this method starts execution of the applet's thread.
//------------------------------------------------------------------
public void start()
{
   // TODO: Place additional applet start code here
}


// The stop() method is called when the page containing the applet is
// no longer on the screen. The AppletWizard's initial implementation of
// this method stops execution of the applet's thread.
//------------------------------------------------------------------
public void stop()
{
}



// MOUSE SUPPORT:
// The mouseDown() method is called if the mouse button is pressed
// while the mouse cursor is over the applet's portion of the screen.
//------------------------------------------------------------------
public boolean mouseDown(Event evt, int x, int y)
{
   mousedownboolean = true;
```

```
    mouseupboolean = false;
    anchorpoint = new Point(x, y);
    return true;
}

// MOUSE SUPPORT:
//   The mouseUp() method is called if the mouse button is released
// while the mouse cursor is over the applet's portion of the screen.
//--------------------------------------------------------------------
public boolean mouseUp(Event evt, int x, int y)
{
    mousedownboolean = false;
    mouseupboolean = true;

    if(lineboolean){
        drawtopoint = new Point(x, y);
    }
    else{
        drawtopoint = new Point(Math.max(x, anchorpoint.x), Math.max(y,
➥ anchorpoint.y));
        anchorpoint = new Point(Math.min(x, anchorpoint.x), Math.min(y,
➥ anchorpoint.y));
        width = drawtopoint.x - anchorpoint.x;
        height = drawtopoint.y - anchorpoint.y;
    }
    repaint();
    return true;
}

// MOUSE SUPPORT:
//   The mouseDrag() method is called if the mouse cursor moves over the
// applet's portion of the screen while the mouse button is being held down.
//--------------------------------------------------------------------
public boolean mouseDrag(Event evt, int x, int y)
{
    if(drawboolean){
        try{
            points[currentpoint++] = new Point(x, y);
        }
        catch(ArrayIndexOutOfBoundsException e){
            currentpoint = 0;
```

```
        System.out.println(e.getMessage());
      }
      repaint();
    }
    return true;
  }


// MOUSE SUPPORT:
//   The mouseMove() method is called if the mouse cursor moves over the
// applet's portion of the screen and the mouse button isn't being held down.
//----------------------------------------------------------------------------
public boolean mouseMove(Event evt, int x, int y)
{
   // TODO: Place applet mouseMove code here
   return true;
}


// TODO: Place additional applet code here

void setallfalse()
{
   mousedownboolean = false;
   mouseupboolean = false;
   drawboolean = false;
   lineboolean = false;
   ovalboolean = false;
   rectboolean = false;
   roundedboolean = false;
}
}
```

That's how we can handle the exceptions that Java throws. However, we can also create our own custom exceptions, and we'll explore that process next.

Defining Our Own Exceptions

You may recall our earlier example named PCs4All in which we allowed customers to select among various computer systems by clicking on option buttons:

```
------------------------------------------------------------
|                                                          |
|  (*) System Package 1           [v] CPU1 system          |
|                                                          |
|  ( ) System Package 2           [v] SVGA screen          |
|                                                          |
|  ( ) System Package 3           [ ] CDROM  (6x)          |
|                                                          |
|     ------------------                                   |
|    |Price: $3000      |                                  |
|     ------------------                                   |
 ------------------------------------------------------------
```

We placed checks in the checkboxes at right, indicating what is included in the computer package the user has selected. Since those controls are checkboxes, however, the user can set those boxes with the click of a mouse, giving the wrong impression of what is included in a specific package:

```
------------------------------------------------------------
|                                                          |
|  (*) System Package 1           [v] CPU1 system          |
|                                                          |
|  ( ) System Package 2           [v] SVGA screen          |
|                                                          |
|  ( ) System Package 3           [v] CDROM  (6x)     <-------
|                                                          |
|     ------------------                                   |
|    |Price: $3000      |                                  |
|     ------------------                                   |
 ------------------------------------------------------------
```

In this case, when the user clicks on one of the computer system component boxes, we will throw a customized exception. Let's name that new exception class componentchanged. We can set up our new exception like this:

```
class componentchanged extends Exception{
}
```

That's all it takes to create a new type of exception; we simply derive our new class from the Java `Exception` class. The methods of the `Exception` class appear in Table 13.2.

TABLE 13.2: The Java `Exception` Class's Methods

Method	Does This
`Exception()`	Constructs `Exception` with no message
`Exception(String)`	Constructs `Exception` with given message

Now let's put this new exception to work. The checkboxes we are watching are named `component1` to `component3`, and we can add code to the PCs4All applet to catch checkbox clicks like this:

```
public boolean action (Event e, Object o){
  if(e.target.equals(Panel1.system1)){
    Panel2.component1.setState(true);
    Panel2.component2.setState(true);
    Panel2.component3.setState(false);
    Panel1.pricetextfield.setText("Price: $3000.");
  }         .
            .
            .
➜   if(e.target.equals(Panel2.component1)){
      .
      .
    }
➜   if(e.target.equals(Panel2.component2)){
      .
      .
    }
➜   if(e.target.equals(Panel2.component3)){
      .
      .
    }

    return true;
  }
```

If any of these checkboxes were clicked, we can throw our new exception, `componentchanged`, this way:

```
public boolean action (Event e, Object o){
  if(e.target.equals(Panel1.system1)){
    Panel2.component1.setState(true);
    Panel2.component2.setState(true);
    Panel2.component3.setState(false);
    Panel1.pricetextfield.setText("Price: $3000.");
  }        .
             .
             .
  try{
    if(e.target.equals(Panel2.component1)){
➜     throw(new componentchanged());
    }
    if(e.target.equals(Panel2.component2)){
➜     throw(new componentchanged());
    }
    if(e.target.equals(Panel2.component3)){
➜     throw(new componentchanged());
    }      .
             .
             .
  }
  return true;
}
```

Now we can catch our new exception. If the user has changed the setting of one of the component checkboxes, we can print that out to the log file in our `catch` block this way:

```
public boolean action (Event e, Object o){
  if(e.target.equals(Panel1.system1)){
    Panel2.component1.setState(true);
    Panel2.component2.setState(true);
    Panel2.component3.setState(false);
    Panel1.pricetextfield.setText("Price: $3000.");
  }        .
             .
             .
  try{
```

```
                    if(e.target.equals(Panel2.component1)){
                      throw(new componentchanged());
                    }
                    if(e.target.equals(Panel2.component2)){
                      throw(new componentchanged());
                    }
                    if(e.target.equals(Panel2.component3)){
                      throw(new componentchanged());
                    }
                  }
→               catch(componentchanged exp){
→                 System.out.println("Component button clicked");
→               }
                  return true;
                }
```

And that's it—now we've created our own exception, as well as
thrown and caught that exception. The code for this applet appears
in PCs4All.java.

> **TIP**
>
> Customized exceptions don't have to denote errors. You can
> throw a customized exception for many reasons—such as sending
> signals to various parts of your code—causing the code in the
> catch block to be executed.

PCs4All.java (with Exception Handling)

```
//*************************************************************************
// PCs4All.java:  Applet
//
//*************************************************************************
import java.applet.*;
import java.awt.*;

//=========================================================================
// Main Class for applet PCs4All
//
//=========================================================================
public class PCs4All extends Applet
{
```

```
  systempanel Panel1;
  componentpanel Panel2;

// PCs4All Class Constructor
//---------------------------------------------------------------------------
public PCs4All()
{
    // TODO: Add constructor code here
}


// APPLET INFO SUPPORT:
// The getAppletInfo() method returns a string describing the applet's
// author, copyright date, or miscellaneous information.
//---------------------------------------------------------------------------
public String getAppletInfo()
{
    return "Name: PCs4All\r\n" +
          "Author: Steven Holzner\r\n" +
          "Created with Microsoft Visual J++ Version 1.0";
}



// The init() method is called by the AWT when an applet is first loaded or
// reloaded.  Override this method to perform whatever initialization your
// applet needs, such as initializing data structures, loading images or
// fonts, creating frame windows, setting the layout manager, or adding UI
// components.
//---------------------------------------------------------------------------
public void init()
{
    // If you use a ResourceWizard-generated "control creator" class to
    // arrange controls in your applet, you may want to call its
    // CreateControls() method from within this method. Remove the following
    // call to resize() before adding the call to CreateControls();
    // CreateControls() does its own resizing.
    //---------------------------------------------------------------------------
    resize(320, 240);
    setLayout(new GridLayout(1, 2));
    Panel1 = new systempanel();
    Panel2 = new componentpanel();
    add(Panel1);
```

```
    add(Panel2);

}

public boolean action (Event e, Object o){
  if(e.target.equals(Panel1.system1)){
      Panel2.component1.setState(true);
      Panel2.component2.setState(true);
      Panel2.component3.setState(false);
      Panel1.pricetextfield.setText("Price: $3000.");
  }
  if(e.target.equals(Panel1.system2)){
      Panel2.component1.setState(true);
      Panel2.component2.setState(false);
      Panel2.component3.setState(true);
      Panel1.pricetextfield.setText("Price: $3500.");
  }
  if(e.target.equals(Panel1.system3)){
      Panel2.component1.setState(true);
      Panel2.component2.setState(true);
      Panel2.component3.setState(true);
      Panel1.pricetextfield.setText("Price: $4000.");
  }
  try{
    if(e.target.equals(Panel2.component1)){
      throw(new componentchanged());
    }
    if(e.target.equals(Panel2.component2)){
      throw(new componentchanged());
    }
    if(e.target.equals(Panel2.component3)){
      throw(new componentchanged());
    }
  }
  catch(componentchanged exp){
    System.out.println("Component button clicked");
  }
  return true;
}


// Place additional applet clean up code here.  destroy() is called
```

```
// when your applet is terminating and being unloaded.
//----------------------------------------------------------------
public void destroy()
{
   // TODO: Place applet cleanup code here
}

// PCs4All Paint Handler
//----------------------------------------------------------------
public void paint(Graphics g)
{
   //g.drawString("Created with Microsoft Visual J++ Version 1.0", 10, 20);
}

//   The start() method is called when the page containing the applet
// first appears on the screen. The AppletWizard's initial implementation
// of this method starts execution of the applet's thread.
//----------------------------------------------------------------
public void start()
{
   // TODO: Place additional applet start code here
}

//   The stop() method is called when the page containing the applet is
// no longer on the screen. The AppletWizard's initial implementation of
// this method stops execution of the applet's thread.
//----------------------------------------------------------------
public void stop()
{
}




   // TODO: Place additional applet code here

}

class componentpanel extends Panel
{
```

```
Checkbox component1, component2, component3;

componentpanel(){
    add(component1 = new Checkbox("CPU1 system"));
    add(component2 = new Checkbox("SVGA screen"));
    add(component3 = new Checkbox("CDROM  (6x)"));
}
}


class systempanel extends Panel
{
CheckboxGroup CGroup;
Checkbox system1, system2, system3;
TextField pricetextfield;

systempanel(){
    CGroup = new CheckboxGroup();
    add(system1 = new Checkbox("System Package 1", CGroup, false));
    add(system2 = new Checkbox("System Package 2", CGroup, false));
    add(system3 = new Checkbox("System Package 3", CGroup, false));
    pricetextfield = new TextField(15);
    add(pricetextfield);
}
}

class componentchanged extends Exception{
}
```

Exception handling can be more involved. For example, what if we set up a `try` block, but there is a call to another method in that `try` block, and the exception is thrown in that new method? Will we catch it in our original `catch` block? Let's look into that now.

Nested Exceptions

Let's suppose that we call a function named `dangerous_function()` and that function can throw exceptions of the `Exception` class `dangerous_exception`:

```
-----------------------------------------------------------
|void dangerous_function() throws dangerous_exception     |
|{                                                        |
|                                                         |
|    [dangerous code]                                     |
|                                                         |
|    throw dangerous_exception;                           |
|                                                         |
|}                                                        |
 ----------------------------------------------------------
```

Now let's say we call `dangerous_function()` from some other method, enclosing our call to `dangerous_function()` in a `try...catch` block:

```
          --------------------------------------------------------
          | try{                                                 |
--------- dangerous_function();                                  |
     |    | }                                                    |
     |    |                                                      |
     |    | catch(dangerous_exception e){                        |
     |    |                                                      |
     |    |   [handle dangerous_exception]                       |
     |    |                                                      |
     |    | }                                                    |
     |     -------------------------------------------------------
     |
     |     -------------------------------------------------------
     |    |                                                      |
----->|void dangerous_function() throws dangerous_exception      |
     |{                                                          |
     |                                                           |
     |    [dangerous code]                                       |
     |                                                           |
     |    throw dangerous_exception;                             |
     |                                                           |
     |}  -------------------------------------------------------
```

We have a `catch` block set up to handle exceptions from `dangerous_function()`. Now let's say that an exception of type

dangerous_exception did occur in the dangerous_function().
What happens next? If there is no exception handler in
dangerous_function(), control comes back to us, and we handle
the exception in our own catch block:

```
          ------------------------------------------------------
        | try{                                                 |
--------- dangerous_function();                               |
|       | }                                                    |
|       |                                                      |
|  -->| catch(dangerous_exception e){                        |
|  |  |                                                      |
|  |  |    [handle dangerous_exception]                     |
|  |  |                                                      |
|  |  | }                                                    |
|  |   ------------------------------------------------------
|  |
|  |   ------------------------------------------------------
--|-->|void dangerous_function() throws dangerous_exception  |
|  | |{                                                      |
|  | |                                                      |
|  | |    [dangerous code]                                  |
|  | |                                                      |
|  | |                                                      |
-------throw dangerous_exception;                            |
|  |                                                         |
|  |}                                                        |
    ------------------------------------------------------
```

When we declare the dangerous_function() function, we have to
indicate that it can throw exceptions, and we do that in function() the
function's declaration:

➜ void dangerous_function() throws dangerous_exception

Let's see this at work. Let's set up a counting program that simply
counts integers, one after the other, starting at zero, and displays
them in a text field. The incrementing and displaying of an internal
counter variable can be handled in this function, displaycounter():

```
    public void displaycounter()
    {
➜      String displaystring = new String("");

➜      text1.setText(displaystring.valueOf(counter++));
    }
```

Now, let's make sure the counter never goes above 500. If it does, we can throw an exception named `over500`, which we add to our applet like this:

```
class over500 extends Exception{}
```

When the counter does exceed 500, we throw the `over500` exception like this in the `displaycounter()` function (we add the keywords `throws over500` at the end of our function to indicate the type of exception this function can throw):

```
public void displaycounter() throws over500
{
   String displaystring = new String("");

   text1.setText(displaystring.valueOf(counter++));
   if (counter > 500) throw new over500();
}
```

Now we've thrown an exception, but `displaycounter()` has no exception handler. We will set up the exception handler in the calling method. That might be a `run()` method like this, where the thread in this method calls `displaycounter()` continually:

```
public void run()
{
   while (true)
   {
      displaycounter();
   }
}
```

To handle the exception thrown by `displaycounter()`, we enclose the call itself in a `try` block and add a `catch` block as well:

```
public void run()
{
   while (true)
   {
      try
      {
```

```
        displaycounter();
      }
→     catch (over500 e)
      {    .

           .

           .
      }
    }
}
```

The code in the `catch` block will be called when the `over500` exception occurs in `displaycounter()`, and we can print out the nature of the exception to the error log, as well as stop the current thread:

```
public void run()
{
   while (true)
   {
     try
     {
       displaycounter();
     }
     catch (over500 e)
     {
→      System.out.println("Over 500 exception occured.");
→      stop();
     }
   }
}
```

We are now able to handle a nested exception. The code for this applet appears in `nested.java`; if you run it, the numbers in the text field will run steadily up to 500 and then stop as the `over500` exception stops the thread. You can see that our nested exception handler applet is a success.

nested.java

```java
//**************************************************************************
// nested.java: Applet
//
//**************************************************************************
import java.applet.*;
import java.awt.*;


//==========================================================================
// Main Class for applet nested
//
//==========================================================================
public class nested extends Applet implements Runnable
{
  // THREAD SUPPORT:
  //   m_nested  is the Thread object for the applet
  //------------------------------------------------------------------------
  Thread  m_nested = null;
  int counter = 0;
  TextField text1;



  // nested Class Constructor
  //------------------------------------------------------------------------
  public nested()
  {
    // TODO: Add constructor code here
  }

  // APPLET INFO SUPPORT:
  // The getAppletInfo() method returns a string describing the applet's
  // author, copyright date, or miscellaneous information.
  //------------------------------------------------------------------------
  public String getAppletInfo()
  {
    return "Name: nested\r\n" +
        "Author: Steven Holzner\r\n" +
```

```
        "Created with Microsoft Visual J++ Version 1.0";
}


// The init() method is called by the AWT when an applet is first loaded or
// reloaded.  Override this method to perform whatever initialization your
// applet needs, such as initializing data structures, loading images or
// fonts, creating frame windows, setting the layout manager, or adding UI
// components.
//-----------------------------------------------------------------------
public void init()
{
   // If you use a ResourceWizard-generated "control creator" class to
   // arrange controls in your applet, you may want to call its
   // CreateControls() method from within this method. Remove the following
   // call to resize() before adding the call to CreateControls();
   // CreateControls() does its own resizing.
   //--------------------------------------------------------------------
   resize(320, 240);
   text1 = new TextField(20);
   add(text1);

   // TODO: Place additional initialization code here
}

// Place additional applet clean up code here.  destroy() is called
// when your applet is terminating and being unloaded.
//-----------------------------------------------------------------------
public void destroy()
{
   // TODO: Place applet cleanup code here
}


// nested Paint Handler
//-----------------------------------------------------------------------
public void paint(Graphics g)
{
   // TODO: Place applet paint code here
   //g.drawString("Running: " + Math.random(), 10, 20);
}


// The start() method is called when the page containing the applet
```

```
// first appears on the screen. The AppletWizard's initial implementation
// of this method starts execution of the applet's thread.
//-------------------------------------------------------------------------
public void start()
{
  if (m_nested == null)
  {
    m_nested = new Thread(this);
    m_nested.start();
  }
  // TODO: Place additional applet start code here
}


//   The stop() method is called when the page containing the applet is
// no longer on the screen. The AppletWizard's initial implementation of
// this method stops execution of the applet's thread.
//-------------------------------------------------------------------------
public void stop()
{
  if (m_nested != null)
  {
    m_nested.stop();
    m_nested = null;
  }

  // TODO: Place additional applet stop code here
}


// THREAD SUPPORT
//   The run() method is called when the applet's thread is started. If
// your applet performs any ongoing activities without waiting for user
// input, the code for implementing that behavior typically goes here. For
// example, for an applet that performs animation, the run() method controls
// the display of images.
//-------------------------------------------------------------------------
public void run()
{
  while (true)
  {
    try
    {
      displaycounter();
    }
```

```
      catch (over500 e)
      {
        System.out.println("Over 500 exception occured.");
        stop();
      }
    }
  }

  public void displaycounter() throws over500
  {
    String displaystring = new String("");

    text1.setText(displaystring.valueOf(counter++));
    if (counter > 500) throw new over500();
  }



  // TODO: Place additional applet code here

}

class over500 extends Exception{}
```

That completes our examination of exception handling for now. As you can see, exception handling helps you deal with problems that occur when the program is running. On the other hand, you can take care of many problems that occur while you are developing your application—by debugging it.

Visual J++ Debugging

Visual J++ gives us excellent debugging support. For example, you can actually debug an applet while it is running in Internet Explorer. You can also examine and change variables as the program is running, examine the stack, disassemble direct binary code, watch variables as they change, single step through your code, set breakpoints, and more.

Let's see some of this in action. We might, for example, have a list of friends that we want to alphabetize and display:

```
Thomas
Nancy
Tim
Edward
Sara
Frank
Todd
Phoebe
Ralph
Alyssa
```

We can alphabetize this list and display it in our applet in a text area control. To do this, create a new applet named debug, omitting multithread support, and open its init() method. We start our code by setting up that text area, an array of String objects named names[], and adding the names we want to alphabetize to that array:

```
public void init()
{
→       String names[] = new String[10];
        resize(320, 240);

→       textarea1 = new TextArea(10, 20);
→       add(textarea1);

→       names[0] = "Thomas";
→       names[1] = "Nancy";
→       names[2] = "Tim";
→       names[3] = "Edward";
→       names[4] = "Sara";
→       names[5] = "Frank";
→       names[6] = "Todd";
→       names[7] = "Phoebe";
→       names[8] = "Ralph";
→       names[9] = "Alyssa";
            .
            .
            .
```

Next, we set up a loop to sort the elements of this array (the loop is not efficient, but it will get the job done—after we debug it!):

```
public void init()
{
   String names[] = new String[10];
   resize(320, 240);

   textarea1 = new TextArea(10, 20);
   add(textarea1);

   names[0] = "Thomas";
       .
       .
       .
   names[9] = "Alyssa";

➜  for(int outer = 0; outer > 9; outer++){
➜     for(int inner = outer; inner <= 9; inner++){
➜         if(names[outer].compareTo(names[inner]) < 0){
➜             String tempstring = names[outer];
➜             names[outer] = names[inner];
➜             names[inner] = tempstring;
➜         }            .
➜     }                .
   }                   .
```

Finally, we display the sorted contents of the names[] array in the text area, which we have named textarea1:

```
public void init()
{
   names[0] = "Thomas";
       .
       .
       .
   names[9] = "Alyssa";

   for(int outer = 0; outer > 9; outer++){
     for(int inner = outer; inner <= 9; inner++){
        if(names[outer].compareTo(names[inner]) < 0){
```

```
                String tempstring = names[outer];
                names[outer] = names[inner];
                names[inner] = tempstring;
            }
        }
    }

→   for(int loop_index = 0; loop_index < 10; loop_index++){
→       textarea1.appendText(names[loop_index] + "\r\n");
→   }
```

We give our new applet a try as written—but the result is shown in Figure 13.1. Our list of names is not only not sorted—it's not been changed at all. It's time to debug.

FIGURE 13.1:

Our debug applet before being debugged

Setting a Breakpoint

We will debug our code by stepping through it one line at a time. You can start this process in various ways. For example, in the Visual J++ menu, choose Debug to open a submenu that contains Go, Step Into, and Run to Cursor.

If you choose Go, the program starts, and since we have not set any breakpoints to halt program execution in the middle, the program will simply finish, giving the same result as before. A *breakpoint* is just what it sounds like—a point in the program where execution "breaks," or stops.

If you choose Step Into, we will start single stepping through the program, line by line, starting from the beginning. Since our bugs are actually in the init() method, that is not so bad, but usually this is not the recommended method. It is far better to set a breakpoint at some location near a suspected troublesome section of code and then single step through that.

If you choose Run to Cursor, you can place the cursor at some line of code and then execute the program all the way up to that point, where execution stops automatically.

In this case, we'll set a breakpoint and run the program up to that breakpoint. We will set our breakpoint at the line of code just before we enter our double loop:

```
names[0] = "Thomas";
        .
        .
        .
➜   names[9] = "Alyssa";

    for(int outer = 0; outer > 9; outer++){
      for(int inner = outer; inner <= 9; inner++){
        if(names[outer].compareTo(names[inner]) < 0){
          String tempstring = names[outer];
          names[outer] = names[inner];
          names[inner] = tempstring;
        }
      }
    }

    for(int loop_index = 0; loop_index < 10; loop_index++){
      textarea1.appendText(names[loop_index] + "\r\n");
    }
```

Now, set the cursor at that line and click on the Enable/Disable Breakpoint button in the toolbar (the button with a hand in it). A small stop sign appears next to the line at which we've placed a breakpoint, as in Figure 13.2.

TIP To edit the placement of breakpoints, choose Edit ➤ Breakpoints.

FIGURE 13.2:

A breakpoint in Visual J++

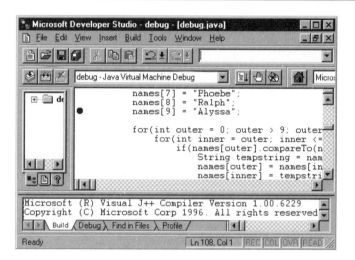

Now choose Debug ➤ Go to start the applet. It keeps going until it reaches our breakpoint, and then execution stops, displaying Visual J++ again, as in Figure 13.3.

FIGURE 13.3:

Stopping Visual J++
at a breakpoint

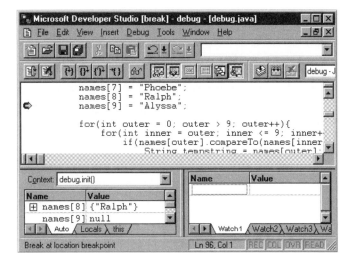

Notice the changed appearance of Visual J++ in Figure 13.3. At the lower left, in the *Variables* window, you can examine the contents of variables and arrays simply by clicking on their names. At the lower right is the *Watch* window. When you type a variable's name in the Name column, Visual J++ displays the variable's value so that you can see how it changes as the program executes. In the *Code* window at the top center, you can see the breakpoint, and the line we are currently executing is marked with a yellow arrow.

> **TIP**
>
> You can change the value of variables in the Watch window (at the lower right in the Visual J++ debug display). Simply enter the name of a variable in the Name column, which displays the current value of the variable in the Value column. To change the value of the variable, edit that variable's entry in the Value column.

We have several single-stepping choices at this point. In Figure 13.3, the Build menu has been replaced by the Debug menu. In the Debug menu, you'll find these items: Step Into, Step Over, Step Out, and Run to Cursor.

If you choose Step Into, Visual J++ single steps execution, stepping "into" all called methods so that you execute each line of every method you encounter. If you choose Step Over, Visual J++ single steps through the code but not through called methods; so you never leave the current method. If you choose Step Out, Visual J++ takes you out of the current method and back to the calling method. If you choose Run to Cursor, you can place the cursor and select an item, and execution will continue to the cursor.

Press F10 now to single step to the next instruction, as shown here and in Figure 13.4:

```
➡for(int outer = 0; outer > 9; outer++){
    for(int inner = outer; inner <= 9; inner++){
        if(names[outer].compareTo(names[inner]) < 0){
            String tempstring = names[outer];
            names[outer] = names[inner];
            names[inner] = tempstring;
        }
    }
}

for(int loop_index = 0; loop_index < 10; loop_index++){
    textarea1.appendText(names[loop_index] + "\r\n");
}
```

This is the beginning of our double loop. We should enter this loop now to see how it functions, so press F10 again.

FIGURE 13.4:

Starting to debug
our loop

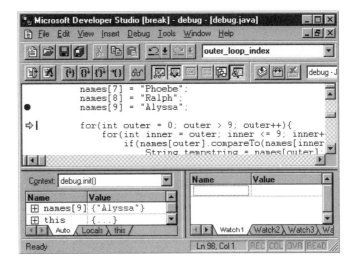

But instead of executing our loop, execution (which is marked by the yellow arrow in the code window) skips down after our sorting loop to the second loop, where we print out the `names[]` array in the text area:

```
for(int outer = 0; outer > 9; outer++){
    for(int inner = outer; inner <= 9; inner++){
        if(names[outer].compareTo(names[inner]) < 0){
            String tempstring = names[outer];
            names[outer] = names[inner];
            names[inner] = tempstring;
        }
    }
}

➜   for(int loop_index = 0; loop_index < 10; loop_index++){
        textareal.appendText(names[loop_index] + "\r\n");
    }
```

In other words, our sorting loop is not being executed at all. A quick look at the `loop` statement shows why. We're trying to sort an array whose elements run from 0 to 9, and it appears that we've got the loop condition for this loop all wrong. We've insisted that the loop continue while the loop index is greater than 9, but, of course, it never is:

```
→  for(int outer = 0; outer > 9; outer++){
       for(int inner = outer; inner <= 9; inner++){
         if(names[outer].compareTo(names[inner]) < 0){
           String tempstring = names[outer];
           names[outer] = names[inner];
           names[inner] = tempstring;
         }
       }
   }
```

We fix that line now so that the loop actually loops over our array of strings:

```
→  for(int outer = 0; outer <= 9; outer++){
       for(int inner = outer; inner <= 9; inner++){
         if(names[outer].compareTo(names[inner]) < 0){
           String tempstring = names[outer];
           names[outer] = names[inner];
           names[inner] = tempstring;
         }
       }
   }
```

Now we rerun the applet, yielding the result in Figure 13.5. Something has changed—but it's just the opposite of the way we wanted it. Instead of sorting the names into ascending order, our applet has sorted the names in descending order. It's back to the debugger.

FIGURE 13.5:

The debug applet,
second try

Start the debugger again, and single step into our loop. This time, we'll follow the name-comparison process. Single step now—by pressing F10 repeatedly—to this line in our code:

```
for(int outer = 0; outer <= 9; outer++){
    for(int inner = outer; inner <= 9; inner++){
→       if(names[outer].compareTo(names[inner]) < 0){
            String tempstring = names[outer];
            names[outer] = names[inner];
            names[inner] = tempstring;
        }
    }
}
```

We'll watch as our program compares the strings in our `names[]` array now. To see what's in a particular variable, we can enter it in the Watch window or examine it in the Variables window at the lower left in Visual J++, but there's an even easier way. Simply select the variable's name on the screen (for example, *names[outer]*) and let the mouse cursor rest over it for a moment. A tool-tip–like window (called a *data tip*) appears, as in Figure 13.6, showing us the value of the variable we have selected.

FIGURE 13.6:

Examining a variable in the debugger

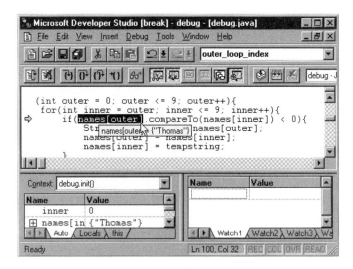

We keep single stepping through the loop until we come to the comparison of Thomas with Nancy:

```
→    names[0]  =  "Thomas";
→    names[1]  =  "Nancy";
     names[2]  =  "Tim";
     names[3]  =  "Edward";
     names[4]  =  "Sara";
     names[5]  =  "Frank";
     names[6]  =  "Todd";
     names[7]  =  "Phoebe";
     names[8]  =  "Ralph";
     names[9]  =  "Alyssa";
```

TIP

A quick way to single step while debugging is to use the shortcut buttons in the toolbar. These buttons display an arrow and a set of curly braces—{ and }. Reading from left to right, the single-step buttons in Figure 13.6 are: Step Into, Step Over, Step Out, and Run to Cursor.

"Nancy" comes earlier alphabetically than "Thomas," so we should see these two names exchanged in the array. Instead, when we press F10 to single step through the process of exchanging strings, we go back to the beginning of the inner loop:

```
for(int outer = 0; outer <= 9; outer++){
➜    for(int inner = outer; inner <= 9; inner++){
      if(names[outer].compareTo(names[inner]) < 0){
        String tempstring = names[outer];
        names[outer] = names[inner];
        names[inner] = tempstring;
      }
    }
}
```

Obviously, we have a problem. We should have exchanged the two strings we were just looking at, but we did not. We examine the string comparison line:

```
for(int outer = 0; outer <= 9; outer++){
    for(int inner = outer; inner <= 9; inner++){
➜      if(names[outer].compareTo(names[inner]) < 0){
        String tempstring = names[outer];
        names[outer] = names[inner];
        names[inner] = tempstring;
      }
    }
}
```

After checking the Java documentation, we see the mistake. When *names[outer]* is "Thomas" and *names[inner]* is "Nancy," we expect names[outer].compareTo(names[inner]) to return a value greater than 0, but we have placed "< 0" in the conditional, as we see above. We fix that like this:

```
for(int outer = 0; outer <= 9; outer++){
    for(int inner = outer; inner <= 9; inner++){
➜      if(names[outer].compareTo(names[inner]) > 0){
        String tempstring = names[outer];
```

```
                    names[outer] = names[inner];
                    names[inner] = tempstring;
                }
            }
        }
```

And now the applet works as expected. We alphabetize the names and display them in the text area, as shown in Figure 13.7. We've debugged our applet successfully. The debugged applet appears in the listing for debug.java.

FIGURE 13.7:

Our debugged applet works as expected.

debug.java

```
//***************************************************************************
// debug.java:    Applet
//
//***************************************************************************
import java.applet.*;
import java.awt.*;


//==========================================================================
// Main Class for applet debug
//
```

```
//===============================================================================
public class debug extends Applet implements Runnable
{
   // THREAD SUPPORT:
   //   m_debug  is the Thread object for the applet
   //---------------------------------------------------------------------------
   Thread  m_debug = null;
   TextField text1;
   TextArea textarea1;
   // ANIMATION SUPPORT:
   //   m_Graphics     used for storing the applet's Graphics context
   //   m_Images[]     the array of Image objects for the animation
   //   m_nCurrImage   the index of the next image to be displayed
   //   m_ImgWidth     width of each image
   //   m_ImgHeight    height of each image
   //   m_fAllLoaded   indicates whether all images have been loaded
   //   NUM_IMAGES     number of images used in the animation
   //---------------------------------------------------------------------------
   private Graphics m_Graphics;
   private Image m_Images[];
   private int  m_nCurrImage;
   private int  m_nImgWidth  = 0;
   private int  m_nImgHeight = 0;
   private boolean  m_fAllLoaded = false;
   private final int NUM_IMAGES = 18;
   int counter = 0;

   // debug Class Constructor
   //---------------------------------------------------------------------------
   public debug()
   {
      // TODO: Add constructor code here
   }

   // APPLET INFO SUPPORT:
   //   The getAppletInfo() method returns a string describing the applet's
   // author, copyright date, or miscellaneous information.
   //---------------------------------------------------------------------------
   public String getAppletInfo()
   {
      return "Name: debug\r\n" +
            "Author: Steven Holzner\r\n" +
```

```
          "Created with Microsoft Visual J++ Version 1.0";
}


// The init() method is called by the AWT when an applet is first loaded or
// reloaded.  Override this method to perform whatever initialization your
// applet needs, such as initializing data structures, loading images or
// fonts, creating frame windows, setting the layout manager, or adding UI
// components.
//--------------------------------------------------------------------
public void init()
{
  String names[] = new String[10];
  // If you use a ResourceWizard-generated "control creator" class to
  // arrange controls in your applet, you may want to call its
  // CreateControls() method from within this method. Remove the following
  // call to resize() before adding the call to CreateControls();
  // CreateControls() does its own resizing.
  //--------------------------------------------------------------------
  resize(320, 240);

  textarea1 = new TextArea(10, 20);
  add(textarea1);

  names[0] = "Thomas";
  names[1] = "Nancy";
  names[2] = "Tim";
  names[3] = "Edward";
  names[4] = "Sara";
  names[5] = "Frank";
  names[6] = "Todd";
  names[7] = "Phoebe";
  names[8] = "Ralph";
  names[9] = "Alyssa";

  for(int outer = 0; outer <= 9; outer++){
    for(int inner = outer; inner <= 9; inner++){
      if(names[outer].compareTo(names[inner]) > 0){
        String tempstring = names[outer];
        names[outer] = names[inner];
```

```
        names[inner] = tempstring;
      }
    }
  }

  for(int loop_index = 0; loop_index < 10; loop_index++){
    textarea1.appendText(names[loop_index] + "\r\n");
  }

  // TODO: Place additional initialization code here
}

// Place additional applet clean up code here.  destroy() is called
// when your applet is terminating and being unloaded.
//-------------------------------------------------------------------------
public void destroy()
{
  // TODO: Place applet cleanup code here
}

// ANIMATION SUPPORT:
//   Draws the next image, if all images are currently loaded
//-------------------------------------------------------------------------
private void displayImage(Graphics g)
{
  if (!m_fAllLoaded)
    return;

  // Draw Image in center of applet
  //-----------------------------------------------------------------------
  //g.drawImage(m_Images[m_nCurrImage],
  //      (size().width - m_nImgWidth)  / 2,
  //      (size().height - m_nImgHeight) / 2, null);
}

// debug Paint Handler
//-------------------------------------------------------------------------
public void paint(Graphics g)
{
  // ANIMATION SUPPORT:
  //   The following code displays a status message until all the
  //   images are loaded. Then it calls displayImage to display the current
```

```
   // image.
   //-----------------------------------------------------------------
   //if (m_fAllLoaded)
   //{
   //   Rectangle r = g.getClipRect();
   //
   //   g.clearRect(r.x, r.y, r.width, r.height);
   //   displayImage(g);
   //}
   //else
   //   g.drawString("Loading images...", 10, 20);

   // TODO: Place additional applet Paint code here
}


//   The start() method is called when the page containing the applet
// first appears on the screen. The AppletWizard's initial implementation
// of this method starts execution of the applet's thread.
//-----------------------------------------------------------------
public void start()
{
   if (m_debug == null)
   {
      m_debug = new Thread(this);
      m_debug.start();
   }
   // TODO: Place additional applet start code here
}


//   The stop() method is called when the page containing the applet is
// no longer on the screen. The AppletWizard's initial implementation of
// this method stops execution of the applet's thread.
//-----------------------------------------------------------------
public void stop()
{
   if (m_debug != null)
   {
      m_debug.stop();
```

```
      m_debug = null;
   }


   // TODO: Place additional applet stop code here
}


// THREAD SUPPORT
//   The run() method is called when the applet's thread is started. If
// your applet performs any ongoing activities without waiting for user
// input, the code for implementing that behavior typically goes here. For
// example, for an applet that performs animation, the run() method controls
// the display of images.
//-----------------------------------------------------------------------
public void run()
{
   m_nCurrImage = 0;

   // If re-entering the page, then the images have already been loaded.
   // m_fAllLoaded == TRUE.
   //--------------------------------------------------------------------
   if (!m_fAllLoaded)
   {
      repaint();
      m_Graphics = getGraphics();
      m_Images   = new Image[NUM_IMAGES];

      // Load in all the images
      //-----------------------------------------------------------------
      MediaTracker tracker = new MediaTracker(this);
      String strImage;

      // For each image in the animation, this method first constructs a
      // string containing the path to the image file; then it begins
      // loading the image into the m_Images array.  Note that the call to
      // getImage will return before the image is completely loaded.
      //-----------------------------------------------------------------
      for (int i = 1; i <= NUM_IMAGES; i++)
      {
         // Build path to next image
         //--------------------------------------------------------------
         strImage = "images/img00" + ((i < 10) ? "0" : "") + i + ".gif";
```

```
      m_Images[i-1] = getImage(getDocumentBase(), strImage);

      tracker.addImage(m_Images[i-1], 0);
   }

   // Wait until all images are fully loaded
   //----------------------------------------------------------------
   try
   {
      tracker.waitForAll();
      m_fAllLoaded = !tracker.isErrorAny();
   }
   catch (InterruptedException e)
   {
      // TODO: Place exception-handling code here in case an
      //    InterruptedException is thrown by Thread.sleep(),
      //    meaning that another thread has interrupted this one
   }

   if (!m_fAllLoaded)
   {
      stop();
      m_Graphics.drawString("Error loading images!", 10, 40);
      return;
   }


   // Assuming all images are same width and height.
   //----------------------------------------------------------------
   m_nImgWidth  = m_Images[0].getWidth(this);
   m_nImgHeight = m_Images[0].getHeight(this);
}
repaint();

while (true)
{
   try
   {
      // Draw next image in animation
      //----------------------------------------------------------
      displayImage(m_Graphics);
      m_nCurrImage++;
```

```
      if (m_nCurrImage == NUM_IMAGES)
        m_nCurrImage = 0;

      // TODO:  Add additional thread-specific code here
      Thread.sleep(50);
    }
    catch (InterruptedException e)
    {
      // TODO: Place exception-handling code here in case an
      //    InterruptedException is thrown by Thread.sleep(),
      //    meaning that another thread has interrupted this one
      stop();
    }
  }
}




// TODO: Place additional applet code here


}
```

Our book is almost over, so let's take the time to get an overview of a Java topic that is steadily gaining in popularity—Java database programming. We'll look at client-server and database programming as we explore the JDBC API.

Java and Databases

Ever since Java came out, it's been a hit. And Sun, taking the hint, has been working on expanding it by supplying new APIs (Application Programming Interfaces). These new APIs are Java packages similar to java.net, which enables you to work with the Internet directly. Probably the most popular of these APIs are the Enterprise APIs, which are targeted at businesses, and the most popular of these is the Java Database Connectivity API, or JDBC for short.

JDBC provides a means of reaching and working with databases that support SQL (Structured Query Language), either locally or remotely. This means that applets can now support airline reservation systems, retail catalogs, and much more.

Java's JDBC

JDBC was inspired by Microsoft's ODBC (Open Database Connectivity) specification, which means that databases that use ODBC can often be connected to your applets rather easily; in fact, JDBC mimics a great deal of ODBC, using ResultSets and connections. You'll need an ODBC driver to interface with your database package—either the standard Microsoft ODBC driver if your database can use that (for example, Microsoft's Access database software) or a custom JDBC driver such as the one that Oracle created for Oracle 7 databases and the one that Borland created for its Interbase databases. In Windows 95, you install ODBC and JDBC drivers by double-clicking on the 32bit ODBC icon in the Control Panel.

TIP You can get a free copy of the Microsoft ODBC driver from the Microsoft Web site, `http://www.microsoft.com`.

JDBC is actually implemented as the package called `java.sql`, and we'll take a look at the parts of this package now.

The JDBC API

The more important classes in the `java.sql` package appear in Table 13.3.

TABLE 13.3: Selected `java.sql` Classes

Class	Does This
`java.sql.CallableStatement`	Holds callable SQL statements
`java.sql.Connection`	Makes the connection to the database
`java.sql.Driver`	Handles a specific database driver
`java.sql.DriverManager`	Tracks available drivers
`java.sql.DriverPropertyInfo`	Tracks property information on drivers
`java.sql.PreparedStatement`	Holds prepared SQL statements
`java.sql.ResultSet`	Holds `ResultSet` from SQL queries
`java.sql.SQLException`	Holds SQL exceptions
`java.sql.SQLWarning`	Holds SQL warnings
`java.sql.Statement`	Holds SQL statements

A typical database access from Java might work like this: You set up a driver using the JDBC `Driver` class and create a JDBC `Connection` object using the `DriverManager` class's `getConnection()` method. Next, you create an SQL statement with the JDBC `Statement` class's `createStatement()` method and then excute that statement object's `executeQuery()` method, which returns a `ResultSet` object. The `ResultSet` object represents the normal result set you get from an SQL query. Using the JDBC API, SQL programmers can feel at home. With JDBC, you can implement client-server applications in Java across the Internet (or an intranet). This is a powerful way to add database programming capabilities to Java programs.

That's It

And that's it for our overview of Java database programming—and that's all for our book. You've seen a great deal of Visual J++ programming in this book, including: text fields and text areas, radio buttons and checkboxes, scroll bars and scrolling lists, image maps, pop-up windows, menus, Card layouts, GridBag layouts and other layouts, dialog boxes, buttons, panels, multithreading, navigating to other URLs, the mouse, resizing images and other image handling, using the keyboard directly, setting thread priority, double buffering, integrating ActiveX, using fonts, graphics animation, suspending and restarting threads, converting images to pixel arrays and back to images, Java applications, nested exception handlers, loading images with a background thread, coordinating multiple threads, debugging Java programs, and more. All that remains now is to put all this Visual J++ power to work! Happy programming.

APPENDIX

A

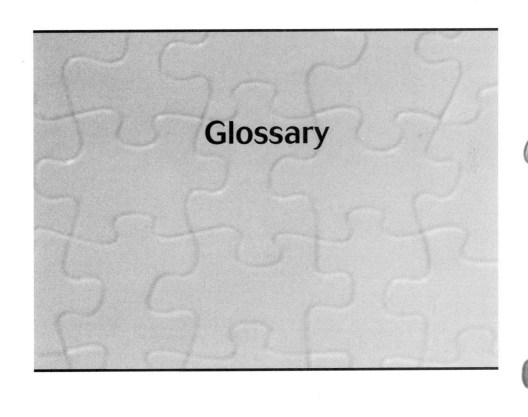

Glossary

A

Abstract Windowing Toolkit
The Java package of user interface methods that handles graphics and windows.

API
See Applications Programming Interface.

applet
A compiled Java program that can be embedded in a Web page and downloaded to run in a Web browser.

Applications Programming Interface
A collection of classes, methods, and datamembers that you can import into Java.

AWT
See Abstract Windowing Toolkit.

B

base class
The class from which another class is derived.

boolean
A true/false variable type; these variables may only be set to TRUE or FALSE.

breakpoint
In debugging, a line of code or a location in a program at which execution halts so that the program state can be examined.

bytecodes
Java excutable binary codes that make up applets; these codes are what the compiler produces and make up .class files.

C

cast
A means of overriding a variable's type, changing that type to another type temporarily.

checkbox group
A collection of radio buttons. When checkboxes are added to a Java CheckBoxGroup object, they become radio buttons.

class
The "template" used to create objects, much like a variable's type (for example, *integer*). A class is to an object as a cookie cutter is to a cookie.

class library
Called a package in Java, a class library contains various Java classes.

client
One half of a client-server pair. Clients rely on a server to perform some task for them.

client-server pair
Splitting an application into two parts, one in the client (that requires a service or data) and one in the server (that provides a service or data to clients), creates a client-server pair.

clipping rectangle
The graphics rectangle bounding a part of the display area to which you want to restrict graphics operations.

compiler
A program that translates source code into runnable target code; for example, a Java compiler translates `.java` files into `.class` files.

constructor
An automatically run method of a class used to initialize an object; run when an object of the class containing the constructor is created.

container
An object of the Java `Container` class; can contain control objects.

control
Any of the various user interface objects—text fields, text areas, scroll bars, buttons, and so on.

critical section
A section of code in which threads should be allowed to undertake their tasks without interference; in other words, noninterruptible sections of code.

D

debugger
An application that lets you execute a program while watching the program's state; execution is often line by line.

double buffering
A graphics method of preparing images off the screen in a memory buffer and then displaying the result.

encapsulating
The process of wrapping both data and functions into classes.

E

event
A user-interface triggered occurrence; for example, a mouse click, a button push, or a key press.

exception
Usually indicates a problem in program flow. For example, when you try to

index an array beyond its boundaries, an array boundary exception occurs.

F
---

frame
The outline or border of a window or an individual image in animation.

H

HTML
See Hypertext Markup Language.

Hyptertext Markup Language
The language used to create Web pages.

I

IDE
See Integrated Development Environment.

image map
An image that has embedded hyperlinks; it is clickable.

inheritance
The process through which derived classes get, or inherit, functionality from their base classes.

Integrated Development Environment
A software package that includes a compiler, an editor, and usually a debugger, such as the Microsoft Developer Studio.

Internet service provider
A company or an individual that provides a machine connected to the Internet that acts as a host machine for individual users.

ISP
See Internet service provider.

J

Java Database Connectivity API
Interface tools providing access to database applications or files from Java.

Java Development Kit
Software package used to develop and create Java applications.

Java Virtual Machine
A system that loads and executes Java bytecode files.

JDBC
See Java Database Connectivity API.

JDK
See Java Development Kit.

L

layout
The arrangement of controls in a Java application or applet, usually handled by one or more Java layout managers.

M

member
Short for a member of a class, meaning a method, embedded data, or a class constant.

method
The member function of a class.

Microsoft Developer Studio
The Integrated Development Environment (IDE) of Visual J++.

multithreading
The basis of multitasking in a program. Each thread represents an independent execution stream within the context of an application or an applet.

N

null
A value usually set to zero in Java.

O

object
The instance of a class. Much like an integer variable is to the Java `int` type: The `int` type acts as a template for the actual variable, and a class acts as a template for an object. A class is to an object as a cookie cutter is to a cookie.

ODBC
See Open Database Connectivity.

Open Database Connectivity
The set of protocols developed by Microsoft to standardize database interfaces.

overloading
In object-oriented programming, the process of defining multiple methods with the same name but different parameter lists so that the method can be called with different sets of parameters.

overriding
In object-oriented programming, the process of redefining a method originally inherited from a base class.

P

package
In Java, a class library is called a package.

panel
A layout construct that holds controls in a specified arrangement for display on the screen.

project
Visual J++ manages program construction in projects; usually you use one project for each applet or application.

R

ResultSet
A JDBC SQL query result. For example, a `ResultSet` can hold a subsection of a database's entries that match a particular criteria.

S

server
General term for a source of data or an application interface with which client programs can interact.

source file
A text file that holds statements of a language to be compiled into an applet or application. For example, a `.java` file is a Java source file.

SQL
See Structured Query Language.

Structured Query Language
The standard database interaction language.

subclass
A class that descends from a given class.

subproject
A Visual J++ project defined inside another project, typically to create a class required by the main project.

superclass
A class from which a given class is derived; same as a base class.

T

this keyword
Java keyword used to refer to the current object; usually passed as a parameter to other methods.

thread
The execution stream in a program; a program may have many threads and therefore be multitasking.

throwable
An object derived from the Java `Exception` class that may be thrown as an exception.

thumb
The small box in a scroll bar that the user manipulates, usually with the mouse.

Web server
A computer on the Internet or on an intranet that interacts with client programs.

Wizard
A Visual J++ tool that creates code or .java files, such as the Applet Wizard, which creates applet source code files.

World Wide Web
Large assemblage of documents interconnected through HTTP, FTP, and other protocols over the Internet. Lots of fun and games!

INDEX

Note to the Reader: First level entries are in **bold**. Page numbers in **bold** indicate the principal discussion of a topic or the definition of a term. Page numbers in *italic* indicate illustrations.

SYMBOLS

& (ampersand) as logical operator, 418

| (bar symbol) as logical operator, 418, 436

{ } (braces), code blocks and, 107

^ (caret) as binary operator, 418

. (dot operator)

    accessing methods with, 17

    executing an object's internal method, 92

// (double slash), commenting with, 50, 93, 101

= (equal to)

    as equality operator (= =), 108

    as inequality operator (!=), 108

! (exclamation point)

    as inequality operator (!=), 108

    as negation operator, 428

    as NOT operator, 418

+ (plus sign) as concatenation operator, 208

; (semicolon), ending statements with, 18

A

access modifiers, 16

accessing methods with dot operator (.), 17

action() method

    in artist applet, 360

    in checkboxes, 162–163, 164

    in dialog boxes, 303, 308–309, 310, 324

    events and, 104–105, 109, 115

    in FlowLayout Manager calculator example, 137–138

    in font handling applet, 428

    in menus, 286–288

    in pop-up windows, 270

    in radio buttons, 172

ActiveX controls, 328–335

    ActiveX to Java data type conversions, 333

    creating wrapper classes for, 329–335

    downloading, 328, 329

    names of classes and methods in, 331

    Variant class Get and Put methods and, 334–335

    Variant data type, 333–335

D

E

G

I

J

K

L

M

S

T

U

X

Y

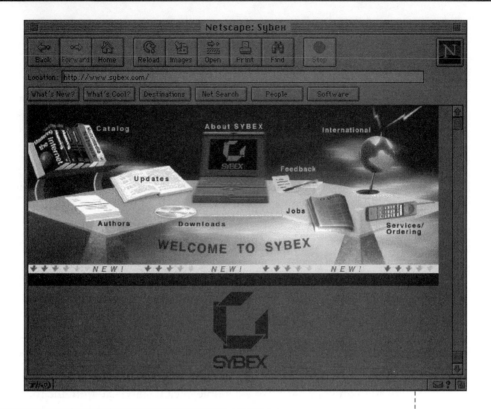

Look What's on the CD

The *Mastering Visual J++* CD contains:

- All code and examples from the book
- Microsoft Internet Explorer 3.0 browser
- ActiveX Control Pad 1.0

The contents of the folders you'll find on the CD, and the steps for installing the various programs, are described below:

 To install Microsoft Internet Explorer, double-click the msie301m95.exe file (located in the Microsoft directory).

 To install the ActiveX Control Pad, double-click the setuppad.exe file (located in the Microsoft Directory). You must already have Microsoft Internet Explorer 3.0 installed on your computer.

If you are using Windows 95 or NT:

Use the self-extracting file—it will copy the project files to the proper location on your hard drive. Double-click instalvj.exe from the root level of the CD. The self-extracting installer will prompt you to extract the project files to c:\vjpp.

In order for these files to run, they must be installed to c:\vjpp. The self-extracting installer will create the directory and subdirectories for you if they don't exist. It is not necessary to use c:\vjpp as your base directory, but if you don't, you may have to rebuild each project's .mdp file.

If you are using a system other than Windows 95 or NT, or prefer not to use the self-extracting installer:

Simply copy the whole vjpp folder on the CD to c:\vjpp. From MS-DOS, use this command: copy *.* c:\vjpp /s. This creates the subdirectories c:\vjpp\application, c:\vjpp\artist, and so on, one for each project on the CD-ROM.

To open a project in Visual J++, open the project's .mdp file, such as application.mdp, artist.mdp, and so on.